ROBERT J. O'CONNELL, S.J. is
Professor of Philosophy
at Fordham University.

Images of Conversion
in St. Augustine's *Confessions*

IMAGES OF CONVERSION IN ST. AUGUSTINE'S *CONFESSIONS*

by

ROBERT J. O'CONNELL, S.J.

Fordham University Press
New York
1996

© Copyright 1996 by FORDHAM UNIVERSITY PRESS
All rights reserved.
LC 94-24023
ISBN 0-8232-1598-9

Library of Congress Cataloging-in-Publication Data

O'Connell, Robert J.
  Images of conversion in St. Augustine's Confessions / by Robert J.
O'Connell.
     p.   cm.
  Includes bibliographical references and index.
  ISBN 0-8232-1598-9.
  1. Augustine, Saint, Bishop of Hippo.   Confessiones.
  2. Conversion—History of doctrines—Early church, ca. 30–600.
  I. Title.
  BR65.A62025   1995
  242—dc20   94-24023
                                                            CIP

Printed in the United States of America

To the memory of all those who,
like Sister Joseph Eileen, O.F.M.,
Robert Clancy, and
John Julian Ryan,
labored so generously
to replace my native ignorance
with some semblance of wisdom

CONTENTS

III
The Gift of Stability

IV
The *Confessions* at Cassiciacum

ACKNOWLEDGMENTS

My thanks, in the first place, go to the authorities of Fordham University, who generously awarded me the Faculty Fellowship year during which the major part of this study was composed. I must also thank the National Endowment for the Humanities for the generous grant which helped defray expenses for that year. Thanks, as well, to the authorities of Duke University for having welcomed me as Visiting Scholar for that same period. Special mention in that connection must go to Professors Elizabeth Clark and Edward Mahoney, of Duke University's Religious Studies and Philosophy departments, respectively, for the many kindnesses they tendered me during my sojourn there.

I have also been lucky enough to have Frs. Thomas V. Bermingham and Joseph T. Lienhard as brother-Jesuits and good-natured live-in consultants on matters classical and patristic; but it has also been of no small moment to have an editor like Dr. Mary Beatrice Schulte, whose competence is all the more priceless in that she is no stranger to classical lore.

ABBREVIATIONS

Atti	Acta of the International Congress on St. Augustine on the 16th Centenary of his Conversion. 3 vols. Rome: *Studia Ephemerides Augustinianum,* 1987
AS	*Augustinian Studies*
BA	Bibliothèque Augustinienne series of the works of St. Augustine (Paris); BA 13, for example, indicates Volume 13
Collectanea	*Collectanea Augustiniana* (Villanova, Pa.) Volume specified by subtitle: "Founder" = "Augustine, Second Founder of the Faith," 1990 "Marquette" = "Marquette University Conference," 1991
RA	*Recherches Augustiniennes*
RE	*Real-Encyklopedie der Klassischen Altertumswissenschaft,* Pauly-Wissowa-Kroll-Witter (Stuttgart, 1984ff.)
REA	*Revue des Études Augustiniennes*
TA	*Thesaurus Augustinianus*
VC	*Vetera Christianorum*

All translations are my own, but I have consulted three vernacular translations of the *Confessions,* referring to them by the translators' names; thus:

Bourke	Saint Augustine. *Confessions.* Trans. Vernon J. Bourke. New York: Fathers of the Church, 1953
Ryan	*The Confessions of St. Augustine.* Trans. John K. Ryan. Garden City, N.Y.: Doubleday Image, 1960
Tréhorel-Boissou	*Les Confessions.* Trans. Eugène Tréhorel and Guilhem Boissou. BA 13–14. Paris: Études Augustiniennes, 1962 (introduction and notes by Aimé Solignac, S.J.)

Out of regard for Augustine's professional sense of Latin, I have found *The Oxford Latin Dictionary*, edited by P. G. W. Glare (Oxford: Clarendon, 1982), an especially helpful resource. I regret that James J. O'Donnell's three-volume work on *Augustine: Confessions* (Oxford: Oxford University Press, 1992) saw publication only after this study had reached completion.

ABBREVIATIONS USED FOR AUGUSTINE'S WORKS

Acad	*Contra Academicos*
Civ	*De civitate Dei*
Conf	*Confessiones*
En(n)	*Enarratio(nes) in Psalmos*
Ep(p)	*Epistulae*
EpJo	*Tractatus in Joannis Epistulam*
Faust	*Contra Faustum Manichaeum*
GenLitt	*De Genesi ad litteram*
GenMan	*De Genesi contra Manichaeos*
Immort	*De immortalitate animae*
InJo	*Tractatus in Joannis Evangelium*
Jul	*Contra Julianum Pelagianum*
Lib	*De libero arbitrio*
Mor	*De moribus ecclesiae et Manichaeorum*
Mus	*De musica*
Ord	*De ordine*
Oros	*Ad Orosium presbyterum*
Praed	*De praedestinatione sanctorum*
QQEv	*Quaestionum Evangeliorum*
Quant	*De quantitate animae*
Retr	*Retractationes*
S(S)	*Sermones*
Simp	*Ad Simplicianum de diversis quaestionibus*
Sol	*Soliloquia*
Trin	*De Trinitate*
UtCred	*De utilitate credendi*
Ver	*De vera religione*
Vita	*De beata vita*

PREFACE

Ideally, the reader of this book should come to it after having read my *Soundings in St. Augustine's Imagination*. In that work, I hope to have shown the surprising extent to which Augustine lived in a vividly imagined world, picturing the universe and the drama of man's interactions with God which transpires there in terms of three fundamental images. First and basic to the other two is Augustine's picture of the *Omnia*, the hierarchic assemblage of "all things"—visible and invisible—which the God of Genesis created. That cosmic image provides the stage setting for fallen humanity's *peregrinatio*, our common departure from and return to God and to the higher spiritual world. But that drama of "wayfaring" is criss-crossed by the lines of a third image, depicting God's various modes of exercising His—or is it, rather, Her?—parental "care" for wayfaring humanity. I have named this after the verb which regularly expresses the multiple aspects of that Divine Care: the *fovere* image.

That liminal study, to which I shall henceforth refer as *Soundings*, could easily be viewed as competing with Suzanne Poque's two-volume work on *Le Langage symbolique dans la prédication d'Augustin d'Hippone* (Paris: Études Augustiniennes, 1984), as this volume might seem to compete with Patrice Cambronne's megabook in microfiche format, *Recherches sur la structure de l'imaginaire dans les* CONFESSIONS *de saint Augustin* (Paris: Études Augustiniennes, 1979). But my research for both these books was launched well before any knowledge of Cambronne's and Poque's works came to my notice—launched on different bases, and to achieve a different set of aims.

The major differences are these: instead of following Poque and Cambronne by first erecting a methodological framework inspired by previous studies of how "the imagination" (in general) works, then searching Augustine's works to reach a comparable set of speculative findings on that same anonymous imagination, I have chosen to walk a lower road. My reason for doing that was the conviction that there were still numerous places, especially in his *Confessions*, where we scholars simply did not understand what Augustine himself was trying to communicate to his readers; hence, my aim all along has been precisely that of deciphering what Augustine is telling us. Little by little, starting some thirty years ago, it dawned on me that one way of accomplishing that task might be to examine the arsenal of images he deploys in his effort to communicate: in my Introduction to *Soundings* I have listed, gratefully, the number of fellow-scholars who encouraged me, in one way or another, to strike out on that road.

As to the basis of my explorations: for my launching platform I chose not to start from previous studies, however prestigious, on "the imagination"; such studies might be helpful in scouting the twists and turns of Augustine's individual imaginative workings, but then again, they might not. The danger inherent in such an approach is that of imposing on Augustine's individual imagination a heuristic grid derived from some modern individual's theory of *l'imaginaire*, "the" imagination.

In hopes of obviating that danger, I chose to begin my survey mainly with the images contained in Augustine's preached works. That made it possible to select, in a second stage, a set of problematic images (or, more frequently, image-clusters) from the *Confessions*, then re-examine his *Sermons, Enarrationes,* and *Tractatus* on St. John's Gospel and First Epistle in as close to chronological order as our knowledge permits. So doing, I strove to follow the genesis, growth, the frequent fusions and cross-fertilizations, and the final blossoming of those image-clusters. Starting with each image-cluster in its nascent form, and tracing its genesis and growth, I hoped to become as confident as one can in such matters that I was witnessing how Augustine's individual imagination worked—"reading *his* mind," so to speak—and learning what these various image-clusters eventually came to mean for *him*, and for the "ideal reader" he was hoping to communicate with.

I do not for a moment wish to depreciate the value of what Poque and Cambronne have accomplished. The interested student of Augustine's mind will find precious fuel for thought in both their studies. Allow me, though, to alert my reader to a set of findings on the working of Augustine's imagination which I must suppose as established by the explorations which went into the writing of *Soundings*. Neither Poque's nor Cambronne's succeeds,

I submit, in bringing these "laws" as clearly to light as a more genetic study can.

The first of those "laws" I have already mentioned in passing: Augustine works more regularly with clusters of imagery than with isolated images; furthermore, those clusters sometimes develop according to a logic that is entirely comfortable to the conceptualizing intelligence. Thus, the image of water can evoke companion-images of bathing or drinking, of coolness and refreshment, of shaded springs or peaceful plashing fountains.

Instead of always moving out that way, however, along a fairly predictable line of kinship-development, a growing image-cluster can sometimes veer toward its natural opposite, so that water recalls filth and the need for washing, thirst and discomfort, or the menace of crashing ocean-waves, vertigo, shipwreck, drowning. So, too, an image of tender maternal care can summon up a mother hen bravely protecting her chicks—or a doctor whose care takes the cruel form of cutting or burning. What the conceptualizing mind finds unendurably contradictory, imagination can find quite serenely acceptable; where reason insists on either/or, imagination may cheerfully embrace both/and!

That process of growth can sometimes take the form of one image clustering with, running parallel to, a partner-image until suddenly the two appear to have "fused," melted into identity with each other: all at once it becomes impossible to decide whether the Odysseus, say, whom we have been following on his laborious sea-voyage, is Odysseus no longer, but St. Luke's Prodigal instead, exhausted from his land-journey into a far country. Or, unaccountably, the nursing mother becomes severe, chastising father—and still, somehow, retains the traits of nursing mother!

Kinship-growth, a logic of opposites, fusion—all three of the above processes have to do with how Augustine's image-clusters develop. There is a final process worth attending to, but it has more to do with the linguistic correlates which act as vehicles for those images: I have adopted the term "recession" to express the process I have in mind. An example will best illustrate my meaning.

Early in his writing career, Augustine is obviously struck by that gothic image the author of Ecclesiasticus (10:9–15) uses to reinforce his assertion that "the beginning of all sin is pride." The preacher describes the "earth and ashes" he identifies as the "proud" man this way: he has "turned away" and "departed" from God, and "in his lifetime, has spewed forth his insides" (*in vita sua, projecit intima sua*). The first time Augustine appeals to this image, in his anti-Manichee commentary on Genesis (2.6), he justifies his use of it by actually quoting a conflation of verses 9 and 14 from the biblical text—*Quare superbit terra et cinis? Quia in vita sua projecit intima sua*—"Why does earth and ashes pride itself? For in his lifetime he has spewed forth his insides." He does much the same thing in (an apparently later allusion from) *De musica* 6.39.

By the time he writes his *Confessions*, however, he can portray "iniquity" (obviously, a stand-in for pride, the "beginning of all sin") as the *perversitas* of the will "twisting itself away from . . . God toward the lowest of realities, spewing forth its insides and swelling to the outside" (*proicientis intima sua et tumescentis foras*) (7.22). The only elements here which are strictly identical with those from the original linguistic correlate are those three words *proicientis intima sua*; they express the very heart, one may think, of this ultra-baroque image. Yet they entirely suffice to link the *Confessions* version with its source in Ecclesiasticus, despite the fact that the original "turning away from God" (*apostatare a Deo*) is now being expressed by a different linguistic form, *detortae*, and associated with that product of Augustine's subsequent metaphysical development, the technical term *perversitas*. The underlying image remains identifiably the same, even though the original linguistic correlate has been markedly reduced: that linguistic correlate has gone into what I shall term "recession." The same process becomes even more marked when Augustine later describes the soul's fall into the multiplicity of temporal existence. He tells us that his "thoughts, the inmost bowels [*intima viscera*] of [his] soul," have become "rent asunder" (*dilaniantur*). Here, the original linguistic vehicle has been even further reduced, has gone deeper into recession; and yet, that residual image of his *intima viscera* being rent asunder and (obviously) "spewing forth" clearly suffices to link this latest version of the image to its counterpart in Ecclesiasticus.

Two observations on this phenomenon of recession, and we shall have done. The first is this: from the point of view of method, recession warns us that the persistence of the linguistic correlate may sometimes be of only secondary importance in the business of identifying the source, model, inspiration (what have you!) of an image or an element in an image-cluster: at the limit, it is quite thinkable that every single element of the original linguistic vehicle can vanish or be replaced by another, and still the original image remain detectable.

A second observation: the fact that the linguistic correlate of an image has gone into recession does not necessarily indicate that the persisting image is working less powerfully in an author's poetic subconscious. Indeed, quite the contrary is more likely to be the case. The fact that Augustine can continue to imagine the soul's fall into temporal reality in terms of a man's insides distending and bursting outward, without the persistent influence of that image depending on its consorting with a particular linguistic expression, testifies to the robust capacity of that image to stand on its own, so to speak—to assert its identity despite any number of changes in linguistic wardrobe. Paradoxically, insistence on the evidence of "black and white on paper"—that is, on verifiable *linguistic* evidence for linkages of this sort—is often the most effective way of blocking off access to the most significant and telling of such linkages.

What I hope to accomplish in this book, then, is to apply that same approach, image-analysis, to ferreting out what Augustine had told us in his *Confessions* about those three crucial turnings in his life-story, the "conversions" he relates in Books 3, 7, and 8. I must confess that it surprised me how much I still had to learn, personally, about those pivotal episodes and their implications for an understanding of the man's life and view of human life. If the reader of this book comes to share something like that revelatory experience, I shall consider it ample reward.

A closing suggestion: it has been pointed out to me that readers might find it useful, before proceeding further, to acquaint themselves with the main lines of Augustine's fundamental *Omnia* image. For full details of that image, the reader might wisely consult the opening chapter of *Soundings*, but I have also presented a summary description of it on pp. 105–106, below.

Images of Conversion
in St. Augustine's *Confessions*

I

Cicero's *Hortensius* and Augustine's "First Conversion"

A Young Man Reads a Book

AUGUSTINE TELLS US that in his nineteenth year he read a book which turned his world upside down. Remarkable book, one is tempted to say; remarkable nineteen-year-old as well. The book was a Dialogue of Cicero's entitled *Hortensius*. Modeled on Aristotle's *Protrepticus*, it represented Cicero's invitation to embrace the philosophical way of life.

Augustine narrates this episode enthusiastically in the third book of his *Confessions* (3.7–8),[1] but then, as if to stress the importance that experience had for him, he recalls it in Book 6, and again in Book 8 (6.18, 8.17). Moreover, he thrice recalls the same occurrence in the Dialogues he wrote during his vacation-retreat at Cassiciacum, soon after his conversion at Milan (see *Acad* 1.4, 3.7, 31; *Vita* 4; *Sol* 1.17); indeed, he tells us he had made that work of Cicero's "required reading" for the two young students he was tutoring there (*Acad* 3.7). Finally, as if to show that it was not just some intellectual romance of youth, he alludes to it in passing any number of times, and as late as Book 14 of his work *On the Trinity* he actually quotes, approvingly, a generous passage from Cicero's little work (14.26).

The importance Augustine accorded to the reading of the *Hortensius* has not been lost on scholars; they have returned again and again to ferret out the implications of the various accounts he has given of it.[2] For there is something inexhaustibly suggestive in Augustine's various accounts of how the *Hortensius*—if I may hazard a contemporary idiom—"blew his mind." And here, one has to mean by "mind" what Augustine meant by "heart," for it was the entire manifold of his thinking, feeling, hoping—and even praying—which Cicero's meditations managed to shake up. Over the course of time, moreover, the suggestions which Augustine drew from the *Hortensius* rechanneled his life-direction into an entirely different course.

Scholars have labeled this episode Augustine's "first conversion," and rightly so.[3] Indeed, it can be argued that it was "first" in at least two senses: not only did it temporally precede, but in significant ways it also set the pattern for those subsequent twinned conversions that occurred in Milan some thirteen years afterward. It hardly needs repeating in this connection that understanding the inner workings of his conversions remains the privileged entryway into understanding Augustine's mind and soul. But it is also true that to understand his first conversion more exactly is to better understand its later counterparts, and vice versa.

Still, it might be objected, we must tread warily here: understanding Augustine's conversions may not come down to exactly the same thing as understanding his *accounts of* those conversions. The nagging problem of the "two Augustines," as old at least as Gaston Boissier's unsettling article from the year 1888,[4] dogs our effort to understand the *Hortensius* episode as well as every other feature of Augustine's account of his soul's odyssey: has the Bishop, writing between the years A.D. 396 and 400, theologically doctored the more ingenuous view he presented of this incident in the Dialogues of the year 386? A comparison of earlier and later accounts may help to answer that question, particularly if it is conducted with a sensitivity to the language of Augustine's imagery. For the imagination does not lie so readily as calculating reason can.

Augustine's Earliest Accounts

The first account of this incident which we have from Augustine's pen occurs in the Prologue section of the *De beata vita* (4), completed in A.D. 386. He is addressing the man who appears to have been the central figure in a circle of Catholic Neoplatonists at Milan, Manlius Theodorus. He describes his past life, figuratively, as a sea-voyage which first headed away from, but then swung around to return to his original spiritual homeland. The account bristles with metaphorical imagery drawn from Homer's *Odyssey*: in those days, and particularly in Neoplatonic circles,

Odysseus' voyage away from, then back to his home in Ithaca was considered a poetic symbol of the soul's "fall" from and "return" to the higher world of the spirit.[5]

Augustine implies that his own "return" started some fifteen years earlier, for, as he puts it:

> Ever since my nineteenth year, after having made the acquaintance in rhetoric school of that book of Cicero's entitled *Hortensius*, I was enflamed [*succensus*] with such a love of philosophy that I pondered immediately [*statim*] changing over to [devote myself to] it [*ad eam me transferre meditarer*] [*Vita* 4].

The Erotic Aura

Notice especially in this sentence the unabashedly erotic tone of Augustine's reaction: he has been "inflamed" with "love" for philosophy (and it is by no means irrelevant to recall that *philosophia*, in Latin, is feminine in gender). Augustine seems incapable, in fact, of dwelling on *philosophia* without personifying her, and immediately resorting to erotic language and imagery to express his attitude toward her; some lines further in this same paragraph we read of his wishing to fly into the "bosom" (*gremium*) of "philosophy," of "bearing himself away" and "finding rest in that bosom" (*me . . . in illum sinum raperem ibique conquiescerem*).[6]

"Conversion" to Philosophy

A second feature to be noticed in Augustine's account is that expression *statim ad eam me transferre*. Augustine will make it clearer further on what that terse expression already imports for him; but it is indispensable that we grasp something of that import from the outset. He is not talking about running down to the neighborhood library with a list of recommended readings, or enrolling at some nearby university for a series of evening courses in critical thinking. His situation resembles somewhat more closely that of a university student who finds himself tempted to change his "major" from accounting to philosophy; this comparison, though still remote, at least catches the fact that he has been stirred into giving serious thought to changing his very career, to "shifting over" (*me transferre*), radically and abruptly (*statim*), from being that man on the make, the professional rhetorician, to becoming that quaint and impractical oddity, a philosopher.

Philosophia means for him, accordingly, not just some subject of school or university study, but a way of life, to which one "gives oneself" without reserve. To accent the solemnity of the life-decision we are talking about, the men of those times had coined precisely that expression: "conversion to philosophy."[7]

But giving oneself over to the philosophical way of life had certain clear implications in Augustine's day. To grasp those implications as they would have affected Augustine himself, compare the philosopher's lifestyle to that of the professional *rhetor*.[8] The *rhetor* could begin by teaching others the art of rhetoric, as Augustine himself eventually will do; but if he had the talent and ambition for it, he could hope for a brighter future than that— and notably, for example, a future in politics. This would entail catching the eye of those in power, courting their friendship, devoting himself to the busy (and often tiresome and self-abasing) round of being seen in all the right places, on all the appropriate occasions, and in the right company. Adoption as the protégé of a rich and influential patron, like Augustine's patron Romanianus, would also be a step up the ladder to becoming, perhaps, official *rhetor* of some important municipality, like Carthage, Rome—or, why not?—the imperial city itself, Milan!

Imagine acting as official spokesman for the emperor himself, helping to articulate, publicly explain, and defend his imperial majesty's policies and decisions. Think of what it would mean to be quite comfortably wealthy, to move in all the best circles, to have one's name a household word, to be highly thought of, admired and envied throughout the Roman world, and able to look forward, as Augustine tells us he himself could (6.19), to a provincial governorship—perhaps even (picture the triumphal return!) in his native North Africa? Not a paltry list of *honores*, that, for the country-boy son of an ambitious widow from obscure Thagaste. . . .

Detachment *from* Honores

Adopting the philosophical life, however, would mean turning one's back on all the intoxications of worldly success. Cicero, of course, that prince of *rhetors*, had drunk of that heady brew during his political heyday, but then he had fallen out of favor. Thereupon he left Rome for his country villa, and gave himself over to the philosophical way of life. It was a simple life, compared to what he had known: spare to the point of being spartan, poor as Socrates had been poor. All he required was a modest table, his books and writing materials, and peace, blessed peace and leisure. His hours passed serenely in reading, meditation, writing, dwelling among the loftiest ideas and ideals to which human minds had risen. All the mad running about, currying of favor, soliciting and preparing of briefs, the sheer busy-ness of those former days was now behind him. More than that, all the menace of daggers, cabals, plots and counterplots, and, most fearful of all, the venomous slander whispered into an anxious emperor's ear, none of that need he fear any longer: here were only *pax, otium, quies, contemplatio*—peace, leisure, restfulness, and the contemplative spirit's soaring voyages out of time.

It is plain both from his *Confessions* and from his early Dialogues that these were the lures the young Augustine saw Cicero's *Hortensius* displaying to "convert" him to "philosophy." It tells us much about that nineteen-year-old that Cicero succeeded in stirring him so deeply, moving him to ponder that invitation with such evident seriousness. To set off the psychic tremors it did, the *Hortensius* must have been a book Augustine was profoundly "ready" for; he must have been psychologically pre-attuned to the contemplative life to which Cicero invited him. Never afterward would he succeed in extinguishing the lingering attraction it exerted on him.

Error and Superstition

But to continue with the *De beata vita* account: Augustine goes on to describe how his efforts at directing his life's course toward this "haven" of philosophy were impeded by both "clouds" and "sinking stars." It is essential to recognize that Augustine is still talking metaphorically here, still picturing his life as a seafaring Odyssey.[9] If this be kept in mind, then the sentences following make it clear that the "clouds" stand figuratively for the "superstitious" authoritarianism of the *Catholica* he knew in Africa, which discouraged any efforts of "inquiry" in hopes of understanding the difficult points of the Church's belief. The "sinking stars," for their part, stand for the competing doctrines of the Manichees, who catered to inquiring minds like the youthful Augustine's, but then fed those minds on teachings which could not, in the long run, stand up to the test of searching intellectual scrutiny: like the sinking stars which every seasoned mariner (like Odysseus[10]) learns to distrust, those teachings could not be relied upon for guidance on life's voyage.

In the course of this *De beata vita* account, Augustine speaks of a crucial moment in his youthful development when he "became"—or "was made"—"more erect" (*erectior factus*) than he had been heretofore. His habitual use of that term *erectus* illuminates what he means by it here: he learned (in a first movement) to "stand up" on his own intellectual feet, as it were, to shake off the yoke of dependence on authority, and to reason things out for himself.[11] (We shall see that becoming "erect" could refer to a second movement beyond this, but we should not anticipate that part of our story just yet.) One would like very much to know what influences may have fed into this declaration of maturity. Was it the acquaintance with the canons of philosophic inquiry he had drawn from the writings of Cicero, or of philosophers more generally? Or, could it be that Augustine is tacitly acknowledging a debt he owed to the Manichees, and to what was valid in the taunts they leveled against the "blind faith" of African Catholics?[12] We may well be assisting at the birth of Augustine's teaching on "understanding" the faith; it would be gratifying to learn more of that infant's lineage. But this passage of the *De beata vita* leaves us, for the moment, in semi-darkness on that question.

The Contra Academicos *Account*

The proëmium of the *Contra Academicos*, addressed to his former patron Romanianus, shows an Augustine still partial to the seafaring metaphor when describing the storms and maelstroms of human life (1.1). In this context *Philosophia*, still an unmistakably feminine figure, offers a haven of safety after a battering voyage (1.3). Feminine, she evokes the erotic response we have already examined; she boasts bosom and breasts (*gremium, ubera*) to receive the lovers who fly "panting" (*inhiantes*) (1.4) to embrace her (1.2–3). But she is also maternal: she "nourishes and tenderly cares for" her devotees (*nutrit ac fovet*) (1.3); her breasts are suckling breasts, from which "no age group need complain of being excluded" (1.4).

Augustine attributes the eagerness which his youthful students display for philosophy, predictably, to their having imbibed the lesson of the *Hortensius* (1.4), the same work which, he recalls afresh, had originally inflamed him with his early passion for the philosophical life. That flame had meantime come to burn more slowly, but had more recently been revived by the incredible conflagration—*incredibile, Romaniane, incredibile*—ignited by his readings in Platonic philosophy (2.5). It was, he now realizes, the religion of his childhood which was "bearing [him] away, all unknowing, to herself" (*me ad se nescientem rapiebat*) (2.5): like Homer's *Odyssey*, Augustine's is a voyage of return to a belovèd formerly abandoned!

Augustine tends to imagine everyone else's conversion on the erotic model of the one he himself has experienced; the same reaction, he dares conjecture, would overtake even that legal adversary who is currently making trouble for Romanianus. Should "*Philosophia* show her face" to him, he would surely "cast away and leave behind" (*abjiciens et relinquens*) all rival conceptions of happiness, and "take flight toward her beauty, a chaste and holy lover, marveling, panting, burning" (*mirans, anhelans, aestuans*) (2.6). Once granted that vision, "how delightedly would he plunge into Philosophy's bosom" (*quanta voluptate philosophiae gremium se involveret*) (2.7).

The Soliloquies: *What Augustine Was Converted From*

Augustine's early accounts of the *Hortensius* incident cast an interesting light on the nature of his more mature conversion experience at Milan. Everyone will agree that he had to break away from attachment to sexual activity, but was that all there was to it? A most revealing mention of the *Hortensius* occurs in that intimately revealing work, in which Augustine dialogues (or "soliloquizes") with personified Reason. Reason compels him at one point to examine himself on the purity of his desire to see God (1.12–15), or, depending on the paragraph one is reading, to behold (once again, a personified, and unmistakably feminine) Wisdom herself: *Sapientia* (1.22). Reason comes around to asking (1.17) whether he still has any desire for riches. "It is almost fourteen years ago," Augustine replies, "that I left off desiring them. And if by some chance they should come my way, I would

look on them as a means for providing my own necessary suste-
nance, and for liberally dispensing them to others." Then he goes
on to give credit where credit is due: obviously referring to the
Hortensius, he avows that "A single book of Cicero's persuaded
me entirely and easily that we should by no means desire riches,
but that if they came to us, they should be administered with the
greatest of wisdom and prudence."

Significantly, however, when asked about his attitude toward
that cluster of goods the Latins grouped under the rubric of *honores*, Augustine must confess that he left off desiring them only
"quite recently," indeed, he could almost say, "in the course of
these days" spent at Cassiciacum (*modo, ac pene his diebus*). That
avowal chimes in perfectly with what Augustine tells us in the *De
beata vita*: he portrays himself as one of those souls who had to
snap the bonds of both "pleasures and honors" (*voluptatum honorumque*), and one readily guesses that the "anxiety–producing
difficulties of worldly affairs" (*negotiorum anxiae difficultates*) he
speaks of in the very next sentence were connected with that quest
for "honors" (2). The same diagnosis is repeated two paragraphs
further on: the bonds which had held him were the twinned desires "for a wife and for honors" (*uxoris honorisque*), and it was
his professional activity which risked his foundering against the
Sirens' isle of vainglory (4).[13] Indeed, even after his arrival in the
haven of the philosophical life, he sees clearly that the temptation
that recent converts have to avoid most sedulously is that of seeking for "most vain" and "most empty glory" (*vanissimam . . .
inanissimam gloriam*) (3). Moreover, the *Contra Academicos* seems
at one point to make even more of Augustine's desire for "honor
. . . , human vanity and empty reputation" (*honor . . . hominum
pompa . . . inanis famae cupiditas*) than it does of his attachment to
sexual pleasure (2.5)! When we come to compare what the *Confessions* tells us about Augustine's attitudes at the time of his Milanese
conversion, we shall have to recall both these avowals to mind.

The Erotic Quest for Wisdom

The *Soliloquies'* mention of the *Hortensius*, however, occurs without explicit evocation of the erotic echoes we noticed in the *De
beata vita*. Or it would be more accurate to say, rather, that the
erotic echo in the immediate environs appears initially to be a

negative one. Reason asks Augustine (1.17) how he is disposed toward having a wife, one whom Reason goes on to portray as the type of companion who would make an ideal helpmate in his pursuit of wisdom. Augustine repels the suggestion passionately, for nothing, he thinks, so interferes with the virile life of lofty thought as womanly caresses. But then he adds, more positively, that day by day "the stronger my hope of beholding that [Divine] Beauty grows, that Beauty which I burn [*aestuo*] to see, the more my love and delight becomes totally centered on Her" (*tanto ad illam totus amor voluptasque convertitur*). His sexual ardors have been "sublimated" (in one meaning of that Freudian ambiguity), redirected toward pursuing and embracing Divine Wisdom.

Reason returns to this erotic note a few paragraphs further, and in a perfectly parallel context: she inquires once again how well Augustine qualifies as a "lover of Wisdom." Imagine, she suggests boldly, that he were afire with love for a beautiful woman (*si . . . pulchrae feminae amore flagrares*). He would not expect her to yield herself did she find that he loved some other besides herself. So now with his love for Wisdom (Reason's metaphor now becomes even bolder), Augustine desires to "behold and clasp her nude, as it were, with the purest of gazes and embraces, no veil intervening" (*nullo interposito velamento*). But, Reason asks, does he imagine "this most chaste beauty of Wisdom will show herself to you, unless you burn [*arseris*] for Her alone" (1.22)?

This, though, is only the most striking among many such instances in these early Dialogues, when Augustine comes to speak of devoting himself to philosophy and (what evidently comes to the same thing for him) of his hopes for coming to enjoy the direct and immediate vision of God, or personified Wisdom: the atmosphere immediately becomes charged with erotic overtones. This is especially striking when the discussion is triggered by mention of Cicero's *Hortensius*.

But there are occasions where something like the converse occurs: where the erotic charge precedes and only afterward evokes mention of the *Hortensius*, thereby suggesting that the memory of that book, with all its erotic associations, has been exercising an underground influence all along. Consider, for example, the passage already mentioned, where Augustine, writing to his former patron, describes how he was forced by illness to "seek refuge in the bosom of Philosophy" (*in philosophiae gremium*). This brings him to describe how she "nourishes and cares for" him (*nutrit et fovet*), and promises to introduce him to the vision of the "most true" God Himself (*perspicue se demonstraturum promittit*). For no age group need feel themselves excluded from suckling at her breasts (*uberibus*). Only then does Augustine come around to mentioning the *Hortensius*, which has implanted in his students the same "ardent" enthusiasm (*inhiantes*) toward the philosophic life which it had years before instilled in him (*Acad* 1.3–4).

The Confessions *Account: Again, the Erotic Aura*

It is striking how his accounts of the *Hortensius* episode, both in the early Dialogues and in the *Confessions*, testify to the consistency of Augustine's imaginative recall of this episode. The seafaring metaphor, which accompanied the erotic metaphor in the early Dialogues account, is conspicuous in the earlier books of the *Confessions* (1.23–26, 2.24), but it surfaces only discreetly in the *Hortensius* account (3.3), whereas the entire array of sexual elements seen in his earlier accounts is again embedded in both content and context. Indeed, the *Confessions* account goes a long way toward explaining the erotic character of those earlier accounts.

And first, the context: it could be argued that the first moment in his *Confessions* when Augustine becomes clearly recognizable as an individual self is during his portrayal of the outbreak of youthful sexuality in the opening paragraphs of Book 3. In Book 1, he admits, he has drawn himself, not from life, but from observations of other infants and from speculative inferences based on those observations. Something very similar is true of his portrait of boyhood: the Augustine who comes through is far more "your typical growing boy" than the unique, irreplaceable lad he surely was.

Book 2, it is true, had momentarily promised to be different. It opened with the freshness of one man's individual memory, as Augustine described the turbulence and confusions of puberty, the storms of adolescent sexuality. But then Book 2 quickly subsides into that lengthy meditation on the theft of pears. Here, the lines of individuality lose sharpness; we are confronted with a theological icon, your typical child of Adam, rehearsing the ancient sin of Eden.[14] Book 3 opens, and Augustine returns to his youthful struggles with sexuality: he is nineteen now, far from

home in that "cauldron" of lusts, Carthage. But as with the opening paragraphs of Book 2, we detect once again the vividness
of direct recall, the sharp poignancy that only personal memory
can engender.

Augustine's account of his wrestling with sex, love, and friendship will culminate in his entering into a common-law marriage.
He then goes on to tell of two other turning points which seem
to have occurred in that same nineteenth year: his encounter with
the *Hortensius*, and his conversion to Manichaeism.

He narrates these three events serially, as would have seemed
natural to him; he focuses on each in turn, with the results that
their episodic distinction from each other sets each of them "outside" the other two, as it were. But first of all, we have been
advised not to trust the chronology of Augustine's *Confessions* too
literally;[15] and, secondly, common-sense psychology warns that
those chronological distinctions may do a certain violence to Augustine's unity of consciousness. If, on the contrary, we strive to
set all three episodes into organic relation with each another, we
may come to a more adequate understanding of each of them. In
particular, we may succeed in grasping why the *Hortensius* episode
took on, in Augustine's memory, the overtly sexual coloration
which saturates all his portrayals of it, early and later.

I shall begin, accordingly, by following Augustine's own procedure, analyzing each episode in and for itself. But then I shall take
a second view, looking at the marriage and Manichee-conversion
incidents "through" the *Hortensius* story, and vice versa. The composite picture resulting from that second view will, I hope, make
greater sense not only of the *Hortensius* episode, but of all three
occurrences taken from Book 3.

THROUGH THE LENS OF AUGUSTINE'S SEXUALITY

We have seen that by the time Augustine wrote his Cassiciacum
Dialogues a host of erotic associations had come to cluster about
his memory of the conversion inspired by Cicero's *Hortensius*. To
understand how those associations formed, however, one must
turn to the account of that episode which he composed in his
Confessions. For it is significant that he introduces his *Confessions*
account of that occurrence almost immediately after describing

his battles with sexuality at age nineteen. He is broadly hinting, I suggest, that our understanding of his *Hortensius* conversion will hinge importantly on our understanding the role sexuality played in his youthful years, and perhaps throughout his life.

Yet so much has been written about Augustine's sexuality, and by experts so varied in their approaches and qualifications, that the layperson feels shy about risking still another opinion. To what extent should one intend to rely on this or that among the batteries of psychoanalytic models which have been trundled into position and aimed at what Augustine tells about himself, or fails to tell, and by failing betrays, or misrepresents, whether consciously or unconsciously—or indeed, whatever admixture of the above one chooses to favor![16]

One's hands are already overfull with taking the measure of this particular individual, Augustine of Hippo: of his language, imagery, intellectual development both philosophical and theological—and all of this against the background of the historical period in which he lived. Meanwhile, one listens fascinated while the analysts debate among themselves as to which of their various models is more applicable to this particular client. Should we look for an Oedipal story here, or a pre-Oedipal narcissistic drama? Should we lean on Freud—whether early or late—on Jung, on Kohut? So busy do those liminal issues keep the psychological experts that they seldom if ever allow themselves the time to reckon with the number of facets that make this particular client so *desperately* particular. It may not be sheer impertinence, accordingly, to suggest that the professional analysts have been less than uniformly successful in understanding Augustine's language, much less in illuminating his psyche.[17] These remarks are not intended as a know-nothing plea to reject wholesale everything psychoanalysis may have to say on the subject of Augustine's sexuality; but every shoemaker has his own individual last; he must acknowledge that his minuscule island of competence is surrounded by oceans of relative ignorance; he must apply his particular set of skills as carefully, and modestly, as he can. The analyst who knows much about the psyche in general may know next to nothing about Augustine's Latin, or culture, or theology; but the student of Augustine who is more classically equipped must own up to having corresponding gaps in his equipment. For the "lay" student of Augustine's personality, therefore, modesty requires that he keep a weather-eye out for what psychoanalytic models may contribute to illumine Augustine's account of himself. But he has no other choice but to place primary emphasis on interpreting that account as his scholarly skills qualify him to read it, even if that involves handing over his findings, in a second stage, to professional students of the psyche.[18]

Augustine's Sexual Metaphors

That procedure may help to avoid some of the gaffes which past scholars have committed, by underestimating, for example, Augustine's penchant for figurative language. He had, moreover, the *rhetor*'s tendency toward hyperbole, and the hyperbolic expressions he found in Scripture only encouraged that tendency. How frequently, for example, the author of the *Confessions* accuses himself of "fornication"; sometimes, but not always, the term is further specified as fornication "against God." The unwary reader might not realize that Augustine's use of the term regularly reflects the way he interprets its occurrence in Psalm 72:27: the term "fornication against God," he explains in his *Confessions* (1.21), applies to any act whatever, sexual or not, which expresses the soul's attachment to a creature in preference to God.[19] *Tantillus puer et tantus peccator* is how he labels himself as a little boy (1.16), and the average reader can scarcely contain a skeptical "tut-tut." But we shall come to see that there is more to that hyperbole than immediately meets the eye.

Something similar applies to Augustine's use of the term *cupiditas*: as the opposite of *caritas*, by which Augustine means the desire to rest in the "enjoyment" of God, *cupiditas* signifies any desire whatever which is blameworthy because it deflects the soul's desire toward a love-object which is other than God. Translators have been known to render *cupiditas* as "lust," but sexual lust is only one form of such blameworthy desire. The sinful "love of the world," which St. John censures in his First Epistle (2:15–16)—a text which became central to Augustine's moral theology—could take one of three forms, and sometimes a combination of all three: the desire for pleasure (concupiscence of the flesh, "lust" in the usual sense of that term), "curiosity" (concupiscence of the eyes), and pride. Augustine could apply the term *cupiditas* to any one of, or any amalgam of, the three. For that reason, it seems faintly suspicious when a recent writer speaks of Augustine as the slave of his (presumably sexual) "insatiable lusts,"[20] when that identical expression (*insatiabiles cupiditates*) occurs in the first book of his *Confessions* (1.19), where Augustine is reflecting on the years of his childhood, well before he describes the precisely sexual form of lust as surfacing in his sixteenth year (2.1). Furthermore, Augustine never formally characterizes sexual *cupiditas* as more or less "insatiable" than its partner-members in the triad of sinfulness, the reason being that, like a good Platonist, he understood that such bodily desires in any form are by their very nature "insatiable."[21]

Failure to understand the highly colored language that Augustine uses when speaking of sexuality accounts in large part for the extravagant judgments that have been leveled about the "terrible strength" of his passions. This "'profligate bishop,'" we are told, became the "'fountainhead of that pruriency'" which has since defiled Western theology.[22] He was, we are more recently informed, "a man who never married, and whose experience of sexual pleasure was illicit and guilt-provoking."[23] In contrast with angry volleys like those, one is grateful for John O'Meara's more informed evaluation of Augustine's pre-marital exploits as just about average for the Carthaginian collegian of his time, and Peter Brown's careful estimate that his relationship with the mother of his son was an arrangement deemed respectable by both civil and ecclesiastical authorities of the epoch.[24] Despite Augustine's guardedly expressed depreciation of it as "not what is called [*vocatur*] a legitimate marriage" (4.2), it was looked on as a kind of "second-class" union, and its closest contemporary equivalent would be, not concubinage, but common-law marriage. So, Brown is very probably correct in conjecturing that it provided Augustine "nine years of unproblematic enjoyment of sexual companionship."[25] This does not completely resolve all the conflicts of interpretation which turn on the question of Augustine's sexuality, however; surely a measure of closer study cannot do irreparable harm.

What, then, was Augustine's sexual experience like, and how did his resulting attitude toward sex figure into his "conversion" at the age of nineteen, and, later, at thirty-four? Our soundest strategy is to follow the story as he tells it in the *Confessions*; that work has invariably been the primary focus for discussions of Augustine's sexuality, mostly for the excellent reason that it represents our richest source of evidence. That does not mean, of course, that we shall entirely ignore what Augustine reveals on the topic in others of his writings.

Sexuality in Augustine's Relationship with God

It requires no great insight to recognize that, especially when dealing with a God-haunted man like Augustine, the sexual implications of his God-image are of first importance. The *Confessions* are quick to reward the researcher on this issue: the moment the reader gets past the proëmium (1.1–6), Augustine plunges into a description of infancy, dominated by images of maternal breasts.[26] Soon we are told that the milk that nourished the infant Augustine came, not from, but "through" those human breasts, from God Himself—or should we say "Herself"? Here, as so often throughout the *Confessions* (and his preached works, also), Augustine images God as a nursing, consoling, tenderly caring Mother. To be sure, he had plenty of Biblical encouragement for this imagery (and for the effect which doubtless accompanied it); Isaiah alone provided a wealth of inspiration on which he clearly drew.[27] But many another preacher and writer has been exposed to the same Isaian mother-imagery without its inspiring him to compose the symphony on God's maternal "care" which the *Confessions* represents from prelude to final coda. Here, as in all such cases of "selective influence," we are being told a great deal about the predispositions which any "influenced" individual brings to filtering, and attributing importance to, the "influences" playing on him: no two individuals will come away from reading the same poem, say, with the identical baggage of impressions. No one ever read Isaiah exactly as Augustine did.

The "maternal" character of Augustine's infancy idyll might tempt us to think that his Mother-God was ideally suited to him as Monica's "mama's boy." Yet on closer inspection, the picture complicates: for one thing, a number of his feminine God-images are undisguisedly more "spousal" than maternal in character.[28] On this score, also, Augustine received considerable encouragement from Biblical as well as from pagan literature.

Finally, it must be acknowledged that Augustine's "masculine" images of God are (at first blush, anyway) of a much sterner stamp: they regularly have to do with chastisement and judgment;

even when they deal with healing, cure is regularly attained through burning, cutting, and similar painful procedures. These "paternal" features of Augustine's God might seem to support Joseph Dittes's claim that his God tends to be impersonal and remote;[29] but how Dittes can have missed the balancing closeness, the poignant tenderness of Augustine's maternal and spousal God, it is difficult to understand.

It is significant, also, that Augustine regularly depicts his maternal God in close association with those marvelous paradoxes of omnipresence which manifest his keen awareness that God's "nearness" is not opposed to, but actually requires the "remoteness" of, genuine transcendence: to be integrally omnipresent, God must "remain in Himself."[30] Augustine seems to have sensed, moreover, that God must possess masculine as well as feminine traits if She/He is to exist "beyond" the limitations of being one to the exclusion of the other. In any case, the sensitivity Augustine brought to depicting God's feminine side is altogether remarkable, and, more directly to our point here, the boldness of the frankly sexual imagery he brings to that depiction is utterly disarming. As a result of all this, to anticipate what we shall see further on, Augustine will portray his "conversion" to God under a variety of sexual guises. In every case, though, conversion will be not only a turn, but a "return": of the Prodigal to his Father, of a straying child to his mother, of a wandering Odysseus to Penelope, his faithful bride.

The Language of Soul to Soul

Augustine transmutes much of his account of infancy into a meditation on how humans learn the first rudiments of speech. One need not agree with his psychology of infancy or of language to grasp what the point of his meditation is: he is "exercising the mind" of his readers—a favorite teaching technique of his—to provoke the realization that our human life of consciousness and volition is conducted "inside" the opaque "vestment" or "housing"—*habitus* or *habitatio*—of the mortal body. The opacity of the body prevents our "interior" from communicating immediately— "soul to soul"—with the interior of another; hence, we must resort to all the roundabout techniques of symbolic expression and, while doing so, painfully learn that we can never adequately com-

municate the richness of our spiritual lives by means of blunt
bodily instruments like words and looks and gestures. Conversely, if we so choose, this hiatus between soul and body makes
it possible for us to lie and dissimulate to each other. We shall see
more of that "veiling" image, and of its analogues, as we go
further; for the moment, though, notice that it functions as the
"horizontal" counterpart of a more "vertical" image: as a Platonist, Augustine is convinced that the mental representation, or
"inner word," is always "superior," and the spoken, "outer
word," inferior, to it. However eloquently or artistically crafted
that sensible expression may be, it is always a come-down, a trai-
torous translation at best, of the inner word it was meant to convey. It would never spontaneously occur to Augustine, therefore,
to regard the "bodily" language of sex as an appropriate form
of authentically human "conversation," a gestural "language" in
which spouses could express their tender love for each other.[31]

In a corresponding vertical image, this one depicting the relationship of soul to body, Augustine pictures the soul as ideally
situated "above," and therefore governing, the body which is
"sub-ordinate" to it. But humanity's sinful condition has turned
that order upside down: the rebellious body too often lords it
over the soul.[32] Augustine comes to think of the human genitals
as the primary locus of that unruliness which dislocates body from
soul, and sets the mortal body into rebellious disrelation with the
"I" which he identifies with the mind-soul. This persuades him
to think that, once we begin to play the game of sexual love, we
inevitably get swept away into another game entirely: that of lustful exploitation which the mortal body stubbornly insists on
playing.

Family Inheritance: Monica

In dealing with this topic, it should not be forgotten that we
have to do with a North African temperament. In this regard,
exaggerations are a danger: it is true, for one thing, that we cannot
know for sure the exact blood-mix Augustine received from his
parents. But the resulting solution was almost certainly, as André
Mandouze puts it, "hot, impulsive, and given to extremes."[33] Not
only is that judgment borne out by Augustine's biography, but
it also seems to have been Monica's estimate of her young son.

She quite deliberately delayed his baptism because, Augustine speculates, the guilt of sins committed after baptism would be "greater and more dangerous" (1.17) than those committed by a catechumen who remained unbaptized. The penitential practice of the early Church may also have been a factor: for several centuries the sin of adultery (along with murder and apostasy), when committed by a baptized person, incurred the austere regime of public penance for its remission, whereas adult baptism was considered to cleanse the soul at a stroke.[34]

How was the young Augustine to respond to Monica's half-fatalistic attitude? Did he even notice? Augustine assures us that he did. As a child, he became dangerously ill; while hovering close to death, he begged and pleaded for baptism; his mother was on the point of giving in when suddenly he took a turn for the better. Result: baptismal plans were put on "hold" once again. The memory is evidently a vivid one, and Augustine intimates the message this tactic sent to him: that Monica regarded it as "quasi-necessary that [he] would be stained" by sins as he grew older (1.17). The saying was a common one, he assures us: "Let him be, let him do it—for he is not yet baptized!" And Monica was realistic enough to know "what mighty storms of temptations" would menace her volatile young boy during adolescence (1.18).

Monica exhibits a similar laissez-faire attitude on the occasion when Patricius, in the public baths, detects that his son has become "vested in [a body of] restless adolescence," and exultantly brings the glad news home. Augustine's report of this incident is highly suggestive; his father, formerly a pagan, was by this time a catechumen, but only that; obviously, we are not to expect too much from him. But God "had already begun" (*iam inchoaveras*) to make Monica His Temple; we have a right to expect more of her. And, despite the fact that her son was "not yet one of the faithful," she "admonished" him secretly, and "with immense solicitude, that [he] not fornicate, and, most important of all [*maximeque*], that [he] not commit adultery with anyone's wife" (2.6–7). Fornication was bad, but adultery, obviously, could turn out to be big trouble: there is just a suggestion here of the cynical old nostrum "if you can't be good, be careful." In any event, it was not exactly the kind of advice that would put needed spine into a hot-blooded sixteen-year-old's resolve to remain chaste.

In the very next paragraph (2.8), Augustine underlines Monica's careful blend of worldly policy and moral sagacity. Despite her awareness of the dangers surrounding her growing son, her recommendations of chastity never took the form of practical moves, like the obvious one of arranging a marriage for him. The reasoning he attributes to her (*ita enim conicio recolens*) supports his judgment that she may have fled "the very center of Babylon," that haven of evil, but was "still loitering in its outskirts." Her inaction in regard to marriage had nothing to do with his hopes for the next life; she was concerned for his future in *this* life: she feared that a wife who was not from the higher echelons of society might prove an "impediment" to the worldly hopes that both she and Patricius were pinning on their brilliant son!

And sure enough, Augustine is soon afterward sent (without, apparently, any practical concern for his supervision) to pursue his studies in Madaura, and subsequently in Carthage—a city notorious for the opportunities it afforded for every form of vice. Here, as we know, Augustine contracted that liaison with the girl who became the mother of his son, Adeodatus. We must examine that episode more closely further on, but it is worth noting, for now, that while Monica barred the door to him when he converted to Manichaeism, something which occurred around the same time, Augustine records no such complaints when he brought his bed-companion home. After her subsequent reconciliation with her son, Monica seems to have lived at peace with his common-law wife, both at Carthage and at Milan.

Years later, when Augustine's Milanese conversion approaches, Monica's attitude and tactics remain much the same: Augustine awakens one day to find that the mother of his son has been sent home to Africa, evidently as part of a deal which will ensure him the high-society marriage that will further his brilliant career (6.19). Once penned up in that corral of safety, though, Augustine can also think seriously of baptism. But until this arrangement for her son's worldly future had been nailed down, it is something of a question how very high either his baptism or his chastity ranked among Monica's effective priorities. Augustine takes an interim mistress; again, we do not hear of a whisper of complaint from Monica. Her devotion to Augustine had much of the "daughter of Eve" about it (5.15), and the message was not lost on her son.

Patricius' Contribution

But where, all this time, was Augustine's father? And what was
Patricius' influence on his son? Ah, dear old Patricius: I cannot
help feeling he has been given (forgive the expression) a "bum
rap," first by his son, then by interpreters of the *Confessions*. What
do we really know of him? Very little, but that little has gone far in
firing the inventiveness of later generations. Dittes, for example,
speaking of Patricius' proud discovery that his boy was growing
up, blackens the incident with the rancid label "bawdy locker
room initiation."[35]

It is not surprising that Patricius, a *petit fonctionnaire* of the
imperial bureaucracy, of limited means and enjoying no particular
prestige, shared Monica's ambitions for their son. Even Augustine
seems to have been impressed by how far he strained his income,
even going temporarily broke, in his efforts to finance the best
possible education for the boy (2.5). A pagan when he married
Monica, he was eventually won for the faith, and was baptized
before he died (9.22). But he seems to have remained a pale and
formless presence to his brilliant son; Augustine's narration does
not provide any substantial evidence that he was the object of the
"Oedipal rage" some analysts have claimed he was (or, perhaps
more accurately, *must* have been). The poor man dies, and Augustine only adverts to that fact several biographical paragraphs
later (3.7)! Aha! a Freudian slip! But must all such slips be genuinely Freudian?

But Monica, her son tells us in his little biography of her in
Book 9, "endured [Patricius'] injurious treatment in her marriage
bed" without making any great fuss about it (9.19). Interpreters
have regularly interpreted that expression *toleravit cubilis iniurias*
as meaning that Patricius was "unfaithful" (Elaine Pagels inflates
this to "habitually unfaithful") to his wife.[36] Further, they tacitly
assume that the boy Augustine must have been aware of this—in
which case Patricius, too, would have to bear his share of guilt
for undercutting his son's resolve in his adolescent sexual conflicts.

Were that interpretation sound, however, we would hardly expect Augustine to have done the portrait of his father in the
washed-out tones more appropriate to a figure who was never all
that emotionally important to him. Augustine tells us at one point,
in a chilling sentence, that Monica strove determinedly to make

God, not Patricius, Augustine's "true father" (1.17). She may have succeeded all too well.

But we have no warrant for inferring from the Latin expression Augustine employs that the "injurious treatment" Monica suffered from her husband took the form of marital infidelity. The term occurs immediately after Augustine has assured us that Monica's character made her *pulchram . . . et reverenter amabilem atque mirabilem*, "beautiful and [the object of] reverent love and wonder" to her husband, and it takes no great leap of the imagination to conjecture that Augustine may be referring to an excess of sexual ardor on Patricius' part rather than the reverse. We must always remember that the expression comes from the same Bishop of Hippo who urged abstention from marital relations during Lent (*SS 207, 208, 209*), preached that marital intercourse was always venially sinful and justified only for purposes of procreation (*S 51* 21–22), and mocked Julian of Eclanum so bitingly on his rosier view of sexuality.[37] It would scarcely surprise if he was here imputing to his mother his own (and perhaps North African Catholicism's) puritanical view of married sexuality. While still a pagan, of course, Patricius would not consider himself bound by Monica's views in the matter; the hypothesis I am proposing would furnish a natural explanation why his conversion resulted in that change in behavior Augustine later recounts, and recounts precisely in the terms he uses: once Patricius had become a "believer," Monica no longer had to "complain of that which she had had to bear with when he was as yet an unbeliever" (9.22). It comes as something of an intellectual shock, no doubt, when received opinion on a question like this is abruptly turned on its head; but I may be excused for repeating that, once one presses the Latin Augustine employs, the older interpretation does not seem to have much ground to stand on, after all. And, in any event, as long as the one I have proposed remains a plausible competitor, it seems extremely chancy to erect any inferences concerning Augustine's sexual attitudes on the questionable premiss that he knew his father was something of a rake.

Sexual Imagery in Augustine's Literary Studies

Augustine tells us that his first experiences of sex came at second hand, when he was put to studying literature. He will try, in an

afterthought, to exculpate Monica by speculating that she hoped
the normal course of studies would "be no obstacle, but even
some help to [her son] toward attaining [God]" (2.8). But while
it was probably true that he took delight in reading about the love
affairs of Dido, Aeneas, and Jove (1.20–26) we now know enough
about his figured language to realize that the "fornication against
[God]" he sees in all of this means only that "friendship with this
world" St. John warns against in his First Epistle (1 Jo 2:15–16).

But it is worth noticing that Augustine archly intimates that his
soul's original "fornication" from God was in fact a pre-temporal,
archetypical act whereby "I forsook You, and went chasing after
the lowermost of your creatures; I, who was earth, going toward
earth" (1.21). This, I can only suggest for now, is one of Augustine's images for the primal "iniquity" (7.22) which "weighed
down" our souls when their desires turned "earthy," and plunged
them from the heights of angelic bliss into the restless pursuit of
the pleasures promised by the "lowermost" of bodily realities
(7.22). In his treatment of infancy, he asked two troubling questions and left them both unanswered: before he existed in this
mortal life, was he anyone, anywhere (1.9)? And could that have
been where and when he contracted the "iniquity," the sinfulness
in which Scripture assures us each of us is "conceived" (1.12)? He
has already begun to hint at the answer to both those questions:
the dynamism of our soul's original "fall," figuratively replayed
in the famous "theft of pears" (2.9), is still working its way
through the activity of infant, child, adolescent, and adult, un-
masking even a "little lad" as quite literally (in that phrase we saw
earlier) a "great sinner" (*tantillus puer et tantus peccator*).

But this is only one such instance where what initially seemed a
specimen of overblown rhetoric discloses, when pressed, a deeper
stratum of dark ironies. Even childhood peccadilloes, Augustine
is convinced, are surface revelations of a sinful dynamic whose
venom wells up from an act once performed in the unconstrained
plenitude of angelic freedom. In consequence, that plenitude of
freedom has been lost to us (8.22; cf. *Lib* 3.34–35), yet even the
acts we now commit out of moral "ignorance and difficulty" can
contain a gravity and poignancy which fully justify, Augustine
thinks, expressions which we could mistakenly read as rhetorical
overkill. For according to his theory, every sin we commit, including that of bodily fornication, is a renewal of our primordial

"turning away" to love "this world" in preference to God, a fresh ratification of our soul's original "fornication" from Him.

Augustine's Sexual Awakening

As we remarked earlier, sexuality in the proper sense of the term (*pace* Freud) makes its massive entrance in Augustine's sixteenth year, when he enters on adolescence. He opens Book 2 with a barrage of near-Swiftian imagery: filth, corruption, fevers mingle with the stench and stain of rank jungle growth. He accuses himself of "varied and shadowy loves," inspiring one interpreter, less acquainted with Augustine's Latin than he might have been, to imagine him engaging in homosexual adventures.[38] Like the Prodigal, he kept going farther and farther from his heavenly Father, while (simultaneously!), like Odysseus, he was "tossed about and spilt forth" into the stormy seas of passion. Suddenly, the metaphor of fluidity takes a frankly biological turn: his "fornications made [him] boil over and flow outward in all directions." The result: he is overcome by a "restless weariness" (*inquieta lassitudine*) (2.2).

That phrase is a near-perfect match for the one Augustine will use later: artists who observe no norm for the "use" of their beautiful productions succeed only in "wandering farther away" from God and "spew forth their strength into wearisome languors" (*in deliciosas lassitudines*) (10.53). Augustine is picturing those artists, and himself, as a composite of those two ancient world metaphors for the wayfaring soul, the Prodigal and Odysseus. Both encountered sensual temptations, the Prodigal among harlots, Odysseus on Circe's island—but amid the Lotus-eaters' "languorous weariness" as well. For both, the great danger was that they might "forget" that they were on a homeward journey and tarry, regarding the beauties surrounding them not as objects of "use," temporary "stop-overs" to help them voyage farther, but as "places to stay," "abodes" at which their journeying could be considered at an end. Instead of regarding them as *stabula*, travelers' "inns," and journeying farther, the soul was in danger of taking them for *mansiones*, permanent dwellings meant to be terminally "enjoyed."

Augustine is saying, then, that the sexual form of *cupiditas* induced him to consider the bodily charms of those who gave him pleasure as objects of terminal "enjoyment," coaxed him to mur-

mur languidly, like the Lotus-eaters of Tennyson's poem, "leave
us alone, we will not wander more." The image is a daring one;
it speaks volumes on how Augustine regarded sexual self-
indulgence: having "spewed forth" the strength he should have
conserved for journeying back to God, he then experienced the
"weariness" of post-coital languor, a weariness both cloying and
at the same time "restless," for it cannot entirely silence the nagging voice of duty, somnolently deferred.

Sex and Friendship-Love

But there is a hidden irony here: Augustine's scheme implies that
had he loved his sexual partners with the more appropriate love
of "friendship" (*amicitia*), he would, in a real sense, have loved
them less! For, then, he would have loved them, not with the love
of "enjoyment" (which he reserves to God, exclusively), but with
the love of "use." This corollary of his love-theory has been
pointed out, in tones of disappointment, by a number of his critics, and their case is a strong one.[39] Augustine has, in fact, adopted
an overly simple set of categories for thinking out the various
forms of love—we "love" either for "use" or for "enjoyment"—
and when striving to situate our love for other human beings in
terms of those categories, he has applied them all too inflexibly.
Even our dearest and noblest friends must be loved as objects of
"use," to bring us closer to the God Whom alone we should aspire
to "enjoy." True, he does experiment in his work *On the Trinity*
(11.20) with a hybrid form, *frui in via*, permitting us to "enjoy"
our human loved ones "along the way"; but then he warns that
we must never allow those loves to detain us, or slow us down
from our homeward journey; hence, when all is said, he is approving a form of "use," after all.

  The hidden irony involved here is this: Augustine will quite
soon tell us of his first literary product, a little work on aesthetics
called *De pulchro et apto* (4.20ff.). The title itself betrays the basic
distinction presiding over the work. In the first place, there is a
kind of "good" which is so in the sense of being *aptum*, "fitting"
or "befitting." It "goes well with" (is *conveniens* to) the other being
"for which" it is considered "good": so, a "good" shoe "goes well
with" a person's foot. But there is another kind of "good," to
which Augustine accords the title "beautiful" (*pulchrum*): such re-

alities are good in and of themselves; there is no need for their goodness to be grounded on any relationship of being "good-*for*" some other being (though they may also have that kind of goodness, as well).

Here, though, Augustine has put his finger on a property which "beauty" shares with the ideal sort of "friend" which Aristotle described in Book 8 of his *Nichomachean Ethics*, and which must surely have been familiar to Augustine through Cicero's dialogue *On Friendship*. Both of them, the beautiful object and the ideal friend, exhibit a type of excellence which invites, even compels, us momentarily to suspend all traces of self-interest and self-concern—all "narcissistic" considerations, if you will—and simply lose ourselves in admiring the excellence of the friend, or the beauty of the phenomenon before us. This, I take it, is the attitude to which narcissism theory refers as genuine "object-love." Oliver O'Donovan, in his study of "self-love" in Augustine's thought, classifies it as "rational love";[40] but there is some question about whether he has sufficiently acknowledged how regularly it gets mentioned precisely in an aesthetic context. For tracing the development of Augustine's aesthetic thought shows that virtually every time the rights of this "rational" form of love are challenged by the "use-*vs.*-enjoyment" scheme, the quasi-terminal quality of "un–self-concern" evanesces, its *frui* character boiling down to a form of *uti*.

That kind of reductionism is at work in the passages on sex and friendship we have just been considering. Similar reductions can occur quite abruptly. To anticipate for a moment: one such occurs in Book 4 of the *Confessions*, the book in which Augustine outlines the *De pulchro et apto* thesis which should have obviated it, and in the very paragraphs which precede (14–15) and follow (30) the discussion of that little work. There, Augustine counsels us not to love even our dearest and best of friends the way he loved that young man whose death pierced him with such agony. We must love everything temporal with the love of "use," or, in an alternative formulation, we must love them all "in God." But only the formulation is new: loving our friends "in God" comes down, on examination, to the same thing as loving them with the love of "use."[41]

One can only conclude that Augustine's appreciation of "rational-" or "object-love" was unsteady, at best, too weak to stand up against the momentum of his *uti–frui* distinction. The contemporary thinker, enriched by the contributions of intervening centuries, has a larger number of avenues for approaching these questions. One cannot help wondering what would have eventuated had Augustine been prompted to explore the possibility we mentioned earlier: that sexual activity could become a genuinely expressive "language," especially had that idea been combined with the insight that one could behold and cherish a true "friend" as a thing of beauty.

But the melancholy truth is that Augustine never seriously pursued such alternatives. Isn't it possible, the heart protests, that this bloodless and abstract *uti–frui* distinction may have ranked (in Newman's classic terms) among Augustine's "notional," rather than among his "real," assents? For we are, after all, talking about a full-blooded individual who, by all accounts, had a positive "genius for friendship," who "lived" his friendships far more faithfully, even passionately, than this chill theory would sanction. Besides, the mental gymnastics to which he put himself in his work *On the Trinity*, even if they eventually afforded him no escape from it, clearly point to his chafing discomfort with this distinction. Augustine was at least as intelligent as we moderns, and even if his mind was insufficiently stocked with alternative categories for dealing with the question, he must have felt keenly how tight this mental straitjacket fitted.

We have to sympathize with such protestations; and yet, we must also come, at the last, however disconsolately, to face the cold facts of the matter. Understanding Augustine's conversion, in all its connected facets, necessarily entails trying to understand what he himself has told us. True enough, we must strive to expand on what he told us consciously, by ferreting out as best we can what he has betrayed through the more occult conduits of imaginative communication; but we can never entirely escape the predicament which binds us to interpreting what Augustine himself has told us, and how Augustine himself, on both conscious and less-conscious levels, "understood" his own experience. Nor can we alter the way he understood his own experience by wishing, however fervently, that he had understood it otherwise.

Moreover, Augustine himself has alerted us, with stunning insight, to the osmotic interrelationship which bonded his personal experience to his ongoing reflection on it: he was one, he assures us, who "kept writing as he kept progressing, and kept progressing by writing" out the record of his progress (*Ep 143* 2). This is a special type of person: he was positively driven to understand his ongoing experience by transmuting it into written expression; but then, the expression he gave it inevitably caromed back to shape his ongoing experience. At a number of points, what "actually happened" to him became less decisive than—indeed, *became*, simply—very much what he thought and felt and imagined had happened.

But this only made Augustine a specially pronounced case of that power common to all conscious human agents: each of us "creates" modes and limits of feeling and evaluating which, over time, can inhibit, recast, even to some extent "falsify," our saner, more spontaneous, and "natural" ways of feeling. Every physician knows that the psychosomatic headache "hurts" just as much as a "real" one, just as every therapist must deal with patients who have come "really" to live in the forest of neurotic fantasies they have constructed about them. Persuade yourself deeply enough that friends must not be loved except with a love of "use," and that persuasion is bound to alter your more spontaneous attitude toward your friends. So also (to anticipate for a moment), when we come to Augustine's life as a Manichee, we must not allow our conviction that Manichaeism is a farrago of nonsense, to prevent us from acknowledging that over a good span of years Augustine's world, both inner and outer, "*was* that way" for *him*.

I know of no more convincing evidence that Augustine came to view his loves and friendships in line with the strictures of his *uti–frui* distinction than the recurring image which sums up for him, more poignantly than any other, his feeling for our entire human situation: the image of life as *peregrinatio*. Like the Prodigal, we are wayfarers; like the Israelites, wanderers in a desert; like Odysseus, voyagers. It would be our greatest tragedy, heartbreaking failure, to get so comfortable with the amenities of our journeying as never to "arrive": back to our Father's house, back to the breasts of the Heavenly Jerusalem, our Mother, back to the spousal embrace of Penelope, that ancient figure of Wisdom, whom we long ago left behind, but never completely forgot. Strangeness, alienation, insecurity and danger; hunger, thirst, and insatiable longing; restlessness—these are the feelings Augustine

entertained for "this" twilight world, this "region of darkness."
Not only did he entertain them, he deliberately cultivated them,
and strove tirelessly to persuade his flock to cultivate them as
well.[42]

The "Ascetical Model" for Sexuality

This was Augustine's individualized backdrop for what Peter
Brown has termed the "ascetic" paradigm for viewing human
sexuality. Something of the sort was "in the air" of late antiquity,
Brown observes; it received especially forceful expression from
the "radical wing of ascetical Christians," and quite notably from
Ambrose and his circle. Adam and Eve, these people thought,
were created by God to be, and to remain, asexual beings, in
"angelic" bodies, "untouched by sexuality." All their original
bliss, Brown goes on to say, derived from their "'angelic' contemplation of God." But from that blissful condition they "fell" into
the "present 'material' mode of being," into a condition of sexual
differentiation, as well as into the "'cares of this world'" which
have since become familiar to us all. Hence, Brown concludes,
withdrawal from human society to embrace the ascetical life was
looked on as a partial return to the angelic joys of Adam and
Eve's pre-fallen state.[43]

Brown's picture seems to me to this point unexceptionable;
moreover, it chimes in quite well with the view of human sexuality we are about to see Augustine develop in his *Confessions*. I
would suggest only one alteration; it may be more a matter of
emphasis than anything else. We are about to see that in the case
of Augustine's version of the paradigm, at least, the label would
more appropriately read "ascetical–*mystical*." For Augustine will
insist that the withdrawal to the "ascetical" life is in the first instance a surrender to the peaceful joys of contemplation, and possibly to the ecstasy of mystical union as well. He never tires of
stressing, moreover, that we must be "drawn" upward from the
delights of bodily sex by the appetite for "spiritual" beatitude;
that beatitude, he promises, is only the more attractive for embodying, on a higher, spiritual level, all the allures of sexual union.
And, strangely enough, his earliest formulations of this "mystical"
view of sexuality seem to have been encouraged by his reading,
of all people, Cicero!

Adolescent Sexual Experiences

We have already seen that Augustine recounts his experience of adolescent sexuality in two stages, covering his sixteenth year at the very beginning of Book 2, and his nineteenth year at the beginning of Book 3. He begins Book 2 with the first of several word-plays on the term for love: he is, he tells his God, about to confess all this out of love for God's love: *amore amoris Tui*. He tells us that he "burned" at age sixteen (*exarsi*) with love for this world's beauties (2.1), but on reflection he now sees that beneath the surface of those loves what really delighted him was to "love and be loved" (*amare et amari*) (2.2). There is something diffuse, undirected in all this—call it something "oceanic." Augustine himself calls attention to that property a bit further on (3.1): arrived at Carthage, he realized that "I did not yet love" (*nondum amabam*) but "I loved loving" itself (*amare amabam*). And "Since I loved loving, I sought for something to love" (*quaerebam quid amare*). So he battened in love on the sensible beauties in the world about him, but tasted only disappointment and frustration: his love had not yet found its true object.

Nineteen years of age, away from home, and buffeted by the psychic storms of adolescence, it should be no surprise that Augustine sometimes failed in drawing the line between love and lust, or that he failed to discern how the bright reality of friendship might consort with the feverish tides of sexual passion. We have already observed how deceptive Augustine's lurid metaphors in this connection can be; they scarcely entitle us to depict him as a randy monster of sexual indulgence.[44]

An "Assignation" Made in Church?

It would seem in this connection that Augustine's undeserved reputation for juvenile profligacy has engendered still another classic misinterpretation, one which has gained broad acceptance.[45] He is in the midst of recounting his youthful sins; he has begun with his failings in the sexual area, but these he deals with in exactly one paragraph (3.1). He then changes focus and spends the next two entire chapters, totaling five paragraphs of text, on his sins of "curiosity."

He opens the topic of curiosity by depicting the delight he took in "vain" theatrical spectacles (3.2–4). He then passes on to a chapter which might well bear the title "Service of Demons" (3.5–6), for he portrays the "sacrilegious desire" he had for "knowledge" as a desire directed toward the "deceitful service of demons" (3.5). He must admit that he was not so evil as to engage in those more seriously "demonic acts" which the Carthaginian gangs of "overturners" (*eversores*) perpetrated (3.6), but he depicts his application to his studies as constituting a "sacrifice" to "demons" nonetheless (3.5).

Now, this is the identical expression he earlier used in an identical context: speaking of the "vanity" of his poetry studies—"all smoke and wind"—he sums them up as a "sacrifice offered to the transgressor angels" (1.27). Augustine's reasoning is that the vain "curiosity" which is deployed in the pursuit of the worldly "knowledge" promised by such "secular studies" is demonically "sacrilegious," precisely because it is a mocking *simulacrum* which draws the soul away from the salutary love for Divine Truth. This connection, between curiosity, vanity, the devotion to "secular studies" and the service of "demons," is made clearer in his exegesis of the Prodigal parable: the "husks" which the Prodigal fed to "pigs" (standing for demons) were the "secular studies" which "make demons rejoice."[46]

It is precisely in this context, focused exclusively on "curiosity," not sexuality, that Augustine tells us that, even in church, he "dared to desire [*concupiscere*] and to carry out business [*agere negotium*] for procuring the fruit of death" (3.5). Everyone I have seen comment on that expression assumes that Augustine meant he was making a sexual assignation; but study of his metaphors shows clearly that *concupiscere* can take the form of "curiosity," exactly as the image-context suggests; it is far more likely, then, that he is here telling us that he was making some kind of secular business deal (*negotium*), probably to advance his rhetorical career.[47] And so another brushstroke in the portrait of Augustine, prince of roués, has to be erased.

A Romantic Idealist

But any man with a memory of his own adolescence will resonate with the other side of the picture Augustine presents of himself, a side which is too often ignored. For those troubled years were also, for him, a time for lofty ideals, for dreams of heroism, for those "thoughts of youth" which are "long, long thoughts." The same emotional fires may burn in both the sexual and the heroic passions. "I was in love with love": to attribute its proper weight to that phrase, we must first evoke, but then transcend, the echoes it prompts from the popular song. While on the subject, though, we must observe that Augustine was clearly a young romantic, but a romantic idealist as well. How strongly he was moved by the passions and partings of Dido and Aeneas—but of that Aeneas, remember, who was almost inhumanly dedicated to his ideal dream of Rome. That same idealistic streak kept him from joining or approving those gangs of *eversores* who ran wild in Carthage. And when he agreed to a common-law marriage (for, again, that is the closest modern analogue we have for that type of union as sanctioned by Roman law), it must be kept in mind that this was a quite respectable living arrangement, even in the eyes of the Church at that time; it is an historical anachronism to picture the young Augustine as snatching his sexual satisfactions along with someone he regarded, guiltily, as his mistress, or concubine—but in either case a woman closer to whore than to legitimate spouse. It is well to remember, also, that this man who seems so anxious to tell us as little good about himself as possible lets it slip out, as it were, that he lived in fidelity to the mother of his child for all the fifteen years or so of their union (4.2).

How soon after his arrival at Carthage did Augustine contract this marriage? Less than a year, Brown calculates,[48] and then infers that "Far from being the libertine that some authors have imagined . . . Augustine was, in reality, a young man who had cut the ebullience of adolescence dangerously short." In any case, the testimony of Vincentius, later a Rogatist opponent, but his onetime fellow-student at Carthage, lends added credibility to that judgment: the Augustine he knew was a quiet, well-behaved young man (*Ep 93* 51). At the same time, the garish picture of Augustine, Carthaginian playboy with his endless list of sexual conquests, appears less and less persuasive.

Alongside the normal tumult of adolescent sexuality, therefore, not in opposition to it (I suggest) but as integral part of that ambiguous passage to adulthood, Augustine fell in love, not simply with this girl or that, but—*amare amabam*—he fell in love with love. What does this Bishop hope his readers will detect in that expression?

A Clue from the De Trinitate*: On "Loving Love"*

Looking back on this period of his life, Augustine is telling us
that he now realizes that his hunger for some satisfying love-
object could be stilled only by that other-worldly reality, God
Himself. But those word-plays, *amare amabam, amore amoris*, in-
sinuate that he gleaned, even then, some measure of that self-
knowledge from his youthful experience of love. If we may be
permitted an Augustinian interpretation of Augustine, the self-
knowledge gained then was of the sort he later terms, in the *De
Trinitate, notitia* (14.7–11): that vague and implicit awareness which
even the sinful soul has that it is *imago Dei*; it needs but to love
love itself—*diligere dilectionem*—in order to "embrace" by that love
(albeit *nesciens*, Augustine would add) the very God Who is love
(*Trin* 8.12).

It may initially sound forced to claim that as early as his nineteenth year Augustine had already descried a connection between
sexual passion and the burning desire for an other-worldly vision
of a "Beauty, ever ancient, ever new." But close examination of
the next episode in his story—his reading of Cicero's *Hortensius*—
confirms that this is what Augustine himself is claiming.[49]

THE *HORTENSIUS* AND AUGUSTINE'S ROMANCE WITH WISDOM

It is remarkable to see how much sexual coloration Augustine
contributes to his account of a philosophical book which impressed him at the age of nineteen. But in order to gauge what that
sexual coloration implies, the reader must apply the interpreter's
imperative which Olivier Du Roy illustrates on virtually every
page of his painstaking analysis of Augustine's early works: to
understand Augustine, we must learn how to capitalize a number
of key terms in his writings—especially the terms which are his
code-words for the Eternal Christ: words like Philosophy, Reason, Intellect, Order, Truth—and Wisdom.[50] *Augustine's Quest of
Wisdom* was an excellent title for Vernon Bourke to choose, but I
submit that in nine-tenths of its occurrences in the text Wisdom—
the object of the other-worldly vision Augustine is "questing"
for—should have been capitalized. Capitalize that term as it occurs
in the *Hortensius* account, and that slight orthographic alteration
brings one to the very center of Augustine's thought-world.

Recall for a moment exactly how Augustine tells the story in his *Confessions*. In the ordinary course of study, he came upon the dialogue *Hortensius* which, he tells us, contains Cicero's "exhortation to philosophy." "This book changed my heart-set": he has already implied this in his early Dialogues, and will assure us of the same thing twice more in his *Confessions*. Here, as there, he also lays stress on the moral and religious aspects of what we could otherwise mistakenly think of as a purely intellectual experience:

> It turned my prayers [*preces*] to You Yourself, Lord, and redirected my purposes and desires [*vota ac desideria*]. My every vain hope was suddenly cheapened for me [*viluit mihi repente omnis vana spes*], and with incredible ardor of heart [*aestu cordis incredibili*] I yearned for the immortality of Wisdom. I began to rise up, in order to return to You [*surgere coeperam ut ad Te redirem*] . . . [3.7].

Augustine has obviously seen that in exhorting his readers to *philosophia*, Cicero was urging them to abandon the life of worldly activity altogether, along with all the "vain hopes" bound up with such activity. (We shall come to see presently that "vain hopes" is Augustine's cliché for "empty" aspirations after "secular" or "this-worldly" distinction.) Cicero was urging his reader to become, in a word, a kind of secular monk. The dramatic effect this book had on him shows, again, that Augustine was peculiarly "ready" for it: as early as his nineteenth year he must already have been sensitized by a lively inclination toward that kind of contemplative life. Was he a "born mystic"? Perhaps not; but he was certainly a born contemplative.

An Other-Worldly Soul with Other-Worldly Longings

Most of what I have said thus far one could glean from Testard's treatment of this episode in his *Saint Augustin et Cicéron*.[51] But Testard places much less emphasis on the erotic aura which saturates this experience as Augustine recounts it both here and in his early Dialogues. That erotic quality, already hinted at by the *aestu cordis incredibili* quoted above, becomes more intense as we go on:

> How I burned, O my God [*ardebam*, the same word we saw a moment ago in a sexual connection], how I burned with desire to fly back to You from earthly things [*a terrenis*] . . . for Wisdom is with You [*apud Te est enim Sapientia*]. . . .

I have taken the liberty of capitalizing the "W" of Wisdom; we shall see justification for that quite soon. But for now observe the multiplication of fire- and flame-words, and the lexicon of sexual passion more generally:

> What delighted me in [Cicero's] exhortation was only this: I was stirred up, and enkindled, and enflamed to love, to seek after, to attain and strongly embrace, not this or that sect, but Wisdom Itself, whatsoever Wisdom might be.

Not only is Wisdom, *Sapientia*, a feminine noun in Latin, but Augustine is here envisaging Wisdom as an unmistakably feminine target of erotic desire; hence, the translation would more accurately say that he longed to embrace "Wisdom *Herself, Whoever she* might be."

> In so great a blaze, only one thing held me back: that the name of Christ was not in it. . . . Whatever lacked that name, no matter how well-written, polished, and truthful it might be, could not wholly bear me away [*non me totum rapiebat*] [3.10–11].

Here Augustine is probably revealing as much what he himself brought to his reading of Cicero as what Cicero actually wrote. In any case, he is telling us that he envisaged the contemplative life as a search, not for this or that version of "human wisdom," not for the doctrine of this or that competing philosophical sect, but for "Wisdom Herself": Wisdom personified, absolutized— Wisdom, in short, with a capital "W." The exact wording he uses tells us he "desired the immortality of Wisdom," and it is surely not pure coincidence that the author of the Book of Wisdom asserts (8:13) that he "will have immortality through her," that is, through that beauteous "Wisdom" he has come to love and wed as the "spouse of his soul" (8:1). Indeed, I hope shortly to publish the mass of evidence arguing that Augustine's portrait of Wisdom as a feminine hypostasis owed much to the images he gleaned from the Old Testament Wisdom books.

Notice, however, that the relation between any sectarian instance of human wisdom and supernal Wisdom Herself perfectly parallels the relation between any human love-partner and the transcendent Love Augustine truly loves; again, however distant the materials might initially seem to be, Augustine's imagination structures them in surprisingly consistent ways.

But Wisdom, "Whoever She might be": Augustine soon quali-fies that mysterious "whoever" with some telling specifics. And, first, the pursuit of Wisdom Herself implied flying upward from all "earthly realities": that generality covers both sexual attach-ments and this-worldly hopes, both of which "weigh" the soul down, each after its own fashion.[52] (We shall see more of this later.) But in any case it is becoming much clearer now that Au-gustine is thinking of that "Wisdom Herself" along the lines of an unworldly Platonic reality, or of a Biblical personification, or (more probably) as a fusion of both. Wisdom is beginning to take firmer shape as a fullness of Wisdom somehow apart from, in another, higher "world" from, all human wisdoms.

At this juncture, the picture fills out significantly: that other-worldly Wisdom is to be found "with God" (*apud Te*). That telltale preposition, *apud*, seems to have been meant to alert Augustine's readers to the fact that he is thinking of this celestial Wisdom as identical with the Eternal Christ, the Divine Word, which, St. John's Prologue twice tells us, is "with God": *apud Deum* (Jo 1:1–2).[53] This identity was undoubtedly part of the reason why Augustine was so disappointed that the *Hortensius* stopped short of mentioning the name "Christ."

The Prodigal and the "Loss of Wings"

The next two features to observe about this episode form a pair: first, Augustine describes himself as beginning to "rise up" in order to return (*redirem*) to God: *surgere coeperam*, he tells us. Sec-ond, in another metaphor, he puts it that he burned to "fly back" to God from "earthly things" (*revolare a terrenis ad Te*). "Flying back," of course, is a stock expression from the Platonist lexicon which described our souls as once, previous to this "earthly" life, winged, and dwelling in the heavenly realms; we have lost our wings and fallen from that realm, but even now, when suitably reminded, we yearn to sprout those wings again and fly back to our heavenly abode. This same *revolare* image of ascending return occurs in the *Hortensius*, and in a climactic passage which, years afterward, Augustine quotes, without the faintest sign of de-murral, to climax the fourteenth book of his *De Trinitate*. We shall examine that quotation shortly.

The former of the two expressions, *surgere coeperam*, Augustine has taken from the fifteenth chapter of St. Luke's Gospel; there it applies to the Prodigal Son, whom Augustine invariably takes as a figure of fallen humanity.[54] The Prodigal journeys far from the celestial mansion of God, his Father, collapses out of hunger and exhaustion, but eventually "rises up" in order to "return" to his Father. But just as the soul now shorn of its wings once dwelt in heaven, so too the Prodigal once dwelt in the Father's house to which he is now resolved to "return." The soul, we are invited to infer, is other-worldly not only in its destiny but also in its origin.

Augustine is telling us, in sum, that he found Cicero's *Hortensius* awakening a deep nostalgia for "returning" to the other-worldly God, from the earthly realities toward which, until now, he had misdirected both his ambitious hopes and his human affections. That same God he had once abandoned, but was still in love with, unbeknownst to himself, as the deepest dimension of all his other loves—including his sexual loves. Augustine can, moreover, depict his "return" either in the Platonic metaphor of the wingèd soul or in the Gospel metaphor of the wandering Prodigal; there is not the slightest reason to believe that he himself sees any conflict whatever between those metaphors: the Prodigal simply is, for him, the Christian equivalent of the classic Platonic metaphor for our condition as fallen souls.

Augustine's "Erotic Intellectualism"

Notice once again, though, how consistently Augustine's imagination works when recalling this episode. In the first place, just as in his earliest Dialogues, it comes back to him as charged with an unambiguously erotic tonality. Indeed, when working at its intensest pitch, Augustine's intellectualism invariably assumes this erotic quality. Here, he would have us believe that Cicero's invitation electrified him in much the same way as, centuries later, Dante's first glimpse of Beatrice electrified him. He "burned," Augustine tells us, burned with desire, with "incredible ardor of heart." He cannot find synonyms enough to dramatize his reaction: he was stirred up, enkindled, enflamed, to love, seek after, attain, and strongly embrace. . . .

That unmistakably feminine *Sapientia* puts one in mind of the equally feminine figure of *Philosophia* in the *De beata vita* (4) and *Contra Academicos* (1.3–4), or (most striking of all) the *Soliloquies'* unabashed evocation of Wisdom as a beautiful woman whom her ardent lovers are on fire to behold, stripped of "every intervening veil."[55] We shall also have occasion, further on, to compare her with the Lady Continence who, shortly after a final recall of this same *Hortensius* incident, appears to Augustine at the climax of his conversion-struggle in that garden at Milan. But, once again, the Bible was teeming with examples of the sort: one has only to think of those poetic images of Wisdom which Ecclesiasticus, Proverbs, and the Book of Wisdom string together, all of them alluringly feminine. . . .

Augustine's "Rehearsals" of Conversion

The close analogies one finds between the imagery of the *Hortensius* account and the images to which Augustine resorts in connection with his later conversion at Milan point to a habit of composition which we encounter repeatedly in the *Confessions*. Augustine tends to "see" earlier incidents, and often incidents which happened to someone else besides himself, as anticipating or prefiguring some crucial incident which later happens to him. More often than not the anticipatory incident will prefigure some aspect or phase of the conversion at Milan which he describes in Books 7 and 8. Let me refer to these anticipatory episodes as "rehearsal" passages. They are especially interesting because Augustine frequently includes details in the "rehearsal" account which he omits, elides, or expresses more cryptically in his later description of conversion. In cases like that, a backward glance over one or other "rehearsal" passage will often clarify any ambiguities in the later conversion account. We shall see, when we come to it, that if we use the "first conversion" he experienced on reading the *Hortensius* as a standard of comparison, it will illuminate several features of Augustine's description of that Milanese conversion.

The Hortensius and Augustine's Sexuality

For the time being, however, the *Confessions*' account of the *Hortensius* episode lends definiteness to the answers that Augustine's earlier description of his sexual awakening left relatively hazy: we know much more explicitly now, when he found himself in love with love and had to search about for some object on which to

fix his love, what—or Who—that anonymous object was. For
Augustine counts on his readers' knowing that God is as "feminine" as He is "Father," as much sheer Wisdom as He is pure
Love. Indeed, his earliest Dialogues show Augustine using Wisdom, *Sapientia*, as his preferred name for God's Eternal Son; nor
will it take him long to affix the name Love to the equally divine
Holy Spirit.[56]

We can now understand more clearly, too, why he found no
creaturely love-object capable of satisfying him, any more than
this or that limited version of human wisdom could still his hunger for Wisdom Herself. He still has some growing to do before
this relatively vague *notitia* becomes fully explicit *cogitatio sui*. But
from this time forward, the architectonic lines of his thinking
have taken form and will never substantially alter. He has located
the center from which, henceforth, all his thinking and aspiration
spring. He has come to the conviction that we are beings whose
native air was once the loftier world where beauteous Wisdom
dwelt with God. We have sinfully fallen into this lower realm of
darkness, struggle, and misery; and we long to fly back to the
bright home, to the rapturous embrace we spurned and left behind. Nothing less, he is unalterably convinced, can possibly satisfy us.

Augustine's earliest Dialogues already reveal an unbreakable
bond between the sexual and the mystical components in his spiritual experience; one has to read the *Confessions* with that bond in
mind in order to catch him tracing out its genesis: whatever other
psychological forces may have been at work, that process was
catalyzed when his reading of the *Hortensius* coincided with the
onslaught of youthful sexuality which climaxed in his getting
married. From that moment on, the sexual would always resonate
with mystical overtones for him, and mysticism invariably find
its most natural expression in sexual metaphors.

Whatever doubts Cicero himself may have had on the subject,
this is the truth Augustine found adumbrated in the final paragraphs of the *Hortensius*, if we may judge from the way he quotes
and comments on it in his *De Trinitate* (14.26). "Commending
this contemplative wisdom" about which he himself has just been
discoursing, Augustine quotes Cicero as writing that, "If we
sharpen our understanding, which is the eye of the mind, . . .
and if we live in philosophy," and if, further, as "the greatest and

by far the most illustrious of ancient philosophers have agreed, we have eternal and divine souls," then we are entitled to think and hope that the life lived in philosophy will "make the ascent and return [*reditus*] [of those souls] to heaven so much the easier." The philosophic way of life, the sharpening of intelligence, the growth in contemplative wisdom: this was the road-map which the *Hortensius* furnished Augustine for the fallen soul's return to heaven. It is also suggestive that Cicero mentions the philosophical view that our souls have been joined to bodies, as living to dead, to atone for some sins (*scelera*) we committed in a higher existence, one which we enjoyed before our birth into this world.[57] It will take Augustine some years to entertain with any sympathy that hypothesis of a sinful fall. But that was largely because Manichaeism, as we shall see, offered a much more flattering account of how we were plunged into this world of pain and misery.

AFTERMATH OF THE *HORTENSIUS:* CONVERSION TO MANICHAEISM

Augustine leaves us in no doubt whatsoever on how powerfully Cicero's *Hortensius* affected him. It is hardly surprising, therefore, that he feels obliged to explain why he did not respond to its invitation to embrace the life of philosophic contemplation. "It did not wholly bear me away," he tells us (*non me totum rapiebat*). And the reason he gives is this: that the "name of Christ was not in it."

We shall have occasion presently to weigh that remark about the absence of the "name of Christ," but I mean, for the moment, to call attention to that pregnant term which Augustine uses: that Latin term *rapere*.

At first blush, the word seems innocent enough. And yet, that word eventually becomes the nucleus of one of Augustine's favorite "conversion" images. The reason for that becomes startlingly clear in Book 8, where its original source in Matthew's Gospel (11:12) is made unmistakably evident. "The kingdom of heaven suffers violence," Jesus said, "and the violent bear it away" (*rapiunt eam*). I have dealt elsewhere with the early image-connotations Augustine attached to this term,[58] so I may be permitted to summarize them briefly now.

Augustine sees Matthew's use of *rapere* as (initially) implying that a vigorous, even "violent" act of exertion, of something like "will-power," apparently, is needed in order to make the human decision involved in conversion. Hence, associations with terms and images of *vis* and *violentia*, with force, violence, resolve—all of them, incidentally, the manly, "muscular" qualities of the *miles*, the soldier—will gradually build up around the root-term *rapere*, as well as around its composite terms, like *arripere, corripere, diripere*, and so forth. This, I am persuaded, represents the story of Augustine's use of the term *rapere* throughout his earlier works.[59]

But it would appear that later on, and notably after his having pondered the questions addressed to him by and composed his answers *To Simplician*, it became sorely questionable in Augustine's mind how much we humans could claim to achieve by our natural powers. Then the term *rapere* tends to shift into the passive voice so that we "are borne away," or, if it remains in the active voice, as here, the subject of the verb is some power beyond ourselves which "bears us away." Eventually, Augustine begins to identify that force beyond ourselves with the sweet power of love, and more precisely with the power of Divine Love as personified in the Holy Spirit. But then, predictably, the Holy Spirit's working will result in inflaming us, making us ardent, thus "lightening" us to fly up on the "wings" of charity in order to "cleave" once again to the Eternal God Who is Wisdom and Love: that "Beauty, ever ancient, ever new." We shall have occasion to explore this cluster of motifs, however, when treating of the conversion Augustine describes in Book 8.

A New Look into Scripture

Augustine's nostalgic attachment to Christ prompts him, now, to take a fresh look into the Scriptures. The paragraph which recounts this exploration (3.9) is a veritable jungle of intertwining images, so various in provenance and subtly diverse in import as to make this one of the most strained pieces of prose to be found anywhere in the *Confessions*. Let me first offer a literal translation, then go on to justify that translation by explicating the various images Augustine employs in his text:

> So I decided to apply my mind to the holy Scriptures to see what they were like. And lo! I see a reality [*rem*] which is not uncovered

to the proud or bared to boys [*non conpertam superbis neque nudatam pueris*], but is lowly with respect to her entryway, but lofty as one progresses further [*incessu humilem, successu excelsam*] and veiled in mysteries [*et velatam mysteriis*], and I was not the sort [*talis*] who could enter into her, or bend my neck at her doorway [*intrare in eam . . . aut inclinare cervicem ad eius gressus*]. . . . For my swelling [*tumor*] was repelled by her modesty [*modum eius*] and my gaze [*acies*] did not penetrate her inmost parts [*non penetrabat interiora eius*]. And yet, that [reality] was such as to expand along with [the growth of] the little ones [which she enveloped] [*quae cresceret cum parvulis*], but I disdained to be a little one and, puffed up with arrogance, I seemed to myself a big fellow [or: a grown-up] [*dedignabar esse parvulus et turgidus fastu mihi grandis videbar*].

The first image-register we encounter sets the "reality" which Augustine "saw" (*rem*) over against the "veil" which half-conceals and half-reveals it: Augustine is talking about the interpretation of Scripture, and is evidently applying the *res–signum* couple which he frequently employs in that connection. The "veil" he refers to, we may safely infer, is the clothing of "signs" in which the authors of Scripture enveloped the "reality" they were striving to convey. That reality is the Divine Truth which is identical with the Eternal Christ; but the Eternal Christ, as we so recently saw, is one with the Divine Wisdom to which Cicero's *Hortensius* pointed.

This accounts (in a second image-register) for the manifestly feminine character of that reality, Who here (like the beauteous Wisdom of the *Soliloquies*) "is not uncovered to the proud or bared to boys" (*non conpertam superbis neque nudatam pueris*).[60] Now, a *puer*, in Augustine's frequent usage, is the symbol of that impudent presumption which distinguishes him from the authentic *parvulus*. He is, in fact, a "little one," but in puerile fashion insists on being treated as a *grandis*, a "grown-up," or in this case a self-styled "big fellow."[61]

Augustine is suggesting that in order to enjoy the naked vision of beauteous Wisdom one must either consent to be as humble as a *parvulus*, or grow up to attain the stature of an authentic *grandis*.

He is subtly reminding us (in a third image-register) that the only males in the household who are permitted to draw delight from the mother's breasts are, not the "boys," but the unweaned infant or the grown-up husband and father. Now Augustine is emboldened to shift into a sexual image of such boldness as to shock the over-fastidious. The bond linking sexuality and mysticism was never more candidly displayed. Though this feminine reality is, he tells us, lowly in respect of her entryway, *incessu humilem*, she is "lofty upon further advance" (*successu excelsam*), lofty and "veiled in mysteries" (*velatam mysteriis*). Now Augustine admits to finding that he was not of the sort (*talis*) able to "enter into her" (*ut intrare in eam possem*); he was incapable of exercising the husband's right. Nor could he enter as a *parvulus*: he was unable to "bend [his] neck" humbly before her "doorway" (*inclinare cervicem ad eius gressus*). The modest style of Scripture, when compared with Cicero's, repelled him, much as a narrow entryway would repel someone who was grossly tumescent; he was too swollen with pride, and his spiritual sight "did not penetrate her inmost parts" (*non penetrabat interiora eius*).

Those inmost parts, Augustine now realizes, like the mother's insides, were such as would "expand [*cresceret*] along with the little ones," the *parvuli* they enclosed: Scripture reveals deeper and richer messages to the believer as he advances from spiritual infancy to spiritual maturity. Only a *parvulus*, therefore, a "little one," can hope to enter that narrow passageway into the very womb of Scripture, and be carried about safely within it. In that womb of security the little one can hope to mature, eventually emerge, suckle on the "milk of faith" at the naked maternal breast, and in time become a *grandis*, a grown-up capable of enjoying that "food of grown-ups," *cibus grandium*, the direct and immediate vision of God (7.16). Only then can he hope to behold Wisdom naked, as a husband may, and so "enter" and "penetrate" to her inner mysteries (*interiora*). Not so, however, the arrogant *puer* Augustine was then.

We shall come to see that Augustine is once again rehearsing a central feature of the dynamic which will afterward structure his Milanese conversion: at nineteen, he thought himself a subject sufficiently "grown up" to "penetrate" and "feed upon" a direct and unmediated vision of that supernal "reality," Divine Wisdom, when in fact a long road lay ahead of him before he would become capable of that more modest achievement, the filtered vision of "understanding."

A Convert's Attitude Toward Sex

But there is a quality running through Augustine's evocations of the sexual metaphor which has scarcely received the notice it deserves. The French would call it *désinvolture*, an ingenuous matter-of-factness which is something close to disconcerting. Were he the former monster of lust now become the guilt-ridden convert, as he has sometimes been depicted, we would expect him to be much more inhibited in his references to sexuality, more guarded than he is—in a word, at the same time more re-pressed and puritanical. But the evidence shows that he does not hesitate to image his desire for the vision of God in candidly sexual comparisons, and do so repeatedly; and when a nocturnal incident informs him that the flames of desire are not nearly so safely banked as he had previously imagined, we hear about it in his *Soliloquies* as though that self-revelation were the most natural thing in the world (1.25–26).[62]

The Augustine Who Became a Manichee

This, then, was the human bundle of adolescent passion, self-conceit, and contemplative idealism who married, happened on Cicero's *Hortensius*, and a short while later, or more likely around the same time, yielded to the attractions of Manichaeism. Again, we must not permit Augustine's serial narration of these episodes to lull us into focusing on each of them as though it stood apart from, "outside," the other two. Not only were all three incidents closely related chronologically, they must have been psychically "interior" to one another. His enrollment as a Manichee must certainly have been the fruit of a growing acquaintance with that sect and its adherents, and that growing acquaintance must have run concurrently with his sexual difficulties, marriage, and read-ing of the *Hortensius*. Hence, the young man who read the *Horten-sius* was at the same time grappling with the problems of youthful sexuality which eventually landed him in a common-law mar-riage; but by the same token, that same young man was also, in all likelihood, already mulling over objections which his Manichee acquaintances were throwing out against his faith as a Catholic, as well as pondering the Manichee hymns and scriptures which celebrated our souls' kinship with the glorious kingdom of Light.

So too, given the underlying continuity in these episodes, Augustine's youthful idealism and contemplative affinity must have been as thoroughly interwoven with his earliest encounters with Manichaeism as with his reading of the *Hortensius* and his experiences of sexual passion and noble love. Indeed, just as we detected a parallel structure between Augustine's way of envisaging sexuality in its relation to the Christian God of Love, so too, we should fully expect to find a similar structural relationship running through his conversion to Manichaeism.

In the light of that hypothesis, let us pause for a moment and try to take the measure of this fairly normal adolescent, sexually sensitive but also romantic and idealistic, who had, on the one hand, found Cicero's *Hortensius* so wildly inspiring, and settled, on the other hand, into the rather tame domesticities of a common-law marriage. How would such a youth respond both to the Manichees' objections to his Catholic faith, and to that side of Manichaeism we may be less inclined to take account of, its exuberant imagery of that radiant world of Light?

In answer, let me hazard this portrait of Augustine at this stage of his existence: the quotidian domesticities of marriage must, in time, have de-romanticized his sexual fantasies to some extent, draining them of the adventurous, even dangerous aura which can make sexual exploits (not unlike a nocturnal theft of pears!) so bewitching to the roving young blade. Marriage invariably proves that the promise forbidden sex holds out to the callow adolescent is an extravagant promise which sex itself can never truly fulfill.

But Augustine must also have begun to suspect that what is true of sex is equally true of so many of "this" life's other extravagant promises: of security, of loving and being loved, of worldly achievement, success, even glory. "Vain hopes," he calls the whole array of "this life's" promises; and yet, those promises are there. Is the world which holds them out to eager adolescence no more than a giant deception? Or could it be that, just as all human wisdoms only stammer hints of Wisdom Herself, and all human love-partners merely suggest the Love we truly love, so every promised fullfillment awaits in another world from the one we inhabit? Could it be that security, love, achievement, glory, as well as the unabating ecstasy so fleetingly promised by sexual union, are hints, suggestions—what Plato would call "imitations"—of a perfect fullfillment which can occur only in a world we dream about, long for—or (is it possible?) a world which we "remember"?

That, we know, is what Augustine later came to believe: we once knew bliss in a "remembered" world. But if all that be true, then (in a phrase Augustine will shortly use in a related connection), he may already have begun to suspect that the ideal world of our hopes and dreams must be *aliud, aliud valde,* "other, vastly other" from "this" world of our experience. What could possibly have gone wrong to account for this radical dislocation, our alienation in "this" frustrating world of misery and disappointment?

Here we must suspend our memories of Augustine's insistently negative portrayals of Manichaeism, and strain to get inside the head of the young man on whom this religion once exercised a positive appeal, an appeal strong enough that he broke with his mother, Monica, and presumably with a number of his Catholic friends. Remember, too, that he remained a Manichee for something like ten years.[63] What aspects of Manichaeism must he have found attractive, and how would they have related to his sexual experience, as well as to the appeal exercised by Cicero's *Hortensius*?

The Appeal of Manichaeism

For one thing, the Manichees offered Augustine a version of the happy life remarkably in accord with the one that Cicero's work intimated to him. The Manichees insisted that our souls were other-worldly beings, both in origin and in destiny. They trumpeted an ascetic ideal of purity, and notably of sexual purity, and by this time I hope to have sanitized whatever lurid misrepresentations of "Augustine as young roué" my readers might formerly have found credible. Augustine was already enough of a "divided man" that he very likely found such ideals of "purity" highly attractive! Finally, the Manichee depreciation (at least in principle) of earthly achievement may well have resonated with what Testard describes as Cicero's austere ethical counsels.[64]

But in addition, Augustine tells us, the "name of [God] and of our Lord Jesus Christ," which he had missed so sorely in the *Hortensius*, that name was forever on the Manichees' lips (3.10). Indeed, Mani proclaimed himself the Apostle of Jesus Christ. Years later, moreover, Augustine is able to remind the Manichee bishop, Faustus (*Faust* 15.5–6, 20.9),[65] of that tenet of theirs which must have made a deep impression on his youthful mind, their teaching on the Luminous Christ and His mythical analogue, the *Splenditenens*: the One who held the world of spiritual splendor in his hand.[66] That *Splenditenens* Augustine will none too subtly recall by the striking expression he coins in the *Confessions* (7.21): the all-upholding creative Word of God is *Omnitenens manu veritate*, "All-holding by His Truth-Hand."

The appeal of Manichaeism brings us back, accordingly, to that immortal Wisdom Who is also Truth and Word "with God"—*apud Deum*—that other-worldly hypostasis Whom Augustine glimpsed between the lines of Cicero's *Hortensius*. But this was only one more feature of Manichee teaching which answered to the young Augustine's most cherished religious and moral ideals. We must not forget that he could, and almost certainly did, feel that in adopting Manichaeism he was not apostasizing from, but actually adopting, a purer, more "spiritual" form of Christianity than he had found in the North African *Catholica* of his day.

Mani and the Esteem for Intelligence

But another characteristic common to the *Hortensius* and to Manichaeism, one that strongly appealed to the young Augustine, was the high regard for the workings of human intelligence they both displayed. Augustine is so insistent about this feature in the Dialogues written shortly after his conversion that one might almost be tempted to think it was the only reason for Manichaeism's appeal to him. He was *factus erectior*, he tells us, he was "made more erect" (*Vita* 4);[67] and he explains that phrase as meaning that he was no longer content to bow down before the *terribilis auctoritas* of North Africa's preachers, and believe unthinkingly in what they "commanded" him to believe. It is significant that he applies the same interpretation to the phrase which describes what the Prodigal did in the Gospel: he "rose up" to direct his gaze toward the higher world of truths which only the power of understanding can grasp (*QQ EV* 2.33, *UtCred* 2–3).

So the summons to philosophical meditation he had read in the *Hortensius* chimed in with the challenging promise the Manichees held out to him: that they would never require him to believe anything which they could not explain to him so cogently that he would see the truth of what they taught by the light of human reason.

But there is a significant distinction between the contributions Augustine describes as Cicero's, on the one hand, and the Manichaeans', on the other. It is a distinction which must be kept in mind whenever we use that famous phrase "faith seeking understanding." Augustine is obliged to credit the Manichees with encouraging him to reject the authoritarianism of "infantile" blind faith, and "rise up" to stand on his own two feet as an adult rational being, capable of thinking for himself (see *Mor* 1 and *Util*, passim). Undoubtedly, the Manichees had more in mind than this: the whole point of their religion was the soul's recovery of that tranquil immersion in the Divine which had been disturbed by the primordial "invasion" of Divine Light by the jealous hordes of Darkness. But for some reason, when he speaks of "faith seeking understanding" in a Manichee-related context, Augustine more often has in mind the need to moderate this imperative of moving from an infantile dependence on authority to the mature reliance on reason.

Now Augustine credits Cicero with urging the same transit, to autonomous thinking (*Acad* 1.8, 24). But he also credits him with more: Cicero's invitation to *philosophia* suggested to him (for whatever reasons) that attaining the capacity to reason things out for oneself was not simply a kind of natural right owed to one's human maturity: that would place it in too close a neighborhood with free-thinking pride.[68] Progress from faith to "understanding" was, in Augustine's eyes, a genuinely *religious* exigency.

For he regards the capacity to think things out for oneself as only a halfway-house: the reach of the human mind went beyond those operations of discursive reason. Reasoning things out might possibly succeed in establishing this or that version of human wisdom against its competitors, though Cicero, the convinced Academic, seems to have been somewhat pessimistic in that regard. For one thing, that exercise of self-justification all too frequently descended to the level of acrid contentiousness and sectarian rivalry, the sort of thing of which Augustine had seen too much among his rhetorician colleagues.[69]

But in any case, "understanding" in the full sense aimed well beyond that task of reason. For, Augustine found Cicero suggesting to him, the human mind hungered for a vision that would be ecstatic union with Divine Wisdom Itself, or, more exactly now, Wisdom Herself. Our soul's reach stretches into another world entirely, the world from which we originally came. And Cicero seemed to suggest that growth in "understanding," during this embodied life, would constitute progress toward that eventual vision.

Augustine's "Image" of Understanding

We have already gleaned hints of the image—or cluster of images—which Augustine regularly employs to "picture" (quite literally that!) the operation of "understanding." Various though they are, all these images—and they begin to make their appearance from his earliest Dialogues onward—share the same essential structure: there is invariably some object of vision (more often than not luminous, radiant, or beautiful) which is hidden, or partially hidden, behind some sort of veil or scrim. The soul yearns to behold it as immediately and directly as can be, but the radiance (to settle on that example) can reach the soul only as filtered through the intervening veil or scrim. So the soul must content itself with an "intel-ligence" of the desired object, quite literally a "reading between" the obstructing lines of the intervening veil: *inter-legere* in its exact etymological meaning.

So, for example, we have seen Augustine portray Wisdom's lover as anxious to behold her beauty "nude, as it were, without any veil intervening" (*Sol* 1.22); we saw him apply that identical image to the mysterious "Reality" which is half-veiled, half-revealed by the humble language of Scripture (3.9); his explanation of language subtly implied a similar image of intelligence as having to "pierce through" the screen of symbols (1.17). Augustine twice resorts to a variant of the same image to describe how he has "glimpsed" (*conspeximus*) Romanianus' interior virtue: it leaps forth like lightning from the enveloping clouds (*nubibus quasi fulmen involvitur*, and *fulgura fulminibus propiora conspeximus*) (*Acad* 2.2). We shall see that Augustine reads Paul's text from Romans (1:20) along precisely the same lines: God's invisible attributes are "glimpsed" (again that term, *conspiciuntur*) *through* created realities (*per ea quae facta sunt*), meaning, as Augustine understands the text, that the divine attributes, whose radiance pierces through the intervening scrim of creatures, are glimpsed with the eye of "understanding": God's attributes are precisely *inter-lecta*.

But Augustine draws what is perhaps his most telling image for intelligence from his image-cluster of the cosmic "All" (*Omnia*).[70] In this version, he pictures our situation as though we were standing beneath a cloud-covered sky; a friend has assured us that the sun is shining beyond those clouds, but we are unable to penetrate the cloud-cover and catch sight of it. Yet we believe and trust our friend (faith must often precede understanding!) and are persuaded that he knows what he is talking about. So, we keep gazing steadily in the direction indicated, until we glimpse a hazily luminous point where the sun's rays are filtering through. Now we, too, "know," have come to "understand," that the sun is really there. And that filtered vision inspires the hope that someday the cloud-cover may break, or even that the clouds may entirely disappear, and we will be able to gaze on the Sun directly and immediately. This, I submit, is also the image which subtends the more abstract descriptions of faith, hope, and charity which Reason gives in the *Soliloquies* (1.12–13).

If asked to guess where Augustine drew his most telling inspiration for this image, I would still have to suggest the scene of Christ's Transfiguration; but the interested reader can find substantiation for that claim elsewhere.[71] Again, though, in writing to Romanianus, Augustine gives expression to the core-image by claiming that the personified figure *Philosophia* was already granting him a glimpse of God *per lucidas nubes*, "through light-filled clouds." Just as the believer yearned for the glimpse of understanding, so, too, the deepest yearning of one who has come to undertand is for those clouds to disappear entirely, leaving him to behold that Sun directly, immediately.

The image, and its associated conviction, were both durable: "Love, love understanding," Augustine exclaims years later in that famous exhortation to Consentius (*Ep 120* 13); but why? Ultimately because that way lies our hope of attaining, perhaps even in this mortal life, to the "very summit of contemplation," the unmediated "vision" which Paul describes as "face to face" (*Ep 120* 4, 8).

This dynamic linkage of faith to understanding, but also of understanding to immediate vision, held a seductive power for Augustine which goes far toward accounting for one notable feature of his conversion to Manichaeism. From what he says later about it, we might be tempted to think of his becoming a Manichee as though it represented an apostasy, a falling away from the Catholic faith he had drawn in with his mother's milk: as just another step in Augustine the Prodigal's *aversio*, his sinful journey *away* from God. But again, the remarkable fact is that Augustine himself considered his conversion to Manichaeism as a *conversio*, a *positive* and progressive step: it carried forward the spiritual momentum generated by his reading of the *Hortensius*; it fitted right in with the logic of his "becoming more erect," "rising up" like the Prodigal, in order to "return" to God. But he accomplished all this precisely by abandoning the "superstitious" blind-faith religion he had encountered in North Africa's *Catholica*, and stepping upward to a type of Christianity which proclaimed, whatever be its other shortcomings, that faith was meant to lead onward to understanding. Only along that path did the hope of eventual vision lie.

In his *Quaestiones Evangeliorum* (2.33), Augustine's exegesis of the Prodigal parable suggests a confirmation of this estimate of Manichaeism's place in his religious development. Significantly, this little work dates from around the year 400, exactly when Augustine must have been putting the finishing touches on his *Confessions*. There, the Prodigal is pictured as exhausted upon a dung-heap; the memory comes back to him of how many "hired servants" in his father's house—*mercenarii*, in the translation Augustine was using—had plenty of bread. Who were these *mercenarii*? The Father's servants, to be sure, but servants who worked mainly for earthly gain: exactly like the self-interested preachers of the word toward whom St. Paul takes, when all is said, so tolerant an attitude (Phil 1:12–19). For it was the word of God the Manichees preached, and it must have been their preaching (Augustine reasons) that awoke the Prodigal to that memory of home. Despite their not being as selflessly dedicated as Paul, accordingly, they nonetheless performed a signal service by reanimating that memory which might otherwise have remained forever dormant. For in doing so (Augustine's exegesis continues) they stimulated the Prodigal to "rise up" and "return"—along the path of faith seeking understanding—to the Father.

Here, I submit, Augustine must solicit Luke's text so cruelly, in order to justify an interpretation which corresponds suspiciously to his own experience, that the inference seems unavoidable: he has approached the text pre-convinced that preachers like the Manichees must have some role to play in the parable, and he is able to tailor Luke's *mercenarii* to fit the role—the decidedly positive role—which he felt the Manichees had played in his own conversion. A similar conclusion is suggested by that moving prayer to God the Father, in opening his *Soliloquies*, to "take [him] in" now as he flees from the "enemies" who had so long deceived him: "Take me in, Your child, as I flee from them, for they, even they, took me in when, a stranger, I was fleeing from You" (1.5). He was a stranger, and they took him in; they may not have been Catholics, but Augustine must acknowledge that on more than one occasion they acted toward him like true Christians.

Manichaean Morality and Its Influence

But how was Augustine's attitude, particularly toward sexuality, marked by Manichee moral teaching? We know that they laid claim to a higher "purity" than their Catholic rivals: that conviction was partly grounded on their dualistic view of the human being as an amalgam of impeccable soul and evil body. Our souls, they taught, were sparks of the divinity, which the founder-teacher Mani had identified with sheer, transcendent Light; those souls had been taken prisoners by the opposite cosmic principle, evil and filthy Matter. Hence, the greatest sin a Manichee could commit was that of procreating, which would result in imprisoning a spark of the divinity for at least another generation.

But there was a twist: the "auditors," or rank-and-file Manichees, could marry and even engage in sexual intercourse. Filthy though it was in principle, Mani assured them that all such activity was not really their doing, but the doing of their bodies, of the evil Matter which was an alien nature opposed to their genuine, divine selves. They must, however, take careful steps to ensure that procreation did not result, and the Manichee devices on this score, including suprisingly detailed instructions about calculating the woman's "safe period," must have induced a certain measure of anxiety on the couple's part. But what a breeding ground for psychological complexes: sexual intercourse, in and of itself, was utterly guiltless, indeed, had no moral qualification whatever, was neither good nor bad; and yet procreation, its natural sequel, was the greatest of sins!

This paradoxical teaching was further complicated by the fact that the sect's inner circle, the "elect," were required to live in unsullied celibacy and sexual purity! These were the only members of the group who could hope, at death, to escape their matter-prisons and be re-united with the Divine Light. Here was a gaping inconsistency, one that an Augustine would have felt keenly, even if he failed to conceptualize it explicitly. It would seem that there must be something reprehensible about sexual activity, after all, if it could prevent a serious aspirant from attaining to "first-class citizenship" in the Manichee religion. And Augustine, who never settled contentedly for second class, clearly implies that he was, for a considerable time, "determined to advance in that sect" and was making positive efforts to do so (5.13).

Yet he also tells us that this doctrine of guiltlessness continued to appeal to him, even after he had left Manichaeism (5.18). But this is no iron-clad guarantee that he actually *felt* all that guiltless: the very opposite *could* conceivably have been true. Add to that ambiguous admission the equally ambiguous fact that, very early in their marriage, he and his companion had a child, a brilliant and charming boy: and they chose to name him Adeodatus, "Gift from God." What did Augustine intend by choosing precisely that name? It may well have been the Latin form of a common Punic name, and yet no one was ever more sensitive than Augustine to the meanings of words and the implications of names! Was there a hint of subconscious defiance here, a personal protest that, whatever Manichee teaching might claim, this remarkable child must indeed be just that, a gift from God?

What is one to conclude, then? One could, if one chose, selectively stack the evidence that Augustine furnishes in the *Confessions* to sustain a one-sided case either for or against the view that Manichaeism succeeded in complexifying his attitude toward sex. Yet the one clarity that emerges is that this precise issue, up to this point at least, remains unclear. Our best evidence may come from the attitude Augustine subsequently demonstrates: that candid, uninhibited *désinvolture* with regard to sex which surfaces especially in his Cassiciacum Dialogues, and particularly in his *Soliloquies*. But Augustine will tell us more as we follow his account to that fateful crisis in the garden at Milan.

THE *HORTENSIUS* AND AN IMPORTUNATE DREAM

As we know, the young Augustine managed for years to resist the powerful pull of Cicero's invitation to the life of philosophic contemplation. Time passes; he continues with his rhetorical training, and eventually sets himself up as teacher of rhetoric, first in Thagaste, subsequently in Carthage. Later still, he crosses the sea to Rome and, sign of his growing success, is soon selected to take the important position of municipal *rhetor* in what was then the seat of imperial governance, Milan. A North African provincial, still unable to erase the giveaway traces of his foreign accent, he has nonetheless risen to being official spokesman for the imperial might of Rome (*Ord* 2.45).[72] Monica has been amply rewarded for all the stubborn plans and costly sacrifices she made to ensure her son every opportunity for so brilliant a career!

Despite this series of successes, however, Augustine's life has turned into one long misery. He has told us that as the result of reading the *Hortensius* his "earthly" hopes had become "cheapened," yet if we follow his life-story, he seems still to have remained the plaything of those worldly ambitions. The *Soliloquies*, we noted, would assure us that the *Hortensius* experience liberated Augustine definitively from all attachment to wealth for its own sake. But when it comes to those other two "earthly" desires—for worldly honors and for the pleasures of sex—the story is markedly different. And yet, each time Augustine is tempted to resign himself to the type of contentment to which worldly success would appear to have entitled him, the memory of the *Hortensius*, and of the promise it had once held out to him, returns to haunt him: the dream of contemplative happiness refuses to die.

To measure the enduring power of that youthful experience, and to understand the way the rest of Augustine's story unfolds, we must turn to explore how Augustine's imagination portrays his struggles with "vain ambitions," and with the form of *cupiditas* directed toward all such vain ambitions: "curiosity."

THE HOLLOW BURDEN OF "VANITY"

One result of his having read the *Hortensius*, Augustine tells us, was that his every "vain ambition" (*vana spes*) was suddenly "cheapened" for him (*viluit*). The context makes it clear that those vain ambitions aimed at his becoming an "outstanding" professional rhetorician (*eminere*), and gathering all the kudos that went with such eminence. It will become apparent, a number of extant translations to the contrary, that Augustine did not mean that those aspirations became utterly worthless, for his subsequent story shows that he still had to battle, not only against the "concupiscence of the flesh," but also against the hopes for worldly glory which he associated with the "concupiscence of the eyes" of St. John's First Epistle.

The point has its importance. We shall have occasion to see that more than one scholar has argued for the view that Augustine's adult conversion some nineteen years later, in the year A.D. 386, should be understood principally, if not exclusively, as a triumph over his attachment to sex; that represents a view of his conversion which entails a number of corollary implications about Augustine and his story.

We have seen that the attitude toward sexuality described in his *Confessions* would give considerable encouragement to that view, or at least to something very close to it. And yet, we have also seen that in the autobiographical sections of his early Dialogues, he regularly portrays himself as having been converted from two distinct forms of cupidity—from the desire for sexual satisfaction, but also from the desire for worldly honors. Accept this picture, and it follows that the *Hortensius* may have dampened the strength of Augustine's worldly hopes, but failed to extinguish them.

Once alerted to this anomaly, the careful reader will begin to inquire whether the *Confessions* account still discloses residual traces of the twin-attachment featured in the Dialogues. There is no room for doubting the reality of Augustine's sexual attachments; but at several crucial moments in his Milanese conversion account he makes it clear that there was more to his conversion than that. At a crucial moment of his conversion, for instance, he credits God with having closed his eyes lest, in the Psalmist's image, "they look on vanity" (7.22); later, in that Milanese garden, he will picture himself as striving to shake off the *sarcina saeculi*, the *sarcina vanitatis*, by which he means ridding himself of the weighty burden (*onus*) of his "secular" service of the emperor— an activity which, we are about to see, he regularly associates with the image of "vanity" (8.11–12, 18, 26).

Augustine's Image of "Vanity"

But what exactly does Augustine mean by "vanity"? To postpone textual evidence until later: for now, how is the finished image-complex structured? In their gem-like study of how Augustine uses this term,[73] Rondet and Chevalier correctly point out that he was obviously inspired by the famous phrase in Ecclesiasticus 1:2, but the Latin translation he originally followed read, not "Vanity of vanities," but "Vanity of those who are vain" (*vanitas vanitantium*). This suggested to him that "vanity" could designate the subjective condition of persons who are "vain," or the objective quality which rendered the realities they prized "vain" realities. Further, Rondet shows, objective vanity appears to be the result of humans' having become "vain"—meaning sinfully fallen—or perhaps (I suggest) Rondet's point might have been put more exactly by saying that our sinful "fall" accounts for our immersion in the realm of objective "vanities."

Rondet goes on to show that something could be vain in the objective sense if it were deceptive, false, a "lie" or an illusion; the polar opposite of *vanitas* in this sense is *veritas*, truth—or, more exactly, the transcendent *Veritas* Who is Eternal and Unchanging. That identification accounts for the next set of properties Augustine attaches to vanity: just as *Veritas* is the source of our ultimate bliss, is eternal and unchanging, so vanities are changing and temporal, hence deceptive in the sense of ephemeral and disappointing—like everything "under the sun" (*sub sole*) (Eccli 1:3). Similarly, *Veritas* is solid and supportive, something on which one can take a "stand," whereas vanity is empty, has no such solidity, inevitably gives way from under and "lets us down."

Here, once again, Augustine's imagination is vividly active. Having associated vanity with all that is empty, hollow, vacuous, *inane* in the literal Latin meaning of that term, he sees vanity as sheer façade with nothing substantial within or behind it. It is like a billow of smoke or mist; it looks impressive, can even appear to be solid, but the moment the beholder passes from seeming to reality, it is no more than a great big nothing, doomed to evanesce on the instant. Hence, too, the special association Augustine establishes between vanity and delighting in the "illusions" of theatrical "spectacles": particularly those that are "all show," like circuses or gladiatorial contests.

Vanity and "Curiosity"

That evocation of shows and spectacles, however, suggests the relationship that most directly links vanity with the second member of Augustine's triad of sins, "curiosity." Along with pride and concupiscence of the flesh, Augustine views curiosity as one of the three *capita iniquitatis*, the fontal kinds of sinfulness: all other varieties of iniquity are combinations and variations of them (3.16). Consistent with that conviction, those three *capita* eventually provide the headings for his examination of conscience in Book 10. But it is very possible that the description he gives there of those three forms of primal sin introduces a systematic neatness into Augustine's thinking, whereas his earlier development left a certain number of loose ends showing.

That untidy quality especially characterized Augustine's successive depictions of "curiosity." There was little room for confusion about what St. John's First Epistle could mean by "concupiscence of the flesh" or by "pride." But the notion of "concupiscence of the eyes" was indeterminate enough that it left Augustine room to maneuver, and to shift its meaning noticeably in order to adapt it to his adversaries of any particular moment.

One of his first moves in this connection was to link this form of concupiscence with the elastic notion of curiosity which he appears to have found in Plotinus' treatise *On Eternity and Time* (3.7). "Curiosity," for the Neoplatonist of Plotinus' sort, is both concomitant cause and persistent resultant of the soul's original fall from eternity into the temporal world. Augustine, for his part, pictures the soul as having fallen from the leisure, the *otium*, of contemplative "rest" (*quies, requies*), into the "unquiet" and "disquieting" busy-ness (*negotium*) of action.

Hence, it was the soul's original *curiositas* which begot its present condition of *vanitas*. The soul became wearily "sated" with contemplation, and an unquiet "itch" to be busy "doing something" enticed it down from those heights. That descent from the fullness of the One to the dispersion of the temporal many "emptied" the soul (*evanescit, inanescit*) of its interior spiritual resources, which it poured "outside" itself (*foras*) into "hands-on" activity amid the realities of the temporal world.

The soul has thereby forfeited the breadth and power of its former intellectual survey and governance of the sensible universe, from aloft and afar, as it were, exchanging it for the narrow immediacies of "experimental" knowledge. Hence, Augustine's observation that curiosity implies the love of experimental knowledge—even of unpleasant realities—for its own sake (10.55).

The insatiability of its curiosity now prods the soul toward more and more active, "experimental" contact with the bewitching flux of temporal realities. But now, by an ironic backlash, the unremitting chase after the elusive things of time inevitably brings on frustration after frustration, so that "curiosity" assumes another form. For "curiosity," Augustine reminds his readers,[74] comes from the root-term *cura*, meaning "care." So, its continually frustrated chase after the fleeting realities of time gives birth to a fretful, disquieting sense of "restlessness," making the soul more and more "care-worn."

Vanity and Pride

One of the soul's chief motives for engaging in this "action" on temporal realities is the exhilarating sense of achievement which it hopes will result from exercising its powers effectively; it feels it has "excelled," distinguished itself, and thereby earned "honor" and "glory" from its fellow-*vanitantes*, equally "vain" souls who put an equally false value on this sort of activity.

That lust to excel, *eminere*, with its accompanying delight in praise and reputation—*honores, gloria*—tends to draw vanity into the orbit of pride, *superbia*. On closer inspection, vanity takes that weakened form of pride which Augustine calls "vainglory"—not so much the contemptuous will to be feared as the yen to be liked and admired. But in any event, praise and reputation, the accolades which come from other human beings, turn out all too often to be "vain": empty, hollow facade without solidity, evanescent as any smoke-cloud.

Rhetoric and Vanity

From the vantage point we have now reached, it is easy to understand why Augustine's own profession of rhetoric falls quite especially under the indictment of "vanity." What is it, after all, but an art of illusion, of glittering surfaces, aimed at "clothing" one's thoughts and sentiments impressively and attractively, or serving up a treacherous mix of solid truth and hollow falsity on shining "platters" (*ferculae*) of eloquence?

The *rhetor* is, moreover, a specialist in those adult games called debating contests and contentious courtroom rivalries; it is surprising how much importance Augustine attaches to the acridly "contentious" atmosphere he found impregnating his professional activity. And what, after all, are they contending for? So many hollow victories, the fickle prizes of momentary popularity, of "this world's" empty praise, fame, reputation, or (to use that inflated term) "glory."

The Burden of Being a Lightweight

In terms of the *pondus* theme taken from Augustine's *Omnia* image, accordingly, both the products of the active life, and the "honors" accorded them, are like so much smoke and mist, contemptibly "lightweight"; they have no genuine importance, no enduring solidity. But the life itself of "this-worldly" or "secular" action inevitably can become, on the contrary, a heavy "burden," an *onus*, *sarcina*, to the agent who is harried by its constant busyness and worn down by its "cares." Though the *works* of action may be flitting and weightless, therefore, the active life itself "weighs down" the agent, pinning him to "earth" like a heavy load which he has taken onto his shoulders.

It will not have escaped the reader that his conversion from "vanity"—however inchoate it turns out to be—prompts Augustine's imagination to evoke the same two-world structure as did the topics of Manichaeism, sexuality, and the *Hortensius*'s invitation to the contemplative life. His imagery on this point is nothing if not consistent. Hence, when he claims that the *Hortensius* made his "empty ambitions" lose much of their luster, he is implicitly claiming that this disaffection toward "vanities" was the obverse of his "conversion" to the quest for Wisdom: it corresponded to a shift of aspirations away from noisy worldly achievement to the quiet serenities of contemplative joy, from temporal activities toward other-worldly "Truth."

The Story of Augustine's Wrestling with "Vanity"

But it is time to detail how these motifs come to expression and articulation in the *Confessions*. Augustine wastes no time in introducing the topic of vanity, and he does so with acid irony:[75] it is a childish sin which, he archly suggests, makes self-important adults act like tiny boys. This is what he himself did: instead of those solid and substantial "useful" studies of spelling and counting, as a child he preferred "vanities" like playing "games" and chasing after "victories in competitions [*certamina*] . . . and to have his itching ears [*scalpi aures*] tickled with fictional fables that made them only itch the more" (*quo prurirent ardentius*). All this, he tells us, was motivated by the same "curiosity" which made his "eyes glitter for shows [*spectacula*], those games of grown-ups. For the producers of those games are held in such high esteem [*ea dignitate praediti excellunt*] that almost all parents desire it for their children."[76] Fictions, shows, spectacles, and every variety of falsity, along with competition for hollow victories—the lexicon of "vanity" is rapidly expanding.

But Augustine is also thinking here of both his parents, Monica and Patricius; they may not explicitly have entertained the precise "wish" that he "arrive" at the distinction of putting on similar plays, yet they were anxiously concerned that their brilliant son, the *rhetor*, enjoy all the educational advantages which would equip him to capture his share of worldly glory (1.16).

And still the little scamp persisted in finding his elementary studies in Latin, and all his studies of Greek, "punishingly burdensome" (*onerosas poenalesque*). That attitude he now ascribes to the "vanity" of human life, which makes all of us, in the Psalmist's image, so much insubstantial "flesh, and a breath [*spiritus*] that goes and does not return" (1.20). For he set higher store by "vain" and "useless" fictional tales like Vergil's about Dido and Aeneas than he did on the things he learned—to count, to spell—which still prove "useful" to him now (1.24).

And what did it profit him to imitate the anger of the goddess Juno in that juvenile rhetorical contest he once managed to win? He can still recall it as a "disquieting business" (*negotium . . . inquietum*) with "praise as its prize" (*praemio laudis*). The boy who would speak in the most praiseworthy fashion (*laudabilius*) had to ape the goddess's emotions most effectively, and "dress up" her sentiments in the most suitable language (*verbis . . . vestientibus*). What did all this amount to, Augustine now reflects, but so much "smoke and wind" (*fumus et ventus*), so many "empty trifles" (*inania nugarum*) (1.27).

But then, was it any wonder that he was "borne away" (*ferebar*) from God into such "vanities" when the masters appointed for his imitation so obstinately valued surface over substance? "Elegance" of expression counted more in their eyes than the truth or justice of what was expressed, and they gloried in the praise they won by such performances (*laudati gloriabantur*) (1.28). They would have been mortified to be heard mispronouncing the word "human," but when one of them, bent on winning "fame for eloquence," spewed forth enough oratorical bile upon some courtroom opponent to get a living man unjustly sentenced to death, he never turned a hair (1.29). And to please such men as these, Augustine was given to believe, was what "honorable living" (*honeste vivere*) was all about!

Yet he was as vain as they, though in boyish fashion. Out of a "vain desire for distinction," he cheated his companions and won "false victories" at games. Likewise, he gulled his teachers repeatedly out of "love for play, eagerness to see frivolous shows, and the restless hope of imitating what had been played on stage" (*amore ludendi, studio spectandi nugatoria, et imitandi ludicra inquietudine*) (1.30). That final indictment reads almost like a deliberate summary of what Augustine denotes by the term "vanity."

Augustine opens Book 2 of his *Confessions* with a hymn of praise to the God Whose "sweetness" has now become a conquering delight, the God Who is now, he confesses, "collecting me [*colligens*] from that dispersion into which I was shattered and sundered, when I turned away from [God], the One, and emptied myself out [*evanui*] upon the many"—upon the manifold of lower, temporal realities. This compact evocation of the original "fall" anticipates in remarkable detail the description at Book 11.39 of the soul's fall from the contemplative "collectedness" of eternity into its present dispersion among the realities of time. Viewed from that perspective, the "fall" gives birth to the entire realm of "vanity," and Augustine summons up that vision with the striking term *evanui*. *Confessions* 11.39 will picture Augustine as plunging down into "times," shattering apart, and spilling forth his "insides." At Book 7.22, he will evoke the very same image but in language much closer to that of Ecclesiasticus 10:9–14, the original inspiration for this somewhat baroque image-complex (*GenMan* 2.6). Here, like a marksman with a single shot in his magazine, Augustine makes do with that single word, *evanui* (2.1).

The next two paragraphs (2–3) we have already examined: in a cluster of images quite distinct from the *vanitas* cluster which interests us for the moment, they describe his sexual awakening. At the end of paragraph 2.4, however, another indictment gets under way: neither Monica nor Patricius, Augustine complains, took any care to arrange a marriage for their son. Their motive for that, he goes on to explain, was the "vanity" of ensuring him a successful worldly career: "Their only care was that I should learn to make the finest orations and become a persuasive speaker." Patricius went to extraordinary lengths to stretch and supplement the family budget in order to pay for Augustine's educational expenses in nearby Madaura; he was anxious that his son become "cultivated in speech," but was uninterested in his spiritual development (5). Monica warns her son to avoid fornication, or at least to stay clear of adultery, yet she stays well short of exercising "definitive care for this," by seeking to arrange a marriage for him. Her motive, too, is "vanity"; she had lofty worldly ambitions for her bright young son, and feared "that [his] prospects would be hindered by the impediment of a wife." Besides, and here Augustine admits he is conjecturing, she may have thought that the education she and Patricius were paying for would not constitute an obstacle to Augustine's becoming a good Christian (6–8). The "vanity" of this-worldly hopes, then, found comfortable haven in Monica's heart, as much, or even more so, than in her pagan husband's.[77]

Augustine spends the remainder of Book 2 on the famous theft of pears, but he returns to the motif of vanity when opening Book 3. Here he sketches a summary picture of his spiritual state. The triadic categories which guide him in that brief self-estimate are his accustomed ones, but in this instance he reviews only two of the three sins St. John speaks of in his First Epistle. He opens by alluding to both forms of concupiscence, of the flesh and of the eyes (3.1), then passes on to dwell on his sins of "curiosity" (3.2–6). In case his readers fail to catch what he is about, he summarizes the entire sin-triad explicitly at paragraph 16; this occurs, understandably, in the context of his treatment of Manichaeism.

The topic of curiosity evokes some fresh variations on the familiar images associated with "vanity": Augustine's "emptiness" of the only "interior food" that could have fed his hunger, God's Truth; his itchy yen to be "scratched" by the outer realities of the sense world (3.1); his avid fondness for theatrical "spectacles"; the "falsity" of real sorrows directed toward "fictional" people (2–3); and, once again, the theme of his ulcerated soul's itching and yearning for the "surface" pleasure of being "scratched" (3.4).

The complete picture is filling out: *vanitas* is the "false" or "lying" counterpart of *Veritas*; it is empty and hollow, while Truth is solid and filling; it is all exterior surface, whereas Truth is interiorly substantial; it provokes a superficial "itch," whereas Truth answers to the soul's profoundest hunger.

At this point, "vanity" momentarily betrays a certain kinship with pride: we have already examined the way Augustine connects his "sacrilegious desire" for the experimental knowledge of sense—the shadow-counterpart of the contemplative knowledge his soul has forfeited by its fall—with the worship of demons. "Proud of neck" (*praefidenti collo*), he wanders like the Prodigal, "far" from God (3.5). His studies only reinforce the appeal of vanity; their entire point is to prepare him to "shine" (*excellere*) in those "litigious forums" of the law-courts, winning "praise" for the accomplished "fraudulence" of his victories there, and "glory" in his very blindness. He was top boy in his rhetoric school, and "proudly rejoiced, swollen up with vanity" (*gaudebam superbe et tumebam tyfo*).[78]

He introduces the *Hortensius* episode now, but with one last slant at his studies in "eloquence": he confesses that he himself desired to excel in them (*eminere*), "toward a damnable and windy purpose, and for empty human joys" (*per gaudia vanitatis humanae*) (7). As we noticed earlier, Augustine tells us that the reading of the *Hortensius* resulted in an ardent yearning to fly away from "earthly realities" in general, and that, more specifically, his every "vain hope" (*vana spes*) was suddenly "cheapened" (*viluit*). I have already suggested[79] that the more general expression "earthly realities" most probably covers the objects both of vain "curiosity" and of sexual lust, whereas "vain hope" clearly evokes the more specific register of "vanity" associations. Hence, it might be translated quite accurately as "this-worldly hope" or "secular ambition."

Augustine's Requisite: Certainty

Part of the reason why he clung to those secular hopes lay in an important difference Augustine had with Cicero. As an Academic,

Cicero was convinced that one should be content to pursue the truth, and, indeed, derive one's happiness from that pursuit, even when persuaded that truth could never definitively be found. Augustine, however, could never be satisfied with Cicero's claim that, in the terms he borrowed from the Gospel of St. Matthew, the "seeking" (*quaerere*) alone should make the "philosopher" happy, even if the "finding" (*invenire*) was indefinitely deferred—indeed, was clearly acknowledged from the start as unobtainable. Hence, he deliberately alters the terms of Cicero's "invitation to philosophy," and instead promises himself that from the moment he is certain that he has "found" the truth, he will then put aside all the secular ambitions which prevent his embracing the philosophical form of life, shuck off the life of worldly activity, and devote himself undividedly to the contemplative pursuit of otherworldly "Wisdom" (6.18, 8.17). In the meantime, although the objects of his secular ambition have loosened their hold on him, he cannot see his way to abandoning them entirely until he is *certain* of having something "solid" to put in their place.

From this point in his story, up until his dramatic experience with those "Platonist books" at Milan, we shall see Augustine at grips with that "quest" for "certainty," a quest which becomes more and more anxious as year follows year. It will be important to discern why the attainment of certainty became so intense an obsession for Augustine—and also, precisely what certainties he strove so stubbornly to attain.

The Burden of Worldly Ambition

Augustine's quest for certainty will run concurrently with a competing tendency, the continued pursuit of worldly success; and the conflict between those two pursuits will exact a cost which Augustine finds increasingly demanding, and ultimately intolerable. For he will pass, in time, from the cocoon of rhetoric school to assume the responsibilities of a teacher of rhetoric in his native town of Thagaste. From there he will move to the wider and more challenging arena of Carthage, then to Rome, and finally, the loftiest rung of ambition's ladder, to the imperial city, Milan. With each successive upward move, his responsibilities grow heavier, the competition grows fiercer, the demands on his time and attention leave him less and less room to catch his breath, less and less leisure to search for the certainty which continues to elude him.

In that quest for truth, moreover, the Manichees turned out to be more and more a disappointment. One of his persistent indictments of them, leveled from his later vantage point, was their "vain" habit of dressing up their doctrine in glittering imagery to disguise the emptiness of its falsity. The *Hortensius* had made his soul hunger for the solid nourishment of Truth, but all he received from this new religion was counterfeit nourishment, "empty figments" (*figmenta inania*), despite their being served up on decorative "platters" (*fercula*) (3.10–11).

"Seduced and seducing, deceived and deceiving" is how Augustine describes himself as teacher in Thagaste, "proud" as well as "vain." He "chased after the emptiness of popular glory" (*popularis gloriae sectantem inanitatem*), living a round of "contests" and "competitions" (*contentiosa carmina*), with "garlands of grass" as prizes. He even stooped to seeking "applause in the theater" by acting in a number of "foolish plays on stage" (4.1). He depreciates his teaching of rhetoric as a business of "selling" a speaking skill "designed for winning courtroom battles" (4.2). Contests, competitions, courtroom litigation: the competitive edge of his profession bites into him more and more intensely, and Augustine discovers how some of his colleagues would go to any lengths to assure themselves of victory (4.3).

A dear friend dies, a youth of Augustine's own age. The moving account of his inconsolable grief subtly veers into a meditation on the vanity—though the word is never mentioned—of placing one's happiness in fleeting temporal realities: they never "stand" still for us; the moment we think we have caught hold of them, they slip out of our grasp. We can never find in them the "rest" we forfeited when we turned away from the Eternal One for the variegated many. If we ourselves would "stand" and find "rest," we can do so only by loving everyone we love "in" the Eternal God Who "stands" immovably (11–18).[80] But to escape his grief, Augustine can think only of moving—from Thagaste to Carthage.

Meanwhile, he begins to find discrepancies between the beliefs of the Manichees and the findings—particularly the astronomical findings—of contemporary "physical philosophers" (5.3–7).[81] He is assured that all his difficulties will vanish once the famous Manichee bishop, Faustus, comes to speak to his flock in Carthage. He waits and waits; when Faustus eventually arrives, he is a galling disappointment. Charming, glib, but shallow, he dishes out more empty Manichee eloquence, serving up fake food in elegant serving-ware (*vasis urbanis*) (5.10). He leaves Augustine with all his intellectual difficulties intact.

This is where Augustine tells us that he now abandoned his efforts and resolve to advance from the outer circle of "auditors" to the inner circle of Manichee "Elect" (5.13). He will remind us of this decision a few paragraphs later (5.18). It must have cost him dearly. Augustine is now twenty-eight or twenty-nine years of age; he has been a Manichee, and a formidable proselytizer for that sect, for upward of nine years; it cannot have been easy to digest his feelings of deception at the failed promise Manichaeism represented.

But this episode should most of all erase any residual doubts about how seriously Augustine took Manichaeism; he would scarcely have endured those months and years of awaiting Faustus' arrival, in doubt and suspense, unless he did so. There is a more general conclusion to be drawn, as well: from everything we know of him, at least from his nineteenth year forward, Augustine was always a seriously religious person. And so, we must be disposed to believe him when he tells us that the period of drift he is about to enter, cut loose from all religious moorings, was especially painful to him.

The Peregrine in Italy

Now he decides to leave Carthage and try his fortunes across the sea in Rome. He tells us why, but in a curiously hesitant way: he went to Rome in hopes of finding students who were less unruly and undisciplined than the rowdies of Carthage; it was not, he assures us, the hope of more money which drew him, or aspirations toward "greater honors" (*dignitas*); and yet—he now hedges that assertion—"such things also influenced my mind at that time" (*quamquam et ista ducebant animum tunc meum*). So, the ambiguous best he can offer to explain his move is this: the prospect of teaching more disciplined students was "the greatest and almost the sole reason" (*causa maxima et paene sola*) for his going to Rome. Had the "vain hopes" which the *Hortensius* so dampened been entirely extinguished? "Yes," Augustine would like to be able to say, but when push comes to shove, he must answer: "No, almost, but not quite" (5.14).

But alas, just when he is getting to become "known" in Roman circles, he finds his students there too clever for him, especially when it comes to slithering out of paying their tuition fees (5.22). Besides, word comes to Symmachus, who had formerly been municipal *rhetor* at Milan and now held the powerful political office of City Prefect in Rome, that Milan had need of a new municipal *rhetor*. By this time in history, Milan has succeeded Rome as the imperial city; Symmachus' subsequent advancement testifies to the political importance of the post of municipal *rhetor* there; North African or no, Augustine is reaching the top of his profession.

Applying for the position required that Augustine deliver a trial speech. It is unclear whether this was a competitive test, but if it was, Augustine beat out all his rivals; in any case, he won the post. More than ever assured of being a "comer," he packs off to Milan, where the Catholic Bishop is a redoubtable man named Ambrose.

Augustine has heard of Ambrose's reputation as a preacher, and will form the habit of assisting at his sermons, and yet (sign of his own persistent "vanity") to study the man's rhetorical manner, not his theological matter. But he cannot help observing that, in a reversal of the equation that held for Faustus, Ambrose's manner is less flashy, but the content of his preaching far more solid (5.23). Between them, the two bishops represent the poles of vanity and Truth.

The Burden of Activity, the Chains of Sex

While discharging his duties at Milan, Augustine tells us, he was "avid for" (*inhiabam*) honors, money, and marriage (*honoribus, lucris, coniugio*), desires that made him "suffer most bitter hardship" (*patiebar . . . amarissimas difficultates*). Coming, as they do, after the lukewarm ambiguity of his professed motivation for transferring to Rome, the three ends listed in that assertion, one suspects, did not actually rank as equal as Augustine's phrasing suggests. Everything we have seen and will see argues that he would have desired money only as a means for pursuing worldly honors. Something similar must be said about his desire for "marriage" (*coniugium*). Events will show that he is not using that term exclusively to designate his habitual desire for a sexual partner; the mother of Adeodatus seems to have served quite satisfactorily in that capacity. Rather, both he and (quite especially) Monica— who by now has followed her golden boy to Milan—appear to be on the lookout for prospects of a "first-class" marriage to a more socially distinguished spouse: again, the demands of Augustine's promising career claim first priority.

Even that qualified reading of the text suggests, however, that the "vain hopes" that the *Hortensius* threatened to quench appear to have sprung into new life. It could be that the collapse of his Manichee beliefs left Augustine with no other-worldly object to give direction to his life, while his growing success (and Monica's prodding?) revived "this-worldly" aims as something to fill the vacuum. But the strains involved in pursuing those aims have seriously intensified: Augustine has entered the most demanding arena for a professional *rhetor* to deploy his skill. The upshot is, he has only one word to describe his state of soul: *misera*.

Augustine illustrates his wretchedness with a vivid memory: he pictures himself as the complete creature of "vanity" in all its darkest aspects. One day, as he is heading off to make an important speech "in praise of the emperor"—*imperatori laudes*, one of his official duties as municipal *rhetor*—he espies a drunken beggar, already in his cups, joking with the passersby and wishing them well; it suddenly occurs to Augustine with overpowering force that this creature is actually happier than he is! After all, he is merry and cheerful, while Augustine's heart is "pounding with cares" (*curas anhelaret*). In the speech he is about to make he will tell "many a lie" (*plura mentirer*), and those "lies would win the favor of men [*mentienti faveretur*] who all knew that [he] was lying."

We can almost see Augustine, striding along the streets of Milan, dragging the "burden of his misery" along behind him (*infelicitatis meae sarcinam*), his life one wearying round (*ambiebam*) of "toilsome twists and scheming turns." He sees now that he was seeking a false happiness through all sorts of "roundabout plans" (*ambitionibus*), "troubled" and "full of fear" (*anxius, trepidus*). His "very vitals," he tells us in that striking metaphor, again, were "torn out with cares" (*curis eviscerarer*) in his efforts to "please men [*placere*], not to instruct them, but" (fickle and uncertain business), "merely to please them" (*placerem*) (6.9).

And do not tell Augustine that his motive is higher than the beggar's; he does it all for "glory" (*gloria*). But it was "no true glory," just as it was "no true joy" which he was pursuing, burdened with "cares and fears" (*curis timoribus confectum*). True joy was worlds away from this hollowness he was living (*incomparabiliter distat ab illa vanitate*).

The Torment of Deferral

This was his life, then; how long could he go on this way? He answers in one of his favorite metaphors, that of sleeping and waking: night and day he "lay down to sleep and got up again, and would again lie down to sleep and get up again, and for—count them—so many, many days" (*vide, quot dies*)! In sum, despite all the trappings of worldly success, things were "going ill" with him (6.10).

Sleeping and waking, day following day, the endless deferring of the life-decision to "leave all things and be converted to [God]" (*relictis omnibus converteretur ad Te*); the train of images makes it clear that Augustine is "rehearsing" the dramatic "awakening" he will describe in Book 8.

But here his two close companions are as involved as he is; the same tormented question—"How long?" (*Quamdiu haec?*)—comes from their lips as well. For the same sense of tedium and pointlessness is afflicting not only Nebridius, but also his longtime friend Alypius—whom Augustine now portrays (6.11–16: a rehearsal within a larger rehearsal!) as the typical "man of curiosity."[82] All three of them are "inflamed" with the search for "Truth and Wisdom"; all three suffer from the emptiness of "want" till God (in the words of Psalm 144:15, which was used even then for "grace before meals")[83] should give them "food in due season"; together they taste the bitterness of longing for the "life of happiness" (*beatae vitae*) while compromisingly engaged in "this-worldly activities" (*saeculares actus*). All three are wavering about the "manner of life" (*vitae modus*) they should adopt, but they nonetheless persist in deferring the decision to "leave all those things" (*illis relictis*)—until they have first caught hold of some kind of "certainty" to guide them (6.17).

Certainty, Truth, and Happiness

With that explicit introduction of the expression *beata vita*, Augustine brings to the surface a connection which has been active in subterranean fashion ever since the *Hortensius* incident. We have seen and will see more of the importance Augustine accorded to the matter of attaining certainty; now he has told us that his two dearest friends shared that same preoccupation. As moderns, we might be tempted to think that these men were raising a good deal of fuss about an issue of concern only to professional eggheads: as though they were perplexed about the purely intellectual problem of how to escape from Academic skepticism. Augustine has only begun to describe the mental agony and frustration they were suffering through, and we could mistakenly assume that it arose from an anxiety over finding the "truth" about such questions as whether that famous oar the skeptics ran on about was really bent once dipped into the water.

But Augustine is reminding us that, ever since the reading of the *Hortensius*, his concern went to deeper issues than epistemological ones: or, more exactly, that he measured the importance of epistemological problems precisely by how closely they touched on the vital question of happiness. Despite all of Cicero's own reservations on those issues, we have seen that his *Hortensius* insinuated to Augustine this thrilling possibility: that happiness might lie, not in "seeking" and "finding" some particular truth and sectarian wisdom of this or that human group of philosophers, but in the "finding," meaning no less than attaining to the blissful "vision," "embrace," and "possession"—of an other-worldly Truth and Wisdom and Beauty all compacted in a single radiant She. This was why the doubts now gripping him caused such torment: they penetrated to the very heart of that possibility, insinuating that no such other-worldly Truth-Wisdom existed, after all; that She was all dream-stuff; that either "Wisdom" was a "nothing," or, at very least, that humans could never be certain that such an Ideal Beauty, such a bosom of happiness, truly existed. And if Verity did not exist, then it must follow that all, all is vanity. . . .

This was the problem of "certainty" as Augustine envisaged it; what he is implying now is that his two companions, Nebridius and Alypius, viewed that problem in substantially the same existential—and vaguely Platonic—terms. Now, as if to sharpen the conflict he was in, and also to clarify its terms for us, the memory of Augustine's first conversion comes flooding back:

> It caused me the greatest wonder when I reflected anxiously on how long a time had passed since my nineteenth year, when I had first been enflamed with the desire for Wisdom. For then I had determined that, once Wisdom had been found, I would leave behind [relinquere] all the empty hopes and deceptive madness of my vain desires. Yet here I was in my thirtieth year, still caught fast in the same mire through my avidity to enjoy realities of the moment that kept flitting from my grasp and sapped my energy. And all the while I kept saying to myself: "Tomorrow I will find it! It will appear clearly to me and I will take hold of it" [6.18]!

"Tomorrow, tomorrow": *cras, cras*. But again, he is resolved to break with his "empty hopes" only *after* this supernal Wisdom has allowed him to glimpse Her. Book 8.12 will re-express it as "*Modo, modo; sed modo et modo non habebat modum*. But Augustine the preacher seems to have delighted in imitating that ugly syllable, *cras, cras*, which he likens to the hoarse-throated call of the crow; it is emblematic, for him, of the would-be convert's tactic of deferring, endlessly deferring, the moment of surrender.[84]

He insists he must first lay hold of *perspicua veritas*, but "where is it to be found?" Ambrose might be of some help, he tells himself, but Ambrose himself "has no time off" (*non vacat*). Augustine has introduced a new key term, *vacare*, into his lexicon for the life of contemplation. But now his fevered desperation shows vividly through his text: he himself, he tells us, has

> no time off for reading, either [*non vacat*]. Where, for that matter, could we look for the books we would need? Borrow them, but from whom? We *must* set time aside, *must* make up a schedule for the good of our soul!

But his frantic round of secular activities makes "time off" an unattainable dream:

> Our students take up the morning hours; how do we spend the rest of the day? Why not do our studying then? And yet, if we did that, when would we go visiting our influential friends, whose backing we need? And when would we prepare classes for our students? And what time would we have for relaxation and escape from these cares and tensions [18]?

"Perish all of this!" Augustine exclaims in desperation; "Let us dismiss these vain and empty concerns" (*dimittamus haec vana et inania*). "Let us devote ourselves to the search for Truth and that alone!" But this is only a half-resolve, recalling the half-resolve arising from the *Hortensius* incident. He still insists on first finding something certain to light his way.

By this time, though, the life of "philosophy" has taken a more outspokenly turn, for (using the word *vacare* in an ironic sense now) Augustine admits he has come to acknowledge that the worldwide spread of Christianity can be "no idle and empty thing" (*non vacat, non est inane*). "Why do we put off leaving all worldly hopes behind [*relicta spe saeculi*], why not devote ourselves unreservedly to seeking after God and" (the equation is revealing) "the life of happiness" (*ad quaerendum Deum et beatam vitam*) (6.19)? But "Wait a bit!" he stops himself; the charm of those "worldly hopes" beguiles him still:

> These things still bring us joy; no little sweetness attaches to them. It is not an easy thing to go without them, and it would be shameful to abandon and then go back to them. See, too, how much has already been accomplished toward procuring a post of distinction [*aliquis honor*]. What more do you want in this regard? You have plenty of important friends; if nothing else is in the offing, and you want to hurry matters, it is likely you might be granted a governorship somewhere. You could marry a wife who has some money, so as not to increase your living expenses—that way, greed will be held within bounds. Many a great man, well worth imitating, has devoted himself to the pursuit of wisdom while being married.

Again, the Burden and the Chain

Compromise, rationalization, delaying tactics—Augustine the Bishop sees that more clearly now. And through it all, "time was passing, and I still kept delaying my conversion to the Lord; day after day I kept putting off the moment when I should begin to live in You . . ." (6.20). He was afraid that he would be "entirely too miserable if deprived of womanly embraces." And now he confesses to his greatest error: when he thought then of the virtue of "continence," he considered it—wrongly—as something he would have to achieve by his "own powers." And he was at least clear-sighted enough to see that such a thing was beyond his powers (6.20).

So his attachment to sexual delights has become a "chain" (*catena*) he must drag along; a prisoner, he is terrified of being freed! Well may he point to the example of those great men who searched after wisdom in the married state, but if it came to the truth of the matter, he was far from their "grandeur of spirit" (*granditate animi*) (6.21). Indeed, he was being hypocritical, for "whatever conjugal beauty there may be in the duty of regulating marriage and in caring for children, it did not attract [him], except very slightly" (*nisi tenuiter*). On the contrary, he was "in great part" (*magna . . . ex parte*) a "captive" to the habit of satisfying his sexual desires. That enslavement was a torment to him (*excruciebar*), but there, he would have us believe, was the unromantic fact of the matter (6.22).

And yet, there is a curious hint of reserve in Augustine's self-accusation: *nisi tenuiter . . . magna . . . ex parte*. A sudden flash of honesty seems to have reined in his inclination to indict himself more flatly. But Augustine is making it progressively clearer: he is resolved to keep the desire for money within reasonable "measure," but the "chain" (*catena, vinculum*) of attachment to sexual pleasure is primarily what also binds him to the ever more irksome "burden" (*onus, sarcina*) of secular activity. Primarily: but not solely. His eyes can still light up at the prospects of success, honors, glory. And so, one suspects, can Monica's.

Now he illustrates how much he was no *feminae imitator* but a mere "slave to lust": he tells that troubling story about the arrangements for his prospective marriage. Monica has found a socially acceptable young girl who will make a more presentable bride for her rising star of a son. She succeeds in persuading the mother of his child to clear off and return to Africa (vowing, Augustine says admiringly, never to have another man). But he himself seems to have awakened one day to discover how successful Monica's machinations were: his former "bed-mate" was gone, and he does himself the small justice of admitting that the realization caused him acute suffering. But he finds it impossible to endure the two-year wait the new girl's tender age imposes: he takes an interim mistress (6.23, 25).

And still, the suffering of separation from Adeodatus' mother continues unabated. The expression Augustine uses in this connection is revealing: she had been "torn from his side" (*avulsa a latere meo*) and, in consequence, his "heart, to which she adhered, was torn and wounded, and left a trail of blood." One translator takes romantic flight at this point, inserting a "because I loved her dearly" which has no foundation in the Latin.[85] But however unwarranted, that mistranslation calls to mind the charming dialogue which once took place between two distinguished French scholars: Pierre Courcelle had inferred from Augustine's marital fidelity that Manichee morality on that score must have been fairly exigent; to which Henri–Irénée Marrou replied by asking, "Dare I pronounce, in a stage whisper, the word 'love?'"[86]

Despite the admirable finesse of that rejoinder, however, I must confess that I find it disquieting that, in this context, Augustine never seems to have been able to pronounce that word. This seems just one more instance where he fell short of integrating sexual attachment with the "object-love" more appropriate to the "friendship" relation. Examination of his imagery here shows that it is sexual attachment, not love, that he is talking about. *Ubi adhaerebat*: we moderns can say we are deeply "attached" to someone, without adverting to the origin of that metaphor. But study Augustine's usage in this connection, and he is quite consistent;[87] he employs the various cognates of *haerere* (*adhaerere, cohaerere, inhaerere*) to convey the literally "adhesive" property whereby the lover becomes "stuck on" the object of his love, so that the partners become "nailed" or "glued" to each other. Pull them apart, the metaphor implies, and that abrupt action will inflict a wound on both of them; like Augustine separated from his bed-companion, they will "trail blood."

This was a stock Platonic metaphor,[88] and was often fraught (as here) with pejorative connotations: when focused on an "earthly" object, such loves as Augustine believed he experienced made the lover as earthly as the object of their love, and (in the language of the *Omnia* image-cluster) "weighed" the lover down. But if the love was "spiritual," it could "lighten" the lover and "bear him upward" to "union" with the belovèd (see 13.10).[89] In expressing that union, Augustine's "ascetical–mystical" paradigm for sexuality stimulates his imagination to leap from "vision," or "beholding," to "embracing," then to complete "one-ness" with the belovèd. So, he will remind us, St. John assures us that when we come to "see" God, we shall be assimilated to Him, "be" like

Him (1 Jo 3:2). Only the spiritual love of the purified contemplative, Augustine is intimating, climaxes in the perfect bonding of lover and belovèd which the act of physical intercourse dimly foreshadows.

It has been pointed out innumerable times that Augustine never tells us the name of his longtime consort; but then, he never names that most dear young friend of his youth in Thagaste, yet no sensitive reader of the *Confessions* will ever forget his moving account of that untimely death and how it tore his heart to ribbons (4.9–13). Though the young man remains nameless, Augustine's story has rendered him immortal; the same is true of the mother of his son, Adeodatus. Could it be that Augustine's failure to utter the word "love" in connection with her is one more of his artistic master-strokes, leaving his readers to wonder why? But perhaps this would be bending over backward to "save" Augustine . . . or would it?

In sum, Augustine seems to have wanted throughout this section of the *Confessions* to portray himself as a "slave to lust" (*libidinis servus*) and little more; and yet, for some strange reason, when read with an ear for its subtle false-notes, that portrait keeps falling shy of absolute conviction.

The Dream of the Contemplative Life Returns

Meanwhile, he and his companions earnestly discuss the possibility of turning their backs on the "turbulent botherations of human life" for which they entertain a common "detestation." Unsurprisingly, that possibility soon begins to take the shape of a communitarian response to the invitation of the *Hortensius*.

Augustine relates how he and his companions "thought about and jointly discussed living a life of tranquil leisure [*otiose vivere*] apart from the crowd, and had almost reached the point of deciding on . . . [this] life of leisure" (*otium*). The group of companions would number about ten; they would pool all their goods, possessing them in common; two of them would be appointed for a year's term to take care of temporal necessities, leaving the others undisturbed (*quietis*). A lovely plan: what went wrong? Alas, several of them already had wives, others were planning on marriage, and the wives (*mulierculae*: again, Augustine's chauvinist irony is showing!) would never put up with such arrangements! And so "the whole project, which we had so well worked out, collapsed in our hands." And back they had to go, to the daily round of activities and cares they had come to hate (6.24).

For one brilliant moment, the dream of Augustine's nineteenth year was almost a reality. His disappointment is bitter, all the more so since he must admit to himself that the principal obstacle lay in the iron logic of his own weakness: to have a wife meant the possibility of having children, which meant the obligation of making money to support both her and them, which meant, in turn, settling for the round of this-worldly activities he had come to "detest." Once again, in Augustine's imaged language, the weighty "chain" of enslavement to sex binds him also to the heavy "burden" of "worldly action." Between them, they both hold him down to "earth."

But though the plan of a contemplative community was dashed to pieces, the dream refused to die. Augustine assures us that God was laughing at their plan, even while He was readying a plan of His own. We shall see that God's plan will fulfill the dream; it will remain in continuity with the *Hortensius*, but a *Hortensius* set in a Christian key.

The Hortensius: A Conversion Unconsummated

The *Hortensius* experience did, therefore, truly represent a "first conversion" for Augustine. But it must be reckoned, in the first place, as a companion experience to the idealistic dream his dawning sexuality awakened in him. Not only did Augustine find Cicero encouraging a brave venture toward understanding, but he read that encouragement as also suggesting that sexual passion would attain sublimated fulfillment in an erotically charged quest for a beatifying vision; the supernal Wisdom promised by the *Hortensius* served to clarify the lineaments of the "love" he had fallen in love with. To Augustine's erotic intellectualism, Wisdom and Love had to be one and the same.

But both those stimuli must be viewed in tandem with the kindred promises held out by Manichaeism: for Augustine viewed his entry into that group as an equally positive, progressive step. Far from being an "aversion," it must be coupled with the *Hortensius* incident as an integral moment in a genuine "conversion."

Finally, it must be borne in mind that his meditations on the

Hortensius conspired, in all likelihood, with the other-worldly aspirations of the Manichees to instill in Augustine's heart a jaundiced attitude toward the "vanity" of this-worldly accomplishment, of all human "labor under the sun." That attitude will intensify, over time, until it becomes a positive detestation.

Granted: Augustine is looking back on all the events narrated in Book 3 from the perspective of his more developed thinking; from that vantage point, they reveal an identical dynamic: they all tended to prompt this young man to think of, and "feel" himself as, a *peregrinus*, a stranger and sojourner on this alien planet, a visitant fallen from another, higher world. The diffuse yearnings provoked by his sexual awakening could not put a name on what he longed for; he knew only that he had come to love some vast vagueness, call it love, or loving. Next the *Hortensius* suggested that it might be the Beauty of Wisdom which somehow haunted his memory; but in any case, his conviction has gained both clarity and firmness: only in some higher world would he ever find that immense Love, Radiant Wisdom, solid Truth, in the thrill of lasting embrace.

It should be no surprise that to this mélange of intellectualism and ultra-spiritualism, and apart from whatever exegetical difficulties may have bothered him at the time, Manichaeism seemed a religion with greater appeal than the more pedestrian North African Catholicism. Augustine could quite plausibly imagine that, having recognized that everything "under the sun" was vanity, his adhesion to Manichaeism put the religious seal on his conversion: he had changed his life-direction, and, however falteringly, turned his steps homeward.

On three decisive counts, however, that conversion remained unconsummated. As for Manichaeism, it eventually turned out to be a deception; as to sexuality, only years later did Augustine finally succeed in sublimating those urges in pursuit of an otherworldly ideal. Only then could he respond fully to that third, and most imperious, aspect of his "first conversion," the summons to adopt the life of "philosophy." But this will mean accepting a new invitation, from that mysterious symbol of sublimated sexuality, Lady Continence. She will urge him not merely (in the Gospel phrase which has subtly begun to sound like a recurrent refrain) to "leave all things" (*relinquere*), but, more energetically still, to "cast away" (*abicere*) all his hopes of worldly honors, along with his desire for the pleasures of marriage, and to don the livery of a soldier of Christ.

But, as was suggested earlier, not only was the *Hortensius* conversion the first in a temporal series of conversions, it remained the enduring core about which each of Augustine's successive conversions would have to build. More than ten years after reading that seminal work of Cicero's, he is still nostalgic for the contemplative life—albeit Christianized—whose peaceful *otium* it had invited him to enjoy.

Counterpulls to Conversion: Sex, or Honors, or Both

There can be little doubt that Augustine's attachment to sexual pleasure did much to impede his responding to that invitation. But it is clearer now that there was another obstacle, one not to be underestimated. Augustine had been encouraged by both his parents, and they carefully, expensively educated him, to polish and sell the glitter of eloquence, to compete for prizes of praise and name and honors: a heady brew for this heady North African. But there is something puzzling about the account the *Confessions* gives us of Augustine's attitude toward all the "vanities" success has crowned him with, and promises to crown him with still more lavishly. We saw that at *Confessions* 6.9, while already at Milan, Augustine tells us that he was "longing for honors, wealth, and marriage," making it sound as though all three were on the same footing. Even taking into account that the triad may have run off his pen with the facility of a cliché, the attitude toward "honors" expressed there does not clash terribly with his account ten paragraphs later, at Book 6.19; there he records that he found the perquisites of his position "agreeable" and "possessing no little sweetness of their own" (*non parvam dulcedinem suam*).

The decision to abandon his "worldly hopes" did not seem an "easy" one; after all, not all the drunken beggars in Milan could make the prospect of a governorship something lightly to be dismissed. True, the "burden" of his professional life is weighing heavier on him now, while the competing dream of peace in a contemplative community has been reborn with fresh intensity. It is also true that the wine of success has an exciting bouquet, but once actually tasted it can turn flat on the tongue. Nonetheless, it comes to the reader as surprisingly abrupt when Augustine tells us, in the very next paragraph (6.20), that he thought he would be "too unhappy entirely, if deprived of woman's embraces," and goes on from that point on to talk as though his captivity to sex and sexual satisfaction was his dominating, if not his unique, reason for "putting off conversion."

Now, conversion clearly did require that Augustine be liberated from the "chains" which bound him to sexual enjoyment. But there is almost a cliché about his conversion which runs through his early Dialogues: he had to break clear of *two* attachments, to marriage, *and to honors*.[90] The *Confessions* account, one might object, does not deny this; it merely makes clear that sexual attachment was the primary problem, and that Augustine looked on his commitment to the life of "secular activity" as a necessary means for supporting his sexual partner, whether she be wife or no.

And yet, the question still teases at the corner of the mind. Augustine has stressed the toll exacted in terms of cares and anxiety by the fierce competitiveness and tense uncertainties of his profession and his new-won eminence in it. But we cannot help divining that there must have been another side to that. It is not at all difficult to imagine that the exercise of his brilliant talents must also have procured Augustine many a moment of electric excitement and thrilling victory. So, the question keeps returning: to what extent did his conversion at Milan have to work against a residual attachment to the prizes of that "secular activity"? We shall have to remain alert for the answer to that question; any sound interpretation of his conversion depends importantly on getting it right.

The Other-Worldly Augustine

One final observation: the *Hortensius* episode was probably the most important one of the three pivotal experiences recounted in Book 3 of the *Confessions*. But all three of those experiences reciprocally reinforced each other. They all conspired to awaken Augustine to the possibility that, like the Prodigal and Odysseus, like the wingèd soul of Platonic myth, he may have fallen from a world of tranquil contemplation of Beauteous Truth into this harrying and distracting world of vanity and busy-ness, and he would find no lasting rest except by returning to that other world.

But if, as he depicts himself, he has been con-verted, literally "turned around," one can only infer that up until this point in his *Confessions* he has been a soul "turned away," *aversa*, in a flight that continues the alienating flight of his primordial "fornication from God." Given the way Augustine's rhetoric loves to balance such key expressions, the *conversio* of Book 3 must correspond to and correct some preceding *aversio*. Which leaves us with the troubling question: When could that *aversio* possibly have occurred?[91]

This much, at all events, is clear: from the moment the dawning of sexuality prompts him to suspect that he was fashioned to fall in love with love, he already senses vaguely that sex and passion of every sort point upward to a Beauteous Wisdom Who was somehow strangely familiar, somehow dimly remembered. From that moment forward, "philosophy," for this man, became the single-minded pursuit of a happiness which the contemplative soul had once enjoyed, wrenched itself away from, but restlessly longs to embrace again, this time forever. To this born poet, contemplative, and maybe even mystic, not only sex, but every delight, every pang, absolutely everything and everyone we encounter on our journey here below, eventually became sign and shadow of that splendorous reality waiting for us on our return to the home we once left. Compared to every such sign and shadow, that Reality was *aliud, aliud valde*: "other, vastly other." Which is why Augustine tirelessly wrote, and preached, that we humans—or, better, we fallen and wayfaring souls—must settle for nothing less.

But we have left Augustine at that juncture in his story where he could still question whether that "other, vastly other" realm of happiness really existed. We must follow him, now, as he labors to reach "certainty" on that vital issue.

NOTES

1. In citing the works of St. Augustine chapter number (conventionally indicated by small Roman numerals) are here regularly omitted except for those works where they are indispensable (for example, *Retr*). Only Book and paragraph divisions are given, both being written in arabic numerals. Thus, for example, *Conf* V.x.19 will be shortened to *Conf* 5.19.

When commenting continuously on the same work, so that no confusion should result, I shall give the title of the work at the start of the commentary, but only Book and paragraph will be indicated thereafter. The numbered reference will normally appear at the end of the appropriate section of commentary.

2. See Maria Peters, "Augustins erste Bekehrung," in *Harnack-Ehrung: Beiträge zur Kirchengeschichte* (Leipzig: Hinrichs, 1921), pp. 195–211; Michele Pellegrino, *Les* CONFESSIONS *de saint Augustin* (Paris: Études Augustiniennes, 1961), pp. 87–92 (henceforth: *Les* CONFESSIONS); Pierre Paul Courcelle, *Recherches sur Les* CONFESSIONS *de saint Augustin*, 2nd ed. (Paris: E. de Boccard, 1968), pp. 269–90 (henceforth: *Recherches*); Maurice Testard, *Saint Augustin et Cicéron*, 2 vols. (Paris: Études Augustiniennes, 1958), I, 19–30 (henceforth: *Cicéron*); André Mandouze, *Saint Augustin: L'Aventure de la raison et de la grâce* (Paris: Études Augustiniennes, 1968), pp. 93–94, 252–58 (henceforth: *L'Aventure*); Robert A. Russell, O.S.A., "Cicero's *Hortensius* and the Problem of Riches in St. Augustine," AS, 7 (1976), 59–68; Leo C. Ferrari, *The Conversions of Saint Augustine* (Villanova, Pa.: Villanova University Press, 1984), pp. 1–17 (henceforth: *Conversions*); Jean Doignon, "Sur l'enseignement de l'*Hortensius* . . . ," *L'Antiquité Classique*, 51 (1982), 193–206; Robert J. O'Connell, S.J., "On Augustine's 'First Conversion': *Factus Erectior* (*De Beata Vita* 4), AS, 17 (1986), 15–30 (henceforth: "*Factus Erectior*").

Jean Doignon presents several objections to this last article in "*Factus Erectior* (*B. Vita* 1, 4): Une Étape de l'évolution du jeune Augustin à Carthage," VC, 27 (1990), 79–93 (henceforth: "Étape"). But see below, note 13.

3. See references to Peters and Courcelle above, note 2.

4. "La Conversion de saint Augustin," *Revue des Deux Mondes*, 85 (1888), 43–69 (henceforth: "Conversion"). Note that Boissier makes the contrast between the "two Augustines" less stark than it often became in later stages of the ensuing controversy.

5. *Soundings*, pp. 174–291.

6. See *Soundings*, pp. 191, 206–209, 213, 267, for justification of this translation of *rapere*.

7. See Arthur Darby Nock, *Conversion: The Old and the New in Religion from Alexander the Great to Augustine of Hippo* (Oxford: Oxford University Press, 1933), pp. 164–86 (on "conversion to Philosophy"), and 259–66 (on Augustine's conversion). Also Ferrari, *Conversions*, pp. 2–4, and the article cited therein, p. 6*n*23; Courcelle, *Recherches*, pp. 58–59.

8. See Claude Lepelley, "*Spes Saeculi*," *Atti* I, pp. 99–117. This excellent study came to my attention only after much of this chapter had already been composed.

9. It is important to recognize that when he writes of "sinking stars" Augustine is continuing to recount his life as a "voyage"; hence, he is still speaking in terms of that navigational (more precisely the Odyssean) *metaphor*. Ferrari (*Conversions*, pp. 34–35) has him switch without warning into a literal register, and tell us of his supposed interest in astrological studies.

Doignon's objection to my interpretation of this episode (in "Étape," note 2 above) also requires that (*a*) one take Ferrari's quite speculative portrait of "Augustine the astrologist" as so solidly "proven" as to qualify as premiss for further interpretation, and that (*b*) one imagine that Augustine, trained *rhetor* though he was, would slip prematurely from the distinctly metaphorical register, which has hitherto presided over the description of his life's "voyage," into this baldly realistic meaning for "sinking stars." This would be much like asking us to imagine that a skillful versifier would insert, unaware, a clumsy extra foot into the final line of a limerick. It seems far more natural to me to interpret these "stars" as an additional element in a navigational metaphor, recalling, indeed, Odysseus' resolve to steer his course only by stars which do not sink into the ocean: so Augustine has discovered that the reliable guidance he was promised by the Manichees turned out to be delusive. For the evidence that the metaphor commanding this passage is thoroughly "Odyssean," see *Soundings*, pp. 174–245.

10. Doignon suggests the *Aeneid* (3.515) as "source" for this "sinking stars" image; this may be just one more instance where Vergil drew inspiration from Homer, and where (consequently?) the Aeneas and Odysseus images tend to "fuse" in Augustine's imagination; see *Soundings*, pp. 8–10, 73–81. (Doignon may have made this suggestion without realizing that it implied a return to the metaphorical key.)

11. Doignon is of the opinion that Augustine's many "occurrences of the verb" *erigere* which I cite in the article he criticizes have "little relation to one another." We have a methodological difference here: the relation I was arguing for derived from the single *image* of "becoming erect" which Augustine has deliberately, and suggestively, evoked in each of these varied instances.

12. On this issue Augustine clearly thought the Manichees were closer to the truth than the North African Catholicism he knew; this was one of the reasons why Augustine could think of his "conversion" to Manichaeism as a progressive step. See *Vita* 4, *UtCred* 2–3; *Soundings*, chap. 6.

13. The Sirens, in Augustine's imagination, stand for the temptation of vainglory which his "worldly" side hoped to satisfy by continuing to bear the *onus* of his rhetorical *professio* (*Vita* 4). See also Jean Doignon,

"Le symbolisme des Sirènes dans les premiers Dialogues de saint Augustin," in *Hommage à R. Chevalier* (Tours, 1986), pp. 113–20.

14. See my *Saint Augustine's* CONFESSIONS: *The Odyssey of Soul*, 2nd ed. (New York: Fordham University Press, 1989), pp. 47–50 (henceforth: *Odyssey*).

15. Courcelle, *Recherches*, pp. 53–46, gives a concise summary of this debate.

16. The literature is immense, but see especially the issues devoted to Augustine's *Confessions* by the *Journal for the Scientific Study of Religion* (henceforth: JSSR), in Volumes 1 and 2 (1965 and 1966), and the studies done more recently, in Volume 25 (1986), particularly: Joseph E. Dittes, "Augustine: Search for a Fail-Safe God to Trust," 57–63; Volney Gay, "Augustine: The Reader as Self-Object," 64–76; and Eugene TeSelle, "Augustine as Client and Theorist," 92–101. Compare the article by Peter Brown on "Augustine and Sexuality," in *Colloquy*, 46 (1983), 1–13, (publication of the Center for Hermeneutical Studies, Berkeley, California), along with responses solicited from J. Patout Burns, Xavier Harris, Margaret Miles, and me (pp. 14–25), and Brown's reply to those responses as well as to other scholars' questions, pp. 28–41. See also Brown's *The Body and Society: Men, Women, and Sexual Renunciation in Early Christianity* (New York: Columbia University Press, 1988), esp. pp. 387–427. More recently, Paul J. Archambault has contributed "Augustine's *Confessiones*: On the Uses and Limits of Psychobiography," *Collectanea*, "Founder," pp. 83–99. I shall abbreviate references to the above, citing them as Dittes, Gay, and TeSelle (all: 1986), and Brown, 1983 and 1988.

17. Paula Fredriksen, in "Augustine and His Analysts: The Possibility of a Psychohistory," in the review *Soundings*, 61 (1975), 206–27, gives a careful summary and excellent critique of some recent attempts to examine Augustine's sexuality through the lenses of various psychological constructs. She surveys studies by E. R. Dodds and C. Kligerman, plus the authors contributing to Volumes 1 and 2 of JSSR, mentioned in note 16: D. Bakan, W. H. Clarke, J. Dittes, and P. Woolcott, Jr., P. W. Pruyser, respectively. (I shall cite this article as Fredriksen, 1978). Though I find the great majority of her critical observations uncannily accurate, I must also suspect, sadly, that in attempting to apply the "narcissistic" construct to Augustine, she herself may have tumbled into more than one fault she finds in others. But I shall spare the reader, for the most part, detailed references to where the reading of Augustine's text I present here clashes with readings given by my predecessors.

18. See TeSelle 1986 and Archambault (cited in note 16, above) for thoughtful observations on this point.

19. *Fornicabar abs Te*, Augustine writes, and clarifies: *amicitia enim*

mundi huius fornicatio est abs Te (*Conf* 1.21); fornication from God can take any of the forms in which the soul can express its "love for *this* world" in preference to God.

20. See Elaine Pagels, *Adam, Eve, and the Serpent* (New York: Random House, 1988), p. 141; see also p. 105 (henceforth Pagels, *Serpent*). (Ernest Fortin has reminded me in this connection of how difficult it is to identify Augustine's "dominant passion," and how dangerous it would be to oversimplify his psychological make-up.)

21. The tradition on this issue traces back to Plato's *Philebus* and *Gorgias*.

22. Quoted by Brown 1983, p. 1.

23. Pagels, *Serpent*, p. 141.

24. See John J. O'Meara, *The Young Augustine* (London: Longmans, Green, 1954), pp. 47–52. Also Brown 1988, pp. 390–94.

25. Brown 1983, p. 3.

26. For documentation, see my articles, "The God of St. Augustine's Imagination" and "Isaiah's Mothering God in St. Augustine's *Confessions*," both in *Thought*: the former in 57 (1982), 30–40; the latter in 58 (1983), 188–206; *Imagination and Metaphysics in St. Augustine* (Milwaukee: Marquette University Press, 1987); and, more recently, *Soundings*, pp. 95–142. See also Tarcisius Van Bavel, "L'humanité du Christ comme *lac parvulorum* . . . ," *Augustiniana*, 7 (1957), 245–81; Margaret Miles, "Infancy, Parenting, and Nourishment in Augustine's *Confessions*," *American Academy of Religion*, 50 (1982), 349–64, and Marsha Dutton, "When I Was a Child . . . ," *Collectanea*, "Founder" (1989), pp. 113–40.

27. See both my articles cited in note 26, above.

28. As the two articles cited above show; but we shall see more of this below. Compare Dittes 1986, p. 183.

29. Dittes 1986, pp. 61–62.

30. See my "*Ennead* VI, 4–5 in the Works of St. Augustine," REA, 9 (1963), 1–39.

31. For fuller development, see my *Art and the Christian Intelligence in the Works of St. Augustine* (Cambridge: Harvard University Press, 1978), pp. 57–58, 201–202 (henceforth: *Art*).

32. Brown 1983, pp. 28–29; cf. *Mus* 6.13–14.

33. See *L'Aventure*, p. 74. Mandouze, be it noted, has lived much of his life in North Africa.

34. See TeSelle 1986, p. 86.

35. Dittes 1986, p. 61.

36. *Serpent*, p. 122.

37. See *Jul* 3.28, especially in what Frederiksen 1978, p. 226*n*26) wittily terms the "energetic translation" found in Peter Brown's *Augustine of Hippo* (Berkeley: University of California Press, 1967) p. 391 (hence-

forth: *Augustine*). (When this chapter was presented in an earlier form, as a discussion piece, both Karen Jo Torjesen and Jean Bethke Elshtain expressed their reserves on the possible anachronism they detected in my depiction of Patricius: the pagan marriage mores of the time would have sanctioned his expending his sexual energies on slave girls and/or concubines. No need for him to be a nuisance to Monica. But is it entirely too innocent to imagine that Patricius may have just plain loved his wife more than such [twentieth-century?] promiscuity would imply? Augustine's elaborate description of Patricius' regard for her, especially since it occurs in the immediate context, is striking. In any case, I would still hold to my main conclusion: we cannot be sure that Augustine is telling us Patricius was unfaithful, and so would be ill-advised to use that shaky assumption as premiss for drawing further conclusions).

38. Fredriksen 1978, p. 210 (cf. p. 207), cites Bonner and Marrou as students of Augustine who were "annoyed" (and justly so) by such wildly suspicious readings of Augustine's text.

39. See Donald Capps, "Augustine as Narcissist: Comments on Paul Rigby's 'Paul Ricoeur, Freudianism and Augustine's *Confessions*,'" *Journal of the American Academy of Religion*, 53 (1985), 115–17; Fredricksen 1978, pp. 222–23.

40. TeSelle 1986, p. 99, gives a partial defense of Augustine, referring to Oliver O'Donovan's work *The Problem of Self-Love in St. Augustine* (New Haven: Yale University Press, 1980), pp. 29–32.

41. O'Donovan, *Problem of Self-Love*, p. 32.

42. See *Soundings*, pp. 69–94.

43. Brown 1983, pp. 5–6; 1966, pp. 396–408.

44. See above, pp. 15–17.

45. Some authors (Brown, O'Meara) wisely leave this incident unmentioned, but Courcelle cannot resist chuckling (*Recherches*, p. 56n6), while Pincherle (*Vita di Sant' Agostino* [Rome: Laterza, 1980), p. 15) simply refers to the incident as involving an assignation with a woman.

46. See *Soundings*, pp. 143–73, on Augustine's interpretations of the Prodigal parable.

47. TA indicates that this is the only occurrence of the couple *fructus mortis* in Augustine's works. There is no warrant, accordingly, for interpreting the expression as implying one specific kind of sin (fornication) rather than another.

48. *Augustine*, p. 39.

49. After writing this section, I came upon Tarcisius Van Bavel's remarkable lecture on "The Double Face of Love in St. Augustine (*Atti III*, pp. 69–80). Van Bavel situates Augustine's first quotation of St. John's "God is Love" as occurring in the year 393 (*De fide symb* 19); in the year 405, however, Augustine gives first expression to the "daring

inversion" of that expression, now affirming that "Love is God (*In Jo Ep* 14). That would, suggestively, situate the *amare amari* formula from the *Confessions* as roughly midway along this line of development, quite possibly as presaging what he expressly affirms later.

50. See his *L'Intelligence de la foi en la Trinité selon saint Augustin: Genèse de sa théologie trinitaire jusqu'en 391* (Paris: Études Augustiniennes, 1966), pp. 109–206, passim (henceforth: *Trinité*). See especially the Trinitarian "triads" he lists on pp. 537–40.

51. *Cicéron*, I, 19–39.

52. The reader need only accept this as a working hypothesis for now; confirmatory evidence will come below.

53. Of the 42 occurrences of the term *apud* in the *Confessions*, 19 take God as their direct object, while most of the others betoken the similar kind of intimacy (*apud me, apud amicos*, etc.) which the proposition *cum* need not imply.

54. *Soundings*, pp. 69–94, 143–73.

55. *Sol* 1.22: *nullo interposito velamento, quasi nudam videre . . .*

56. See again the *loca citata* in note 50.

57. Fragment 97 (see Testard, *Cicéron* II).

58. *Soundings*, pp. 192, 206–209.

59. A developmental study on this would be well worth some scholar's while.

60. Compare the language, and especially the image, exemplified in note 55 above.

61. For some examples, see *Enn 44* 1, *46* 203, *82* 2. Scriptural context sometimes compels Augustine to adopt a more neutral interpretation of the term *puer*.

62. Sublimation is a tricky notion, and I am not suggesting that Augustine's sublimation of his sexuality was an unqualified success; nor is that assumption necessary for the case I am making.

63. See Leo C. Ferrari, "Augustine's Nine Years in the Manichees," *Augustiniana*, 25 (1975), 208–15.

64. *Cicéron*, I, 24–27, and 131–54. Some caution is appropriate here: Testard may have yielded to the temptation of attributing broader influence to Cicero than he actually exerted.

65. See Samuel N. C. Lieu, *Manicheism in the Later Roman Empire and Mediaeval China* (Manchester: Manchester University Press, 1985), pp. 134–35.

66. Augustine may also be calling attention, subtly, to the difference between a God Who is *All*-holding, *Omni-tenens*, and a *Splendi-tenens* whose power embraces only spiritual realities.

67. See above, at note 2.

68. Thus Courcelle, *Recherches*, p. 274. In reply to Doignon's "Étape"

article, I would argue that Augustine wanted to show that he was sensitive to this possibility, suggest it to his readers, and counter it by appeal to the more acceptable resources of the *erigere* image.

69. We shall see more on this theme below.

70. See *Soundings*, pp. 55–56.

71. See *Art*, Appendix A, pp. 175–77. When dealing with an image-cluster, however, there can frequently be more than one root and mode of genesis, even when one or other has primacy. Thus, while the Gospel story of the Transfiguration seems first to have suggested the image of glimpsing the (divine) Sun through cloud-cover, that Gospel origin seems subsequently to have brought all the furniture of the cosmic *Omnia*-image into play.

72. See also Brown, pp. 69–72, and Lepelley, "*Spes Saeculi.*"

73. Louis Chevalier, s.j., and Henri Rondet, s.j., "L'idée de la vanité dans l'oeuvre de saint Augustin," REA, 3 (1957), 221–34 (henceforth "Vanité" and attributed for simplicity to Rondet).

74. For what follows, see my *Early Theory*, pp. 173–82.

75. Augustine is implying that adults who take these childish playthings seriously are nothing but "big babies."

76. He means, I take it, that parents wish their children might one day enjoy the honor attached to such acts of patronage; they would very probably also hope for the wealth implied, as well.

77. Lepelley, "*Spes Saeculi*," pp. 100–105.

78. The term *superbe* suggests that vanity can hover into the area of pride, as well.

79. See above, p. 63.

80. Suzanne Poque makes the soldierly quality of the *stare*-image primary, whereas I tend to make it secondary to the more metaphysical implication: even in its soldierly connotations, to "stand" is, at bottom, to share in the immovable solidity of God's own eternity. See the Epilogue to *Soundings*.

81. I am unable to find Ferrari's case convincing (*Conversions*, pp. 46–47, and the articles referred to in the notes) that Augustine became an enthusiast of astrology in the proper sense; the hard evidence for that view seems fragmentary in the extreme, and needs to be sutured together by generous appeals to likelihood and tenuous inference. The resulting edifice I find so shaky that I question whether it should be required to bear the weight of additional interpretation Ferrari builds on it.

82. Note that Alypius is portrayed in this section as taken with "spectacles," especially when they have a competitive edge and offer experiences of a "sensational" and/or horrific sort, along with rewards of praise and adulation. His admiration goes to the Manichees' "show" of conti-

nence (which Augustine implies was mostly façade), but does not prevent him from being morbidly "curious" about Augustine's attachment to sexual activity.

83. The *Oculi omnium* verse (15) accounts for the fact that Psalm 144 was used by the early Church (as by traditional religious communities even today) as the prayer of "grace" before the principal meal (see Artur Weiser, *The Psalms* [Philadelphia: Westminster, 1962], p. 826.) Any contemporary reader would have recognized that, in his repeated allusions to this psalm, Augustine was suggesting his attitude of growing desire and readiness to receive the food of Truth from God's "opened hand"; most would also have caught the further implication that, despite his anxious impatience, God would accede to his hunger only *in tempore opportuno*, at the "providential" time.

84. Several examples among many: *SS 82*, 14; *224* 4; *En 102* 16.

85. *Saint Augustine's* CONFESSIONS, trans. R. S. Pine-Coffin (Harmondsworth: Penguin, 1961), p. 131.

86. Marrou, review of Courcelle's *Recherches*, REL, 29 (1951), 406.

87. See the texts listed in Isabelle Bochet, *Saint Augustin et le désir de Dieu* (Paris: Études Augustiniennes, 1982), pp. 93–95. esp. p. 94n3.

88. See Jean Pépin, *Ex Platonicorum persona: Études sur les lectures philosophiques de saint Augustin* (Amsterdam: A. M. Hakkert, 1977).

89. For fuller detail, see *Soundings*, pp. 52–54, 64–65.

90. We shall see more of this further on, but for the moment the reader might consult *Vita 2* (*voluptatum honorumque*), 3 (*uxoris honorisque*); *Acad 2.4* (*cupiditatum vinculis . . . oneribus curarum*), 2.5 (*honor . . . pompa . . . mortalis vitae fomentum*); *Sol 1.17* (*honores, uxor*).

91. When interpreting Scripture, particularly, Augustine lays considerable stress on the exact force of the words as a (Latin-speaking) *rhetor* would measure it; when Paul speaks of our *re-novatio*, for example, Augustine spontaneously understands him to mean that we shall "be made new again," that is, returned to a condition of "newness" which we must once have enjoyed and then lost. See a telling example of this turn of mind in *GenLitt* 6.37–39.

II

Augustine's Quest for
Certainty

AMBROSE, FAITH, AND CERTAINTY

WHILE LIVING IN Milan, Augustine decided to frequent the cathedral where Ambrose preached regularly. He was interested, he tells us, less in the substance of Ambrose's sermons than in his technique. But some of the substance managed to filter through nevertheless. Augustine found himself gradually realizing that the Manichees had merely caricatured the teaching of the *Catholica*—at least as Ambrose purveyed that teaching, in "spiritual" terms and by means of a "spiritual" (read: allegorical) style of Scriptural interpretation. Slowly he began to experience a quiet joy in finding that Catholic teaching was exempt from a whole series of errors of which the Manichees had accused it (6.4–6).

But at this stage of his development, Augustine was incapable of forming a correct notion of "spirit" or of spiritual reality, incapable of deciding whether the so-called "spiritual realities" Ambrose spoke of were anything more than airy nothings. In short, however comforting he found Ambrose's message, he had no intellectual yardstick for judging whether the man was speaking the truth (5.24–25). He could not be certain.

He realized he could no longer continue as a Manichee; the skepticism of Academic philosophy now made a strong appeal to him, but since the name of Christ was missing from it (just as it had been missing from the *Hortensius!*) he could not fully commit himself to Academicism. He resolved, as an interim measure, to enroll as a catechumen in the Church of his childhood (5.25).

"Understand, in Order to Believe"

His willingness to believe has been abused twice already, by the authoritarianism he met with in the North African church, and by the false promises of the Manichees; so, he finds himself resistant to any new invitation to commit himself unreservedly in faith.

And while nothing that Ambrose said "caused [him] difficulty, still, he would affirm things that [Augustine] did not as yet know to be true" (*utrum vera essent adhuc ignorarem*). There is a desideratum implied by that complaint, and Augustine promptly spells it out: "I wanted the things I did not see to become just as certain to me [*ita me certum fieri*] as I was certain [*certus*] that seven and three were [*sint*] ten." For despite the momentary attractiveness of skepticism, he assures us that he was never so "mad" (or "sick-minded," *insanus*) as to think that a proposition like "seven plus three are ten" could not be "known," meaning known with certainty (*comprehendi*). "But," he goes on to explain, "I wanted other things" to attain the same status, that is, to be known with the same certainty as that mathematical formula. Among those "other things" he lists first "bodily things not present to [his] senses," then the kind of "spiritual realities" (*spiritualia*) about which Ambrose habitually discoursed. But a central difficulty blocks him still: he "did not know how to think about" spiritual realities "except in a corporeal way" (6.6).

Augustine has told us several important things here. First, he has made it clear that for *him*, given his past experiences with belief, it was psychologically indispensable that he arrive at some certainties of the order of human "understanding" *before* he could reopen his heart and mind to believing. He admits in the very next sentence that believing would have "healed" his ailing power of intellectual vision, by "directing" (somehow or other: *aliquo modo*) his "purified" gaze toward God's Eternal Truth. But as his story unfolds, it will become clear that this need for certain liminal insights of "understanding" was an indispensable part of Augustine's own individual process of conversion.

That passing allusion to the role of faith deserves a moment of attention. It illustrates how Augustine can combine, almost casually, two quite distinguishable ways in which he thinks of faith as operating to bring the unbeliever to the stage of "understanding." The first way is familiar from the "image" of understanding itself, which we examined earlier:[1] the fallen soul, now situated in the lower world, cannot see the light of the Sun because of the intervening cloud-cover which separates the higher and lower worlds; hence, someone who "knows" must "direct" his gaze toward where the Sun is situated, in hopes that the clouds may thin out, and the searcher glimpse the sunlight filtering through.

But this notion is here juxtaposed with another: the soul's fall has infected its power to see the eternal Light, making it "infirm" in the double sense implied by the Latin term *infirmus*: "weak," but "sickly-weak." So, as here, its "healing" would strengthen it by making it *purgatior*, as though some kind of impurity, like an unhealthy film, or some specks of dust—or a cloud of buzzing insects, like the gnats or flies which plagued the Egyptians (7.11; cf. *En* 118, *S 24* 4, *InJo 102* 4)—were blocking its vision. It should be said in passing that the first image, of "direction," is easily enough grasped if one assumes Augustine's image of the *Omnia*; but I have yet to find any place where Augustine satisfactorily explains how the image of faith as "healing" the eye genuinely illuminates the role faith plays in the Christian's spiritual progress.[2]

Augustine's Criterion for Certainty

Equally deserving of attention, though, is the criterion Augustine espouses for certainties of the "understanding." He has told us earlier (5.19) that he was tempted to agree with the Academics who were "commonly held" (*vulgo habentur*) to believe that "all things must be held doubtful" and "no truth" whatever "could be comprehended by human beings" (*ab homine comprehendi posse*). Augustine confesses that he himself shared this common view of their philosophical position, but goes on to say that he was wrong in doing so; he "did not yet understand their intention." Augustine reveals how he later came to understand their "intention," their philosophical strategy, so to speak, in his early dialogue "against"—or "about"—the Academics.[3] Their skepticism, he tells us there, extended only to our sense knowledge of the visible, corporeal world; like Augustine himself, they were not so "mad" as to doubt that mathematical formulae like "seven plus three are ten" could be "comprehended" by human beings. But the reason for that, Augustine's theory held, was that the Academics considered such formulae as not derived from that untrustworthy source, sense apprehension. They were purely intelligible propositions; essences like "three" and "seven" and "ten" were invisible, incorporeal "realities,"[4] and the mind's capacity to "comprehend" them testified to the existence of a higher, intelligible world to which, despite its immersion in sense realities, the human mind still had access. Augustine's "Academics" are, in a word, crypto-Platonists, lineal descendants of Plato himself, and forerunners of that *Plato redivivus*, Plotinus![5]

This view of Academicism had as one of its consequences that it confirmed Augustine's estimate of Cicero's *Hortensius* as Platonic in inspiration and import: we may, accordingly, expect a strong current of continuity to link his "first conversion" with the later conversion at Milan, which was sparked by his reading of certain "Platonist books."

But a second consequence is contained in that little surprise-step that Augustine executes when he reveals his criterion for certainty. We fully expect him to say that he wanted "spiritual realities" to be as manifest to his mind's eye as bodily realities are when indubitably present to the bodily eye. The instinct for placing spiritual and bodily vision in parallel would rather prompt us to ask, for instance, that God, the "spiritual Sun," reveal Himself as directly and immediately to our "spiritual eye" as the corporeal sun in a cloudless sky becomes indubitably manifest to our bodily eye. And, in fact, this is exactly the way Augustine puts things in his *Soliloquies* (see 1.12), a way which seems far more natural to us; for most humans seem instinctively to think of "knowing" primarily in terms of such unimpeded acts of "direct acquaintance."

It is significant that in his *Confessions* Augustine takes a different tack. He no longer draws his normative ideal, his optimal example of certainty, from the "direct acquaintance" class of sense experiences suggested by vision of the corporeal sun. His acquaintance with Academicism may already have instilled a suspicion of such sense-apprehension models of knowing. In any case, he is telling us here that his model for certainty was already the more Platonic model suggested by mathematical and geometrical "insight." And, for our purposes, two features of that model are worth remarking.

First, it presents itself as, *prima facie* at least, a "propositional," rather than a "direct acquaintance," model of knowing: *what* we come to know and affirm is, in the first instance, a *relationship* between the subject and the predicate term of a proposition. In other words, we "see," in the sense of coming to the "intellectual insight," that, between the composite term "seven plus three" and the term "ten," there exists a necessary and universal relationship of identity: seven plus three *are* always and without exception ten (*sunt decem*). When I "see" the sun, on the other hand, I come to "know" that sun by direct acquaintance. It would be forced and unnatural to claim that in such a case I "assent to a proposition," however implicit, like "the sun exists." It would be truer to my experience to say that I come to "know-the-sun" (explicitly) and that (implicitly) I come to know it "as-existing."

But the situation is not quite so unambiguous as I have made it out to be: behind the camouflage of the propositional there also lurks a set of "direct acquaintance" apprehensions. For when driven to his trumps, a Platonist like Augustine would claim that his insight into the relationship of seven, three, and ten to one another follows upon his having "seen" what each of those integers individually "means." And one of the mental habits which marks him as a Platonist springs from his conviction that "seeing" the meaning of any such intelligible reality is tantamount to seeing *what* that reality essentially is; from there it is a small step to envisaging that act of "seeing" as a "beholding"—the mental contemplation of an essence, or set of essences, as possessing a reality in a disembodied world of essences, shorn of all sense properties.

Augustine is soon to describe an absolutely capital contribution to his conversion: his reading of certain "Platonist books." When we come to the way in which he expresses what he "saw" as a result of those readings, we shall see how that final ambiguity—propositional insight or contemplative vision—comes into play.

Augustine's Further Progress

But to return to Augustine's story of what went on before his "Platonist" readings: he tells us that he eventually began to ruminate on how human beings of every stamp must place faith in any number of things they are asked to believe. What would happen to the fabric of human society if every little Augustine began to question who his father or who his mother was (6.7)? In short, despite the scalding experiences in his past, he was beginning to find believing, both in matters human and in matters religious, a reasonable and acceptable proposition.

So much for Augustine's growth in readiness to believe. But again, he was looking for more than belief; he felt the need of biting firmly into some certainties, certainties accessible to human "understanding." So, for instance, in the lines he wrote immediately before describing the illumination he was about to receive, he tells of the "impatience" he felt "until [God's] existence should become certain to [him] through the inner gaze" of his mind. It is significant that Augustine attributes that impatience to God's activity within him (*stimulis internis agitabas me*) (7.12).

Augustine's "Required Certainties"

But how many certainties, and about what questions, did Augustine require before the assent of faith was possible for him? Answering that question with some precision might equip us to approach the account of his Platonic readings with a more focused set of expectations.[6] And yet the question, put that way, is not an easy one to answer.

Consider, for example, the two certainties we have already seen him mention: should certainty on God's existence be reckoned as distinct from the "mathematical" certainty on the reality of the spiritual—or did Augustine count God as one among those spiritual realities? Or consider another case: when Augustine finds that Ambrose's preaching had succeeded in leaving both Catholic and Manichee positions "equal in their defenses," he resolves to find out whether he can "convict the Manichees of falsity" by any "certain proofs" (*certis aliquibus documentis*). Is this to be regarded as a second or even third instance, or type, of "required" certainty? Again, the answer is doubtful: Augustine immediately subtends that the job would have been done had he only been able to form an adequate notion of spiritual reality (*si possem spiritalem substantiam cogitare*) (5.25). That would seem to imply that the certainty which would settle the Manichees was precisely a certainty about the existence of spiritual reality, and could, therefore, include the existence of God.

But however one estimates the number of certainties Augustine required before assenting in faith, this much is clear: the dramatic illumination he is about to detail for us includes a much larger number of certainties on a greater number of issues than his previously expressed desires would seem to account for. But perhaps there is a reason for that: Augustine may have more than one way of suggesting the range of exigencies which confront the effort to "understand the faith" of Christians.

One way of suggesting those exigencies was Augustine's favorite educational technique, the *exercitatio animi*. That technique normally involved a master and a disciple (or disciples) engaged in dialogue: Augustine's early Dialogues furnish excellent illustrations, and show how much faith he reposed in this technique.[7] Before he ever delivers the terminal discourse in which he resolves the various problems he has been discussing with them, the master guides the minds of his disciples over a series of intellectual hurdles; he is "exercising" their wits on a skein of preliminary questions, ensuppling them in preparation for the final effort at understanding which he has in store for them. The wise master knows that unless his disciples are first genuinely bothered by the question, and their minds actively engaged in endeavoring to resolve it, the "answer" will mean almost nothing to them.

That was one of the techniques which dictated how Augustine wrote his *Confessions*. His first book, for instance, invites his readers to share a meditation on how the immense and omnipresent God can be conceived of integrally as present "in" each of His creatures (1.1–3), then goes on to hint at the paradoxes involved in the conventionally accepted list of divine attributes (4). His readers may never have thought about these matters, but Augustine's brush with the Manichees had shown him how perilous it could be for a Catholic to have confused ideas on such questions. Augustine's birth raises the question about infant sinfulness, and pushes it further back until it becomes the darker question about whether and where we may have existed—and sinned—before we even entered our mother's womb (7–10). The account of how Augustine learned his native language turns into a meditative query on what the need for speech insinuates about our human predicament (11–13), and so on, and so on. Every reader of the *Confessions* remembers the riveting *exercitatio* on the nature of time in Book 11, but the power of that outstanding achievement should not be allowed to eclipse the less spectacular uses of the same technique throughout the *Confessions*. Quite especially throughout the first seven books, biographical narration repeatedly serves to tease the mind with questions, puzzles, paradoxes until, Augustine hopes, the reader, too, has become what Augustine became, a *grande profundum*, a *magna quaestio*: a riddling abyss of mystery.

Looked at in the light of the *exercitatio animi* technique, it becomes evident that Augustine intended his *Confessions*, among other things, to insert a generous array of questions into his readers' minds, to which he would then reply in his account of the intellectual illumination that resulted from his reading of the Platonists. But even then, as we shall see, his replies tend to be so concise as to be riddling, enigmatic: Augustine meant his readers to push on attentively, to the very end of Book 13, before their minds would be entirely satisfied.

Augustine's Addressees

Moreover, the number and kinds of certainties Augustine felt obliged to furnish depended partially on the readers to whom he was addressing his *Confessions.* Among the readers we may assume he had in mind were those conservative African Catholics who considered his efforts to "understand the faith" by means of the thought-categories of pagan philosophy a perilous venture. Certainly it would have kindled the righteous ire of that prince of African theology, Tertullian. What compact, after all, could exist between Athens and Jerusalem?

At the other extreme Augustine hoped to make one more heroic effort to persuade non-Christian devotees of Roman and Greek philosophy that his understanding of the Christian faith was compelling and sophisticated enough to appeal to the most critical spirits among them. His eye must also have been on the Donatists, who fueled their resistance to the *Catholica,* in part, with their suspicions about this brilliant Bishop's scandalous past. Each of these groups posed special questions which Augustine felt obliged to answer with his understanding of Catholic Christianity, but none more so than his former co-religionists, the Manichees.

The Challenge of Manichaeism: The Question of Evil

The question that the followers of Mani delighted in brandishing in order to torment young Catholics like Augustine was, of course, the question about evil, that dark obverse to the question about happiness: "Why are we so unhappy?" And the Manichees immediately translated: "Why is the world we live in so rife with pain and suffering, and with evils of every sort, like snakes, scorpions, and mosquitoes, which inflict those pains and sufferings?"

Hone that question a bit, and the anti-Catholic (and anti-Juda. too, because anti-monotheistic) edge shows more clearly: "How can all this be, if these things were made by one God Who is, as Catholics claim, creator of all things, visible and invisible, bodily and spiritual?" For Catholics claim in addition that this One God is also All-Good: but, the Manichees objected, "How dare they blaspheme Him by insisting that He is to blame for the evils we see all about us in this bodily, material world?"

The Manichees answered their own question by attributing everything good to a true God, all Light and Spirit and Goodness, whereas everything evil came from a kind of anti-God, all Darkness and Matter and Evil. That "race of darkness," they taught, had invaded the realm of Light and carried off our souls, fragments of that Divine Light, and—through no fault of theirs—imprisoned them in the befouling Matter of this lower, visible world. The main business of salvation, therefore, required that we, first, be awakened to our souls' divinity and to our monstrous situation in this enmattered world, and, second, that we bend every effort to "return" from this lower world to the higher Divine realm—by rites and practices the gospel of Mani prescribed.

There were a number of more particular issues which bothered Augustine, but chief among Manichaeism's appeals to him was this dualistic solution to the problem of evil: it appeared to safeguard God's goodness more "piously" than the *Catholica*'s monotheism (5.20, 7.20).

Manichaeism on Faith and Understanding

The Manichee claim that everything they taught made transparent sense to human reason provided them with a second weapon against the Catholics of North Africa: their authoritarian pastors intimidated their flock into accepting Church teaching blindly, without any questioning—even about aspects of Church teaching which might easily create difficulties for human reason.[8]

This was a particularly sore point for the young Augustine. He had a lively and inquiring mind, with an insatiable thirst for making sense of life through exercising his understanding. He had already run into some bruising conflicts with authoritarian representatives of North African Catholicism, and the Manichee promise to treat him as an intelligent adult was powerfully attractive.[9]

What specific certainties would Augustine require in order to combat these tenets of Manichaeism? Let us begin with the relationship of faith to understanding.

Augustine's Attitude: Belief Seeking Understanding

By the time Augustine came to hear Ambrose preach, he had already become largely disaffected from Manichaeism. The Manichee claim that their beliefs would stand up to the test of reason had eroded, and eventually dissolved, as Augustine tested them against the physical and astronomical lore of his age. But Augustine felt obliged to show to the Manichees, as well as to the conservative Catholics who found this message suspect, that the *Catholica* did not insist that her children believe her teachings blindly, avoiding all effort to raise their faith to the level of understanding; the love for wisdom and understanding, he argued, was preached not only by the New Testament, but by the Old Testament (which the Manichees rejected) as well (*Mor* 1.26–32). At the same time he strove to make the Manichees (and conservative Catholics) acknowledge that the faith must be understood in spiritual terms, of the sort he found employed both in Ambrose's preaching and in the writings of the Platonists.

The Metaphysics of Being, Truth, Good, and Evil

It was chiefly the Manichee stress on the question of evil, however, which compelled Augustine to expand the list of certainties he required in order to develop an adequate understanding of Catholic teaching. The fool, it has been said, can ask more questions than a wise man can answer: certain it is that a seemingly simple question like "why did your Catholic God create the scorpion?" compelled Augustine to elaborate a subtle and wide-ranging metaphysics in which the nature of good and evil had to be correlated with the nature and operations of being, truth, beauty, sinfulness, freedom, divine and human agency, spirit and matter, time and eternity, *und der Gleiche mehr!* And as if to demonstrate that he knew how to write a masterly book when he chose to do so, Augustine has taken every philosophical issue he eventually includes in the account of his Platonist illumination and made it the focus of at least one "exercise of the mind" in some previous chapter of his *Confessions!*

Particular Certainties, or a New Mode of Thinking?

We have seen that Ambrose's preaching cleared up a number of fraudulent difficulties Augustine had had with Catholic teaching, and helped him see the option for belief as more and more acceptable; but that preaching did not deflect Augustine's determined struggle toward achieving the kind of certainty which only the insights of understanding can provide. He may gradually have come to suspect, however vaguely, what he later came to discover: that the certainties which eluded him were all *of a kind* which the Manichaean style of thinking was unable to furnish; their minds worked far more comfortably along lines of mythical and imaginative conceptions than with the incorporeal mathematical abstractions and metaphysical realities familiar to the Platonists.

This suggests a fresh way of formulating our question. When Augustine expressly talks about the certainties he felt the need to attain, there is a common property in all three of them: they all involve the need for changing his whole *manner* of thinking. Hence, he may not be asking us to focus on the *topics* of his desired certainties so much as on this common property: they all required that he learn to form a correct idea of spiritual reality.

One might wonder how explicitly Augustine formulated his need for a more "spiritual" way of thinking about spiritual realities *before* he "read the answers," so to speak, in those Platonist books. There does not seem to be any way to answer that question confidently, but he tells us that he ran up against intellectual roadblocks any number of times, particularly when coping with the question of evil posed in corporeal terms, and we may safely conjecture that Ambrose's emphasis on "spiritual" realities also insinuated the inadequacy of all such sensist epistemologies. Besides, we have seen that Augustine had already become partial to the mathematical model of "understanding," so integral to the Platonist style of thinking which will eventually satisfy his questing mind, but we have little idea about whether, or how clearly, he recognized that kinship.

Let me propose, for now, what I take to be the most probable answer to the question of Augustine's "required certainties." Looking back on the tortuous process that culminated in his conversion, Augustine came to see that the core of all his intellectual difficulties lay in his manner of thinking: he was unable to conceive of spiritual reality in anything but corporeal terms. But once he had made the necessary breakthrough to that spiritual manner of thought, thanks to his readings in the Platonists, he was enabled to reflect upon what he had read, and elaborate a systematic view of reality. That view of reality, he was convinced, also constituted a valid understanding of the very same reality as the Catholic faith portrayed it. But that view of reality embraced, of necessity, a considerable number of propositional certainties, a far greater number than the three (or two, or one) which he only *seems* to be enumerating, when in fact he is uniformly pointing to his need for this new manner of thinking.

But that proposed solution can only be provisional at this point; we shall have to return to this question later. I suggest, however, that the view I have just presented seems to receive confirmation from the way Augustine presents the lengthy section we are about to examine, *Confessions* 7.16–26. I hope to show several things about this section: that it is a wide-ranging view of reality; that Augustine will stress that a breakthrough to a spiritual way of thinking lies at its core; but that he will do so precisely in order to commend to his readers the comprehensive world-view which emerged from that breakthrough.

Platonists' Gold Without Their "Idolatry"

While that world-view was the fruit of his own personal reflections, it was prompted in great part, Augustine candidly admits, by what he read in what he calls "books of the Platonists" (*libri platonicorum*). Those books were, accordingly, pagan rather than Christian, a fact which some conservative Catholics would find shocking. Hence, Augustine's first impulse when speaking of those books was to show how much of their teaching closely corresponded to what Catholic Christians believed—his enthusiasm for them would, therefore, be shown as legitimate, on that score at least. But, second, he had to admit that there were both omissions and positive errors in those books. While admitting that, however, he also claims that he was alert to their omissions and careful to avoid their errors: like the Israelites who carried off their enemies' idols when they fled from Egypt, but melted them down for the pure gold they contained, he purified the Platonists' teachings of what he terms their "idolatry" and accepted from them only what was God's own truth (13–15).[10]

AUGUSTINE'S ARRIVAL AT CERTAINTY

"I Saw, and Came to Know"

Augustine now goes on to detail the complex of insights to which he came, prompted by the reading of these books. Exactly when did he come to those insights? He does not tell us. Was it immediately on reading those books, or shortly, two or three days—or perhaps even months, or even years—afterward? It is important to realize that Augustine simply does not say.

Let us shelve that problem for the moment, and concentrate on this tripartite question: What were the insights he says he came to, how do they connect with each other, and to what extent did Augustine think of them as necessary in order to answer the questions that were plaguing him? Much of the answer I am about to offer now will strike the reader as highly condensed, and for that reason sorely questionable; I present it initially in this condensed fashion purely for purposes of clarity, but I mean, in a subsequent step, to spell out and substantiate that answer in greater detail.

Augustine's World-Image: The Omnia

As we work through this central section of the *Confessions*, it will become evident that Augustine's view of reality, however metaphysical we judge it to be, is nevertheless sketched against a background *image*. In order to grasp his world-view clearly, even to understand the language he is about to use, one has first to grasp the contours of that "world-picture." To begin with, Augustine's imagination accords to God, and to each of the "all things" (*Omnia*) which He created, what he calls their proper "places" (*loca*). Those places are arranged hierarchically as in the following diagram.[11] Before we proceed, a few explanatory clues may be helpful. Notice, first, where the crucial dividing line occurs between these two "worlds": it separates visible from invisible, or, what comes to the same thing, bodily from spiritual realities.[12] Augustine frequently calls these the two "regions"—higher and lower—of the *Omnia* which the God of Genesis created. He will also often call that higher world simply "Heaven," so that its upper reaches represent the "Heaven of Heaven"; correspondingly, he will call "this" entire lower world (designated depreciatingly as *iste mundus*) simply "earth," the sun and stars being situated in the "heaven of earth."

Unum, Summum,	GOD	*Aeternum, Immutabile*
The One, Highest		Eternal, Unchangeable
Superiora, altiora	*Angels and Souls*	*Spiritualia:* Spirituals
		(even bodies)

Above this line: *Invisible, suprasensible, Intelligible realities:*
i.e., "*Heaven*" and "Truth"

Below this line: *Visible, sensible, "opinative" realities:*
"*Earth*" and "*Vanities*"

Multa, Inferiora	Sun (Heat)	*Temporalia,*
Mutabilia		Temporals,
The Many, Lower		Changeables
and the	Air (Dryness)	*Corpora*, Bodies
Infima, Extrema	Water (Dampness)	
Lowest, "Last"	Earth (Coldness)	

Furthermore, Augustine pictures "this" lower world as arranged according to the weight (*pondus*) of whichever "element" dominates in the make-up of any particular being or type of being: those elements were most frequently viewed as four, ranging from "earth" as heaviest, through water, then air, and finally, lightest and therefore highest of all, fire.[13] The "weight" of a being, therefore, caused it to rise or descend, depending on whether its dominant element was light or heavy, and finally come to "rest" in its appropriate "place." That law of "weight" applied primarily, of course, to physical realities, but we shall see that Augustine pictures it as having a spiritual counterpart as well.

The World-View of Confessions 7.16–26

When sketching the world-view on which he asks us to meditate with him, the first thing Augustine tells us he came to see (*vidi*), in the sense of "glimpsing" it with the "interior" eye of understanding, is that God existed, somewhat in the way Light existed

(7.16). But he does not mean by that any kind of visible light, like ordinary sunlight which is spread out through mile on mile of spatial immensities; he came to "see" that God was "other, vastly other," a *spiritual* kind of Light which could be be grasped only by the mind. Augustine realizes that this insight into a superior, spiritual realm of existence sprang from a radical break with the sensist mode of thinking, the mode of pseudo-understanding which he, like the Manichees, formerly espoused. That sensist way of thinking looked upon the "spiritual" as simply vacuous, an empty "nothing" (*nihil*).

Augustine is implicitly telling us that he has just taken his first step toward a fresh world-view, the kind of world-view he needed in order, among other things, to respond to the array of questions posed by the problem of evil. That problem, he is saying, along with all the sub-problems undivorceably connected with it, could not be resolved to the mind's satisfaction unless one first "saw" that a higher, spiritual world really existed, and unless one learned to think of that spiritual reality in appropriately spiritual terms.

But *vidi*, "I saw," *cognovi*, "I came to know," *manifestatum est mihi*, "it was made manifest to me"—these are all terms which Augustine employs to stress the fact that he has passed beyond the need to "believe" the truths he is talking about, on the authority, say, of Ambrose; he has passed from the stage of "belief" and come to knowledge, insight, understanding: certainty. But this does not mean that Augustine can be fully satisfied. Spiritually he is still a child; he is hungry for the enduring, unbroken vision of God, but that unbroken vision, he realizes, is food for spiritual "grown-ups," and Augustine has considerable growing to do.

The second insight he came to (7.17) is more a corollary of the first: turning his attention to created realities, he "saw"—came to understand—that God alone "existed" in the fullest sense of the term. Augustine's reason for this is significant: God was unchangeable, and only the unchangeable truly "existed." "Other" beings, inferior to God, were changing beings, including the bodily beings Augustine had formerly thought of as the only "really existent" realities. They were constantly changing, from what they had *been* to what they had *not been*; they were an unstable amalgam of being and not-being, existence and non-existence.

But change affects Augustine also, making him not "truly" existent. This allows us to understand a curious expression he had ed earlier (7.16): "I saw that I, the one who saw, did not yet exist" (*nondum me esse*). Though now immersed in change, he writes as though he hopes at some future moment to become truly "existent," become unchangeable!

Thus far, Augustine has come to understand that there are two distinct realms of beings, a higher, spiritual, and a lower, bodily, realm. Moreover, he has come to understand that beings are variously, are more and less, "real," depending on how subject they are to change. Now he is about to apply that being-insight to the property of goodness.

Before doing so, however, he takes a slight detour: he borrows an insight from Aristotelean philosophy and argues (7.18) that "evil" is not some positive reality, but a kind of defect in a being. Oddly enough, Augustine may have become acquainted with Aristotle's theory by reading Plotinus' refutation of it in his treatise on "The Origin of Evil" in *Ennead* 1.8![14] In any event, Aristotle terms evil a "privation," a form of non-being inasmuch as it was the absence of some perfective property which should be present—but present in a being that possessed the positive value of existing, and existing at a certain grade of reality-perfection. This is his answer to the first question the Manichees *should* have asked about evil: "what" evil is. It is nothing positive, nothing substantial; it is sheer privation. Hence, *pace* the Manichees, it is simply nonsensical to ask why God created evil; for creating evil would be equivalent to creating nothing, hence, not creating at all!

Everything that exists, accordingly, is good, inasmuch as it possesses some grade of reality-value, but (Augustine returns now to the relativity principle established above) not everything is *equally* good. Therefore, if this or that being is not so good as some other, one should not complain, much less call it evil; for it is good in its own way and at its own reality-level. Augustine now articulates his *Omnia* principle: this inequality among beings makes the hierarchized variety, the entire assemblage of realities—the *Omnia*—not simply good, but, as the Creator in the Book of Genesis found it, "very good."

But the goodness of anything can be looked upon from two angles (7.19): a being can "suit" or "befit," can be "good *for*" another, as a shoe fits someone's foot; or, a being can be good in and for itself. Augustine is here basically recalling the insights he encased in his own youthful work *On the Beautiful and the Fitting*,

where he calls this latter kind of goodness "beauty" (*Conf* 4.20).
Contemplate the entire panoply of realities now, he is telling us,
and you will find things that may not be good "for" you—mosquitoes, say, or scorpions—but you will find nothing that is not
good "for" some other being (the male for the female scorpion,
for instance), and nothing that is not beautiful, good in and for
itself, in some measure or other: how elegantly, for instance, the
humble mosquito is structured! The Manichees complain (and
Augustine admits that he himself formerly did) that if God were
truly good He would not have permitted anything to exist except
the realities of the higher, spiritual world; that only shows, Augustine now contends, that they have not contemplated the graded
beauty of "all things," higher and lower, spiritual and corporeal—
if they had, they would have judged more "sanely" (*saniore judicio*)
that it is better (more beautiful) for "all things" to exist than for
merely the higher, spiritual realities.

At this point, Augustine interrupts the sketch of his world-
view to recall (7.20) how this problem of evil formerly persuaded
him to adopt the Manichee dualism. Subsequently, having abandoned Manichaeism, he admits to having adopted a more Stoic
notion of God. In both cases, though, he was really imagining
God in sensist terms, as spatialized. But now, finally, he claims
to have submitted himself to God's healing action, so that the
"inner" spiritual eye of his understanding has been quickened, and
he has come to "see" that God's infinity does not mean that He
is "in" all created realities, but that the reverse is true: they are all
"in" Him, as though supported by His incorporeal Hand, a Hand
which is identical with Truth Itself—or more exactly, Truth
Himself.

That relationship to Eternal Truth, moreover, prompts the further insight (7.21) that all temporal things are "true"—partici-
pating more or less in God's eternity—in the measure in which
they have reality: the grades of being, goodness, and truth, therefore, are rigorously parallel to each other. All temporal beings,
moreover, derive whatever enduringness they possess from their
Eternal Creator, Who is Eternal precisely because there is no "before" and "after" in His creative activity.

Now (7.22) Augustine brings forward his insight on the rela-
tional character of the good as "befitting" or "good-*for*," and applies it to the question of moral evil. It should be no surprise, he

writes, that the punitive workings of God's justice should displease unjust humans, just as good food tastes bad to one whose palate is affected by disease, or as pleasant sunshine pains the eye that is sickly. This is particularly true of wicked people who complain about the evils besetting them in this lower, corporeal, world. They do not realize that it is their very wickedness which makes it fitting that they be confined to this lower world. That wickedness, in turn, arises from an act of "iniquity" which they committed—like Augustine himself—a free act whereby they "twisted" themselves away from the one Eternal God in order to delight in the many realities of this lower, temporal, world, with the result that they "swelled up and burst, spilling their insides outward."

A mysterious set of expressions, certainly; their import we shall have to probe more carefully further on. But this much should be plain enough: Augustine has here answered, however cryptically, the second part of the question about evil: namely, "Whence do evils come?" We encounter things we are inclined to *call* evil, he has told us, by the very fact that we now inhabit the "lower," corporeal realm of the spiritual–corporeal *Omnia*, where creatures like vipers and worms can torment us. But we have only ourselves to blame, since we freely turned away from God and from our original place in the higher, spiritual world, forsaking Him in order to find delight in the realities of this lower realm. The sufferings they cause us, accordingly, come from the working of God's justice, punishing us (apparently) for that act of "iniquity," but also (as we saw in paragraph 7.16), and what is perhaps more important, "instructing" us.

Augustine next turns to consider (7.23) that other classic property of being, beauty. He is thrilled to have made contact with the very reality of God, and not (as he formerly had) with just some sensist image of Him. But when he finds himself drawn upward by the attraction of God's beauty, he finds the spiritual "weight" (*pondus*) of his sinful carnality, his "corruptible body," pulling him down again to the "lower realities" to which he has become "accustomed." Again, he is unable to "stand," to abide enduringly in enjoying the glimpse of God to which he has risen. But he retains a "memory" of God, as well as the conviction that God's "invisible" attributes can be glimpsed by the eye of his "understanding."

This prompts him to ask how it was that he had been able—even before his reading of the Platonists—to make sound "judgments," correctly evaluating the relative beauty of bodies and, now, of spiritual realities. In answer to his own question now, methodically, step by step, he mounts the ladder of created beauties, up beyond his "reasoning power" to his "understanding," until he comes, once more, to catch sight of the Divine Light he had glimpsed earlier (7.16). But now that Light is identified with the Eternal Beauty Whose perfection acts as the absolute standard for all such relative judgments. Once again, Augustine finds himself unable to make this fleeting vision last; but once again, too, he assures us that he has "glimpsed" God's invisible attributes through created realities with the eye of his "understanding." And he takes with him, once more, a "memory" of God as of a divine banquet—that "food of grown-ups" we noted before (7.16)—which he was not yet able to feed upon.

Augustine's Requisites Fulfilled?

This ends Augustine's outline of the world-view he came to elaborate by reflecting on those "Platonist books" which he had first opened in A.D. 386. He tells us in the next four paragraphs how much more he had to learn and accept about the Jesus Christ Who humbly came as "food" for spiritual children, like Augustine, who needed to "grow up" before being able to feast upon the enduring vision of God. But he is maddeningly vague about how long it took him to learn and accept those truths about Christ, just as he never clearly tells us how long his reflections lasted before they flowered into the fully formed world-vision he has just outlined.

In paragraph 7.26, however, Augustine presents an interesting summary of the principal points of that world-vision. Once "admonished" by these Platonist books to take that first, revolutionary step, and to "seek for incorporeal Truth," he begins by assuring us for one final time that he had succeeded in glimpsing God's invisible attributes by the eye of his "understanding." But because of his darkness of soul he was permitted only to glimpse, and not to contemplate what he had glimpsed in enduring fashion.

But in virtue of what he had come to understand, he became "certain," first, that God was infinite but not in the sense that He was diffused through infinite space; second, that He truly existed, ever the same and without the slightest change; and, third, that all other realities came from Him, as witnessed by the fact that they existed. "I was certain of these [truths], and yet too infirm to enjoy You."

Infinite Being, Eternal Truth, and Loving Creator of all else that exists—abridged and allusive though it is, this Trinitarian formula catches the essentials of the world-view Augustine has just finished spelling out. This was the God Catholics believed in, but grasped, now, with the insightful certainty accessible only to the power of understanding. And so Augustine feels entitled to claim, with that certainty of understanding, not merely on the basis of faith, that this new view of God and creation makes far more sense than the dualistic "madness" the Manichees had long ago proposed to him.

Observe that if one choose to regard the world-view Augustine has proposed here as systematically answering to the questions and problems which were troubling him from his youth onward, it serves that end quite adequately. An inventory will show that most of those problems were raised by his principal adversaries in writing the *Confessions*, the Manichees. Those problems, moreover, extended far beyond an obsessional concern for making quasi-mystical "ascents" to "ecstasy," Plotinian or otherwise.[15] Granted: his discovery of how to think appropriately about the spiritual world, how genuinely to "understand," did allow him to elaborate a technique for making such ascents; but, more important, that discovery opened the door to an entire network of other important insights.

The discovery of the spiritual enabled him, for instance, to transcend the Manichees' monochromatic empiricism, and so enlarge the cosmic canvas as to include various levels of reality, graded according to their relative mutability. This, in turn, made room for his crucial notion of the spiritual–corporeal *Omnia*, which justified the existence of the lower, sensible world as something other than a Manichee hell (or, for that matter, an Origenist prison for sinful souls).[16] Augustine's further claim that evil was that species of non-being called privation, and that lesser goods were not for that reason to be thought of as evils, refuted the Manichee thesis that evils must be positive realities and all on a single level.

But one of Augustine's masterstrokes was the corollary notion of "iniquity" as a primordial "perversity of will" which required no positive cause, yet resulted in the soul's being, not "sent," but "dismissed," into the lower world. This implied that the soul plunged downward by its own spiritual "weight" into the sufferings it encountered amid lower realities; here, then, was a way of understanding the soul's sinful "fall" which blunted any contention that God was ultimately the cause of evils by causing the very iniquity which lay at their source.

Furthermore, by the way these books explained the relationship between eternity and time, they enabled Augustine to reply to the Manichee's mocking question, "What was God doing through all those ages before He created the world?" But that explanation did more: it enabled him to relate God's unchanging providential plan to the diversities of temporal epochs, and to see that everything not only was in its "place" but also occurred at its proper "time"; the Manichee complaint against the God-sanctioned morality of the patriarchs could now be dismissed as an anachronism (3.12–17).

The Value of a World-View

But Augustine must also have hoped that his new world-view would convince conservative Catholic critics that his was a suitably cautious and well-grounded enthusiasm for Neoplatonic categories of thought, pagan though their lineage might be. If critically sifted, they could provide an acceptable framework for understanding the Catholic faith. But it should also impress the conservatives that those same categories could arm the Catholic thinker with weapons against the most virulent heresy that North Africa knew, Manichaeism.

Finally, he could hope that non-Catholic philosophers, and particularly fellow-Neoplatonists, would come to appreciate how sophisticated and attractive his style of intellectual Catholicism could be, and how richly it responded to their own deepest religious aspirations. Augustine seems to have suffered some bruising disappointments of the hopes he had once entertained in this respect, but those hopes appear to have remained relatively bright for some four or five years after his conversion in A.D. 386.[17]

A Personal Conflagration

But it would be mistaken to measure the importance this Neoplatonic illumination held for Augustine personally purely in terms
of its power to furnish him with intellectual weapons of refutation
or even persuasion. The power of these writings went far beyond
that. We must believe him when he tells Romanianus and Manlius
Theodorus that it ignited nothing less than a raging bonfire—
incredibile incendium, incredibile!—in his own mind and heart. That
language forcefully recalls Augustine's stammering descriptions
of the erotic blaze enkindled by the *Hortensius*, a blaze which was
never extinguished, though it had come, in time, to burn with a
lower, slower fire (*Acad* 2.5).

Here too, however, these Platonists did not merely reply to the
soaring promise Augustine had read into Cicero's work, they
went far beyond it. Cicero had suggested that the life dedicated
to the mere "seeking" for Wisdom would be a life of happiness,
even if the person questing never succeeded in "finding" Her.
Augustine, we saw, never contented himself with so limited a
dividend. He could never settle for the tepidities of Cicero's Academic skepticism; if he was to devote his life to a contemplative
pursuit of the other-worldly Wisdom Cicero had enflamed him
for, he must first be certain that She existed;[18] indeed, we have seen
him claim that God Himself kept urging him toward that goal.

This was, moreover, the way he interpreted that favorite text
the Manichees tirelessly quoted to persuade the blind-faith Catholic that Christ Himself urged us to pass upward from belief to
reason: "Seek, and you shall find; knock, and it shall be opened
to you" (see *Mor* 1.24). This will be the text that weaves its way
discreetly through Augustine's early Dialogue on Academic philosophy, where he strives to convince us that the Academics were
really crypto-Platonists, their skepticism a ruse to ready us for
the thrilling message he had recently discovered for himself: that
the certainty of understanding was indeed accessible to one who
rightly "sought" for it. But he would have his readers also realize
that certainty of Wisdom's existence was only a step toward beholding and embracing Her; understanding was the halfway house
toward a more ultimate "finding," where the "door" might be
opened, even during this life in the body, to nothing less than
direct and immediate—vision![19]

Apologetic Value

Yet despite this "surplus" value which the *libri platonicorum* held for Augustine personally, they did represent an apologetic gold-mine as well, particularly for combating Manichaeism. We have already surveyed the many points of contact which exist between Augustine's summary in *Confessions* 7.16–26 and neuralgic Manichaean theses the Catholic thinker would have to refute, or, at the very least, neutralize. But the breadth, subtlety, and elaborately systematic character of the synthesis he presents here underlines the interest of that question we raised earlier: How long did it take Augustine to come to, develop, and interconnect the various insights he found necessary for replying to the Manichees?

We shall deal with that question in due time, but it cannot be answered without first addressing a prior set of issues. Even the most careful readers must have found that the foregoing interpretation of *Confessions* 7.13–26 was so condensed as to raise as many questions as it claimed to answer. What I have so far written on this pregnant section of Augustine's work was meant only as an introductory *tour d'horizon*, not to convince but merely to orient the reader for the more detailed justification that is about to follow. It is time to embark on that justification.

A World-View or a Story?

The reader probably noticed it, but there was an interpretation already embedded in the way I formulated the résumé given above: that interpretation would have it that, in this crucial section of his *Confessions*, Augustine's primary interest went toward outlining a world-view, informing his readers of *what* he came to "see." Assuring those readers *that* he came to see it, or for that matter informing them of *when* he came to see it, was only a remotely secondary part of his intention. Clearly, if he is telling us *what* he came to understand, he is also implicitly claiming *that* he did, as a matter of historical fact, come to understand it, and come to that understanding at some time or at some different times. Hence, he is obliged to use terms like *vidi, cognovi, manifestatum est mihi*: "I saw, I came to know, it was made plain to me." But the last thing he expects his reader to reply is: "Oh, *did* you now, did you *really*? And (or) *when* did that occur?"

From an intelligent reader of this section (as distinguished from that odd specimen, the modern Augustine scholar), the question Augustine would expect as appropriate would be: "Granted you claim to have 'seen' that, does *what* you have seen truly *make sense?*" He has, in other words, presented us—and the Manichees, and conservative Catholics, and fellow-philosophers who are not yet believing Catholics—with what he considers a coherent *Weltanschauung*, a world-view which he feels makes sufficient sense that we should examine it, see if it hangs together, and if it does, adopt it as our own. That world-view was, of course, the product of Augustine's own hard-won insights, and those insights came to him at some particular time or times. But he would not have us be distracted by such irrelevant considerations. This world-view has become true for Augustine, and now Augustine is facing his readers squarely with the challenging question: "Mustn't this be true for you, as well?"

The "Narrative" Interpretation

It must be stressed that such an interpretation differs importantly from one which has gained wide allegiance in most current literature on the *Confessions*: that Augustine is less explaining than narrating, telling a story (writing "history"), relating a series of *occurrences*. That series of occurrences, the narrative interpretation holds, are the sequential *experiences* he underwent, and (presumably) underwent in the spring of A.D. 386, at Milan. In this case, verbs like "I saw, I came to know, it was made manifest to me" are interpreted as indicating (more or less freely?) the temporal stages in that series of experiences.

A Narration of "Mystical" Experiences

But there is a second characteristic which is frequently associated with what I shall henceforth call the "narrative" interpretation, described above. It is this: the "occurrences" Augustine is presumed to be narrating are regularly held to be mystical, or quasi-mystical, experiences. To employ the terminology which has been put into general circulation by Pierre Courcelle, perhaps the most influential tenant of this view: the central burden of the section we have been considering was Augustine's narration of his "frustrated attempts at Plotinian ecstasy" (*vaines tentatives d'ecstase plotinienne*).[20] According to this view, Augustine meant verbs like *vidi*, *cognovi*, and *manifestatum est mihi* to express visions of a mystical sort, momentary though they may have been, and followed by a melancholy descent from dazzling vision to the customary grayness of everyday.

If it was, in fact, mystical visions Augustine was describing, it would be easy to understand his yielding to the overpowering desire to "narrate" the story of such wonder-filled moments; mystics both before and after him have surrendered to that same compulsion. Assume, then, that he is talking about a series of ascents to mystical or quasi-mystical visions, and the "narrative" interpretation is quite consonant with that assumption; the "narrative" and the "mystical" interpretations frequently overlap and become what I shall call the "narrative-mystical" interpretation of this section.

In the explication I have given of Augustine's text, however, I have deliberately called attention to the four distinct times he reminds us that he came to "glimpse" the "invisible [attributes]" of God by the eye of "understanding" and *through* created realities." I have already argued[21] that that formula, from Paul's Epistle to the Romans (1:20), was Augustine's personal code for saying that he did *not* "see" God's reality directly and immediately (as is normally implied by the term "mystically"), but "glimpsed" that reality mediately and indirectly.[22] That is, he "understood" it, "read between" the lines (*inter-legit*) and "through" the scrim of God's creatures (*per ea quae facta sunt*). So, I am claiming, Augustine espied the splendor of the Divine Light in filtered fashion, the way one would glimpse that Radiance through "light-filled clouds" (*per lucidas nubes*) (*Acad* 2.5).

The point I am driving at has this implication among others: if the claim being made here is valid, and it was Augustine's intention to outline a world-view, to tell us *what* he saw, it would be confirmatory of that claim if I could show that he is speaking the language of philosophic insight, that he is telling us how he came to "understand" reality and its interconnections.[23] By the same token, it becomes less likely in this hypothesis that he is "telling a story," conscientiously narrating a series of occurrences *as they occurred*, those occurrences being the sequence of insights to which he came. If, on the other hand, he is talking the language of mystical visions, one could easily understand that experiences of that order, dazzling and powerful, would each have left so strong an impression on him that he would feel compelled to tell his readers about them, would adopt the narrative mode and "tell their story."

It must be kept clear that none of us can afford, in a case like this, to overstate the strength of our arguments; we may not claim *ore rotundo*, for instance, that "mystical visions entail narration of occurrences, but insights of understanding entail description of a world-view." We are interpreting a text written hundreds of years ago, so the best we can hope for is to hit upon the "most natural" of the various plausible ways of understanding it; we must content ourselves with establishing presumptions, evaluating grades of lesser or greater consonance; we have to rely, in short, not on rigorous logic but (in Augustine's own expression) on sound judgment (7.23).

Similarly, it need not be that the two alternatives sketched above are either mutually exclusive or adequately inclusive. Augustine could be shifting from narrative to descriptive and back again; or, his *genre* might represent some mélange of those two modes more elusive than scholars have yet conjectured. We shall simply have to stay awake to the possibility of such surprises.

In any event, we must go over the entire ground more slowly now, and ask which interpretation the text supports, once it is scrupulously translated and meticulously dissected. To express my hypothesis one final time: if I was correct in my original exposition, then Augustine was primarily interested in describing to his readers the outlines of *what* he saw, the view of reality as he came to "understand" it. But, I must confess from the outset, it was also part of the interpretation embedded in the treatment given above that I do not think there are any convincing traces of "narrative intention," and, more specifically, narration of "mystical" or quasi-mystical experiences. But it is time to let a closer study of the text decide.

ANALYSIS OF A WORLD-VIEW

"*I Came to See That Spirit Truly Existed*" (Confessions 7.*x.16*)

Again, *caveat lector*: the very title I have given above, to summarize this chapter of his *Confessions*, supposes the soundness of my hypothesis: that Augustine is outlining the new world-view which his understanding of both the Bible and Neoplatonism prompted him to elaborate. One way to test the accuracy of that hypothesis would be to test whether my chapter titles truly reflect the content of Augustine's text. For in studying these sections I shall, by exception, cite chapter- as well as paragraph-divisions, since there is a real likelihood that the former may correspond to the literary units Augustine had in mind. In any event, he begins with the words:

> And, admonished thence [that is, by those readings] to return to myself, I entered into my inmost reality[ies], You [God] being my leader, and I was able [to do so] because "You became my helper." I entered there and I saw. . . .

Inde admonitus: Augustine employs the term *admoneo*, and less frequently such kindred forms as *moneo* and *commoneo*, again and again in his *Confessions*. It turns out on examination to be as close to a technical term as one is likely to find in his writings. Monica "admonishes" the young Augustine to avoid adultery; her words really come from God, but Augustine pays no attention (2.7). Augustine makes some depreciatory remarks to his class about gladiatorial contests, and they function (without his intending it, or being aware of it) as an "admonition" to his friend Alypius, waking him up, as it were, to the foolishness of his enthusiasm for such shows (6.11). In the case before us, Augustine reads some Platonic books and that reading functions as an admonition, spurring him to abandon the sensist focus on outward, corporeal things which has crippled his previous efforts at understanding reality, and to turn his mental gaze inward and upward toward the immaterial objects to which the Platonist insists on attending. Common to all his uses of the term seems to be this core of meaning: someone is in danger of wandering off or continuing on a wrong path when someone (or something) else brings something to his or her attention, deliberately or not; the result is (ideally at least) that the wanderer changes direction for the better.

But it is not our concern here to haggle about *exactly* how Augustine uses this term. The point, on which most scholars of the *Confessions* have come to agree,[24] is that *admoneo* is a semi-technical term for the Augustine who wrote the *Confessions*, and has something very close to the sort of meaning I have just described. This was not yet clear to the scholarly community at the time when Pierre Courcelle wrote his famous, and influential, *Recherches sur les* CONFESSIONS *de saint Augustin*.[25] Courcelle wrongly inferred that the occurrence here of the term *admonitus* implied that some such "admonition" must have been literally present—a phrase like "turn inward," say—in one or other Platonic book Augustine read, and he settled, after a rather perfunctory search, on Plotinus' *Ennead* 1.6.[26] Courcelle took encouragement, of course, from the fact that Paul Henry had previously argued that the same treatise must have been among the *paucissimi libri*, the "very few books" of Plotinus which Augustine "tells" us he had read before his conversion at Milan.[27]

But, among other things, the results of research on how Augustine himself used the term *admoneo* has cast doubt on Courcelle's entire procedure in this matter;[28] at the same time, Henry's inference from the *paucissimi* phrase has also been been seriously riddled.[29] What is left of their interpretation is this: Augustine found something in one or several places in whatever Platonic books he had read[30] which inspired him to adopt an entirely different mode of thinking. Instead of inspecting the "outer" realities on which his senses reported, he now resolved to turn "inward," by which he means, to shift his focus to what Platonists called "intelligible realities," realities which we might refer to as "mental objects."

His earliest Dialogue on the Academics gives examples of what he means by those intelligible objects: they include the sorts of "analytic" propositions which we confidently judge *must* be true from the moment we see clearly the meanings and the necessary connection beween subject and predicate terms: "there exists either no world, one world, or more than one world." Or, in the example he gives in his work *On the Trinity*, "If I doubt, I must exist" (*Acad* 3.27–29, *Trin* 15.21).[31] Other examples of the same sort can be found in the discussion of "memory" in Book 10 of the *Confessions*. In all these cases, Augustine is arguing that the content of the subjects and predicates being compared cannot have been drawn from "exterior" sense observation. Hence, they must be "interior" realities: realities accessible to the spiritual intelligence which he ranks as one of his own "inmost" realities, *intima*, or, more exactly, interior "powers" (as contrasted with his "exterior" powers like those of bodily limbs or external senses). (That term *intima* one might accurately translate more baldly as "in-sides"; Augustine knows how to put its ambiguity—physical or spiritual insides?—to excellent use.)

Augustine confesses that this inward turn—along with its successful issue, doubtless—was made through God's guidance ("You being my leader": *duce Te*) and because God "became his helper" (*factus es adjutor meus*). Some have attempted to interpret these two phrases as deliberate slants against what they claim was Plotinus' pretension at human "self-sufficiency." In that case Augustine would be pitting his "confession" that he needed and received God's grace in order to make this inward turn against some phrase or other—from *Ennead* 1.6, for instance[32]—in which Plotinus would allegedly have claimed that the human being can "do it all" without any such divine aid. But all such attempts that I have come across, though devoutly apologetic in their intent, fail in one way or another. It is more likely that Augustine found Plotinus talking about our *receiving* divine aid than going without it![33]

Nonetheless, that quotation of Psalm 29:11, "You became my helper," *adjutor meus*, is worth attending to in the above connection. For his preached works show that Augustine has a distinctly personal way of using that term *adjutor*, especially when referring to God.[34] For God is always ready to "take us up" (*suscipere*) in order to "help" us, to "be" our *adjutor*. But, like a querulous sick person who refuses to confide himself to the ministrations of his doctor, we can resist God's aid, and so prevent Him from "becoming" our helper. As happens so often with Augustine's language about God, the claim that He has now "become" *adjutor* in man's efforts toward "returning to himself" and "turning within" tells us more about the man than about God. Augustine means to say that he had come humbly to recognize his need for God's help, and so made room, as it were, for God to "become" his helper.

Without that divine aid, he is assuring us, he would never have been able to "see" what he is about to see. Indeed, he is telling us more: without that aid he would not have been able to perform even the liminal move required for this new kind of "seeing." Even to "return to [him]self" and to his spiritual "insides," he stood in need of God's help. In sum, seeing what he is about to see is not merely an intellectual, but also a moral and religious, achievement: it requires a humble surrender to God's empowering grace.

In passing, it should be noted that this calls into question a way scholars have become accustomed to refer to the two central "conversion" books of the *Confessions*: Book 7, it is often said, recounts Augustine's "intellectual" conversion, while Book 8 recounts his "moral" or "religious" conversion.[35] Here, Augustine's allusion to God as his *adjutor* is the first of several expressions he employs in this section to warn us that there was already a moral-religious—a "grace-component" if you will—at the very heart of his so-called "intellectual" conversion.

It is understandable that such assertions, about God's help and about the "graced" character of this experience, would encourage readers to interpret the "seeing" Augustine is about to describe as something quite extraordinary: he *must* be telling about a "vision" of the sort that the medieval mystics describe and theologians characterize as necessarily grace-infused. Ought we to score this as a point in favor of the "narrative-mystical" wing of interpretation? Perhaps it would be wiser to count it as only a presumptive point: Augustine thinks of grace as required for absolutely every salutary act we perform, whether ordinary or extraordinary; besides, he is about to give us more specifics both on what, and how, he actually saw.

Augustine's Fidelity to His Sources

But, to go back for a moment to the very beginning of paragraph 16: there is a striking difference between Augustine's opening words here and those he uses in paragraphs 13, 14, and 15. Earlier, he repeats formulae like *ibi legi* (13), *Item ibi legi* and *est ibi* (14), and, finally, *Et ideo legebam ibi*. He is plainly stressing that the content he was describing was truly—*ibi, ibi, ibi*—in the books he is talking about. He is insisting on his fidelity to the original tenor of those writings, despite the slightly uncomfortable admission that there may be some freedom in the way he paraphrases what he read there: it was "not said in these words, of course, but [was] altogether the same teaching" (*non quidem his verbis, sed hoc idem omnino*) (13); "it was said variously and in many ways" (*varie dictum et multis modis*) (14). Hence, there just *may* be some question in the reader's mind about whether what Augustine claims was there would have been "there" for other readers, and particularly for readers who had not learned from Ambrose, as

Augustine had done, how the techniques of "spiritual exegesis" could make any text mean virtually anything one wanted it to mean.[36] But Augustine will not have us regard that as grounds for skepticism: what he found written there was truly there, *ibi*. The credibility of his little *apologia* for commending these pagan books stands or falls with that claim.

From the opening words of paragraph 16 until the ending of paragraph 26, on the contrary, he does not utter a single such protestation of "fidelity to his sources." The most probable reason is that he no longer claims to be telling us what he *found in* these books. Instead, he has profited from the central "admonition" they represented for him, and has resolved from this point forward to "return to [him]self" and to that chief among his "inmost powers," his intelligence: Augustine has decided to think for himself. Or, more exactly, he has decided to combine a number of reasoned convictions he had come to earlier with the fresh suggestions drawn from this new source: he will *continue* to think for himself. Oh, he will be glad to consult those books on more than one occasion, and profit from suggestions he finds; but he will not always accept what he finds there, or ever simply parrot what he decides to accept: he will always make those books grist for the mill of his independent personal reflection. We shall be wise to remain open to the possibility that the skein of insights he is about to relate to us is the product, and the relatively "final" product, of a sustained effort of personal reflection.

The Eye Above the Eye

The next portion of Augustine's text confronts us with a translator's difficulty which seems to have baffled the noblest of that profession. Let me first give the Latin, then my own translation, then an attempt at justifying that translation.

> *Intravi et vidi qualicumque oculo animae meae supra eundem oculum a-nimae meae supra mentem meam lucem incommutabilem.* . . .

Augustine is still speaking about "entering" into his inmost self:

> I entered [there] and saw, with an eye of some sort or other of my soul, [an eye] above that same eye of my soul, above my mind, [an] unchangeable light. . . .

The moment one begins to study this sentence several puzzles leap from the page. The first of them: how translate that term *qualicumque*? And, secondly, what can Augustine mean by the phrase *supra eundem oculum animae meae*? What is it that Augustine is locating as "above" that "same" eye of his soul? The point may not be of earth-shaking importance, but it is instructive concerning how to read Augustine's Latin. Finally, though, is Augustine saying he saw "*a* Light" or just plain "Light"?

John K. Ryan's attempt[37] to solve those puzzles is somewhat typical: "by my soul's eye, *such as it was*, I saw *above that same eye of my soul*, above my mind, an unchangeable light." But no good Latin dictionary will countenance translating *qualicumque* by the English "such as it was," or by Vernon Bourke's "whatever its condition,"[38] or by Tréhorel and Bouissou's French "tel qu'il fût";[39] the term means "of some sort or other," and no amount of wanting will change that.

But in order to see how that dictionary meaning fits, one must get straight on the second question asked above. What is it that Augustine is telling us was "above" that "same" eye of his soul, and indeed, above his "mind" as well? Ryan, Bourke, and a host of others reply: "the unchangeable Light." Now, there can be no doubt that Augustine does locate this Divine Light "above" the soul's eye and above the mind more generally; but is this an accurate rendition of what he is saying in the Latin of this particular text? Stare at the word order more intently, and the repeated *supra*s seem more naturally to modify the *qualicumque oculo* that precedes rather than the *lucem* that follows them. Then the answer that Augustine's Latin gives is: "an eye of my soul of some sort or another [which was] above that same eye of my soul [and] above my mind." But this, the average English translator splutters, is sheer nonsense: an eye of the soul above the same eye of the soul—two eyes which are somehow the "same" one eye, unthinkable! Augustine could not have meant such a thing, and so we are obliged to read his Latin—or strategically misread it?—in some way that has him talking sense.

But if we recall momentarily that Augustine may here be tapping the Neoplatonic source-materials he has just finished telling us meant so much to him, then his Latin may make excellent sense: difficult sense, perhaps, as Neoplatonism can frequently be difficult, but excellent sense nonetheless. Assume Plotinus as emblematic of the Neoplatonic thought-world: he will claim[40] that we can mount toward vision by means of that eye of *our individual* soul which we call reason; but at a certain moment in that ascent, what would seem to be another "higher" eye of the soul—common to all of us at our topmost reach—must shift into gear, as it were. *Noûs* itself, the Divine Intelligence if you will, must take over and "become" the eye that empowers our minds to see with the seeing that is *Noûs*'s own.

Olivier Du Roy has pointed to several loci in the early Dialogues where Augustine avails himself of this Neoplatonic thought-device;[41] it would also seem to be the inspiration behind Augustine's habitual exegesis of the Psalmist's phrase *in lumine Tuo videbimus lumen*: "in Your Light we shall see [the] Light" (Ps 35:10). This Augustine interprets (see, for example, *S 126* 15; *En 35* 14–15; *InJo 18* 10, *21* 4, *40* 5) as meaning that in God's own Son, Whom the Nicene Creed calls *Lumen de Lumine*, Light of the Father's Light, we shall see the Father and, indeed, the God-Trinity. So, too, in the evocation of our heavenly bliss with which he ends his *Confessions*, Augustine can dwell on the same insight in that series of incantatory phrases: "Those who see these things through Your Spirit, You see in them" (13.46) and "we see all these things . . . because You see them in us" (13.49), and "You shall rest in us as now You work in us" (13.52) (*Tu vides in eis, Tu ea vides in nobis, Sic requiesces in nobis quemadmodum nunc operaris in nobis*): heaven will be the manifestation of God's profound interiority to all we humans have ever known and done.

Augustine will hint broadly at this same interpretation in paragraph 23 of this same section: there, for the first time, it is beyond question that he is describing the technique of spiritual ascent. At a crucial stage in that ascent, he tells us, his "reasoning power" (*ratiocinans potentia*), discovering its mutability, *erexit se ad intelligentiam suam*, "straightened itself up to [toward] its own [power of] intelligence." How did reason achieve this? It "withdrew its thought from [its] customary mode, taking itself away from the mobs of contradictory phantasms" which it was accustomed to deal with at the lower levels of its operation, "in order that it might find the Light by which it was besprinkled . . . [that Light] whence it knew the Unchangeable [God] Himself . . . and it came [at last: *pervenit*] to 'that which is,' in a flash of trembling regard."

Notice that in that upward passage it is the very same "reasoning power" which changes from its more "customary" mode of operation to the style of operation proper to "intelligence," until it "arrives" at last, succeeds in catching sight of the Unchangeable "That Which Is," God: "reason" remains the lone subject of all the verbs from start to finish of this sentence.

What Augustine has described, then, appears (at first blush) to be an elevating self-transformation of the reasoning power whereby it "raises itself" from its lower occupation with sense-reports and phantasms to the more serene mode of operation proper to "intelligence." This, he implies, is more on a level to contemplate the Unchangeable. (That verb *erigere*, we have seen, evokes the image of the human being as "straightening up"—or "*being* straightened up"?—in order to contemplate higher, spiritual realities.)

Finally, in one of Augustine's cherished metaphors, reason, which up until now has been "seeking" (*quaerens*) and hoping to "find" (*ut inveniret*), "arrives" (*pervenit*) at the term of its journeying. It finds the "Light by which it is besprinkled"—a mixed metaphor encouraged by the fact that Psalm 35:10 calls God both "fountain of life" and "Light" in Whom "we shall see Light." Irrigated by that fountain, which is one with being enlightened by that *Lumen de Lumine*, reason is empowered to judge correctly on matters involving unchangeability: in His Light it sees the Light "which is"—God.

We are tempted to wonder why Augustine does not simply distinguish reason from intelligence, and have done with it. Why not simply allow for our having *two* "eyes of the soul"? Here he confronts us with a translation-conundrum much like the one we met in the puzzling text from paragraph 16: just when we have succeeded in distinguishing two eyes, Augustine flicks his wand and insists that *presto!* they are really only one, but the same eye engaged in various levels of performance. And the highest of those levels is to glimpse the Divine Light Itself.

But reason, even raised to intelligence, cannot glimpse that Light unless it is empowered by that Light—unless (in the language of paragraph 16, now) that Light becomes "some sort of eye," at once *above* reason, but now manifesting itself as what it always has been, the loftier eye "of" reason, "seeing" in and through reason's own seeing.

If we count what we saw in paragraph 16, along with what

we have just examined from paragraph 23, it is now twice that
Augustine has told us that he arrived at a vision of Divine Light,
a vision which, as he describes it, sounds very much as though it
were of a mystical, ecstatic, or at least a semi-mystical order.

To test that possibility, however, we must read further. Augustine continues his description of [the] "Unchangeable Light"
in paragraph 16; that Light was

> not this ordinary light, plain to all flesh, nor as though it were a
> greater [light] of the same kind, as though this [ordinary] light
> were to shine much, much more brightly, and fill the whole [uni-
> verse] with its magnitude. Not such was that Light, but other,
> vastly other [aliud, aliud valde], from all these [ordinary] lights.

Here Augustine is coaching his reader's mind to grasp the distinction between visible-corporeal and intelligible-spiritual realities, between the "ordinary" daylight or sunlight "plain to all
flesh," visible to "exterior" bodily eyes, and this "other, vastly
other" kind of light which only the "interior eye" of the mind can
"see." The technique he employs is much like Plotinus' step-by-
step correction by "dynamic image."[42] His point is to show that
the difference involved must not be confused with a mere quantitative difference in magnitude or expanse, or with a qualitative
difference in intensity of brightness.

The first member of that double correction, however, suddenly
confronts us with a realization: Augustine has not been thinking
in terms of a light-source but, rather, of a light-field. Notice that
in my translation I left this possibility open by bracketing the
English articles, whether definite or indefinite: they do not, of
course, exist in Latin. In that language, then, one can say "I saw
light"—vidi lucem—and that assertion must take the same linguistic form as "I saw a light" or "the light." In the latter two cases,
the object seen is an individual light in the sense of a light-source,
like a star, the sun, or a lamp. But if a Latin-speaker wished to
say that he saw "light," in the sense of "daylight" or "sunlight"—
meaning a field or expanse or "atmosphere" of luminosity, considered quite apart from whatever its source might be—he would
be obliged to resort to the same linguistic form as denotes a light-
source, and make his precise intention clear by some other means.

The fact that Augustine used the term lux instead of lumen does
not create any strong presumption either way; but the manner in

which he describes the first "correction" he brings to his initial image holds a telling clue. For he asks us to begin by imagining this "ordinary" sunlight as becoming *grandior*, "greater" in the quantitative sense of expanding farther and farther outward, "until it [should] fill the whole universe with its magnitude"—*magnitudine*, again, a quantitative term, which strongly suggests that Augustine is coaching us to imagine a light-*field* rather than a light-*source*. This is simply a first stage; the image needs to be "corrected," just as the same image, which Augustine seems to have "rehearsed" earlier, needed correction. There Augustine says he imagined (quite literally that) God's presence to creation by comparing it to the presence of sunlight to what it illuminates: he pictures it as extended in magnitude (*grande*) "through limitless space," in such a way that it "penetrated the entire world-mass and everything beyond throughout endless immensities in all directions" (7.2). We shall see that this distinction between light-source and light-field, however pedantic it may initially seem, will acquire a certain importance later in our study.

But the "corrections" which Augustine has thus far brought to our ordinary ways of thinking still operate on the visible-corporeal level proper to "ordinary" light; they get the mind under way, so to speak, but they do not quite succeed in helping us to vault the chasm separating the visible-corporeal and the "other, vastly other" intelligible-spiritual realm. And Augustine shrewdly suspects that part of the difficulty may lie in the very language he has been using: in that term "above" (*supra*), for example:

> Nor was it "above" my mind thus, as oil is above water, nor as heaven is above earth; but it was "higher" because [in the sense that] it made me, and I was "lower" because [in the sense that] I was made by it.

"Above," "higher," and "lower," Augustine is telling us, should be understood not as indicating *spatial* relationships in the visible-corporeal world, but as expressing the *intelligible* relationship whereby every "maker" is (as Neoplatonism taught) metaphysically "superior" to what it makes, every cause is superior to its effect. Hence, when Augustine speaks of God as "on high," he hopes we will not understand him to mean that God is spatially "up there, out there." (And, we might add, he implicitly hopes he himself will not slip into meaning that, either!)

The Divine Trinity

Now, in a burst of religious enthusiasm, he exclaims:

> One who knows [the] Truth knows [that Light], and one who
> knows It knows Eternity. Charity knows It. O Eternal Truth, and
> True Charity, and Belovèd Eternity! You are my God, and I sigh
> for You "day and night."

Here Augustine is making a remarkable claim: that the Light
which (Whom?) he came to see after heeding the "admonition"
received from those "Platonist books" was identical with the God-
head, and, indeed, with the Trinitarian God worshiped by Christians. Du Roy has shown plainly that in this triadic formula,
"Eternity" is Augustine's name for the Father, "Truth" his name
for the Son, and "Charity" his name for the Holy Spirit.[43] Pagan
though the Neoplatonists may have been, Augustine thinks, there
is after all only one God, and that God is Trinity. Indeed, the
Plotinian triad of One, Noûs, and All-Soul in some respects mim-
icked the Christian Trinity. Hence, Augustine could think that the
God he had come to glimpse, and the God Whom some Neoplatonists came to contemplate at the climax of their mental ascents,
can have been no other than the God Who is, in point of fact,
Trinity. This seems to be the minimal claim Augustine is making here.

In what sense, though, did the Neoplatonists explicitly recognize God as Trinity? And is Augustine implying that he himself,
having mounted successfully and come to "see" this Divine Light,
saw that Light as explicitly Trinitarian in character? These are real
problems, surely, but they would lead us well beyond the ambit
of this study; for now at least, we must leave them for others.[44]

To Be and Not-To-Be

Augustine's account continues by confronting us with another
translation problem. His Latin runs as follows:

> *Et cum Te primum cognovi, Tu assumsisti me, ut viderem esse quod
> viderem, et nondum me esse, qui viderem.*

Allow me to submit, for the moment at least, my translation
of this sentence:

And when first I came to know You, You raised me up, so that I
saw [or: might see] that what I saw existed, and that I, who saw,
did not yet exist.

Here, at first blush, it would seem that Augustine is narrating,
and narrating an occurrence, or at least an occurrence of sorts.
Allow me to explain what I mean by that latter phrase. Augustine
is recalling when "first" he "came to know" God. But several
questions immediately suggest themselves on how we are meant
to understand both those terms.

To begin with, does "when first" Augustine came to know God
refer to one precise *event*, "the first *time*" he came to know Him?
Not necessarily. It could just as easily refer to a more extended
process, as one might say, "That summer, when I first got (i.e.,
was getting) to know you."

Second, is Augustine using the "know" of direct acquaintance
(as my example above would illustrate), or is he implying that he
came to "know *that*" God existed? Notice that either hypothesis
would satisfy the desire he spoke of earlier, to become "certain"
of God's existence. But a knowledge by "acquaintance" would fit
more snugly with the "mystical" theory of this section, whereas
knowing *that* God exists would fit with the "knowledge by understanding" hypothesis for which I have been arguing.

At this point we might be tempted to entertain the possibility,
mentioned earlier, of a "mix" between these two competing
modes of interpretation: even if one were to insist that the *primum*
discussed above can mean "the first *time*," an "event," and only
that, it would still be possible to claim that while Augustine may
here have slipped into the narrative mode, *what* he is narrating is
not necessarily a mystical experience, but a successful venture of
understanding which culminated in his coming to know for certain *that* God existed. But is that what Augustine is saying that he
came to "see"?

We cannot answer that confidently except by unraveling the
second translation-difficulty in this sentence. Let me illustrate the
difficulty once again by indicating the types of rendition which
have been proposed. They will serve to show that the two knotty
phrases are, first, *ut viderem esse quod viderem*, then, second, *et [ut
viderem] nondum me esse qui viderem*. I shall italicize what the various translators make of those two phrases. God, according to

John K. Ryan, "took [Augustine] up, so that [he] *might see that there was something to see*, but that *I was not yet one able to see it.*"[45] Vernon Bourke's version is essentially the same: God took [Augustine] up to Himself that he might "*see that there was something to see*," but Augustine "*was not yet ready for the vision.*"[46] Tréhorel and Bouissou are more puzzling than clarifying: they have it that God acted so as to make [Augustine] see "*qu'il y avait pour moi l'Être à voir, et que je n'étais pas encore être à le voir.*"[47] But their translation is supplemented in a footnote[48] by Aimé Solignac, suggesting "two possibilities" for translating and understanding this sentence: the one Solignac appears to favor comes down to something in the near neighborhood, at least, of the version I have proposed above.[49]

Now, one would have to say that all three translations locate the knottiest difficulty in that phrase *nondum me esse qui viderem*. What can Augustine mean by saying (what the Latin, when taken literally, *does say*) that he, the one *qui viderem*, the one "who saw," saw himself as *nondum esse*, literally, saw that "he did *not yet exist*"? Unable to understand what sense such an assertion could make, all three translators resort to the tactic of supplying a phrase. It is a phrase that Augustine *could* have included. But he chose not to do so. He meant to say, his translators imply, that he was not yet "able," or "ready" (or whatever "*être à*" is supposed to mean), for the vision. So, if we are to credit his translators, Augustine says that he "saw" despite the simultaneous admission that he was not yet "fit" to see. That is hard enough to digest. But then we are asked to believe that this professional wordsmith compounds the confusion by writing a Latin that says he "did not yet exist," when he really meant to write that he was not yet "ready for the vision." Curiouser and curiouser.

Once again, I submit, the problem is that translators have found it beyond them to make sense of Augustine's Latin precisely as he wrote it; so, they have mistranslated that Latin in hopes of making it make the kind of sense they could understand.

The translation I have proposed has the initial advantage of being perfectly literal; but what sense does it make? Start with the second member first, and Augustine is saying that he "did not yet exist." But what does he mean by "exist" in this context? Solignac has seen part of the solution: one of the Scriptural texts Augustine has in mind is God's reply from Exodus 3:14—which

he will actually quote a few lines further on!—"I am Who am."
In the very next paragraph, furthermore, Augustine will tell us
how he regularly interprets that phrase: "that alone truly exists
which abides unchangeably" (7.17).[50] To exist in the "truest" sense
of that term is to be absolutely immutable, whereas changeable
realities are an "unstable" (Augustine's term) amalgam of being
and non-being, existence and non-existence: they are constantly
"flowing" (Augustine's favorite metaphor for changing realities)
from what they were to what they were not, from warm to cold,
ignorant to knowing, living to dead. As a changeable reality,
accordingly, Augustine "does not exist" in the true sense of the
term. But what can he mean by saying he "did not *yet* exist?"

To answer that, one must call to mind a second Scriptural text,
one that Augustine frequently quotes in direct connection with
Exodus 3:19 (*SS 117* 15; *158* 7, 9ff.; *58* 13; *346* 2; *Enn 86* 9, 36;
S 2 8). St. John in his First Epistle (3:1–2) tells his people that we
are now children of God, but do not know "what we shall be"
later. For at the end-time "we shall be like Him, for we shall see
Him as He is." Or, as Augustine would have printed it: "we shall
see Him as He IS." For Christ as Eternal Son of God truly IS,
He EXISTS in the fullest sense of that term.

But Augustine credits St. John with tacitly applying the Greek
philosophical axiom "like knows like": to know the Eternal, we
ourselves must become eternalized, "like Him." And this, he ex-
ults, is exactly what the Evangelist is promising: that from our
present changeable state we shall be united to the Eternal God,
and through that union we shall be transformed. We shall participate in God's own Eternity: we "shall *exist*" in the true sense of
that term. But now, like Augustine, we "do not *yet* exist."

One key to translating the term *esse* in Augustine's writing
consists in knowing when it means "exist, simply," and when he
means us to remember that "existence" can assume what I shall
call the variable "intensities" implied in the text we have just examined.[51] Unsurprisingly, now, we shall see that what worked
for the second member of this text will work also for the first.

God lifted Augustine up, he tells us, *ut viderem esse quod viderem*:
that he "might see," as our three translators substantially agreed
to put it, "that there was something to see." I suggest that this
comes close to what Augustine meant to say: there *was* an object
there, so to speak; Augustine was not deluded, was not hallucinat-

ing; he had made solid noetic contact with a *reality*. So, it is a small step to the translation that has the virtue of being consistent with the second member of the phrase, as we have come to render it: Augustine came to see that "what [he] saw *existed*."

But, more important, that translation also fits with how Augustine shaped the earlier portions of the *Confessions* to prepare our minds for this central illumination. Recall that he has told us that the "greatest and almost single cause" of his inevitable error in thinking about God was his persistence in trying to think of spiritual realities in corporeal terms (5.19, 25). This empirical bent repeatedly resulted in the conviction that non-corporeal realities had no solidity, no substantiality; they must be so many vacuous "nothings." Now he has learned, at last, how to think of spiritual realities in non-corporeal terms; the result is that he has come to "know" that God and spiritual reality more generally are not airy "nothings," after all, but *exist*—in fact, when compared with corporeal realities, the spiritual (when united with God, and like God) exists in a vastly fuller sense of that term!

Understanding, or Vision?

Assuming that this interpretation is correct, we may now be in a position to answer the question we postponed earlier. Can we simply point to the fact that when first he came to "know" Him, Augustine "saw" *that* God exists? This, if it were all Augustine is saying, would come up far short of saying that he "saw God," came to "know" God with something on the order of a "mystical" knowledge by direct acquaintance: it would, on the contrary, be a proposition expressing a truth accessible to the workings of Augustine's "understanding."

That hypothesis has at least the merit of making us re-examine the text more closely. Once that is done, it becomes plainer that Augustine is asserting something oddly different from a merely "propositional" truth of "understanding." For his Latin appears to say that he "saw *that*" (proposition of understanding) "*what* [he] saw" (by direct acquaintance) "existed." And that, to all appearances, is a downright peculiar thing to say. For it seems to imply that he could see something by direct acquaintance, doubt its existence, and have that doubt removed by an insight of the understanding which assured him "that what he saw existed" after all.

Admissible, perhaps, in regard to other objects of acquaintance—near-hallucinatory sense-objects, for example. But such an anomaly, if we are to believe the mystics, becomes very hard to swallow in the case of a mystical or quasi-mystical vision of God. In any case, there is every reason to think that Augustine himself would have considered the direct and immediate vision of God an experience that would leave no room for doubting God's existence. We have not finished with this question; Augustine's account will compel us to return to it, and, let us hope, with more adequate evidence for answering it.

There is a final feature of this puzzling text which should not pass unnoticed: it is that opening image of God "lifting" Augustine up in order to see what he had previously been unable to see. *Assumsisti*: I shall only suggest, for now, that the term evokes associations very akin to the ones evoked by the *adjutor* we saw earlier: that of someone strong coming to the aid of a person who is comparatively helpless. More specifically, I suggest that Augustine hoped this term would leave us with a kind of residual image, that of a mother or father, at the circus or the theater, lifting up a little child so that it can see over the heads of all of those grown-ups who, until now, were blocking the view. But perhaps we shall find evidence to buttress that suggestion further on.

Experience of "Repercussion"

And You beat back the weakness [*infirmitatem*] of my gaze, shining into me most forcefully, and I trembled [*tremui*] with love and with [awesome] dread [*amore et horrore*].

Augustine describes how the power of God's radiance repelled him, much as stepping out into bright sunlight would prompt a person to shield his eyes from it, or even to scuttle back into the shadows. (Note that in North Africa it would not be necessary to stare straight at the sun—the *source* of the brightness—to undergo a similar reaction.) This would be particularly true in the case of eyes which were "sickly," and therefore "weaker" than ordinary; the Latin term *infirmus* means both weak and sickly, and Augustine plays on that connection to suggest that our spiritual "weakness" is the result of our being "sick," with a sickness brought on by our sinful fall. We are about to see that in answer to our "weakness" Christ comes to us as "food" to help us "grow" and become "strong." In answer to our "sickness," He comes to us as *medicus*, a doctor wise in all the arts of healing.

A cursory reading might suggest that Augustine had experienced a single momentary glimpse of God's radiance, and yet (as with the *primum* discussed above) the Latin is patient of a repetitive meaning also—"you kept beating back"—even if that might have been conveyed more clearly by the imperfect tense. Interpreted repetitively, Augustine could easily be talking about a reaction— DeQuincey's "*O altitudo!*"—which he experienced on more than one occasion when striving to "understand" God's utter transcendence. The note of religious enthusiasm is entirely comparable to the one which infused the *Hortensius* account, and could arise here, as there, from Augustine's "erotic intellectualism," compounded by the preacher's eagerness to have his readers share his enthusiasm.

In any event, his reaction is typical of the experience shared by many budding mystics. But it is common to less exalted religious experiences also: in Rudolph Otto's term, the Divine is experienced as *tremendum* as well as *fascinosum*.[52] It is interesting that Augustine describes the sense of awe before the *tremendum* as dominating his initial reaction; the attitude toward God as *fascinosum* is far more characteristic of him; but he will come to express that aspect very soon.

In short, there are features of this "repulse" experience which would initially encourage the "narrative–mystical" interpretation of the entire section, but the grounds for that inference are hardly peremptory, and, besides, we have not yet surveyed all the evidence.

A Region of Unlikeness

> And I found myself [to be] far from You, in a region of unlikeness, as though I heard Your voice from the highest: "Food am I for grown-ups: grow, and you shall feed upon Me. Nor shall you [then] change Me into yourself, as [you do with] the food of your flesh, but you shall be changed into Me."

It might help to recall Augustine's "world-picture" at this point. In that picture, God is, as Augustine mentions here, the "Highest" of realities, and (spatial relationships acting to symbolize ontologi-

cal relationships) Augustine would now be picturing himself as
"down" among the "lowest" of temporal and corporeal realities,
as "far" from God as imaginable, hence, as "different" and "alien"
from Him as possible: in a "region of unlikeness." It has been
suggested[53] that he could have found the phrase in Plotinus' *Ennead*
1.8. That is very likely, but the point can remain secondary; the
image, and perhaps even the verbal formula, could have been
fairly widespread in the post-Platonic tradition—as indeed it became after Augustine's time.

When placed against the world-picture which I have presented
as Augustine's, the increasing "distance" from God to lower, then
even lower, and finally the "lowest" of realities symbolically expresses the increasing "unlikeness" of those lower and lowest realities to God. The "distance" in this case is expressed in the
vertical dimension, from highest to lowest. Recall the twinned
images we saw Augustine evoke in the *Hortensius* episode, and
that verticality corresponds to the Platonic myth of the "wingèd
soul" that has lost its wings and "fallen" from on high.

That vertical image, though, tends to combine (sometimes
quite abruptly) with its partner in the *Hortensius* account, the
"horizontal" image drawn from St. Luke's Gospel parable of the
Prodigal son: he traveled overland, a great "distance" *away* from
his Father's house, to a "far country." Or, that horizontal distanc-
ing can occur on sea rather than land, so that the figure we descry
is that of a sea-voyager: an Odysseus, or an Aeneas. Observe,
however, that for all their differences, these images have the common characteristic of depicting the human soul's journey as a
circular one: in all three cases the distant traveler yearns to "return" to his point of departure, the "home" he originally left
behind.

Heavenly Food: For Grown-ups

Augustine has found himself too "weak" to support the radiance
he has glimpsed; in reply to that weakness, now, God's voice
from on high reminds him that God is "food," spiritual food to
satisfy the soul's profoundest "hunger." (We shall see that God is
also a "fountain" of delights to slake the soul's spiritual "thirst";
these were common metaphors for the soul's relationship to God.)
But God is not food for spiritual "infants" like Augustine. *Tu das*

escam illorum in tempore opportuno went the psalm (144) for graces before meals which Augustine has been citing like a refrain through Books 4, 5, and 6. But it was not yet the "opportune time" for them to "feed" on Him; only spiritual "grown-ups" are strong enough to tolerate, and even to enjoy, the brightness of His splendor in abiding fashion. Augustine must "grow up" before he can feed on God in that way. And when he does, the result will be the opposite of what occurs in the process of nourishment he is familiar with: Augustine will become assimilated to God, rather than assimilating God to himself. Earlier, we saw him anticipate the possibility that he might later come to "exist," might ultimately be "eternalized"; now God has promised that exactly such a transformation can in fact occur.

Iniquitas

But if Augustine cannot hope to feed on God Himself, how can he hope to "grow" up and become "strong" enough to abide in the vision he hungers for? That question is left hanging for the present, while Augustine goes on to enlarge on our state of "unlikeness" to God:

> And I came to know that "You have instructed man on account of [his] iniquity, and You have made my soul shrivel away like a spider. . . ."

Augustine here quotes verse 12 from Psalm 38, as he frequently does in his preached works (*Enn 38* 17–18, *143* 11, *122* 6, *89* 9–10), to account for what he considers the misery of our human condition: because of our "iniquity," God has "made our souls shrivel away" as a spider does when it dries up at death to become a brittle, disintegrating mass. The Manichees, of course, thought of our human condition in similarly bleak terms, but they accounted for it by a kind of primitive catastrophe for which we were not in the least to blame. If there was anyone—or anything—to "blame," it was the evil anti-God principle, "Darkness" or "Matter," which had jealously invaded the kingdom of Light and borne our divine souls away as captives in this lower world.

On the other hand, the Manichees contended, the Catholics could not account satisfactorily for our present misery without being compelled to admit that their One so-called "Good" God was, in the last resort, to blame for it. Oh, like the Jews who had adulterated God's revelation to give us such scandalous trash as the Book of Genesis, Catholics claimed that our present misery was God's just punishment for some mysterious "iniquity" we had all committed in the "beginning"—that it was all *our* fault. But obviously, the Manichees insisted, this was only a dodge: push the analysis back, and the Catholics' one God must bear the blame for giving man freedom of choice, despite having foreseen, or perhaps even predetermined, that man would use that freedom in order to sin.

No wonder, then, the Manichees continued, that the Catholic Scriptures so often reverted to portraying God as flying into those terrible fits of anger, jealousy, and spite, like some crochety old tyrant who simply delights in exacting vengeance and punishment (*Mor* 1.16).

That final portrait of God had once made a searing impression on Augustine. There is a particular set of traits, attributed especially to the Old Testament God, with which he deals in especially gingerly fashion: those which would make God out to be a splenetic tyrant of vengeance and punishment.[54] That apologetic reflex contributes to his predilection for that verse from Psalm 38. In the first place, that psalm accounts uncompromisingly for our miserable situation as stemming from our own "iniquity"; the self-exculpation of the Manichee is proud "presumption" where the situation calls for humble "confession." But in the second place, and equally important, that text describes God's response to our "iniquity" not in terms of anger or vengeance or punishment, however appropriate one might argue those responses to be. *Erudisti* is the term the Psalmist addresses to his God. For God's aim in reducing us to our present condition was to "instruct" us, to make us "wiser" than we were when we committed that grand folly which brought on our "fall."

Platonism and Humanity's Penal Condition

One final comment on this sub-section: notice that Augustine's claim is *not* that he has come to believe, or even believe more firmly, in the Catholic account of our iniquity and fall. His claim is far more surprising; he might formerly have believed all this on the word of the Psalmist, or of Ambrose, but now, he is telling us, he came to "know" that it was true (*cognovi*). Through the correct application of his understanding, which he learned, evidently, by reflecting on these Platonic books, he has come to reasoned convictions on these issues. Moreover, these are by no means convictions which exalt the self-sufficiency of man—so frequently the jibe against the Platonists as Augustine, the recent convert, "must" have regarded them—but views which underline, if anything, the dark side of our human condition, and the guilt we must avow for bringing on that misery.

Truth, and Wisdom, Really Exist

Augustine will have much more to say, both about our "iniquity" and about the workings of the divine justice which resulted in our "fall"; for the moment, however, he circles back to the first of the series of convictions he gained from his reflections:

> . . . and I said: "Isn't Truth, then, not a nothing, because of its not being diffused through either finite or infinite local spaces?" and You cried to me from afar: "Perfectly true: 'I am Who am.'" And I heard, as one hears in the heart. . . .

To "hear" with the "heart" is equivalent, for Augustine, to "seeing" with the inner eye of the "mind" or understanding.[55] It would appear, then, that he is closing this first paragraph of his account with an insight of understanding. It turns out to be the same insight, at bottom, which he has already placed at the center of that account thus far: that Truth, meaning True spiritual being, is not some vacuous "nothing" because of its being inextended, un-diffused in space. Spatial spread-outness, corporeality, whether finite or infinite, simply is not a requisite for a being to be "real." And Augustine clearly understands that the God of Exodus, the God Who "Is," stands as guarantor of that insight.

> . . . and there was absolutely no further ground for doubting, [indeed] I would more easily doubt that I lived than that Truth did not exist [sic]—[that Truth] which is glimpsed "by [the eye of] understanding, through the things which have been made."

Augustine's Latin tumbles over itself in this closing sentence: he obviously wants to say that he could no longer doubt the existence of this incorporeal Truth; but there are so many negatives running about in the sentence that, in hopes of making his affirmation turn out positively, he puts in an extra *non*, and winds up saying he no longer doubted that Truth did *not* exist. Once that little snarl is untangled, however, what abruptly dawns on the reader is how remarkable an affirmation Augustine is making: he claims to be *more* certain that Truth exists (my capitalization here is quite deliberate) than that *he himself* exists!

His claim is vintage Platonism, so that we may fairly conjecture that Augustine's mind is moving this way: in order for the particular proposition "I exist" to be true, it must "share" or "participate" in Truth Itself; hence, the universal proposition "Truth exists" must be true. But the same thing must hold for any and every particular proposition that purports to be true: for any such particular proposition to be true, it must share in Truth Itself; hence, its truth entails that Truth Itself must exist.

Now go back to the proposition "I exist." That proposition is only "contingently" true. It is true as a matter of fact, but it need not be true; it could conceivably be untrue: the temporal universe could quite possibly run its course from its beginning to its ending without my ever coming into existence. But, Augustine's reasoning runs, if it be *de facto* true that "I exist," then it is necessarily true that Truth exists.

That same conclusion can be reached from another angle: even were the proposition "I exist" untrue, it would still be true that it was untrue; even for it to be untrue, therefore, Truth must necessarily exist. And this is what Augustine claims to have "seen": that "I exist" need not be true, but that "Truth exists" must necessarily be true.

But that explanation of his reasoning is purely abstract. As with his more generalized view of "understanding," however, there appears to be an imaged justification backing up that reasoning process. Unsurprisingly, the best approach to grasping that image is to start once again with the citation from Romans 1:20.

This is the first of four distinct times in this section that Augustine explicitly quotes this text. He will do so in paragraph 26, where he gives a condensed retrospective summary[56] of this entire section; he does so here, where it has a similar ring, very much resembling a summary-conclusion of paragraph 16. And he quotes it twice in paragraph 23, which describes, again, the only unquestionable "ascent of the mind" in this section of his *Confessions*. Take all these three paragraphs together, and it is significant that Augustine quotes this text each time he comes to speak of having glimpsed that "Light": it seems to represent, for him, a commentary-statement on what he *means* by saying he caught such a "glimpse" (*conspexi*).[57]

Augustine's interpretation of Romans 1:20, as we saw earlier, provides a luminous insight into how he "imagines" the workings of the "understanding": as an act of peering through a veil or scrim, or a cloud-cover, so that the "sunlight" of the divine Truth is "glimpsed," as it were, "through light-filled clouds" (*Acad* 1.3).[58] In every case, though, the "glimpse" is filtered, mediated, indirect; the luminous reality is glimpsed precisely as *inter-lecta*.

Now apply this image to the kind of "seeing" one does in the process of "understanding." Consider one of Augustine's own favorite examples: "seven plus three is ten." Notice that, as a mathematical proposition, it is the kind of necessary and universal "truth" on which the typical Platonist centers his interest. But how does one come to know it as true? The Platonist answers that, if you know clearly what the essence of "seven-ness" is, and the essence of "ten-ness," and what is meant by the operation expressed by the term "plus," then you must "see"—mentally, intellectually—you must "understand," that the sum of seven plus three is ten, *must* be ten, is *necessarily, unchangeably, eternally* ten; it could never possibly be otherwise, in any imaginable universe.[59]

But those properties make it an entirely different kind of truth from a contingent truth like "I exist." It would seem, in fact, to share somehow in the very unchangeability and eternity of Divine Truth. But how can this be? Augustine's imaged thinking seems to follow this path: "eternal" truths like those of mathematics exist in a higher realm of reality, in the spiritual region of the *Omnia* to which only intelligence can attain. There they are bathed in the Light of Divine Truth itself, which "charges" them, as it were, with God's own eternity, and so makes them luminous with a spiritual, intelligible luminosity.[60]

Consequently, when any particular intelligible truth becomes luminous to my mind, then I must be seeing that truth as bathed *in the Light of* Truth Itself. At this point Augustine seems tacitly to infer that seeing that a particular truth is immutably true is equivalent to seeing "through" that particular truth to the "background" Light of Immutable Truth Itself.

But at this juncture we must recall the distinction we saw earlier between "*a* light," meaning a light-*source*, and "light" (without the article, either definite or indefinite), meaning a light-*field* or luminous atmosphere: Augustine is evidently imagining those intelligible truths as bathed in the "field" of intelligible Light. He knows in a concomitant way, of course, that that field of luminosity must be emanating from the Divine light-source, but that light-source is not what he is focally attending to. The act of "knowing" he is depicting is focused precisely on the particular truth "I exist," and the universal truth "Truth exists," along with the necessary relationship disclosing itself as linking them. Also (in a peripheral, or perhaps subsequent, act of awareness) he realizes that all those three elements are being illumined by the Light-field of Eternal Truth.

Examine it patiently, therefore, and the logic of his imagery is unambiguous: Augustine is emphatically *not* claiming here that he caught a glimpse of God as Divine Light in the sense of Divine "Sun," *Source* of all intelligible Light.[61] On the contrary, he has glimpsed a Light-field *inter-lecta*, shining "between" and "through" the scrim of particular truths which Paul's "created realities" stand for in Augustine's mind. Hence, the translation I have proposed: the Light has been "glimpsed by [the eye of] understanding," the spiritual eye which can "read between" the lines of created realities to the presence of divinity behind them. Clearly, then, Augustine is not describing a direct and immediate mystical vision, but an insight of the understanding.[62]

Conclusion: A "Vision" of the Understanding Eye

Thus far, therefore, Augustine has told us that at Milan he had at last come to "see" that the spiritual realm that Ambrose discoursed about, and where the *Hortensius* had insinuated he might attain happiness, was not just vacuous dream-stuff. This was central among the certainties he had yearned for.

But notice that in order to buttress that central conviction, he had to come to a number of supporting convictions as well: among them, that there were higher and lower grades of reality; that this spiritual world was real, truly and unchangeably real, with a reality thrillingly "other, vastly other" from any sensible reality; that he himself had been confined to this lower "region of unlikeness" on account of some mysterious "iniquity" he had perpetrated.

In addition, he has also come to realize that he had reached that insight by means of an "eye above the eye" of his soul, the eye of reason raised to the power to *inter-legere*, to glimpse God's radiance by "reading through" the intervening screen of created realities. Yet however mediate and indirect that insight, it was the assurance he required that the God for whom he had "sighed, day and night," the heavenly food for which his soul had so long hungered, was real with a reality far superior to anything his mind, locked into spatial and corporeal categories of thinking, had previously been able to conceive of.

The title I offered earlier read: "I Came to See That Spirit Truly Existed." It was an attempt, more or less successful, at encapsulating the core-content of what Augustine was about to tell us. And yet, the moment one begins to unpack any single one of its terms, it becomes plain how skeletally spare any such summary turns out to be, when compared with the rich, complex, and highly sophisticated tapestry of supporting insights with which Augustine has embroidered it. The richness of that embroidery represents, I submit, a substantial difficulty for the proponents of the "narrative" view of this entire section. Let me state the difficulty, for now, in the form of a provisional suggestion: it would seem astonishing that anyone, however talented (and we know that Augustine could lay claim to that), yet possessed of only the slenderest professional acquaintance with the Platonic tradition in philosophy, could have put together so intricate a thought-construction inside of a month, or even a year, of his first exposure to Neoplatonism.

THE ABIDING OMNIPRESENT, AND "THE REST OF THINGS" (7.17)

At this point, Augustine opens a new chapter. The "chapter" divisions in the *Confessions*, indicated by small-capital Roman numerals, may not go back to the author's own composition,[63] but they do have an odd way of corresponding to natural sense-divisions of the text. So it is here. Augustine has finished telling us of his insight into the existence of spiritual reality, and of the precise kind of certainty it brought him. Now, in Chapter xi, paragraph 17, he shifts his focus to the changing visible world around him:

And I turned my regard to the rest of things, those below You, and I saw that they neither altogether exist nor altogether non-exist; indeed, they exist because they are from You, but non-exist because they are not what You are. For that alone truly exists which abides [*manet*] unchangeably. "But for me, it is good to cleave to [*inhaerere*] my God," for if I do not abide [*manebo*] in Him, I cannot even [abide] in myself. But He, "abiding in Himself [*in se manens*], makes all things new"; and "You are my Lord, because You have no need of my goods."

The first portion of this paragraph makes more explicit what we have already unfolded from the implicits in paragraph 16, above, the key insight being (again) that "true" existence belongs only to the unchangeable God. Hence, whatever is changeable—and this holds *de jure* for all "the rest" of beings "below" God—is (again) an amalgam of existence and non-existence. Insofar as they exist, changeable beings derive all their reality from the God Who alone "Is" and confers on them the share of "is-ness" which makes them distantly "like" Him. Conversely, insofar as they partially non-exist, they are unlike God.

But Augustine here introduces a key term which is worth our attending to, the Latin verb *manere*. Its root meaning is to "re-main," and Augustine regularly sees the term as implying that God (Who alone truly "remains") never stops "being," and never stops "being Himself," never stops being in absolutely every re-spect unchangeably the way He is. (For this reason, one of Au-gustine's favorite terms for God is the Psalmist's *Idipsum*: "the Selfsame").[64]

Different translations of the term *manere* are possible, not all of them equally reproducing the various shadings Augustine evokes by his use of the term. At this juncture, however, I promise the reader that out of all the possibilities—"remain," "endure," "per-sist" are some that could be used—I have elected to translate *man-ere* in its every occurrence by the single term "abide," and at the same time to restrict my use of "abide" to translating or evoking Augustine's use of *manere*. For "abide" seems to me, first of all, to catch the flavor of terms like remain, endure, persist; but it will also serve to reflect another, rather special metaphor which it is crucial to appreciate in order to understand Augustine's thought. I am referring to the second of Augustine's basic image-clusters, the one evoked by the term *peregrinatio* ("wayfaring") and its associations.[65]

One favorite meaning he has for "abide" we English-speakers can savor from the cognate term "abode," used as a noun.[66] A traveler (or "wayfarer," *peregrinus*), when asked about his "abode," will not (if he really understands the language) give the address of the inn or hotel he is "stopping at." For a traveler breaks his journey to "stop at" or "stop over" at some lodging, some "inn" or *stabulum*, which he looks upon as temporary. He does not intend to "abide" there, for he does not regard it as his "abode," his real *home*. This is roughly how, when Augustine is thinking of our human lives as a *peregrinatio*, a "wayfaring" experience, the term "abide" comes to suggest that one has arrived, is finally "at home," and need journey no farther. Nor should it come as a surprise that, fond of word-play as Augustine is, he takes a peculiar relish in the conviction that our soul's only true "abode" (*mansio*) is with the God Who truly "abides" (*manet*).

Further in the imaginative background, *manere* suggests still another image-cluster. For the wayfaring image is simply an anthropological instance of a broader cosmological law whereby bodies more generally are borne by their diverse "weights" to "seek" the appropriate "places" in the universe where they can find "rest." It is as though nothing could find the kind of contentment and happiness appropriate to it except in the place appointed for it to abide, "rest," "be at home."

For Augustine, accordingly, change and movement were essentially symptoms of restlessness and discontent. Humans, blessed (or cursed?) as they are with consciousness, experience this restless discontent in the form of misery and wretchedness. In the world of incessant change which we inhabit, we can never hold on to any scrap of happiness which flits momentarily into our grasp—like the golden hours Augustine shared with that dead friend of his youth, or like the flow of lovely syllables in poetry or song, our moments of bliss are forever escaping into the past. Augustine cannot think of change except as a melancholy reminder of the transiency, the fragility, of all human joys. So here, the thought of the unchanging God awakens the familiar motif of the "happy life," reminds him that nothing in his own life stands still, nothing in his experience "abides" and "rests" as God alone rests and abides. Only by "cleaving" to the Unchanging can he himself attain to unchange; only by abiding in the Ever-abiding God can he enjoy abiding rest. This alone is his "good."

The Omnipresent

But there is still another set of associations which Augustine triggers with the reminder that God "abides" unchangeably. For while suggesting that, unlike some of the angels and human souls He created, God does not "wander off" into wayfaring, does not go on *peregrinatio*, the term also expresses a profound metaphysical insight: that in order to be everywhere, God must "stay at home"; in order to make contact with created realities, He does not have to, indeed He must not, "come down."

One of the absolutely central insights Augustine gleaned from Neoplatonism was that God, and higher spiritual reality more generally, was not simply "present" to lower, corporeal realities, but "integrally omnipresent" to them. And central to Augustine's teaching on "integral omnipresence" was the insight that the spiritual being, and notably God, does not "come down," does not come "out of Himself" as it were, in order to be present to lower realities. This was also central to Plotinus' teaching on the same theme, and there are excellent reasons for thinking that Augustine learned much from Plotinus on this precise issue.[67] But admission of Plotinian dependence is not strictly required for translating Augustine's Latin when he speaks of omnipresence; it simply makes it easier to understand how he came, in time, to so sophisticated a grasp of this difficult insight.

For it was an insight which had caused him persistent difficulties right up to the time when he read the Platonist books. One of those difficulties stemmed from his tendency to think of God's omnipresence as requiring that He be "spread out" like a gigantic corporeal reality. Another erroneous stab at the problem consisted in thinking that God must be "poured out" into created realities as though they were so many "vessels" He somehow needed to "contain" or "support" Him. Both these misconceptions, moreover, shared the common flaw of assuming that God's omnipresence meant He must be "in" all created realities, as though making His "abode" in them. Further, they both imagined the spiritual as present in the way one bodily being is present to another bodily being: as though one were alongside and contiguous to the other, each of its several parts present to some corresponding part of the other. Now Augustine has come to realize that for God to be omnipresent to the world of creatures, He must be *integrally* omnipresent: present in the *totality* of His reality to each and every created being, and to each and every part of every created being. In order to be integrally present, God must be present "to" each one of those beings, and not be present "in" any of them.

But how are we to conceive of so paradoxical a relationship? To the end of his days, Augustine will propose the mind's capacity to think out the paradoxes of omnipresence as the test-case and proof that the mind is a spiritual substance (*Civ* 22.29). For the ability to grasp this insight was, for him, the essential piece of evidence that he himself had arrived at the ability to think of spiritual reality in appropriately spiritual terms.

If we turn back to the previous paragraph of his text, we can now detect traces of the three stages of thought-correction whereby Augustine, much as Plotinus had done before him, leads the mind to this difficult insight. As a first step, we must first imagine God's presence after the manner in which the sun, as light-source, precisely by remaining where it is, illumines each and every sunlit reality. Then, as a second step (since the sun is present to those beings by its power and effects but not strictly in its total reality), imagine the light of the sun as light-*source*, extending outward (as Plotinus suggested) to become a *field* of sun*light*, present to each and every being it illumines. Finally, in a third step, he will ask us entirely to eliminate the first-stage image of the sun as light-*source*, so that we are left with the light-*field* as omnipresent to all it illumines. And so we have come back, by another route, to imagining God (but merely as a first stage in striving to "understand"), not as a light-source, but as a limitless expanse, an atmospheric field of Light, in which all created realities bathe in order to exist at all!

Quite early in his writing career, Augustine came across the text from the Book of Wisdom (7:27) which gave Scriptural expression to what he had come to "know" through reflection on the Platonic books: by "abiding in Herself, she [Wisdom] renews all things." In order to "renew" creatures, that is, to be the ultimate cause of all novelty, of all change among changing realities, Divine Wisdom (which Augustine identified with God's creative Word, the Eternal Son) must "abide in Herself." But that implied that in order to be Omnipresent, God did not have to become present "in" them; indeed, He *must* not. Hence, He had no "need" to be "contained" or "supported" by them. And once again, encouraged by the Platonists as well as by the Psalmist, Augustine finds it a sign of God's utterly transcendent Lordship that He is beyond "need" of any "good" that His creatures could conceivably contribute to His well-being.

This omnipresence insight was doubly devastating to the Manichee conception of their divine principle. Not only did they begin with, they never went beyond, their uncorrected image of "God" as an expanse of light stretching limitlessly in three directions—the fourth being originally occupied by the opposing darkness. Then, when imagining how our souls, sparks of that divinity, came to be present in this evil underworld, they implied that the light was vulnerable to invasion and capture by the hordes of darkness; it was, therefore, changeable. That fundamental error in thinking about God led to two others: the Manichees thought of our souls as portions of the Light who "went out," who failed to "abide" in transcendent unchangeability; in consequence of that, the Manichees were logically compelled to think of the Light as "needing" inferior realities, in the sense that it needed to recuperate the portions of itself which were scattered among those beings, in order to regain the fullness of its own integrity.

Now Augustine has come to understand that he, along with us other human souls in "this" world, has gone on *peregrinatio* into this "region of unlikeness," but (something the Manichees refuse to "confess") in consequence of his own "iniquity." He knows now where his "good," his happiness, lies, and he longs to "cleave," *inhaerere*—literally, "stick to" his God, and so to be "eternalized" through that quasi-osmotic union with the Eternal. Once arrived at that goal, he will be able to stop his restless "wayfaring" and "abide in [him]self" in the only way possible: by resting in the "abiding" God Who has promised to be his eternal "abode."

Once again, we are confronted with an amazingly intricate skein of interconnections—metaphysical, cosmological, anthropological, religious—all tightly bound together in this compact paragraph. Are we to believe that Augustine was capable of forging so subtle and brilliant a systematic during the span of a few months after reading those "books of the Platonists"? Or perhaps the question would be better framed: Is there some way of finding out whether he did, in fact, accomplish that achievement in that short span of time? We shall have to return to that issue, when we have more evidence for dealing with it.

EVIL, "CORRUPTION," AND THE *OMNIA* (7:18–19)

Now, in Chapter xii, Augustine moves on to a second of the classic properties of reality. The Manichee stress on this precise problem obliges him to deal with the question "What is evil?" but he will first clarify that notion by relating it to its more fundamental correlative notion, "good." His analysis will lead him to conclude that evil is in every case what Aristotle termed a *"privatio"*— a "lack" of some ontological perfection that should be present in the being lacking it—but he begins his analysis by using the term "corruption" as a synonym for "privation." One reason for his doing so appears to be this: he has just finished making a veiled allusion to the Manichee notion of their god's vulnerability, or (in the term Augustine regularly uses in his polemic against them), their god's "corruptibility." That choice of term may well go back to the anti-Manichaean objection he attributes to his friend Nebridius, in Book 7.3 of his *Confessions*: Nebridius had argued that the Manichee story of the "invasion" of light by darkness entailed, in one way or another, that the Manichee divinity be "corruptible," that is, susceptible of being "changed to a worse condition . . . from happiness to misery." In any case, Augustine's earliest tilts against the Manichee conception of evil are couched in these terms (*Mor* 2.2–7); and so is his introduction to the discussion now:

> And it was made manifest to me that things that become corrupted are [nonetheless] good; they could not become corrupted if they were the highest goods, [nor could they become corrupted] if they were not goods at all. For if they were the highest of goods, they would be incorruptible; if, on the other hand, they were not goods at all, there would not be anything in them to be corrupted. For corruption does harm, and unless it diminished some good[-ness], it would do no harm. Therefore, either corruption does no harm, which cannot be [the case], or, what is most certain, all things that undergo corruption are deprived [privated] of [some] good.

Evil and Non-Being

Again, as with Nebridius' objection, Augustine's argument takes its start from the definition of "corruption." It was a definition which, he was persuaded, any right-thinking person, even a Manichee in his lucid moments, would accept. We moderns have to rinse our minds clear of all sorts of associations, from biological to ethical and political, in order to focus on the metaphysical purity of the term as Augustine intends it: corruption in its broadest generality means simply "harm," meaning "diminishment of good," which in turn means a "change to a worse condition." All these expressions, Augustine assumes we will agree, are perfectly interchangeable.

For clarity's sake, apply this notion first to the lowest rung on the being-ladder, then push the application upward. Even the lowest or "least good" of realities must possess *some* measure of goodness if that goodness is to be "diminished" and the reality in question "harmed," "corrupted." There must be some measure of "goodness" attached to its condition if it is to be "changed to a worse condition." At the asymptotic limit, a reality that possessed no good properties at all would not even possess existence; it would be a non-reality to which no predicate, not even the predicate "evil," could possibly apply!

Running up to the higher ranges of the being-scale, we have already seen that God, the "Highest" of beings, must be absolutely unchangeable, hence, absolutely incapable of being "changed to a worse condition"; He is, therefore, absolutely incorruptible. Between the lowest and the Highest, we have the intermediate types of beings which range, so to speak, from lower goods to middling goods to higher goods: these are all susceptible of being corrupted, but precisely insofar as they all possess some measure of goodness.

Having clarified that much, Augustine refreshes our minds on the implications of the definition of evil: corruption must do harm, must entail a "privation" of some good. With that phrase he has also bridged the terminological gap between evil as "corruption" and evil as "privation." As he pushes his analysis further, he will employ the term "privation" interchangeably with the term "corruption." To keep the reader reminded of its technical Aristotelian sense, I shall do the same, concocting the verb forms "private" and "privated" for the purpose.

But were [the beings the Manichees consider to be evil] to be privated of all good, they would altogether non-exist.

With this assertion Augustine accomplishes the final refutation of the Manichee conception of evil: they would have it that "evil" is so utterly evil as to be lacking in any good property whatever. But, concludes Augustine, pursuing the same logic as we analyzed above, that would mean that evil lacked even the "good" property of existing, which makes complete nonsense of their position.

At this point Augustine's argumentation seems to unravel somewhat. He appears to lose confidence in the *reductio ad absurdum* he has achieved with his last assertion. Perhaps it seemed to him too brisk, or bloodlessly abstract; in any case, he evidently feels the need to try another tack. The argumentative line he is about to follow does not entirely cohere with the neat logic of the position he has already developed, but perhaps the best way of making sense of it is to recall in more concrete terms how the Manichees conceived of the evil "race of darkness."

They described that "race" as a teeming, smoky, stinking, howling *Walpurgisnacht*, a strident and maddening nightmare surpassing any of Hieronymus Bosch's most grotesque creations. They strained their imaginations, in other words, to portray evil as *positively* repulsive, *positively* ugly. But that, Augustine reasons, is what defeated them in the end: by endowing evil with such positivity, by depicting it as a substantial reality, they turned the "race of darkness," ironically, into a kind of "good." For the least that could be said of any of its denizens is this: it possessed the "good" of existing, and of being endowed with some "form" or other. However ugly *we* may consider any particular form to be, it does at least this much "good" for the being endowed with it: it holds its matter together in the unity of a single being.[68]

Yet the Manichees would obviously wish that evil could be utterly defeated, stamped out of existence entirely. But that, we watched Augustine argue up to this point, would mean that the race of darkness would be "deprived of all good," even the good of existing at all. Now, apparently having momentarily lost confidence in that last proposition, he feels the need either to buttress it with, or to transform it into, a dilemma:

For if they [evils] existed and could no longer undergo corruption, they would be better [than now] for they would abide incorruptibly. And what is more monstrous than to say that things, by losing all their good[ness], would [thereby] be made better?

Augustine is here hypothesizing that the Manichees' wish to eliminate evil has been realized; in that case, one of two things would follow. Either the race of darkness would still exist, or (as he has already argued above) it would no longer exist. But in either case, the Manichee position collapses. For if evils still retained some measure of existence, while at the same time the Manichee wish to eliminate evil were successful, then stripping them of all corruption and (Augustine now adds) of all corruptibility would have the ironic reverse effect of making those evils "better" than they were before; if made incorruptible and yet left in existence, they would then "endure incorruptibly" (*incorruptibiliter permanebunt*), just like God Himself! But if the Manichees choose the other horn of Augustine's dilemma, and concede that stripping evils of all corruption would reduce them to nonexistence, they would find themselves equally impaled: for what more "monstrous" assertion could be dreamt of than this, that things would be "made better" by "losing all their good[ness]," that is, by being reduced to non-existence?

There is something distressingly maladroit about this argumentative parenthesis. For a parenthesis is exactly what it appears to be: in the very next sentence Augustine is comfortably back on the track he was pursuing earlier; in fact, he takes up so smoothly from where he left off two sentences before that one suspects we have just finished examining a later, and none too coherent, insertion. In any event, he now goes on to argue:

Evil as Non-Existence

> Hence, if [evils] were to be privated of all good, they would be absolutely non-existent; therefore, as long as they exist, they are good. Whatever things exist, accordingly, are good, and that "evil" about which I sought "whence" it could be is not a substance, because if it were a substance it would be [a] good. For either it would be an incorruptible substance, hence, a great good indeed, or it would be a corruptible substance, which could not undergo corruption were it not a good.

The bulk of Augustine's argumentation here is virtually a repetition of what we saw earlier: if everything that exists has at least the "good" of existing, then all that exists is good insofar as it exists. "Evil," therefore, cannot be a positive reality, much less the "substantial" kind of positive reality the Manichees claimed it was. For (ranging substances on the ladder of realities, again) whether corruptible or incorruptible, all substances must exist, and therefore be good.

But these two sentences also contain one small sign of things to come. Augustine has quietly introduced the distinction between those two related questions: "Whence" is evil, and "what" is evil. His early anti-Manichaean writings show the importance he attributed to that distinction: it entitled him to charge the Manichees with the methodological blunder of venturing an answer to the "whence" question before they had gotten to a satisfying answer on the prior question, "what" is evil (*Mor* 2.2). But coupled with his passing mention of "iniquity" in paragraph 16, this is another hint that he is aware of his own obligations in the matter; when the time comes, he must furnish a satisfactory answer to the "Whence comes evil?" question.

The Omnia

But before that time comes, he still has further work to do in clarifying "what" evil is. It induces him now to unfold the crucial insight that lies at the heart of the cosmic image we traced above, the *Omnia*:

> Thus I saw, and it was made manifest to me, that it was You Who made "all things" [to be] good, and that there was no substance whatever that You did not make. And because You did not make all things to be equal, for that reason do "all things" exist, because each individual thing is good, and at the same time "all things" are very good, because our God made "all things" to be "very good."

In composing this paragraph (7.xii.18), Augustine seems to have expected his readers to recall that in the account of the six days of creation in the Book of Genesis God "sees" the result of His creative activity after each individual day, and each time sees it as "good"; *singula bona sunt*, Augustine puts it. But on the final day, He looks upon the "all things" He has created, and sees that in their entirety they are "very good": *fecit Deus noster omnia bona valde.*

But what would a Manichee think of that account? The answer

is, much the same as any Gnostic would, including those earlier
Gnostics against whom Plotinus in his time mounted so fierce a
campaign to justify the beauty, and the very existence, of the
lower, visible world.[69] The Manichees thought it a positive scan-
dal that Catholics approved of the Jewish notion of One God Who
was creator, not only of the higher invisible world, but of the
lower visible world as well—*creator visibilium et invisibilium*, as the
Nicene Creed expressed it. For that lower world was, they
claimed, the prison in which the anti-God, Matter, held our divine
souls captive; whatever traces of order or beauty it displayed were
the result of the Light-God's struggle to release and recuperate
those souls. Strictly speaking, though, the Manichees were convinced that the visible world ought never to have existed.

Observe, once again, that Augustine is not proclaiming here
that he came to *believe* what Catholics believed about the goodness
of the visible world. "I saw, and it was made manifest to me," he
assures us (*vidi et manifestatum est mihi*). He is talking the language
of understanding, of certainty, and of a certainty that he attributes, once again, to his reflections on those Platonist books.
What is more, the emphasis implied by his use of that doubled
term should not be overlooked: not only did he "see," but it was
"made manifest" to him. We shall come to see that, given the
nature of the insight in question, that emphasis is well worth
pondering. At very least, it indicates the importance Augustine
accorded to this *Omnia* insight.

But now to the structure of the *Omnia* insight: Augustine reminds us again that each individual reality God created is "good,"
but that the *simul omnia*, the "all things" taken together, in a single
sweeping glance, as it were, that *omnia* is "very good." But Augustine also gives us the reason why it is such an *omnia*: *quoniam
non aequalia omnia fecisti*, because God did not make everything
equal. Instead of complaining, as the Manichees did, that God
should never have created the inferior realities of the visible world,
Augustine has come to "see" that it is not simply "good," but
"very good," that God create an array of creatures running from
higher to middling to lower and even lowest. And his reasoning
is authentically Platonic, and substantially the same as Plotinus'
reasoning against his Gnostic adversaries: it is more eloquent evidence of the divine fecundity to produce not only the higher intelligible realm, but also the lower, sensible world that is its image.[70]

For the result is the ordered splendor we now behold: a hierarchical cascade of variegated forms whose rich diversity and gradations in beauty contribute to the poetry of the whole.

It is highly significant that this *Omnia* insight furnished Augustine with a justification for the existence of the lower, visible world which was far more positive in tone than the one which Origen had proposed a century earlier. For Origen, as Augustine was to learn some years after having completed his *Confessions*, thought that God must have created the visible world subsequent to the sin of angels and of human souls, so that they could expiate their celestial transgression in a bodily "prison" perfectly appropriate to the gravity of their sin. That as a motive for God's having created this lower world Augustine will find flatly unacceptable.[71]

An Aesthetic Judgment

But notice that Augustine's reasoning on this score is fundamentally aesthetic in nature: his argument appeals to the beauty of a hierarchically ordered variety of created forms. Only a world of the most consummate possible beauty would be worthy of the Creator. There is little difficulty in recognizing the central insight from his own early treatise on aesthetics, in the way he traces the cosmic picture in paragraph 7.xiii.19:

> And for You [God], evil in no way exists. Not only [is this true] for You, but also for the universe which You have created. For there is not anything outside of You that could break in and corrupt the order You have imposed on it.
>
> Among its parts, certain things are thought to be evil because they do not go well with certain other things; but those very things [which are thought to be evil] do go well with other things and are [in that sense] good; and [furthermore] they are good in themselves.
>
> And all these things which do not go well with each other nonetheless befit the lower part of reality which we call "earth," [an earth] having its own cloudy and windy heaven congruent to it[self].

I have divided Augustine's longish paragraph into three sections representing distinguishable sense-units. In the first of these sections, he is recalling the (more or less Stoic) cosmic image he had been experimenting with earlier (7.7); in it, God was envisaged after the fashion of an infinite sea surrounding and penetrating the created universe as water would penetrate a sponge. In terms of that image, Augustine had asked where evil could have come from. Could it have "slipped in" somehow from outside the universe so pictured? Now, he has come to realize, his re-formed conception of the ordered *Omnia*, along with the insight that evil is not a positive reality, relieves him of the need to picture some paradoxical nothing-something as though starting from "outside" the universe of being, and "breaking into" that universe to "corrupt" its order.

In the second of these sections, Augustine sets out to apply the central distinction which was the pivot of his *De pulchro et apto*. When we say that something is "good," we often mean that it is good-*for* some other being, *aptum*, that it "fits" or "suits," "goes together with" it, as a shoe "fits" the foot, or fair weather is favorable to the human constitution. *Convenit* is the word Augustine uses here (I have translated it as "goes well with"); the idea is the same as he had come to in that early publication. However, things can also be "good in themselves" (*in semetipsis bona*), good with a kind of "goodness" for which Augustine earlier reserved the term "beautiful," *pulchrum*.

Now Augustine goes on to make a breathtaking claim: everything in the visible universe, he tells us, "goes well with" *something* else in that visible universe; it may not suit me, or my brother, or my pet alligator, but even the male scorpion, *pace* the Manichees, "goes well with" its female counterpart. And likewise everything in that visible universe is "good in itself," "beautiful." Cleanse your mind for a moment, Augustine asks his reader, of the self-concern that makes you ask only if the mosquito "goes well with" *you* and your comfort; assume the attitude of detached objectivity which is the properly aesthetic attitude, and for once *behold* the mosquito: what a marvel of exquisite symmetry and design, how "beautiful" it turns out to be!

But, one might object, there are so many things in this lower, visible world which "do not go well with" so many other things! Augustine seems to have some such objection in view in the last of these three sections. He replies that they all fit together with "earth" itself, by which he makes it clear that he means the lower world. They all "belong" here, all have their place. Whereas, the implication seems to be, they would be "out of place" in the higher, spiritual world.

His Own Earlier View

Augustine now goes on to make a critical admission: he acknowledges that he formerly regarded the realities of this lower world (*ista*: the term denotes depreciation) exactly as a Manichee would; if he had had his wish, they would not even exist:

> Far be it from me any longer [*iam*] to say, "these [lower] things ought not to exist," for even if I beheld only them, I might indeed yearn for better things; but even for these [lower things] alone, I ought still to praise You, because [all of them] show forth that "from the earth" You are to be praised. . . .

That depreciatory evaluation must not have been a matter of how Augustine thought about material realities merely, but of how he felt about them, as well. It would seem, moreover, that not all of those negative feelings had been neutralized by the time he wrote his *Confessions*, for the very way he expresses himself hints at a lingering ambiguity: even if all he could behold of God's creation were these visible, corporeal realities, he ought still to praise God—and yet, and yet, he "might indeed yearn for better things" than they, might still feel the thorn of discontent with living among "these," *ista*, and yearn to dwell in the higher, spiritual world instead.

What Augustine does now is simply quote ten verses from Psalm 148 (which I need not reproduce here). It is a psalm which enumerates an entire panoply of creatures, exulting in the "praise" their very being gives to God. Augustine himself calls attention to the fact that verses 7 to 12 (which he quotes first) catalogue the various creatures—from dragons and trees to princes and judges—who praise God "from the earth," while verses 1 to 5 list the creatures—like angels and stars, sun and moon—whose praise comes "from the heavens." Augustine has successfully insinuated that the Psalmist himself would second his image of the *Omnia*, composed of beings "visible and invisible," reaching from the lower world of "earth" to the higher world of "heaven," even as high as the *caeli caelorum*, the "heavens of heavens." Augustine ends with an expression of his current attitude toward the two realms which the universe as he sees it comprises:

> No longer did I yearn for better things, because [now] I thought
> [in terms of] "all things," and with a saner judgment esteemed
> better things higher [or: superior] to lower things, of course, but
> "all things" as better than those higher things alone [7.xiii.19].

This assertion, if accepted without question, would initially
seem to cancel out the "hint" we saw Augustine drop just above,
about his "yearning" for the "better things" of the higher world.
In dropping that hint, he had hypothesized (in the contrary-to-
fact mode) that the "lower" world *could* have been all he could
see (*cernerem*); on that hypothesis he *would* still have yearned for
"better" things (*desiderarem quidem meliora*). Now the subjunctive
mood has vanished, and everything is expressed in the indicative:
he has "seen" that an *Omnia* of both higher and lower worlds
exists, and (in consequence?) he no longer "yearns," in fact, for
those "better things."

But it is not easy to understand why the addition of a higher
world to his vision of the cosmos would *eliminate* all yearning for
that higher world. It would appear far more plausible, psychologically, that his present knowledge that a higher world existed
would precisely stimulate a yearning for it, whereas his former
state of ignorance about that higher world would have left him
undistracted by any such yearning, readier to "accept the universe" in the incomplete version he had come to behold as simply
the only universe that existed.

Or, is Augustine being even subtler here than we might imagine? Is he anticipating a topic he means to introduce shortly, and
archly suggesting that our dim "memory" of the higher world
would have prodded us into a dumb feeling, at least, an obscure
suspicion, that any version of the universe which omitted a higher
world was an "incomplete" version? If so, he could be insinuating
that our mute, uncomprehending sense of its incompleteness
would stab like a thorn of discontent, promoting the "yearning"
he claims he *would have* felt. In that case, he would be consistent
in insinuating that his arrival at a more satisfying vision of the
cosmos as an *Omnia* had a pacifying effect; it assured him that
"everything was all right after all," that there was no fundamental
reason for being discontented or plaintive about the human situation, that things "were in place" and would work out if given
time.

But if that was Augustine's intention, why does he say that, even while entertaining that incomplete version of the universe, he would have been obliged to praise God for as much as he had managed to see? And again, if that was his intention, one would have to admit that he was being far too subtle for the majority of his readers.

Perhaps the safest course is to fall back on what one senses from habitual acquaintance with the man: Augustine seems always to have felt "out of place," never truly "at home" in the world he frequently labels *inferi*, the "lower regions" or "under-world" (*Mor* 1.3, *Mus* 6.8, *Conf* 3.)[72] More than one translator has been tricked by that nomenclature, and rendered it as "hell." In the words of the ancient wheeze, though, those translators may have been incorrect, but they may also have been right; Augustine's mind may furnish the words while his heart composes the melody, but they are not always collaborating on the same song. Despite what he tells us here, his persistent yearning for the higher world is a matter of record.

A final observation before moving on: in telling us of the conviction he has come to—that an *Omnia* was better than a universe consisting only of a "higher" world—Augustine claims he came to it by a "saner judgment" (*saniore judicio*). Judgment: Augustine uses that term uniformly to connote an evaluative assertion, normally ethical or aesthetic in nature;[73] we shall see him discuss that kind of intellectual performance just a few paragraphs further on. But what does he mean by the term *sanus* in that connection? Literally, the term means "healthy," so that the translation which readily suggests iself would be "healthy-minded" as opposed to "sick-minded," or, as I have written, "sane" as opposed to "mad" or "insane." "Sound judgment" would do in a pinch, but it loses too much of the sick-*vs.*-healthy association Augustine means to evoke: subsequent paragraphs in this section will confirm that view. We would not trust the judgment of a sick man, Augustine will remind us, on how tasty his food was; a sick man's judgment in such matters is too liable to be a sick judgment, just as a madman's judgment is likely to be insane.

But now, notice what Augustine's use of such terms implies about the way we make one of the most radical and basic decisions of our intellectual, ethical, and religious lives. When it comes to how we decide whether the universe as a whole is "good" or "evil," Augustine thinks, we make that evaluation in either a "sick" or a "healthy" fashion, either more or less "sanely." It is significant that some time later, when he is first informed of Origen's view that God created the visible world as an assemblage of prisons for fallen souls, Augustine will want to reject it in the most condemnatory terms he can find; but the strongest language he can honestly employ is that Origen's theory offended against Christian "sanity." We shall see more of this shortly, but it seems good to point out in passing that, for Augustine, "judgments" of this breadth and universality seem to depend for their validity less on clarity or firmness of evidence than on the healthy-mindedness of the person judging.

Perhaps this hint of subjectivity explains what we noted above, that Augustine feels obliged to emphasize both that he "saw" and that it was "made manifest" to him that an *Omnia* of unequals was "very good" (18), when that evaluation is plainly the product of aesthetic "judgment." In making that double claim, could he have been "protesting too much"? We must not altogether forget that question as we go further.

A Question: Mystical Narrative or Religious World-View?

The two chapters we have just finished studying raise the question once again: What is the nature of the account Augustine is giving us? Had he stopped after composing the first chapter (x) of this section, there might have been some justification for thinking he is narrating an experience, and of an intensely religious, if not a quasi-mystical, sort. Chapter xi could conceivably be read as confirmation of that view: when discoursing, especially in his preaching, about the mind's ability to think of God as Omnipresent, Augustine frequently rises to a pitch of religious enthusiasm which borders on the mystical or quasi-mystical.

Yet, to put the argument on a purely quantitative level for the moment: after some forty-one lines of text devoted to what a generous interpretation might concede was the topic of "vision," we have now seen him devote fifty-five lines of text to the topic of good and evil—and he is far from done with the matter. Those who argue for the narrative–mystical interpretation of this entire section regularly lift out and focus upon a mere three chapters of Augustine's account, and tacitly ask us to think of the remainder as incidental window-dressing. And yet, that "remainder" is, in quantitative terms, far too extensive to be fairly counted as mere remainder. And, far more to the point, if we examine the matters Augustine deals with in the non-mystical portions of this account, and weigh them in the light of the importance he felt obliged to accord them in his early writings, the problem of evil and of its consequences immediately asserts itself as claiming as much of his attention as the ascent to vision does (or more of it), or even (for all of its unquestioned importance) the breakthrough to a spiritual mode of understanding.

A second and related question suggests itself as well. Are we, again, to understand Augustine as telling us that he came to all these insights during those months at Milan, and possibly at Cassiciacum? We shall come to see that the *Omnia* insight, with all its rich implicits, is particularly interesting in this connection: interesting, and revelatory.

A Brush with "Insanity" and a Healing Insight (7.xiv.20)

At this juncture in his account, Augustine does launch into a parenthesis which is indubitably narrative and autobiographical, but instead of focusing on something that happened in A.D. 386, it has to do with a time well before his Milanese experience:

> "There is no sanity" in them, to whom anything in Your creation is displeasing, just as [there was no sanity] in me when many things that You had made displeased me. And since my soul dared not have my God be displeasing to it, it refused [to regard] as Yours whatever displeased it [7.xiv.20].

Non est sanitas: "There is no health." Or, does Augustine really mean "sanity"? Unfortunately, there is little to be gained from examining *Enarratio 37*, on the psalm from which this phrase is drawn, for there Augustine travels down an exegetical path quite different from the one that might illumine his use of that psalm verse here. But what Augustine goes on to say makes it clear that he is referring to sanity of mind or (as he would put it) of heart—or, even more precisely, to sanity of "judgment." For it is an evaluative judgment that is being made by the people, the Manichees obviously among them, whom Augustine is condemning. They have looked at various of the creatures in the visible world about them and found them "displeasing." Their sense of propriety, by which Augustine earlier indicated that he means a sense of religious piety (5.20), forbids their attributing those "displeasing" realities to the creative activity of an all-good God.

At this point it becomes evident that the term *displicere* is being used in a very robust sense. A "displeasing" reality in the meaning Augustine implies here must be more than merely distasteful or annoying; there must be something reprehensible about it, something that would make a person of developed moral sense want to "have nothing to do with it," least of all admit to responsibility for having brought it into being. Augustine would not have "dared" accuse his God of having made these things! In a word, "displeasing" in this context means nothing short of "evil." And since Augustine feels he has already proven that there is no such thing as real "evil" in God's universe, there must be nothing in that universe which a person of sane judgment should find valid reason to complain about. And yet, he admits, there was a time when he thought differently, and consequently decided that the realities he regarded as evils could not have been created by the same one God Who created the good:

> And thence [my soul] strayed into the [Manichee] opinion of two substances, and found no rest in it, and uttered madness.

The dualistic world-image of the Manichees appealed to him for a while as more satisfying than the Catholic way of resolving the problem of evil, but that satisfaction did not last. It turned out to be only a transitional stop on Augustine's journey toward understanding. Like a place where a moving body has temporarily paused, but which is not the natural "place" befitting its "weight," this world-view was one in which he could find no "rest"; he could not feel comfortably "at home" with Manichee teaching. His allegiance to Manichaeism, he tells us, resulted in his talking what he calls *aliena*. The term *aliena* has puzzled translators: Ryan gives "the errors of other men," while Tréhorel and Bouissou have him saying he "talked a foreign language." "Nonsense," the version which Bourke has proposed and I was tempted to reproduce here, seems to me too bland to fit Augustine's intention.[74] I suggest that he meant to tell us that he now realizes he was talking "madness."

My reasons for that suggestion are several: Augustine has been ringing variations on the theme of "insanity" for several paragraphs now; he has opened this particular section by admitting that there was no "sanity" in him, by which he obviously means a mental rather than a physical condition; moreover, when a person is "insane," he is an "alien" in the sense of "not himself," and we used to say that he ought to consult an "alienist," a specialist in mental disorders. So, the *Oxford Latin Dictionary* lists for *alienus*, albeit as its twelfth meaning, the synonyms "mentally disturbed, upset, frenzied." But, finally, Augustine will shortly remind us that even a person who is physically sick, with a fever, say, will judge perfectly good bread to be flat and tasteless, while the sunlight that delighted him when he was well now becomes an intolerable annoyance. In short, people who are physically "unhealthy" often become a touch "mental" as well. Like the Manichees, they become unreasonably querulous, lose all sense of proportion; they "talk crazy."

The Heart's New Idol

But that Manichee phase eventually came to an end; meanwhile, though, Augustine's wayfaring progress toward understanding made what was to be its final detour:

> And abandoning [that Manichee opinion] it fashioned itself a god [diffused] through the infinite spaces of all places, and thought that god was You, and set it up in its heart, and was once again made the temple of its own idol, an abomination to You.

This is a condensed version of the world-image Augustine was entertaining (7.7) shortly before reading the Platonists. It has all the earmarks of Stoic materialism,[75] God being imaged as a spatialized, an essentially corporeal reality, even if His body is of a tenuous and highly refined sort. But in any event, by using the expression *idolum in corde* Augustine is telling us that he has excogitated one more false idea of, a phantasm or *simulacrum* of, God (*SS 34* 3, *113* 2, *213* 7; *En 128* 8; *InJo 40* 4).

THE COMPLAINER RECONCILED

But God has been working steadily and patiently on Augustine's soul to convert him—literally, to "turn him around." That work of Divine Care is about to bear fruit. Augustine now describes that moment of fruition in an explosion of poetic imagery:

> *Sed posteaquam fovisti caput nescientis, et clausisti oculos meos ne viderent vanitatem, cessavi de me paululum, et consopita est insania mea, et evigilavi in Te, et vidi Te infinitum aliter, et visus iste non a carne trahebatur.*

> But after You warmed [my] unknowing head, and closed "my eyes lest they behold vanity," I let go of my self[-reliance] a little bit, and my madness was lulled to sleep, and I awoke in You and saw that You were infinite in a different way, and that [way of] seeing did not derive from the flesh [7.xiv.20].

Fovisti caput nescientis: for the very first time in his *Confessions*, Augustine resorts here to the Latin word that invariably releases, for him, a fireworks of imaginative associations. Along with the *Omnia* image which has been recurring repeatedly in this central section, and with the image of the *peregrinatio animi*, the "wayfaring soul," the image-cluster which is triggered by that single term *fovere* has to rank no lower than third among Augustine's fundamental, and most cherished, metaphors.[76]

Briefly, the root meaning of the term is to "warm"; but "warming" can take so many forms and apply to so many different agencies of warming! Augustine tends to be partial to those applications of the term which feature agents and processes suggesting "care": the care a mother-bird expends in protecting and fledging her chicks, the tender care a human mother or wet-nurse lavishes on a plaintive infant, the often pain-inflicting care a doctor or surgeon brings to fomenting or cauterizing a wound or swelling, the sometimes gruff and masculine care a father brings to disciplining a wayward son. Read the *Confessions* attentively, with only those four images of "care" in mind, and the power of Augustine's achievement at this central moment of his story will seem almost incredible.

Touch after touch, like a master-*pointilliste*, he has peopled his readers' subconscious with images of mothers, nurses, and squalling infants, doctors, surgeons, and their suffering, complaining patients, mother-birds and their fledglings eager to leave the nest, fathers and their wayward sons. This is how God treats all of us; these are the ways in which he treated Augustine. Since the opening of the great "fugue" which runs from Book 4.1 to Book 5.2,[77] and evokes virtually all these images one after another, two of these many images have emerged into dominance: the relatively masculine image of God applying the "medicine" of growing faith and purifying suffering to the swollen eyes of Augustine's soul, and the far more tender image of that same God's maternal "care" for her feverish, plaintive infant. Both of those species of "care" Augustine can express with the term *fovere*, and when he suddenly and for the very first time employs the term here, those two seemingly opposed kinds of "care" collide with explosive suggestibility: the God Who so often acted like a chastising father, or like an unrelenting wielder of the cruel surgical knife, that same God is as tender as a mother who takes her child up in her arms, draws it to her breast, caresses and comforts and consoles. . . .

The Complainer Healed

Fovisti caput nescientis: observe, first, how this whole series of terms applies to the God Who has been expending His "medicinal" care on his sickly patient. Augustine has repeatedly admitted to being a *nesciens*: he came to Milan, to Ambrose, secretly prodded by God, but unbeknownst to him, *nesciens*; and all of this so that Ambrose might lead him, *sciens* at last, to God (5.23). But his "head" is still "swollen" by the *tumor* of sinful pride, a swelling which has sealed his soul's eye shut; it prevents him from the kind of "seeing," the genuine "understanding," which would make him a "knower" (7.i.11).

Meanwhile, God keeps applying the fomenting *collyrium* of faith and cauterizing suffering (7.12); the mother of Augustine's child is ripped from his side in a final act of divine surgery which leaves him bleeding (6.25); and, slowly, Augustine grows in the faith which will eventually strengthen the intellectual eyesight his soul-sickness has rendered "infirm." But he grows, as well, in humble acceptance of the purifying sufferings which would formerly have made him squall like an angry, petulant infant who had not the slightest idea—*nesciens*—why life was treating him so cruelly.

Augustine has come to admit that he is sick, and that, like almost any "patient," he is a *nesciens* who does not know as much about medicine as his doctor does. He must acknowledge his utter helplessness, entrust himself unreservedly to his doctor's "care," and so "cast all [his] cares" on the wisdom and goodness of the one who has consented to "take up" his case.

And so the doctor-God takes up the care of the swollen head and tumid eyelids of his unknowing patient (*fovisti caput nescientis*); the patient closes his eyes in restful confidence (*clausisti oculos meos*); he is no longer tormented by the worries which so distracted him: he has handed those over to his doctor (*ne viderent vanitatem*). He has resigned himself, now, to the fact that he cannot heal himself (*cessavi de me*), he has put a stop to his unreasonable complaints (*consopita est insania mea*), and drifts off now into a blessèd convalescent slumber.

Clues from a Rehearsal

But, somewhat like a variation on *Rashomon*, one where the identical script can be played over again with a different set of characters, Augustine's scenario serves equally well, if not better, for telling the story of a mother and her infant child. It will come as no surprise that in this scenario Monica frequently stands in for mother-church, and for the maternal side of God, as well. From Book 1 forward, page after page speaks of milky food drawn from maternal breasts, of mother-birds caring for their young, of Augustine ignoring, rejecting, and eventually fleeing the obstinate care of his own mother, Monica. But the most striking orchestration of the theme occurs in the fugal sequence already mentioned, which Augustine develops from the opening paragraph of Book 4 to the second paragraph of Book 5. That entire passage represents an almost deliberate rehearsal, theme by theme, of what Augustine has expressed in far more compressed fashion here, at the very heart of Book 7.

Augustine brings that fugue to its climactic coda by artfully suggesting the image of a petulant, wayward child who has squirmed out of his mother's protective caresses and run off to play with bigger, rougher companions. His puerile audacity is rewarded by knocks and scrapes and the derision of the big boys; now, squalling his resentment, yet still casting jealous glances back toward the world which still seems so fascinating though it has dealt with him so cruelly, back he trips to the mother who awaits the return of her tiny prodigal. At the very last moment, a pang of doubt seizes the little lad: will she receive him back? And if so, how? She has every right to be angry with him. . . .

To his amazement, his mother reaches down fondly, takes him

gently onto her lap, clucking and cooing endearments and reassurances; tenderly she strokes his head and turns it against her breast (*fovisti caput nescientis*); she closes his eyes to keep him from looking back toward his former playmates (*clausisti oculos meos ne viderent vanitatem*); she continues to stroke and caress, and now she suckles him; the angry tensions of his infant limbs soften and relax (*cessavi de me*); in time his querulous squalling is stilled (*consopita est insania mea*), and he sinks peacefully into sleep.

When it comes to understanding the feminine, maternal version of this moving scene of "return," it seems to me that we can do nothing better than turn to the first two paragraphs of the fifth book of his *Confessions*, where Augustine anticipated this conversion scene, and thereby inserted in our memories what I take to be the *interpretatio authentica* of what he hopes we would see in it. Notice how the "unjust" sinner of the beginning is gradually transformed into a weary, fretful infant, tearfully returning to the mother whose care has pursued him everywhere:

> Let my soul praise You [along with] every spiritual being that has its mouth turned back to You . . . so that our soul may arise to You from its weariness . . . and there [find] refreshment and true strength. . . . [Sinners] have fled from You . . . and in their blindness have hurtled up against You. . . . it is against You that the unjust have hurtled and justly been tormented, for they have set themselves far from Your gentleness and hurtled against Your righteousness and fallen athwart. Your severity. . . .
>
> Let them be turned around, then, and seek for You, for You have not deserted Your creature as Your creature deserted You. Let them turn back and seek for You, and see! there You are in their very hearts, in the hearts of those who confess to You and toss themselves upon You and wail on Your lap after all their rugged ways. And tenderly You wipe their tears away, until they wail even louder now, but with tears of rejoicing, because You, Lord, You, not some man, not flesh and blood, but You Lord, their maker, remake and console them [5.1–2].

The convert has drifted off to sleep. As Plotinus advised in that treatise *On Beauty* which keeps popping up throughout the *Confessions*, he has closed his eyes to the ordinary way of seeing, in hopes of opening them upon another kind of vision (*Ennead* 1.6.8): a vision perhaps like the one the slumbering Ulysses thrilled to when he awoke at last on the Ithacan shore and gazed on what the Platonist interpreters explained was the "home" of the wandering soul, the intelligible world (*Vita* 4–5).[78] In any case, anticipating the image of sleeping and waking which will vitally concern us further on, *Evigilavi in Te*, Augustine says: "I awoke in You." "In You": this was a vision, "not derived from the flesh." Augustine means that last qualification to be understood on two levels: first, the vision was not "fleshly," in the sense of being accomplished through our everyday manner of seeing, with the eyes of our mortal bodies. This is the same point he has made several times already: he has finally achieved the breakthrough toward a superior way of seeing higher reality, of seeing that God is "infinite," but *aliter*, in a radically different way—as a spiritual Immensity which is at the same time integrally omnipresent. But on a second level, he also hopes we will understand that it was a God-given kind of vision, one that mortal man could never hope to attain by virtue of his purely human powers; it required that the seer give up his frantic striving, "let go," *cessare de se*, and allow God to "lift" him up in order to see.

This time he will encase that message in another image of uncommon power.

The All-Holding Truth-Hand (7.xv.21)

> And I looked back on things other [than You] and saw that they owe it to You that they exist, and that all finite things are in You, but in a different manner, not as though in some place, but because You are All-holding by Your Truth-Hand. . . .

Once again, an insight into God's reality immediately prompts Augustine, not to maintain his gaze fixed on God, as the narrative–mystical interpretation would lead us to expect, but to turn his gaze toward creatures. Once again he "sees" that they owe their very existence to God, but now, more emphatically than before, he sees that the true notion of omnipresence obliges him to understand that, instead of God's being "in" all creatures, all of creation is, on the contrary, "in God."

The Old Testament speaks on page after page about the "hand of God," *manus Dei*, or "God's right arm," *dextera Dei*. Augustine interprets those images as referring to God's power and activity "extended" or "stretched out" (metaphorically) toward His creation (*SS 20* 1, *23* 5; *Enn 101*; *SS 2 12*, *120* 11). Encouraged, moreover, by texts like St. Paul's allusion to Christ as God's "Wisdom and Power" (1 Cor 1:24), he makes one of those Trinitarian applications he is so fond of, and God's hand and arm come to mean the Second Person of the Trinity, God's creative Word: by Him, through Him, and "in" Him "all things were made" (*Acad* 2.1). Just as all creation was bathed in the "Light of Light," therefore, so too all creatures were in God's Hand; they existed because they were upheld by His Eternal Truth. Augustine strains grammar to the breaking point in an effort to express that insight with suitable power: instead of saying tamely, *manus veritatis tuae*, "the Hand of Your Truth," or something equally conventional, he simply takes the two terms *manus* and *veritas*, "Hand" and "Truth," concrete image and abstract universal, leaves them both in the ablative case, and lets them collide in stunning apposition to each other: "You are All-holding [*omnitenens*] by Your Truth-Hand."

The echoes raised by that term, *omnitenens*, are several: it almost certainly represents Augustine's "conversion" of the Manichee *Splenditenens*, that mythical figure who, we saw earlier, was credited with holding their radiant higher world together (*Faust* 15.5–6, 20.9).[79] There are also, very probably, echoes of the orthodox *Pantokrator*: this "Hand" supports not only the higher world, but the *Pan*, the "All," not alone the spiritual world, but the *Omnia* including higher and lower worlds. And, finally, as I have tried to show elewhere, Augustine was very likely thinking back to that striking illustration Plotinus gave of his omnipresence teaching, the dynamic image of an all-upholding hand.[80] How is God omnipresent to all creation, then? As the same unchanging power of a hand is present first throughout a single book, then a pair, then an entire column of books it supports: but then, in a flash of sudden insight, we must no longer think of a corporeal hand, but presto! the upholding force of Truth Itself. . . .

But the remarkable fact is that, however carefully Augustine had previously rehearsed for it, we shall come to see that this rich and compact image of conversion is itself a rehearsal for what occurs in the final stage of his conversion process depicted in Book 8. All the actors we have seen performing here will come on stage once again, only slightly disguised. Once again they will go through their courtly pantomime: the *parvulus* acting like a big fellow, the plaintive *infirmus* in need of cure, the Divine Hand chastising, healing, tenderly caressing, lifting, and upholding, the *nesciens* having his eyes closed lest he look back on "vanities," and finally being lulled into "letting go," until he awakens to a vision which could never be attained by merely human effort. The steps in conversion are, Augustine imagines, as ritualized and inevitable as any stately Spanish dance.

ALL THINGS ARE "TRUE" AND "ON TIME"

With the introduction of that key word, it dawns on the reader that Augustine has tacitly made a transition to the topic of "truth." But by "truth" he means the "truth of *being*."

> And all things are true, inasmuch as they exist; nor is anything falsity, unless what does not exist is thought to exist [7.xv.21].

Earlier, we saw Augustine establish a rigorous correspondence between a being's position on the scale of reality and its position on the scale of goodness; now he is establishing the same correspondence between the being-ness of things and their "truth" as beings. Here, as earlier, the criterion for "true existence" is unchange, immutability: only the Eternal truly exists, is truly Being. One might be tempted, therefore, to infer that only the Eternal can be "true," and all other realities must be "false." But Augustine refuses to make things that simple. Even changing beings, we saw earlier, are amalgams of being and non-being. Hence, everything has some share of existence, whether inferior or superior. Everything must be "true" in the sense of being truly what it is, and truly existing with a style of existence appropriate to the kind of being it is. Just as we saw him conclude earlier that nothing was genuinely evil, even though *we may wrongly think* of certain things as evil, now we see him draw the identical conclusion with respect to truth and falsity: nothing is "false," unless "what does not exist is thought to exist"—unless, in other words, *we* "make" it false, so to speak, *by thinking falsely about it*. And, for Augustine, the most glaring example of false-thinking is to look on something which does not "exist" eternally, and think that it *does* so exist—to look on some creature and think it is God. "Beware of *simulacra*" Augustine's earlier writings repeatedly warn, for down that road lies intellectual idolatry (*Ver* 68, 95).

But that is not the only type of "false-thinking" possible; for even if the truest of beings must be eternal and unchanging, temporal and changing beings have their measure of truth, and consequently can also be thought about "falsely"; they can be thought to exist when they do not exist, or thought to be what they are not. Augustine's major point, however, remains valid: falsity still remains in the mind of the one thinking falsely, and everything is "true" according to the measure of its existence.

To this point, Augustine has established the connection between absolute truth and eternity; he has also attributed their relative measure of truth to changing, temporal realities. Now he leaps to a remarkable generalization about the entire world of temporal beings:

> And I saw that all things befit not only their places [in the universe] but their times as well. . . .

Once again, Augustine assures us that he "saw," saw with the eye of understanding, became insightfully certain that each of the propositions he is now affirming is true. But once we appreciate the sweep of his climactic affirmation, we might find it hard to imagine even the most pious Christian's "believing" in it; and yet, still reflecting on those Platonic books, Augustine claims that he came to "see" it. Not only does everything, he assures us, occupy the "place" in the universe appropriate to it, but it also comes into existence, lives its appointed temporal span, and goes out of existence at the "times" appropriate to it. Augustine is claiming, in other words, that God's providential governance of the *Omnia* extends unfailingly from top to bottom and from end to end, to every smallest particular. What is more, he is claiming that one who approaches the question rightly can come to "see" the truth of that assertion!

We have already seen how ancient-world physics thought of each being's "weight" as operating to ensure that everything rose or fell naturally to the "place" its weight assigned to it; once arrived at its place, it came to "rest" there. Only some application of "violent" force could prevent beings from "seeking" and settling into their natural place. This is what Augustine has in mind by saying that all things "befit . . . their places" in the universe.

But he is saying more than that: all things befit "their times, as well." In one of Augustine's favorite metaphors, the temporal universe constitutes a universal poem, a *carmen universitatis*, into which the master-artist introduces each word and syllable and letter at precisely the appropriate point, permits it to sound exactly as loud and long as it should, then has it fade into silence and yield the field to its successor; and all of this in order that it will make its assigned contribution to the meaning and beauty of the whole cosmic poem (*Mus* 6.29).[81]

Finally, Augustine is suggesting that each being seeks its proper place and fills its proper time by acting out of the inmost "truth" of its being: just as it falls or rises "naturally," because of *its own* weight, so it enters and leaves the cosmic stage in accord with the role assigned it by its very nature. At this point, though, we must distinguish between the original nature and weight God conferred on the being at its creation (its "first nature," if you will) and the "second nature" and weight the being may have taken on by sinfully refusing to "abide" in its original place in the created order. In both these two cases, however, God's providential governance does not act *on* beings from without, but acts *in* them from within. When He creates a being, He endows it not only with existence, but with a nature in accordance with which He intends that it both exist and operate; the being's own nature, therefore, including the "weight" whereby it seeks its proper place of "rest," is God's providential design, God's governing will, inscribed in it. The same thing holds proportionately for whatever "second" nature and weight the being takes on by sinning: this becomes its new providential design.

So, Augustine is able to ask: "Where are the weights [*pondera*] for such varied kinds of love distributed within a single soul?" And he can answer his own question with the confident belief that while he did the loving and he did the wandering, nonetheless in all his loves and wanderings his course was invariably being "most secretly steered by [God]" (*nimis occulte gubernabar abs Te*) (4.22–23). Augustine would have us see that there is a perfect coincidence between the "point" from which God acts within us and our own inmost depth from which all action proceeds as ours; He sees his God as *intimior intimo meo*, "more inside me than my own insides."[82] One may complain that there are metaphysical difficulties involved in this position, but no one can deny that the thinking that came to articulate it was both intricate and ingenious.

Eternity, Creation, and Time

But that passing mention of creation raises several more immediate difficulties. The Manichees never tired of harping on the first of them. Instead of stating their objection, though, Augustine briefly answers it by telling us what he "saw":

> that You, Who alone are eternal, did not begin to work after innumerable tracts of time, because all tracts of time, both those which have passed away and those which will pass away, would neither pass away nor come to be unless You were at work and abiding [*nisi te operante et manente*] [7.xv.21].

At Book 11.12 Augustine will spell out more completely the Manichee objection which inspired the first of these assertions. They loved to challenge the believing Catholic to explain, "What was God doing *before* He created heaven and earth?" The essence of Augustine's reply will consist in showing that the objection is based on an erroneous assumption: eternity is not what the objector thinks it is, simply an everlasting stretch of time. Hence, the eternal cannot be situated somewhere before or after "innumerable tracts of time," for eternity is entirely above and beyond time. Augustine contents himself, at this point in his *Confessions*, with what amounts to passing allusions to both the Manichee objection and his reponse; he means to keep his reader on the stretch until he treats the problem thoroughly in his later meditation on Eternity and Time.

But there was a second difficulty, to which Augustine alludes in that phrase *nisi Te operante et manente*. He has again resorted to that term *manere* to express how God exists in the condition of absolute unchange which "eternity" signifies. But by coupling it with the term *operante*, he deliberately brought to his readers' minds a difficulty concerning time and eternity on which even Catholic Scriptural interpreters could disagree. For while Genesis tells us that, having finished all His creative activity, God "rested"—"abode"—on the seventh day, St. John in his Gospel seems to contradict that: he reports Jesus as telling the crowd that just as His Father "works until now," so He works also (*operatur*) (*Ep 166* 8).

Augustine answers that the contradiction is only apparent. Since He is eternal, first of all, God does truly "abide" without change (*manet*). The six "days" of creation are not intended to imply that any such temporal intervals affected God Himself. Now, as always, He is truly at "rest," as Genesis puts it.

But this does not prevent Him from exercising from eternity the kind of "operation" John's Gospel refers to: that of providentially governing the world He has created. That "operation," moreover, does not militate against God's eternal "rest," since it is unchangingly exercised in accord with the unchanging plan identified with His Eternal Word.

INIQUITY THE ROOT OF EVILS (7.22)

By any odds, the most neuralgic and explosive question the Manichees raised to Catholic doctrine was "Whence do evils come?" Augustine is fully cognizant that his refutation of Manichaeism will ride or fall on his success or failure to reply to that question convincingly. This is why it has taken him so long to face the question frontally: he had to have all the major lines of his synthesis in place before he could feel ready to wrestle with it; and everything he has written so far will find application in his answer to it. He opens the discussion (7.xvi.22) with two homely examples; I have already anticipated them above:

> And I perceived from experience that it is no marvel that even bread is punishment to an unhealthy palate, [the same bread] which is tasty to a healthy [palate]; and that light, which is lovable to pure [eyes], is hateful to eyes that are sickly.

Once again, Augustine is playing on the word *sanus* and its opposites. I have given the translations "healthy" and "unhealthy," but Augustine hopes that, because it is a question of "judgment" in both cases, we will also catch the veiled suggestion of "sanity" and "insanity." Both these examples illustrate how bodily sickness can affect our everyday judgments, but they have been artfully chosen: for Augustine has already portrayed God Himself as both "food" and "sunlight." Now he moves on to show how soul-sickness can make even God "displeasing":

> Even Your justice displeases the iniquitous, and the viper and the worm displease them much more, which You have created as befitting the lower parts of Your creation. To those [lower parts of creation] the iniquitous themselves are befitting insofar as they are

dissimilar to You, though befitting the higher [parts of creation] insofar as they become more similar to You.

Augustine is again using that term "displease" in the strong sense: people who are themselves unjust hate it, abominate it, when they are dealt with justly. Sinners more generally—the "iniquitous" (a term we have not seen since the very first paragraph of this section)—detest it when God deals with them in a way "befitting" their sinfulness. What they fail to realize is that the only place in the universe which naturally "befits" them, is *aptus* to them, is the very place in which they find themselves, "far" from God in the depths of this lower world, in the "region of unlikeness" to God, amid the vipers and worms which bother them so much. Were they to convert and become "more like" to God, they would gradually become "out of place" in this lower world and more "in place" in the higher, spiritual world to which they would then naturally gravitate. But it is simply unthinkable that they could be sinners and still find themselves "in place" in that higher realm: that would imply that they no longer exist and act out of the "truth" of their second natures as sinners. Or, in the ancient-world "physics" image to which Augustine suggestively alludes in the very next sentence, they would have come to "rest" at a "place" in which their spiritual "weight" would not permit them to "rest."

With that set of insights, Augustine has put his finger on the final piece of the puzzle which so long detained him: he has discovered the key to understanding "whence" evils come. That means he has dissected the anatomy of those interrelated entities "iniquity" and "perversity":

> And I sought for what iniquity might be, and did not find [any] substance, but [the] perversity of [the] will [rather], twisted away [*detortae*] from the Highest Substance, You, God, toward [into] the lowest [of subtances], [and] spewing forth "its insides" and swelling to the outside [*proicientis intima sua et tumescentis foras*] [7.xvi.22].

Earlier, Augustine told his readers that he pondered seriously on a solution to the problem of evil which he had "heard" from somewhere: that evils were of two sorts, the evils we committed, and the evils we suffered (7.5). In paragraph 16 of this section, he claimed to have come to "see" that God had "instructed" man on account of his "iniquity"; he has come to understand, accordingly, that "iniquity" is the name for some evil we have committed, and is also the root-cause of the evils we now experience for our "instruction": for the Lord "chastises" the son He loves (Heb 12:6), not so much to punish him as to make him wiser.

In this way, Augustine has avoided leaving the slightest hand-hold for the Manichees' charges that the Catholic God was like some crotchety old crank who delighted in punishing those who got Him angry. This was why Augustine has gone to all that trouble of constructing an elegant philosophical scheme in which everything, *including the sinner*, acts according to what is, or has become, its nature, the "truth" of its being, its "weight," and its consequent "place" in the universe. This is why he has also tried to show that a being's acting according to that nature is identical with acting in accordance with God's law, God's creative and providential design, *not* as something *imposed from outside*, but as inscribed *in* the very being itself. Again, God's action *upon* beings must be conceived of more precisely as an activity from *within* the being's fontal depths, where He is *interior intimo*, where He and the being coincide as twinned source of activity.

"Whence" do evils come? That was the Manichees' nagging question, and they claimed that the only answer an honest Catholic could give was: "ultimately, from God." For Catholics make Him the ultimate agent of the iniquities they claim humans commit, and they then go on to teach that He is now punishing us for our iniquity. Now Augustine can answer resoundingly: the evils we suffer come from the "iniquity" we have committed; and God could not have remained true to Himself if He strove to prevent our iniquity from naturally working out into its inexorable evil consequences. Furthermore, while we may choose to regard those consequences as punishments, God shows His goodness by using them for our "instruction."

Perversity

The brilliance of Augustine's solution largely resides in his explanation of how our "iniquity" and "perversity" *had* to work out naturally into the "evil" consequences that issued from them. In the first of the images he employs, that of "perversity," he pictures the whole soul, mind and will, as originally oriented on God, the "Highest" of beings. Supplying from the stock of images we have been gathering along the way, we may picture the soul as originally "cleaving," literally "sticking to," God in a contemplative "embrace" of love, and being "eternalized" by that adhesion.

That condition of "eternalization" Augustine images as a kind of super-concentration of being, the very opposite of the "distention" whereby temporal beings are "stretched out" and scattered into both past and future. Imagine, if you will, a temporal being as existing along a durational time-line, future moments slipping one by one through the slit of "the present" to become past moments; then imagine all past and future moments as though they were gathered together, and crammed into and "frozen" in an "abiding" present moment, a pure "now." This is how Augustine pictures the soul's blissful condition when it is contemplatively united to God: it experiences the "All" as "One" in a timeless "now" which has neither past nor future; the soul "IS" because it sees Him as He "IS."

The typical Platonist offers the experience of contemplation as the closest approach we humans can make to this timeless bliss. When the mind has done with the discursive business of reasoning, like an artist who has finished setting the tiles of a mosaic patiently in place, piece after piece, and backs away to take in the completed whole in a single encompassing gaze, time stops, or better, as T. S. Eliot expresses it, we seem to slip into a "moment in and out of time," at "the point of intersection of the timeless with time."[83] It is a moment of stillness, yet the stillness is electric with a kind of activity as intense as it is effortless; our entire being is concentrated into a singleness of ecstatic vision: we have become pure "eye."

But the vision eventually fades, and we come "down" from that condition of "exaltation" (the Platonist's language of ascent and descent seems to express a natural symbolism). The intensity of our concentration slackens, and in place of the "one" thing we were raptly beholding we find ourselves distracted by the "many" details of the everyday world about us. In Augustine's dramatic image, our "insides," the interior powers which had been so unified in that timeless moment of contemplation, have become "distended" and have burst; they have been "spewed forth." From their unifying contemplation of the "One," they are now poured "outward" in "restless" pursuit of the "many," those fleeting realities of the temporal world which rush toward us out of the future, flit tantalizingly by, forever eluding our grasp, and vanish into the past.

But one is tempted to protest that Augustine's image is more dramatic than the situation calls for. The passage from contemplation to ordinary consciousness hardly calls for such violent images as the soul's being "twisted away," "swelling outward," and "spewing forth its insides."

To answer that objection, one must start with the fact that Augustine originally drew inspiration for this image-complex in a strange coincidence: he saw Plotinus' portrayal (*Ennead* 3.7.11) of the soul's self-distention and uncoiling of its inner riches, spewing them forth over the realities of time, as harmonizing with Ecclesiasticus' portrait (10:9–15) of the "proud" man's movement of "apostasy" from God:

> Why is earth and ashes proud [*superbit*] . . . because in his lifetime, he has spewed forth his insides [*projecit intima sua*]. . . . The beginning of man's pride is to turn away from God [*apostatare a Deo*]. . . . For the beginning of all sin is pride.

Notice that Augustine's reminiscence of the Ecclesiasticus text in this particular instance is an excellent example of the phenomenon I have called "recession," the process whereby the linguistic correlate of an image becomes more and more reduced, until only a trace of it remains. Here, for example, the only two words left from the original Ecclesiasticus text are *intima sua*, yet they (along with that telltale *proicientis*) were sufficient to alert the editors of the BA edition of the *Confessions* that the Ecclesiasticus text (or at least its startling image) still lay behind Augustine's. The three other elements—the mention of God as *summa substantia*, then *detortae in infima voluntatis perversitatem*, and, finally, *tumescentis foras*—all represent accretions which, as Augustine's thought developed, came to attach themselves to the core image from Ecclesiasticus. Those accretions are, admittedly, analogous to corresponding elements of the original: the *summa substantia* stands in for the "God" of Ecclesiasticus, the "detorsion" standing in for *apostatare*, and *tumescentis foras* reduplicating the original *proicientis foras*. But that is entirely to be expected: if the "foreign" elements added in later were entirely alien to the original elements they replaced, the "thrust" of the resulting image-complex would become entirely different from that of its forebear. And that seems simply to defy the laws of imagination's working—at least, if the imagination be Augustine's.

Now, one might initially be tempted to surmise that the persistence of so fragmentary a linguistic remnant from Ecclesiasticus testifies to the diminished influence of that text, and of its vivid imagery, over the workings of Augustine's imagination. But we have seen in a number of instances that, for Augustine's imagination at any rate, the very reverse is true: when so slender a linguistic element can still assimilate and bond together a number of "imported" elements into an image-complex, so that the resultant still substantially retains the force of the original, the paucity of linguistic correspondents argues, rather, for the continuing power and subterranean influence, not for any weakening in the force of the original image.

To understand further why Augustine found this image so persistently compelling, recall that he originally saw in the Ecclesiasticus text an imaged description of the fall of Adam and Eve as portrayed in Genesis. So, it was through "pride" that they "turned away," literally "apostatized" from God.[84] Created and elevated to blissful contemplation of God's own splendor, they wrenched themselves away from the Eternal One, the "Highest Substance," and plunged down amid the temporal "many," the lowest of realities (*infima*). By so doing, they forfeited the interior unity of their contemplative collectedness; already "swollen" with pride, they became further "distended," stretched out in a tireless chase after temporal realities, into times past, present, and future; so, like an unhealthy tumor, they "burst" and spilled their insides outward.

Only as dramatic an image as this would serve to depict the most dramatic act, Augustine was convinced, which the human being had ever performed: the act of violently "twisting" itself away from blissful contemplation, and plunging into the world of feverish and futile action.

That act, Augustine tells us, which was nothing less than the primordial fall of human nature from the summit of contemplation into the action and distraction of time, was an act of "perversity." How he revels in ringing the changes on that word *vertere*! "Because we turned away from [You] [*aversi sumus*], we have become perverted [*perversi sumus*]. Let us turn back now, Lord [*revertamur*], lest we be overturned [*ut non evertamur*] . . ." (*Conf*

4.31) is one of the best examples; only his unquestionable favorite, *convertere*, is absent. But it gives a fairly accurate idea of how Augustine intends the term *pervertere*: he thinks of it as an act of "turning in the wrong direction," in a direction in which one *ought not* turn. One of the consequences of such a sinful turn is that one becomes "overturned"; by proudly turning its back on its natural "superior," God, and from loving submission to Him, the soul, which should be "superior" and in control of the body, its "inferior," finds the body rebelliously taking control over its natural mistress. Things are all upside down (*eversi sumus*). So, Augustine thinks, there is a natural and inexorable connection whereby "turning away" from God ("aversion") leads to "perversion," which leads to "subversion" (or "eversion"); and the only cure for this monstrous situation is that we "convert" and "revert," turn around and return to our original contemplative submission to God.

So, too, there is a similar natural and inexorable connection between the soul's proud desire for independence of the One and its "vain" itch to exult in its power to act upon and dominate the many. And, finally, there is a similar connection between the "earthiness" of its desire to experience closer contact with earthly realities and the "weight" which earthly desire contributes to its being: that weight draws it downward to the "place" among earthly realities which "befits" it.

Iniquity

But Augustine feels entitled both to label and to portray the soul's "aversion" and downward movement as *iniquitas*. Certainly, part of his reason for doing so lay in the fact that the term occurs frequently in Scripture to denote grave sin and sinfulness, but so do other terms as well. Why did Augustine's choice fall on this particular expression? The background, once again, is Augustine's *Omnia* image, in the rudimentary form it took in his Cassiciacum Dialogues. Imagine the strata of the universe as depicted in that image, and let the eye run down to the very bottom, as it were, to a point even lower than the "lowest" of earthly realities; having reached that point, mentally write in: "nothingness." Then imagine a soul falling from its original position at the level of the "Highest"; the course of its fall would bring it "downward" from its union with, and consequent "likeness," to God—"being" in the fullest sense of the term—into the midst of beings of lesser and lesser degree, and the "logical" terminus of its downward movement would be ultimate "nothingness." (Granted: Augustine soon came to realize that "nothingness" was an asymptotic destination, so to speak, one which the soul could never actually reach; but it sufficed for his conception that it was in the very "logic" of sinful fall that the falling soul tended *toward* nothingness).[85]

This imagined scenario once set Augustine off on an etymological excursus: "nothingness" in Latin can be written as *ne quidquam*, "not anything," which in turn resembles the term *nequitia* closely enough that *nequitia*, "unrighteousness," becomes a very apt expression for "sin"; for the term implicitly embodies Augustine's entire metaphysic of evil as "corruption," meaning diminishment in being, privative non-being, a self-destructive tendency toward nothingness (*Vita* 30). Finally, the step from *nequitia* to *iniquitas* scarcely requires explanation! The root of all the evils the soul must suffer in this lower world is, therefore, most appropriately expressed by the term *iniquitas*; the expression neatly conveys the downward movement, which Augustine insists is initiated by the soul itself, into the midst of the inferior realities which are by nature "unbefitting" the soul, alien and even hostile to it. Native to the higher world, the soul is simply "out of place," can never be genuinely "at home," in this region of unlikeness.

Notice once again, however, that the consequences flow inexorably from the very nature of the soul's own evil act. Turn away "perversely" from union with the Highest reality, and by its very nature the turn must be a turn toward lesser realities; it can have no other terminus except the "diminishment" and "privation" of being which Augustine equates with "corruption," evil.

Dismissal

Once again, therefore, a Manichee attack has been neutralized: the "punishment" for having abandoned the higher in pursuit of the lower is accomplished "naturally"; it is not imposed from without by some arbitrary whim of a pettish God. Augustine delights in describing God's response to sinful souls in St. Paul's expression from Romans 1:24: he "yielded them up [*tradidit eos*] to the desires of their hearts." This, he explains, is also why Genesis does not

say that God "sent" Adam and Eve out of paradise on the occasion
of their sin: *non misit, sed dimisit*, He "dis-missed" them.[86] For one
may "send" another against his will, but a host is said to "dismiss"
a guest only when the guest is obviously eager to depart. The
natural resultant of the soul's perverse desire for lower realities is,
ironically, nothing else than fulfillment of that desire. And once
that desire takes final hold of the soul, God Himself, it would
seem, can do no other than assent to it.

THE LADDER OF BEAUTIES (7.23)

Now, however, for only the second time in seven paragraphs of
text, Augustine is about to regale us with another ascent to what
could arguably pass for a momentary "vision." But is it really an
ascent to vision which solely, or even primarily, interests him?
For if he has been conducting a kind of metaphysical tour of the
universe, this could simply be the final leg of that voyage. Notice
once again: he has explained what he came to understand about the
various grades of reality, about being as good (and its derivative
property, evil), about being as true (and false). Now he could
simply be rounding out matters by turning to that classic property
of being which fascinated him from his youth onward: beauty.

> And I marveled that it was now You that I loved, and not some
> phantasm in Your stead; and I did not stand to enjoy [*non stabam
> frui*] my God, but was borne up to You [*rapiebar*] by Your beauty
> [*decore tuo*], and soon was borne away from You [*diripiebar*] by my
> [own] weight [*pondere meo*], and rushed downward with groaning
> into these [lower realities: *ista*]; and that weight was carnal custom.
> But with me was a memory of You; nor did I doubt in any way
> whatever that the One to Whom I cleaved existed, but that I who
> did the cleaving did not yet exist [*nondum me esse qui cohaererem*],
> because "the body which undergoes corruption weighs down the
> soul, and [the soul's] earthly dwelling-place presses down the sense
> which cogitates the many." And I was most certain that "Your
> invisible [attributes] from the constitution of the world are
> glimpsed by [the eye of] understanding through the things which
> are made"; and "also [glimpsed are] Your Eternal Power and Di-
> vinity" [7.xvii.23].

Certain features of this scenario are oddly familiar: they read
like a replay of much that we saw in the opening paragraph (16)

of this account. Augustine is once again at pains to make clear the type of mediated "vision" he has momentarily enjoyed: he has succeeded once again in "glimpsing" the Divine Light with the eye of "understanding." Once again, too, he stresses the difference between his new-found way of "seeing" and the subjection to "phantasms"—corporeal images—which formerly hobbled his thought-ways as a Manichee. This brings him to emphasize anew the certainty of God's reality which accompanied the glimpse which has been accorded him; there was no way whatever that he could have "doubted" the existence of the God to Whom, he now tells us, he "cleaved." He also repeats the cryptic formula we analyzed when dealing with paragraph 16: Augustine is stressing his realization that God exists, but that he himself "does not yet exist."

But that mention of his actually cleaving to God may strike a new note. Previously, he had only come to "see" that cleaving to God was his "good." But it is clear that his cleaving was only momentary; as before, he has been allowed no more than a fleeting glimpse. Now, however, he tells us that he has been "borne [away]" upward (*rapiebar*) by the attraction of God's beauty (*decus*), but soon "borne"—or "torn"—away downward (*diripiebar*) by the "weight" of "carnal custom," which he promptly identifies with the weight of the "corruptible" body spoken of in the Book of Wisdom, 9:15.

We saw that Augustine's fondness for the term *rapere* and its cognates hearkens back to the phrase in which Matthew's Gospel (11:12) tells us that the "violent" bear away God's kingdom (*rapiunt*). That notion of "violence" (*vis*) seems at first blush to consort uneasily with Augustine's conviction that even God would not impose force from without to make a free creature act against the tendency inscribed in it by its "weight." That uneasiness is removed, however, once one notices that here, as in the *Hortensius* episode, the "violence" which God uses to "bear away" his new convert is the "sweet violence" of love, working through the attractiveness of God's beauty; the divine beauty has exerted its appeal in the guise of the *delectatio victrix*, the "conquering delight" which, in Augustine's view, characterizes the working of God's grace. Augustine remains consistent: even when "violently" bearing us away, God does not exert force from without, but acts from deep within the creature (*interior intimo*).

That *delectatio victrix* must act against the residual "weight" of "carnal custom," the habitual affective bent which Augustine traces here to our possessing a "corruptible body." Originally, our bodies were "heavenly"—spiritual and immortal in quality—but in plunging into this world of "lowest things" we exchanged them for the "mortal" or "corruptible" bodies which (Augustine implies) "befit" this "earthly" realm.[87]

Augustine seems to have found that text from Wisdom (9:15) quite suggestive—especially when read through a Neoplatonic lens. It spoke to him, first of all, in the same language of "weights" as did another text from Wisdom: Olivier Du Roy has shown convincingly how crucial that "Trinitarian" echo soon became for Augustine's cosmology: that God created everything in accord with "measure, number, and weight" (*pondus*).[88] The mention of the corruptible body "weighing down" the soul may also have suggested, or at least fitted neatly with, the "upside-down" image of *eversio* which pictures the inferior body as having monstrously become the superior of the soul. This was also one of several texts which encouraged Augustine to picture the body as the earthly dwelling or "habitat" (*habitatio*) of the soul, and possibly, along with other Scriptural texts, its "vesture" also (*habitus*) (*SS 252* 7, *166* 2–3, *214* 4–6; *Enn 145* 3–6, *141* 18; *InJo 13* 5).

But most fascinating of all is Augustine's interpretation of that picturesque phrase, which I translate with brutal literalness: the body "presses down upon the sense [*sensum*] that cogitates the many." He seems to have taken this as referring to the change which the fall wrought in the soul's manner of knowing: the body's action of "pressing down" prevents the soul from looking upward toward the unity of the Divine, and compels it, instead, to "think the many" of the lower realm, which it must approach through the various portals of "sense."

To Stand and Enjoy

In the conflict Augustine is describing between soul and corruptible body, the new "delight" he has tasted does "conquer," momentarily; in that brief moment, it succeeds in becoming a new "weight" strong enough to draw his soul upward against the downward pull of "carnal custom." But only for a moment: Augustine succeeds in "cleaving" briefly to God, and undergoes, presumably, a certain measure of transformation from that contact.

But he is too weak to "stand" and "enjoy" his God: and here we have two more semi-technical Augustinisms. We have already seen how the action of "enjoying" can most easily be understood in terms of Augustine's image of human life as a return "journey" to the "home" we once left behind us; we must never make a permanent "stop" short of arriving at our permanent "abode"— must "use" all the inns along the way, however well-appointed they may be, as "stop*overs*," but no more than that. The only reality which we are meant to "stop at" in such a way as to come to ultimate "rest" and restfully "enjoy" is God.

To "enjoy" God involves, then, permanence, an "abidingness" which banishes every suggestion of the temporary, of the changeable; one cannot truly "enjoy" the blissful vision of God unless every trace of "instability" has been removed. But to be able to "stand" (*stare*), at least two things are required: first, one must be solidly supported, on a genuine *firmamentum* or foundation, like a Rock (and yes, God is our Rock!); but, second, one must also have built up one's strength sufficiently to "take a stand"—as a soldier must do in resisting the onrush of the enemy.[89] The want of both those features accounts for Augustine's inability to "stand" and abidingly enjoy the vision he has merely glimpsed: he has already confessed that he needed more "strength" (*robur*) before he could feed on this "food of grown-ups," and he will tell us shortly about his search for the "foundation" which he still lacks.

A Memory of God

For now, however, Augustine is left with a "memory" of God— very much as he was left, earlier, with the memory of that aromatic banquet he was still too weak to enjoy (16). Does he mean to tell us that this "memory" of God was the result of the "glimpse" he has just had of Him—that he had no such "memory" *before* these Platonic readings? Or have these readings served to awaken the memory of God which lurked slumbering in the depths (or heights, or inmost) of his soul, as residue of the vision he had enjoyed before his "fall" into this lower world? The hints Augustine has dropped thus far do not seem conclusive enough to settle that question—yet. But he may give us more to go on shortly.

But whatever his answer may be to that question about memory, this much is clear: Augustine has told us again, and will repeat the same message twice before finishing this section, that it was not a genuine "vision" that he was granted, but only a fleeting "glimpse" of God's beauty, "seen through" creatures with the filtered kind of vision proper to the eye of understanding—*inter-lecta*. So, Augustine still remains a "seeker." The word he chooses to open the ensuing portion of his account is—*quaerens*:

> For, seeking whence [it was that] I approved of the beauty of bod-
> ies, whether heavenly or earthly, and what empowered me when
> I judged correctly about changeable realities, saying "this ought to
> be so, and that not so," seeking therefore this "whence" I judged
> when I so judged, I [ascertained that I?] had found [the] unchange-
> able and true eternity of Truth, above my changeable mind. And
> thus, stepwise, I passed [upward] from bodies, to the soul which
> senses through the body, and then to the interior power of that
> soul to which the bodily senses herald [the existence of] exterior
> realities (the brute beasts are able to do this much). And thence,
> once again, [I passed upward] to the power of reasoning, to which
> what is received from the body's senses is referred to be judged
> upon. [And] when [this reasoning power] discovered that it was
> changeable in me, it raised itself [up] to its [power of] understand-
> ing, and withdrew its thought away from its customary mode [of
> operating], taking itself away from the mobs of contradictory
> phantasms. [This it did] in order that it might find the Light by
> which it was besprinkled when it cried out with no doubt whatever
> that the Unchangeable must be preferred to the changeable, [that
> Light, I mean] whence it knew the Unchangeable Itself. For unless
> it knew [that Unchangeable] in some way or other, it could in no
> way have placed it with [such] certainty above the changeable—
> and [so the reasoning power raised to intelligence] arrived at "That
> Which Is," in a flash of trembling regard [7.xvii.23].

Ascent to Vision—or Arrival at Understanding?

We have already remarked that a great deal of the literature about this section of the *Confessions* has stemmed from Pierre Courcelle's interpretation that it represents an account of "frustrated attempts at Plotinian ecstasy." Augustine, on this view, is recounting the attempts he made at Milan, more or less successfully, to perform the kind of "ascent of the mind" which Plotinus frequently de-scribes as culminating in a mystical union with the One. It must be said for Courcelle's interpretation that the early Augustine seems to have had a lively interest in that sort of thing; in fact, the stepwise procedure he outlines in this paragraph bears close resemblance to descriptions of "ascents" he has left us in at least two of his earliest writings (*Quant* 70–79, *Lib* 2.15–34; see also *Ord* 2.28–44). Moreover, for some time after his conversion in A.D. 386, he evidently cherished the hope that he, like Plotinus and like Catholic representatives of the contemplative tradition, might reach the stage of spiritual purification where he could enjoy an ecstatic unity with God as something like an habitual manner of existence (*Mor* 1.65–67).[90]

But against that view it must be said that this is the only paragraph in Augustine's entire account which incontestably describes such an ascensional process. Even this account, furthermore, is both preceded and followed by quotations of the same Pauline text, Romans 1:20, which, we have seen, Augustine habitually uses to inform us that he has come, not to a kind of mystical "vision," but to a filtered insight of the "understanding." That diagnosis, finally, is supported by close examination of the "ascent" itself.

The Norm of Judgment

Augustine begins his description of ascent with the kind of epistemic act for which he reserves the term "judgment." We have already seen that *judicare*, in his lexicon, always involves taking an *evaluative* stance: deciding which of several things is better or more beautiful than the others, or, in cases where only one thing is being "judged," deciding whether it is as good or beautiful as it could, or, rather, as it *ought* to be (*debet*). It is worth noting, however, that he specifically refers here to judging on the beauty of "bodies" and "changeable realities"—he is referring back in time to the rather modest level of judging he was capable of exercising when writing his youthful *De pulchro et apto*.

It puzzles him that, even then, before making contact with Platonism, he was able to make those judgments correctly (*integre*). For even to judge upon bodily and changeable realities, he must have been acquainted with some unchangeable norm or standard of judgment, the "unchangeable and true eternity of Truth." We have already encountered this reality in paragraph 16; it is the atmospheric "Light" which, "above [the] mind," bathes all particular truths which the mind "sees" as eternally true.

At this point we encounter another translation difficulty. Augustine writes that, seeking the "whence" he was empowered to make these judgments, he came to see that he "had found" (*inveneram*) the Unchangeable Truth. That pluperfect tense seems again to refer back to the time when he wrote the *De pulchro*. Augustine is implying once again that even before reading these Platonic books, hence even *before* gaining the "glimpse" of the Light they coached him to see, he had already been making, and "correctly" making, the kinds of judgments which implied that he must *already* have been acquainted, however dimly, with the norm of eternal Truth. This was my reason for inserting in brackets the suggestion that those Platonic books may have helped him "ascertain" (or "realize"?) the implications of what he had been doing successfully all along.

If my suggested insertion is acceptable, then Augustine has finally given us a clue to the kind of thinking on the "memory" of God which is presiding over this section. That memory can be present and even operative before the one remembering becomes explicitly conscious of it. This is the same hypothesis which was suggested by Augustine's account of his sexual awakening: the soul's memory of itself (and therefore of God) can take the form of *notitia* without having risen to the more reflective form of *cogitatio*.[91] I would also submit that the same understanding of memory fits neatly with the lengthy analysis of it which Augustine gives in the tenth book of the *Confessions*, and especially with the way he drives home his final conclusion: we all understand what "happiness" means, because we all retain a deeply embedded memory of the happiness we once knew but have almost completely forgotten. For it must be the case that we once experienced "joy" at the vision of eternal "Truth" (10.29–30).

The steps in the soul's "ascent" are much what one would expect from having read Augustine's earlier works, especially on "The Greatness of the Soul" (*Quant* 70–79). There he described seven grades of the soul's activity (for Augustine, such things always come in sevens!), of which he omits the first two here; the formation and animation of the body do not directly interest him now. Beginning with sensation, therefore, he moves upward to the "interior power," the "common" sense which even brute beasts possess. Only on the next level does the characteristically human operation of "reason" take place: reason "judges" upon the relative worth of sense realities.

Reason Becomes Intelligence

But reason itself is changeable: in its "customary mode" of operation it concerns itself now with this, now with that item out of the "mob of contradictory phantasms" drawn from the sense world; furthermore, Augustine tells us, he came to "discover" that human reason like his was "changeable" (*Ver* 18);[92] it can pass from ignorance to knowledge, from error to truth. This discovery prompted his reason to "raise itself up to its [power of] understanding" (*erexit se ad intelligentiam suam*)—as the young Augustine himself, following the example of the Prodigal, had become *erectior*, "straightened up" to the spiritually "erect" posture appropriate for contemplating higher realities.[93] Augustine is convinced that this capacity for contemplation lies slumbering in the soul, as it were, even while the soul is still focusing its play of "reason" on the realities of the sense world; as we saw in commenting on paragraph 16, the *intelligentia* to which reason stretches upward was *sua* all along, "its own" intelligence.

But for reason to operate as intelligence it must "withdraw itself" from its "habitual" mode of focusing on the "mob" of "carnal" phantasms the senses report to it; it must pass upward from concern with the ever-changing sensible "many" in order to seek the purely intelligible Light of the Unchangeable "One." Once again, however, the moment reason succeeds in doing this it discovers that, like the *bourgeois gentilhomme* speaking prose, it has been doing it all along. For it has always "known," and "with certainty," that the "Unchangeable must be preferred to the changeable"—something it could not have known (implicitly) unless it "knew" the Unchangeable Itself, "in some way or other." Pascal's brilliant tag was just: "You could not have sought Me, unless you had already found Me." Even before we become "seekers," God is there, in the depths of our "memory," prodding us to seek Him. And Augustine half-hopes that the attentive reader will ask, "Where, and when, do we remember Him from?"

The Momentary "Glimpse"

At the culmination of his stepwise ascent, Augustine "arrived," *pervenit*, and in a "flash of trembling regard" caught sight of the

God Who "IS." Taken out of context, the language would suggest something very like a moment of ecstatic "vision." And yet, the very next lines disabuse us of that notion. Here, Augustine has come to the close of his account, and he closes with a summary of everything that has happened, including the result of this final, and only, unmistakable "ascent" of the mind. His summary runs along the lines which by now have become familiar:

> Then did I truly glimpse "Your invisible [attributes] by [the eye of] understanding, through the things which are made," but I was not yet strong enough to fix my gaze [upon those invisible attributes], and struck back by [my] infirmity, I was restored to accustomed realities; I carried with me only [a] memory, loving and desirous, as of aromatic [food] upon which I was as yet unable to feed [7.xvii.23].

Once again, Augustine has confessed that he was then too "infirm"—too "sickly-weak"—to feed upon the "food for grown-ups," the direct and sustained vision of God. All he had thus far been granted was a "glimpse" of the divine radiance by means of the eye of "understanding" which must peer "through" created realities. He then appends two full chapters (xviii.24 and xix.25) detailing the hesitations and confusions which kept him from fully embracing the Incarnate Christ, Who, like a nursing mother (Augustine now realizes), came to "suckle" spiritual infants, and enable them to grow strong enough to digest the grown-ups' "food" of vision.

Augustine's Milanese Experience: "Through a Glass, Darkly" (7.26)

He interrupts the story of his progressive attachment to Christ, however, in order to give a final retrospective summary of the Platonic illumination he has just finished outlining. Leaving our examination of those Christological passages for another occasion, it will repay us to attend to that summary now.

> But at that time, having read those books of the Platonists, after having been admonished by them to seek [for] incorporeal Truth, I glimpsed "Your invisible [attributes] by [the eye of] understanding, through the things which are made"; and beaten back, I sensed

what I was not yet permitted to contemplate through the darkness of my [own] soul. [I was] certain that You exist, and that You are infinite, even though not poured out in some speciously infinite way through finite places, and that You truly exist, You Who are ever the Selfsame, not other or otherwise [either] in any part [of Your being] or by any movement, and that all other beings were truly from You, on this sure ground alone, that they exist. Yes, I was certain of all these [truths], but, nevertheless, too sickly-weak to enjoy You [7.xx.26].

In his treatment of this account, Pierre Courcelle chose to lift this quotation out of context, and print it as though Augustine were further narrating still another futile attempt at ecstasy.[94] Replaced in its context, however, it is plainly Augustine's final effort to make it pellucidly clear exactly what the nature of this *entire* experience had been and what dispositions of soul it left him with. He rounds off Book 7 with two final chapters on how he began to realize the difference between Platonism and the Pauline stress on our need for contrition and grace; the "foundation" which was lacking to him was, he now realizes, the humble Christ Incarnate. Then, opening Book 8, he summarizes the results of his first experience with Platonism one final time:

> I was certain about Your eternal life, though I saw it "in an enigmatic way and as though in a mirror." Nonetheless, I had been relieved of all my doubts concerning [the] incorruptible Substance, [and] that every other substance sprang from It. What I desired was not to be more certain about You, but to become more stable in You (8.i.1).

Enigmatically, as in a Mirror

This is the third time we have seen Augustine present a summary of his entire experience of reading, and reflecting on, those Platonic books. He did so twice in Book 7, in paragraphs 23 and 26, and now again in the opening paragraph of Book 8. In each of those summaries he strikes three notes clearly and consistently.

First, he came to a certain number of certainties. Second, he was left with a sense that there was a more plenary vision to be "enjoyed," but that he was as yet incapable of enjoying it. And, third (quite plausibly Augustine's underlying explanation of the first two features), the precise quality of the experience was one of "glimpsing" the Divine Radiance "through" created realities, by means of the understanding, "intel-ligence."

The claim I have just made, that Augustine describes his experience as one which was uniformly mediated and indirect, has far-reaching consequences for the interpretation, not only of this entire section, but of the *Confessions* more generally. Yet nothing could be clearer: four distinct times he has described that manner of "seeing" by citing Romans 1:20, and we saw that in his preached works he constantly interprets that text as portraying the filtered vision proper to "intel-ligence."

Now, in opening Book 8, as though to remove any doubts that might have remained, he tells us that he achieved those certainties despite having seen only "enigmatically, as though in a mirror." That, of course, is the expression Paul uses in First Corinthians 13:12 to draw a contrast with direct and immediate vision, "face to face." Hence, the conclusion seems justified: the "mystical" interpretation of this section of the *Confessions* is unable to accommodate itself to Augustine's own Biblical characterizations of his experience, while the counter-theory, that he is presenting us with a world-view, a connected series of insights gained through "understanding," makes excellent sense of those characterizations; indeed, it makes sense of all the details in Augustine's account. I know of no further evidence to bring it into doubt (though we shall come to see additional evidence in its favor); so, permit me to assume that the "world-view" interpretation of *Confessions* 7.16–26 has succeeded in bearing its required burden of proof.

To Become More "Stable"

As to the second feature of his experience, Augustine has expressed it in Book 8.1 in a term we have noticed before: he was left with a desire to become "more stable." Again, this implies that he wishes he were both strong enough, and established on a solid enough foundation, to take a "stand" and maintain it. The term *stare* sometimes finds Augustine picturing a soldier "standing firm" against the enemy's charge; but he can often picture a man struggling (almost always in vain) for a foothold to resist a river-current or an oncoming tide.[95]

This latter association seems more obviously at work in the case before us: for in Augustine's imagination both "rivers" and "tides" figure the onflowing restlessness of time and change, which incurably infect the lower world in which nothing can ever truly "stand." So (the resonances from paragraph 16 are especially notable), finding himself plunged into the temporal world, Augustine has discovered that he does not truly "exist" with the unchanging abidingness which enables only the Eternal to "stand" in the ultimate, metaphysical sense of the term. Or, more exactly, he has discovered that he "does not *yet* exist," that he may hope to exist, to "stand" eternalized, at some future time which is no longer in time.

Yet the term *stare* is suggestive enough to connect with other metaphors Augustine has used. He has, for example, discovered (in paragraphs 16 and 23) that he is a spiritual infant, but he hopes to be given the "strength" which he lacks and requires, in order to "grow" and share the "food of grown-ups." Then, the weakness of infancy behind him, he will no longer require the coddling mediations and indirections of "understanding," or be "struck back" by the radiance of the divine (16, 23); he will be able to "stand" like a spiritual adult—one whose eyes have become strong and healthy enough (22) to find this sunlight "lovable"—and abidingly "enjoy" the vision.

Certainties Won

But the first feature Augustine regularly mentions in summarizing this experience is the "certainty" it left him with. We noted earlier the urgent need he felt—and his claim that it was God Who had inspired him with that sense of need—for certainty on a number of questions, as a kind of natural prerequisite for unlocking, freeing up, his ability to "believe." His friendly argument with Honoratus, *The Usefulness of Believing*, gives the same diagnosis of his psychology in this respect as the *Confessions*: it shows him sorely conscious that his own earlier willingness to believe had been abused both by the authoritarians of North African Catholicism, and later, despite all their voluble promises to do just the opposite, by the Manichees (*Ut Cred* 2).

Again, Augustine's "Required" Certainties

But to return, now, to the question we answered earlier, but only provisionally: How many certainties did Augustine require, and on what topics? If the question posed that way is accepted as well framed, a quandary results which is very similar to the one we were forced to deal with earlier.

For the section we have just analyzed is brimful with truths he "saw," truths which became "certain," or were "made manifest" to him—so brimful, in fact, that it would take considerable logic-chopping to distinguish and accurately enumerate them. Even were we to limit our consideration to the two chapters (xii.18 and xiii.19) which he devotes to the question "What is evil?" how many propositions, sub-propositions, corollaries, and the like does Augustine claim certainty about in those two chapters? One might dispute about the exact figure, but it is at least clear that he has laid claim to a generous bundle of such certainties.

But focus on the three "summaries" Augustine gives of his experience, and the picture alters somewhat. In their terse economy they would recall the three express mentions of his "required" certainties which we examined earlier.

The first of these summaries, which he gives at the end of Book 7, paragraph 23, is relatively unspecific about content. He describes the filtered quality of the experience in the words of Romans 1:20; he tells how he was "struck back" from abiding in it, and he then goes on to conclude that he was left with a "memory" of God. But beyond mention of the Pauline *invisibilia* he tells us nothing further on the precise content of whatever certainties he drew from his glimpse of the divine attributes; he seems far more concerned with assuring us he has made the breakthrough to a spiritual manner of understanding than in describing that spiritual realm in any detail.

We have already observed how the summary which Augustine gives at the end of his account, in paragraph 26, seems to boast an allusively Trinitarian structure;[96] but does it illuminate the problem of Augustine's list of desired certainties? Again, Augustine seems primarily interested in the fact that he had made a breakthrough to a spiritual way of thinking. He describes his "glimpse" of God's "invisible attributes" as answering to the "admonition" he had received from those Platonist books urging him to seek "incorporeal truth." He does not explicitly claim to have gained any such generalized certainty as might be expressed in the proposition "spiritual reality exists." Certainty on that generalization is implicit, but only that, in the more specific certainties he mentions: that God "exists," and indeed that He "truly exists," unchangingly and eternally; and, further, that He is "infinite," though not in a corporeal manner.

But even here, Augustine seems to want his readers to grasp that he had gained access to a realm which was eternal and therefore spiritual and incorporeal. Now he turns once again to "the rest of beings," creatures; their very existence (which, we remember, makes them "good") is the "most solid proof" (*documentum*) establishing that they are all from God. Augustine has finally found the certain *documentum* he was looking for (5.25), proving the "falsity" of the Manichees, but once again, that proof followed from his having gained access to the spiritual world.

The summary Augustine gives in the first paragraph of Book 8 is the last one he furnishes his readers. There he is more directly interested in describing the state of soul in which this Platonist experience left him. He had become "certain," he tells us, about God's "eternal life," and about [God as] "incorruptible substance, and that every other substance was from [Him]." We may, I think, safely take "eternal life" to mean God's existence, but again, His existence as an eternal, hence, a suprasensible, an unchanging "spiritual" reality. But Augustine claims to have found more; the elliptical phrase that follows—*de incorruptibili substantia, quod ab illa esset omnis substantia*—recalls the *cetera vero ex Te omnia* from 7.26 and, like it, is evidently aimed straight at the Manichee heresy. Augustine came to "see," therefore, that God Himself (as Nebridius had argued) must be incorruptible, and that all other substances must be derived from Him, and not from some imagined principle of Evil which would make them evil instead of good. Again, though Augustine does not employ the term, this discovery surely furnished him the *documentum* he had been searching for to prove that the Manichees taught "falsity." And it did so, once again, precisely by enabling him to break through to a spiritual mode of understanding reality, however filtered that understanding may have been.

Augustine's Account: Story or World-View?

It must be said, in summary, that the long and surprisingly technical discussion we have just examined gives little encouragement to the tenants of the "mystical-narrative" interpretation of this entire section. Quite the contrary. There has not been a word about direct and immediate "vision" or "ascent to vision" since the very opening paragraph. Plainly, Augustine's attention is elsewhere. He has been entirely absorbed by the task of carefully positioning the dialectical batteries required for triumphing over Manichaeism.

It seems thoroughly improbable, in that connection, that the labor of forging such pivotal concepts as iniquity, perversity, and dismissal, and thinking out the relationship between temporality and truth, or between Neoplatonic and Biblical images of the "fall," could have been accomplished overnight. The pieces of the mosaic are much too subtle and close-fitting for that. Indeed, every additional word he writes makes it more and more unlikely that Augustine succeeded in elaborating this powerful synthesis in the relatively short time he spent in Milan and its environs before returning to Africa.

One Possible Solution: A Time-Gap

To put the problem another way: whether anticipating what certainties he stood in need of before his Platonist experience, or summarizing what that experience actually brought him, Augustine tends to be more severely economical of detail than the fuller outline of his discoveries would have led us to expect. In both cases, though, the reason may be the same: his retroactive summaries, like his prospective anticipations, seem to focus primarily on the novel *manner* of the experience—on its character as a "spiritual" style of understanding—only secondarily on the *content* of the particular certainties it yielded. But this may only be another way of pointing up the disparity between anticipations and summaries, on the one hand, and the fully detailed account of intellectual contents, on the other; it is the very luxuriance of that detail, and the surprising degree of metaphysical sophistication at work throughout that account, which raises the question: Did Augustine really intend us to believe that he became master of all that luxuriant detail, all that metaphysical sophistication, in a brief span of weeks during the spring of A.D. 386? Such an achievement would be remarkable, especially for one whose philosophical formation was that of a talented, even a brilliant amateur—but an amateur nonetheless. More than remarkable, it would be simply incredible.

But perhaps the disparity we have been considering will become less puzzling if approached from a different angle. It may be that Augustine's terse expressions of his "required" certainties, and his equally economical summaries of the certainties he attained by reading the Platonists, do accurately reflect, after all, what he actually gained from those readings, *in the springtime of A.D. 386.* But *intravi et vidi*: he not only read, but then reflected, and perhaps came to understand more than he had understood, at first. How long did *that* process take? At the risk of sounding puckish, the answer has to be: as long as it took. As long, that is, as it took him to digest the teachings of Neoplatonism, to grow in familiarity with the teachings of the *Catholica*, and to interrelate and adjust the two in such a way as to elaborate the synthesis he outlines so confidently in the seventh book of his *Confessions.*

But how long would that have taken him? Phrased that way, the question has a suspiciously *a priori* flavor. Perhaps a search through his earliest works, inspected as a record of his *de facto* philosophical progress, will give us a more reliable answer.

At the Crossroads

Before prosecuting that search, however, it is worth noting that one common feature emerges from all the summaries Augustine has given of his Milanese experience. Even his most compact list of new-won certainties assured him of this much: that among the realities of that spiritual realm which he had glimpsed was the beauteous Wisdom Whom, so many years before, the *Hortensius* had invited him to "leave all things" and pursue. Now the question was posed anew: Did this contemplative search really offer promise of the "life of happiness" which had so stubbornly eluded him all these years? He had always rationalized his unwillingness to wager everything on that possibility, by arguing that he was not "certain" that beauteous Wisdom was anything more than an illusion, concocted out of dream-stuff in the fires of youthful idealism; lacking all the length, and breadth, all the bodily solidity of the things we know as "real," She could conceivably be just an empty "nothing."

Now that alibi has been wrested from him. The "admonition" has come to show him that She is Truly Real, after all; Providence has set him firmly at a fresh crossroads. Which way will he walk?

This is the challenge which Augustine describes facing as he opens Book 8 of his *Confessions*.

NOTES

1. See above, and *Soundings*, pp. 94–96.

2. Magnus Loehrer, *Der Glaubensbegriff des hl. Augustinus* (Einsiedeln: Benzinger, 1955) fails to illumine this point.

3. *Retr* 1.1.1 gives the title in both forms. The positive evaluation of the Academics' strategy with which the book ends (as does the lengthy *Ep 118* on many of the same issues) would argue for *De Academicis* as more appropriate.

4. Augustine uses the term *res* with the same force in *Conf* 10.19, and 23.

5. See the mentions of Plotinus in *Acad* 3.41–44.

6. Du Roy, *Trinité*, pp. 24–52, furnishes an excellent example of this.

7. See the preliminary discussions in *Acad*, *Ord*, *Quant*, and the first five books of *Mus*.

8. See Brown, *Augustine*, pp. 19–34, for an excellent sketch of North Africa of this period.

9. Augustine tells us of his own experience in this regard in *Vita* 4 and *Ut Cred* 2.

10. See Eugene TeSelle, "Porphyry and Augustine," AS, 5 (1974), 113–47.

11. Again, see the Preface, pp. xv–xix, and *Soundings*, pp. 21–68.

12. Vernon Bourke, in *Augustine's View of Reality* (Villanova, Penn.: Villanova University Press, 1964), pp. 3–7 (henceforth: *View of Reality*) is correct in speaking of three *de jure* levels of reality (the Unchangeable God, spirits and souls changeable only temporally, bodies changeable both temporally and spatially), but Augustine views those three levels as having settled *de facto* into two *regiones*, the higher spiritual and the lower sensible regions. Again, see *Soundings* on the structure of the *Omnia*.

13. An additional higher reach of the sensible universe is often represented as the *aether*, and though it is true that Augustine sometimes mentions that element, it does not feature importantly for our purposes.

14. See *Ennead* 1.8.11. This may be a point on which, quite early on, Augustine showed a certain independence from Plotinus.

15. Cf. the view of Courcelle, *Recherches*, pp. 157–67, as well as Frederick Van Fleteren's similar emphasis in "Authority and Reason, Faith and Understanding," and "Augustine's Ascent of the Soul: A Reconsideration," in AS, 4 (1973), 33–71, and 5 (1974), 29–72. Publication of my

reply to Van Fleteren was unaccountably delayed, but finally published as "Faith, Reason, and Ascent to Vision in St. Augustine," AS, 21 (1990), 83–126 (henceforth: "Faith and Reason"). Van Fleteren replied to that article in the same issue (127–38), and I attempted to show "Where the Difference Still Lies" on pp. 139–52.

16. See my "St. Augustine's Criticism of Origen in the Ad Orosium," REA, 30 (1984), 84–99 (henceforth: "Criticism of Origen").

17. See Brown, Augustine, pp. 146–57.

18. The fact that Augustine was as yet unable to form an adequate notion of the spiritual would not prevent his entertaining the idea—or "image," as he would insist—that such a realm might exist.

19. For the dynamic interrelationship of Faith, Understanding and Vision, see my Early Theory, pp. 203–26 and 227–57.

20. Recherches, pp. 157–67.

21. See Soundings, pp. 55–56.

22. I am supposing that Augustine was reading the verb conspicor as he normally would, in its first meaning: to "catch sight of." Some translations of Romans employ a stronger sense, that God's invisibilia are "clearly seen" ("conspic-uous").

23. One must always keep in mind that, for the Platonist, "understanding" implies a form of mental "seeing." See below for application of this habit of thought to Augustine's text.

24. See Jean Doignon, "La praxis de l'admonitio dans les Dialogues de Cassiciacum," VC, 23 (1986), 21–37.

25. As usual, Courcelle searches for the evidence represented by verbal correspondences.

26. Impressed, apparently, by Fr. Paul Henry's insistence that Augustine must have read only "very few" works of Plotinus, Courcelle (like Van Fleteren) seems to have been tilted toward Ennead 1.6, which Henry also stressed; that alone would condition one's view toward looking for "ascents of the soul" in this section of the Confessions. The case is far different once one admits, with Solignac and Du Roy, for example, that Augustine's thinking here manifests the influence of a more generous number of Neoplatonic treatises; that "releases" the eye to take into account the wider set of philosophical issues (evil, omnipresence, etc.) which Books 1–7 have raised, and to which Augustine appears to be responding in this section. But the question of whether he did intend to respond to those issues can, of course, be decided only by close examination of his text.

27. Plotin et l'Occident (Louvain: "Specilegium Sacrum Lovaniense," 1934), pp. 82ff.; see my Early Theory, pp. 6–10.

28. Courcelle steps off on the wrong foot once he goes looking for a literal "admonition" in Plotinus' text; he further complicates matters by

the scissors-and-paste treatment which lifts out of context and sets into parallel columns all, *and only*, Augustine's purported allusions to attempted "ascents" of the mind to "ecstatic" vision. This leads him to ignore some three-quarters of the issues which preoccupy Augustine.

29. If someone informed a friend that he had just been incredibly impressed by reading "a very small number" of Franz Kafka's short stories (cf. *Vita* 4, *Acad* 2.5), would the friend be entitled to infer that he had *stopped* reading Kafka at that point? Yet this is the inference Henry and his followers have frequently drawn.

30. More recent scholarship has broadened the field of choice considerably beyond Henry's "very few" treatises; see my discussion in "Faith and Reason," pp. 86–87. Cf. Pier Franco Beatrice, "*Quosdam platonicorum libros*: The Platonic Readings of Augustine in Milan," VC, 43 (1989), 248–81, the cogency of whose case depends in great part on how cogent one finds the evidence produced for an "Encratic" source for Augustine's anthropology in *Tradux peccati: Alle fonti della dottrina agostiniana del peccato originale* (Milan: Vita e pensiero, 1978). See also the critique by Goulven Madec in the "Bulletin Augustinien," REA, 36 (1990), 406.

31. See, in this connection, François Masai, "Les Conversions de saint Augustine et les débuts du spiritualisme en Occident," *Moyen Age*, 67 (1961), 1–40.

32. See, for one example, the instance noted in my "Faith and Reason," 94 and 119*n*51.

33. See my *Early Theory*, pp. 207–208, on the importance of *Ennead* 5.8 to the early Augustine.

34. *Soundings*, pp. 102–12.

35. J. J. O'Meara, in *Young Augustine*, pp. 157–90, writes of Augustine's "submission," first of intellect, then of will; Ferrari, *Conversions*, implies an "intellectual," then a conversion "to Catholicism"; Solignac implies a similar two stages in BA 13, pp. 69–72, and so on.

36. So writes F. Homes Dudden, in *The Life and Times of Saint Ambrose*, 2 vols. (Oxford: Clarendon, 1935), II, 459, characterizing the liberties Ambrose could justify under the rubric of "spiritual" interpretation.

37. Ryan, pp. 170–71.

38. Bourke, pp. 180–81.

39. BA 13, pp. 614–18.

40. See *Ennead* 5.3.2; 8.17.

41. See *Trinité*, pp. 141–43 (on *Sol* 1.13), 144*nn*1,2 (on *Quant* 75); see also pp. 145–47, 216–29.

42. Émile Bréhier, *Études de philosophie antique* (Paris: Presses Universitaires de France, 1955), pp. 292–307.

43. See *Trinité*, pp. 72–81, on the Trinitarian aspects of this (what Du

Roy holds to a "mystical") vision, thereupon issuing (from paragraph 17 forward) onto a "new vision of the world."

44. *Trinité*, pp. 413–66. See also Ghislain Lafont, *Peut-on connaître Dieu en Jésus-Christ?* (Paris: Les Éditions du Cerf, 1969), pp. 72–105.

45. Ryan, p. 171.

46. Bourke, p. 181.

47. BA 13, pp. 616–17.

48. BA 13, p. 616*n*1.

49. In a rare oversight, Solignac seems not to have noticed the role that the text from St. John's Epistle played in this development.

50. The thought is difficult, granted; but it is equally difficult to see how Augustine could have expressed his thought more plainly.

51. Gilson, among others, has labeled Augustine an "essentialist." Perhaps, in the light of what we have seen here, some qualification of that judgment is in order.

52. See *The Idea of the Holy: An Inquiry into the Non-Rational Factor in the Idea of the Divine and Its Relation to the Rational*, trans. John W. Harvey (Oxford: Oxford University Press, 1958).

53. Pierre Paul Courcelle, *Les* CONFESSIONS *dans la tradition littéraire: Antécédents et posterité* (Paris: Études Augustiniennes, 1963), pp. 278–88, 623–40 (henceforth: *Tradition*).

54. There are a number of initial indications that the Book of Wisdom suggested (along with other loci, doubtless) the term *admonitio* as expressing the way God might seem to be merely punishing us, when in fact (*pace* the Manichees) He is paternally "correcting" us; see *Faust* 19.28 for how chapters 11 and 12 of Wisdom are made to function this way.

55. Elgardo de la Peza, *El significado de "cor" en San Agustin* (Paris: Études Augustiniennes, 1962). But instead of reducing "heart" to a cold intellectual organ, this identity points up how fundamentally "cordial" or, perhaps better, "erotic") Augustine's notion of intelligence is.

56. Only by lifting it clear of its context does Courcelle contrive to make this obvious *summary* of the entire experience take on the appearance of an additional "ascent" of the soul.

57. On the force Augustine is likely to have attributed to the verb *conspicere*, see note 22, above.

58. See also note 71 in Part I.

59. Note the important break with the "contingent" kind of affirmation of "what is [the case]."

60. The thought-connection involved here seems to run somewhat this way: what is necessarily true must be unchangeably true, hence (since God is, in the first instance, unchangeable), in some way participant in the Divine.

61. As would, I take it, be implied if the vision were truly "mystical."

62. This is another instance of how important the exact meaning of words was to this professional *rhetor.*

63. Henry Chadwick, in *St. Augustine's* CONFESSIONS (Oxford: Oxford University Press, 1991), p. xxvi, reminds us that these small-roman divisions appear to go back no further than the printed editions of the late fifteenth and sixteenth centuries.

64. See J. Swetnam, s.j., "A Note on *In Idipsum* in St. Augustine," *Modern Schoolman*, 30 (1953), 328–31.

65. *Soundings*, pp. 69–92.

66. "Abode" seems to derive from the verb "abide" much as the Latin *mansio* derives from the verb *manere.*

67. See my article on *"Ennead* VI, 4–5," esp. 21–24.

68. See Du Roy, *Trinité*, pp. 188–91.

69. H. R. Schwyzer, "Plotinos," RE 21, cols. 547–48, and R. Harder, "Eine neue Schrift Plotins," in *Kleine Schriften* (Munich: Forschungsstelle für Buchwissenschaft an der Universitätsbibliothek Bonn, 1960), pp. 303–13.

70. See esp. *Enneads* 2.9 and 5.8 for pertinent materials that Augustine is likely to have read.

71. See my "Criticism of Origen," cited in note 16 above.

72. See also *Ver* 101, where *inferiores inferi* represent the place of punishment after death.

73. See Solignac's explanation of *judicium* in BA 14, pp. 631–34.

74. Bourke, p. 184.

75. G. Verbeke, "Augustin et le Stoicisme," RA, 1 (1958), 67–89, esp. 78–80.

76. See *Soundings*, pp. 95–139. Notice that a genetic study reveals that the *fovere* image-cluster springs originally, for Augustine personally, from the "warming" images associated with maternal "care"; its cosmic resonants (like the warming action of the sun) are relatively secondary, though still important. But to gauge the import of the image in any particular context, the reader must keep this double derivation in mind. I do not think Cambronne's method, in *L'Imaginaire*, pp. 91–168, is all that helpful toward making such discriminations.

77. See *Odyssey*, pp. 55–58.

78. See *Soundings*, pp. 221–45.

79. See above, note 65 to Part I.

80. *Early Theory*, pp. 61–62.

81. On the corollary, that punishment is immanent to the sin, see *Conf* 1.19, 4.14, 5.14; see also Solignac's note 1 to BA 13, p. 308.

82. On God as *interior intimo*, *Conf* 3.11; see also *Trin* 3.14 on God's working "from within."

83. From "The Dry Salvages," *Four Quartets* (London: Faber, 1963), lines 201–20.

84. The very term *apostatare* would have suggested to Augustine this movement of "standing away" from God; from there, the linkage to such images as "deserting," "abandoning," "departing from," would have been easy and natural.

85. See Emilie Zum Brunn, *Augustine on Being and Nothingness*, trans. Ruth Namad (New York: Paragon House, 1988), pp. 49–67 (henceforth: *Nothingness*).

86. See *Early Theory*, pp. 169–73.

87. *Early Theory*, pp. 161–66.

88. *Trinité*, pp. 279–81.

89. See above, note 79 to Part I.

90. See also Brown, *Augustine*, pp. 146–57.

91. See above, Part I, p. 40.

92. See also Bourke's *View of Reality*, pp. 3–7.

93. See above, Part I, pp. 35–52.

94. See *Recherches*, pp. 160–64, where Courcelle places paragraph 7.26 in parallel with 7.16 and 7.23.

95. See *Soundings*, pp. 44–45.

96. See above, p. 129.

III

The Gift of Stability

FOR THE TWENTIETH-CENTURY READER of the *Confessions*, Augustine's description of his posture toward Catholic Christianity, at this juncture of his life, is a disconcerting mix of muddle and clarity. But without question, one of the rays of clarity is this: his readings in the "Platonists" have resulted in his attaining the certainties he required in order to ground his "faith" in Catholic teaching—certainties he had earlier felt he lacked. Augustine leaves us in no doubt whatever on this point. We have seen him expressly emphasize that result of his Platonic experience in the two summaries he gives of it in Book 7, and we have also seen how he repeats that affirmation in the opening paragraph of Book 8. From both content and context, moreover, there can be little doubt that in precisely these cases he is speaking of certainties which he was conscious of possessing at that time, during the spring and summer months at Milan, in A.D. 386.

In the opening paragraph of Book 8, for instance, he unleashes a paean of praise to the God Who, in the very next phase of his story, is about to "break [his] bonds" in the final liberating act which climaxes his conversion. "I was certain [*certus eram*] about Your eternal life," he writes; "all doubt had been removed [*ablata*] from me": the expression suggests that doubt had been a weight which was now lifted from his shoulders. Consequently (there is something tireless about Augustine's insistence), "I desired, not to be more certain [*certior*] about You, but to be more stable in You" (*stabilis in te*). A bit further on (11) he confesses that he had formerly deferred becoming a dedicated follower of Christ, because his "perception of truth was uncertain"; but now, he sighs resignedly, he "no longer had that excuse." In the face of these repeated assurances that intellectual certainty was no longer his problem, it is more than a bit bemusing to come upon seasoned scholars who still fantasize upon an Augustine who will shortly address himself to the old priest Simplicianus in order to initiate, they claim, a series of speculative discussions on the consonance between Neoplatonism and Scripture.[1]

The Source of Stability

But what does Augustine mean by saying that he desired, not an increase in certainty about God, but to become more "stable" in Him? We have already noted that he habitually employs this image to express the soldierly firmness and solid footing to "stand his ground" against the onslaughts of the enemy.[2] But here Augustine is also thinking of a dimension well beyond the moral. He hopes to be enabled to stand against the restless tides, the ever-flowing currents of time and change, indeed, to emerge from and rise entirely above them; he aspires to "stand" immutably as God Himself "stands," to "see Him as He IS" and therefore to "BE, like Him," eternalized through that union with the Eternal. He does "not yet exist," but hopes to exist (cf. 7.16).

But the soldier may not be able to "stand" through his own exertions and without God's aid. In fact, he is incapable of "standing on his own," and must learn to take his "stand in God." And this, as Augustine views the matter, will require that radical humility which takes the form of totally entrusting oneself to the "care" of the Incarnate Christ.

Images of Incarnation

Toward the end of Book 7, Augustine has used several of his favorite images to depict what was still wanting to him. The *fovere* image, first:[3] he had to permit the Incarnate Christ to suckle him—as a nursing mother would (*lactesceret*)—with the "food of infancy," the "milk" which would confer the "strength" (*robur*) Augustine needed to "grow up" (as we saw earlier, 7.16) in order to eat the "food of grown-ups" (24). That in turn means to "enjoy" (*frui*) the direct and immediate vision of God in enduring fashion. Up to now, he has only sampled that heavenly banquet in filtered and fleeting glimpses: the strength God gives him, he now believes, will permit him to "stand" in that vision, to "withstand" and endure it, without being "beaten back" by its blazing radiance. In this image, the Incarnate Christ represents Divine "Food" (*cibus*) "mixed with flesh" (as a mother transforms the grown-up food she eats into the milky food adapted to her infant).

For He is at once Divine "Truth" and "Life," but now become enfleshed in order to be our "Way" to Truth and Life.

In another previous rehearsal passage (4.18–19, 27), Augustine expressed a second notion of how the Incarnate Christ helps sinners to "stand." This time the image (7.24) is dominated by a number of elements from the *Omnia* register.[4] He depicts sinful humans as having swollen up with the "tumor" of rebellious pride, and (one has to fill in this detail) having plunged by the "weight" of that swelling into this lower world. We are clothed, in consequence, with the "dwelling of clay," the "coat of skins," both of which symbolize the mortal body appropriate to this lower world.

From His "supereminent" position above all the "higher" denizens of the spiritual realm, God's own "Word" has come down into our lower world, and clothed Himself in our dwelling of clay, in our coats of skin. As Word and Eternal Truth, He "straightens up all who accept His sway" to enjoy contemplative union with Him (*subditos erigit ad seipsam*). But sinful humans are not subject to Him; they "need to be subjected" (*subdendos*). Christ's tactic is to subdue them through the disarming "lowliness" of His humanity, by a humility calculated to "detach them from themselves" (*deprimeret a seipsis*), lest "in their self-reliance [*fiducia sui*] they progress even further away" in their flight from God. God cannot "straighten us up" and make us "stand" without first rendering us prostrate.

As with Augustine himself, therefore, the first movement in conversion requires that we *cessare de se* (7.20), "let go," stop trying to "do it ourselves." We must abandon all the proud self-confidence which originally prompted us to reject our contemplative "subjection" to God and "stand on our own." Totally disarmed, we must let God convert us. And Augustine hopes that, in our headlong race away from Him, we may run into the heart-stopping experience of stumbling across the prostrate God, "Divinity Itself, become weak through having donned our coats of skin." Then, weakened like Him (*infirmarentur*), we may surrender by becoming equally prostrate, casting ourselves wearily upon Him (or Her?) (*lassi prosternerentur in Eam*), and so permit Him to "arise, and bear [us] up" along with Him (*surgens levaret eos*). Whenever he imagines God as taking, lifting, or raising us "up" (*suscipit, levat, assumit*), Augustine insists that we must first confess our helplessness and entrust ourselves unreservedly to His action.[5]

Views of Incarnation, Early and Later

These two images of Incarnation translate, of course, two aspects of the mature view of that mystery which Augustine claims to have mastered by the time he wrote the *Confessions*. That later view (we shall see more of it presently) represents the standpoint from which he is about to criticize what he now considers the more stunted view he had held in those earlier times—weeks? months? even longer?—after his Platonic experience. But both these mature views also translate, each in its way, two images of the achieved "stability" he has told us he still lacked.

The first of those images reflects the text which, subtly but insistently, he injected into our meditations when treating of his own babyhood: that unless we consent to become as humble as a "child again," we shall not enter the kingdom (1.11, 30). The second image reflects the same conviction come at from another angle: it is based on the translation of Isaiah 7:9b which, for some reason, Augustine chose to employ in his *Confessions*:[6] that unless we "stand in God," stop trying to "stand on our own feet," unless we strip ourselves of all pretensions at being able to "do it ourselves," and cast ourselves upon Him in unreserved trust, we "shall not stand" at all. Augustine is already preparing our minds for the climactic conversion scene to come, where both these images fuse in the person of the Lady Continence who appeals to Augustine in terms drawn from both registers.

CLUES FROM REHEARSAL PASSAGES

There is a whole line of interpretation which stresses that Book 8 of the *Confessions* is recounting Augustine's liberation from enslavement to sex, and little or nothing more than that.[7] If that were the whole story, or even the story's central point, then we would be obliged to conclude that in directing our attention to his desire to "stand," and to its theological implications, Augustine is merely dawdling. And yet, there are at least three important rehearsal passages which he devotes to making precisely the same point.

The first such rehearsal occurs in the midst of the "fugue" of conversion imagery to which I alluded earlier. Augustine is speaking of our love for the "changing things" of time (4.18): we must love them "in God" for only "in Him they stand firm" (*fixae stabiliuntur*). He shifts momentarily into the register of "violence": we must "bear them away to Him" (*rape*), "wrench our love round to Him" (*retorque*), "bear them away to God with [us]." Now he returns to the "stability" motif: we must "stand with Him," for only in that way can we truly "stand" (*state cum eo et stabitis*). Why do we wander so restlessly over "rough and laborious ways"? Those tiring exertions avail us nothing; we must learn to "rest in Him" and then we shall truly "find rest" (*requiescite in eo et quieti eritis*). Augustine goes on to portray the work of Incarnation in much the same imagery as we saw above, and climaxes with the paradoxical counsel we have come to expect: "Descend, so that you may ascend . . . for you have fallen [*cecidisti*] by ascending against God" (19). He himself, he concludes by telling us, "desired to stand" but could not, for he was "borne away" to exterior realities [*rapiebar*] and "under the weight of [his] pride sank down into the lowest of things" (*in ima decidebam*). In the image taken from Psalm 50:10, Augustine's "bones" could not "exult, for they had not yet been humbled" (4.27).

The second of those rehearsals we have already seen: at the climax of that same fugue, we saw how Augustine's portrayal of the returning sinner subtly shifted into the gentler register of the *fovere* image—no images of violence here!—until he was gradually transformed into a squalling infant returning to its mother: he was a little one who had run away from her because he so wanted to play with the big boys. Now, bruised and scraped, he returns in tears; he casts himself helplessly upon his mother's breast, and lets her care for him as only a mother can (5.1–2).

The final such rehearsal occurs in Augustine's portrait of Alypius. A chance remark on Augustine's part had served to free him, it seemed, from his mad attachment to such idle spectacles as the circus offered. It was totally unconscious on Augustine's part, he tells us, but God worked that way so that Alypius' "amendment might be clearly attributed to [Himself]" and not to the human agent who had furnished the "admonition" (6.11–12). Augustine now loses no opportunity to depict the "violence" of Alypius' response: he "snatched at" what Augustine had said and immediately applied it to himself (*in se rapuit*), "shook his spirit free [*excussit*] with a strong effort of self-control," and "tore himself up [*proripuit*] from the deep pit" into which he had plunged. Result: "all the filth of the circus was scattered [*resiluerunt*], and he never returned there again." End of story—or might have been, if someone other than Augustine were recounting it.

Alypius then goes off to Rome to pursue his study of law. There, he was "carried off [*abreptus est*] in an incredible way by an incredible passion for gladiatorial shows." How did this happen, since if left to himself (Augustine assures us) Alypius would have opposed and detested all such shows? Certain of his friends, Augustine answers, "dragged him with friendly violence" (*familiari violentia*) to the amphitheater—and we notice that Augustine has artfully inserted the theme of 'friendship too unfriendly,' familiar from the famous theft of pears. We pause to reflect on that "strong effort at self-control" with which Alypius "shook his spirit free" on a former occasion, and suddenly we encounter its sinister aftershadow: Alypius is quietly confident that though bodily present in the amphitheater, he can still remain absent in mind. So, he brags silently, *superabo*: he will "overcome" both his friends and the attraction of the games. We know the rest of the story: a kill is made, a mad shout raised, Alypius opens his eyes momentarily and—himself is spiritually slain. His "spirit," Augustine reflects, was "wounded and struck down" because it was "still audacious [*audax*][8] rather than strong," and "all the weaker because it presumed upon itself, whereas it should have relied on [God]." But, in time, God "plucked him out with a Hand that was"—paradox again—"most mighty yet most merciful," and "taught him to have confidence not in himself but in [God]" (13).

Do not trust in your own efforts, be they ever so vigorous; the violent "bear away" the kingdom, but only if they themselves are borne away by the gentle violence of love. Do not think yourself strong enough to stand on your own; take your stand, rather, in God. Stop trying to be a big fellow; cast your cares on Him as a little child does with its mother. Even when it comes to his liberation from sexual attachments, we shall see that this lesson in profoundest humility is the ultimate "bottom line" in Augustine's conversion story. Far from being one motif among others, though a number of motifs interweave in his account, this theme of absolute humility encloses the fire at the gem's very heart, and its radiance shines out through the stone's every facet.

Augustine's Earlier Notion of Incarnation

One reason why the strength to "stand" in God was lacking to him, Augustine felt, was that he needed humbly to "embrace" (*amplecti*) this Incarnate Wisdom, weak and prostrate for our sins. But he did not yet "hold fast" to Him, "humble to the humble" Christ (*humilis humilem*). Like a typical Neoplatonist, he was more than eager to "embrace" and "hold fast" to the Supernal Wisdom the *Hortensius* had unveiled to him; but the lowliness of Wisdom Incarnate was another matter. One cause for that, Augustine now realizes, was that his entire way of thinking about the Incarnation was defective.

For while he was correct in thinking of the Incarnate Christ as an integral human being, a *totus homo*, with a human soul and mind as well as a human body, he claims (25) that he thought of Him as all too human. He failed to see "through" His humanity to the Supernal Wisdom He was. True, he saw Christ as a wise man, unequaled for His "participation" in (obviously Divine) Wisdom, a participation more "excellent" and "perfect" than any other's; testimony to that excellence was His marvelous birth from a virgin. He was, consequently, both a model "example" (*exemplum*) of the human being's duty to despise all temporal goods in comparison with obtaining immortality; He was also a teacher who had "merited" that God out of His providential care for mankind[9] should endow Him with supreme "magisterial authority."

This was all to the good, and one would never expect Augustine to abandon what was positive in his early view: what, though, was missing from it? Augustine answers in two sybilline phrases: he failed to understand at that time what a "mystery" (*sacramentum*) was constituted by the "Word made flesh," and (what may come to the same thing) he did not see in Christ the *persona veritatis*, the very "person of Truth." But, except for the suspicion that Augustine is thinking of "flesh" and "persona" in terms of his accustomed image of the "veil" which both half-conceals and half-reveals the Reality behind it, we are left to guess what precise force we are to read into those pivotal terms.

How long did Augustine hold to the "inadequate" view he has outlined for us? He admits (*fateor*) that it was "some time later" (*aliquanto posterius*) that he learned how orthodox Catholic teaching differed from the heresy of Photinus. But if he wanted to be both vague and confusing, he could scarcely have chosen a vaguer expression than *aliquanto posterius*, or adduced a more confusing point of comparison than Photinianism: scholars are virtually unanimous that Augustine's early view hardly fits the definitions of Photinianism which he himself has furnished us![10]

So, the fact is that we do not know what *aliquanto posterius* imports; we have passed from clarity into the muddle I spoke of earlier. And one of the factors which keeps the muddle properly muddy is, I am convinced, the same kind of loose assumption we saw prevailing with respect to Augustine's account of his world-view: most scholars tacitly suppose that Augustine is describing here a state of mind which lasted only through the spring and summer of A.D. 386, or, at very most, for several months thereafter. But we are decades before the conciliar definitions of Ephesus (A.D. 431) and Chalcedon (A.D. 451); there is every possibility that Augustine could have held this *totus homo* theory, with the serene conviction that it was orthodox, for a number of years.[11]

The Philosopher Inflated

But it would appear that Augustine wants us to see that there was a deeper reason for his entertaining this view of Christ, which was at the same time the deeper reason why he did not yet "embrace" and "hold to" Him. The notion of Christ as a teacher of "wisdom" may well have been what encouraged Augustine to look on himself as a student of wisdom, indeed, a *peritus*, one who "knew." In any case, he "gabbled on" (*garriebam*) like one, was "puffed up" with self-styled knowledge, and eager to be regarded as a "sage"—exactly the wrong attitude for humbly embracing the humble Christ. But, he now realizes, not without a certain injustice, reading those Platonic books would never have encouraged him to adopt the attitude of humble Christian charity. How providential that he came from reading them to reading Scripture, and not the reverse!

Again the question comes up: How long did Augustine see himself as vainly strutting like a know-it-all? Was he still "gabbling" during the Dialogues he engaged in at Cassiciacum? He will tell us a bit later (9.7) that those Dialogues, though already written in God's "service," nonetheless "breathed forth" the "school of pride." But if that be true of the Cassiciacum Dialogues, what of his later writings, like the *De quantitate animae*, where an insufferably priggish Augustine treats his friend Evodius as though he were a plodding freshman in high school? We are repeatedly faced with that question, "How long?" and just as repeatedly left, exasperated, with little or no evidence for answering it.

READING ST. PAUL'S EPISTLES

The same question arises with respect to what Augustine recounts next. *Avidissime*, he tells us, "most eagerly" he "snatched up" (or "seized upon": *arripui*) the books of Scripture, and especially the writings of the "apostle Paul" (7.xxi.27). *Arripui*: we are encountering once again an example of the "violence" which "bears away" the kingdom.

But the tense of that verb, *arripui*, revives a question which had bothered us earlier on: when Augustine says, in the perfect tense, that he "saw" (*vidi*) or "came to know" (*cognovi*) something (7.xvi.21), does that preclude his having *repeatedly* seen it, or his *continuing* to progress toward a fuller knowledge of what he had once come to know for a "first time"? I suggest that we have a revealing clue to our answer here. For, sometime later, exactly how much later we do not know, a fellow-African named Ponticianus drops in on Augustine and remarks on the volume of St. Paul's Letters which he sees lying on a table, showing that Augustine was *still* engaged in reading them. Moreover, when Augustine later plunges into that garden to undergo the last paroxysms of his conversion struggle, he carries that same volume of Paul's Epistles with him; on hearing the child's voice, he once again "seized upon" (*arripui*) the book to read. His use of *arripui*, therefore, in the perfect tense, does not preclude the verb's having a certain repetitive and/or progressive force. There was, indeed, a single act in the past, a "first time" when Augustine "seized upon" St. Paul's Epistles; but that does not preclude his having taken them up *repeatedly* afterward, and *kept on* reading them. And the same thing could easily apply to those occurrences of "I saw" and "came to know" which bothered us earlier.

A Discovery of Grace . . . ?

Augustine claims to have found three sorts of things during this reading of St. Paul's Epistles. First, while a Manichee, he thought there existed self-contradictions in Paul's own teaching, as well as contradictions between Paul's doctrine and that of the Old Testament; now all semblance of contradiction simply vanished. Second, he claims to have discovered that whatever truths were contained in the Platonic writings (*illac*) could also be found (*hac*) in St. Paul (7.xx.26).

But the third set of discoveries he claims to have made raises all the same questions about "when" and "how long" and "how much later" which have been bedeviling us so persistently. For Augustine *seems* to be claiming that he found in St. Paul, at this early date, substantially the same teaching on grace which he assures us in his *Retractations* he came to acknowledge only some ten years later, when composing his replies to Simplician of Milan (*Retr* 2.1.1; *Praed* 4.8).[12] Let not the Neoplatonist "glory," for he has been "given" not only what he has seen, but the very act of seeing it (*etiam ut videat*). For, to paraphrase Paul, "What has he that he has not received?" And, furthermore, not only do we need to be "admonished to see" God, as Neoplatonists admit, but we also need to be "healed in order to hold fast to" Him. For (Augustine now evokes the image that we are all *peregrinantes*, "wayfarers" far from our homeland) it is one thing to catch a glimpse of one's blissful *patria* from a distant mountain-top, and ignore, or disdain, the "way" leading to it; it is far better to be like many an untutored Christian believer, momentarily incapable of "seeing" that distant *patria*, yet willing to "walk" in the Way "by which he will arrive, and see, and hold fast" to that object of bliss. *Qua veniat et videat et teneat*—the echoes of the erotic imagery of the *Hortensius* episode are distant, but nonetheless real.

Or, in another image, we are sickly weak and in need of healing. There is another "law" in our bodily "members" which resists the "delight" which the "interior man," the mind–soul, may have learned to take in God's "Law." And at this juncture Augustine assumes we will remember that the Eternal Son is identical with God's Eternal "Law" as well as being the "homeland" of Eternal Truth Augustine has recently come to glimpse. And our weakness is the "just" God's "lawful" reply to our sinfulness, iniquity, impiety. Since, moreover, our sin followed the pattern of Satan's own—both of us refused to "stand in the Truth" to which we were invited to cling immutably—it was right that we be delivered over into his power.

God's "Hand," therefore, "has pressed down heavy upon us" (*gravata est super nos*). For again, that "Hand" is none other than His creative Word, the Eternal Truth Who is also His universal Law. And that Law of the *Omnia* decrees that the soul which becomes "heavy" with earthly desires must necessarily "fall," and fall into a "body of death" from which only Christ, Eternal Truth become Incarnate Way—that same Hand, but now engaged in "lifting" us—can "deliver" the fallen soul.

Here, Augustine feels, he has located the central difference between Neoplatonism and the Gospel: he almost certainly understood its leading thinker, Plotinus, as admitting that our "fall" was the "lawful" consequence of a wrongful act of *tolma*, an "audacious" turning away from contemplative subordination in order to delight in the autonomous deployment of our own active powers (*Ennead* 5.1.1). The Neoplatonists, too, had some inkling that the wrongest attitude the soul could adopt was that of "standing" on its own![13] But did they truly appreciate the catastrophic seriousness of all this? Where were their "tears of confession," and, in the first instance, their "confession of sins" (*confessio peccatorum*), for their rebellious abandonment of God? Where was the "sacrifice" which pleased God, "a troubled spirit, a humbled and contrite heart"? How could they fail to realize that sinful souls could never be healed and liberated except by some incredibly gracious initiative on God's part, like redemptive Incarnation and Death?

But most poignant of all, now that God has shown His touching "care" for sinful mankind by condescending to send His Son to live and teach and suffer and die for us—not only to show us, but to *be*, our "Way" home—where was their *confessio laudis*, their "confession of praise," their psalms celebrating "the salvation of the people, the bridal city, the pledge of the Holy Spirit, the cup of our redemption"? Now that the whole world, virtually, had come to believe in that incredible act of mercy, how could these "wise and prudent" philosophers fail to discern the difference between "presumption and confession," and consequently "disdain to learn from Him, because He is meek and humble of heart"?

Alas, *revelasti ea parvulis*: it takes a "little one" to accept this good news.

Here, accordingly, unless I am much mistaken, we have nothing less than the complete theology of grace which Augustine came to formulate only when replying to Simplician's questions on St. Paul. And yet, to all initial appearances at least, he seems to be telling us here that he came to see it in St. Paul's writings, if not in A.D. 386, at least very early in his own career. Could there be some misundertanding in all this?

Perhaps a closer inspection of his language will help. *Et coepi et inveni*, Augustine writes. "So, I started in" as Bourke translates that *Et coepi*; or in Ryan's version, "I made a beginning." Ryan ignores the initial *et*, but both renditions suggest the inception of an extended effort over time. And Augustine's use of the term *inveni* suggests something analogous. One fully expects the term *invenire* to pair off with its usual Augustinian partner, *quaerere*, so that the ear attuned to his prose half-consciously supplies it here: what he has begun is a process of "seeking"—patient and persistent. "And I found," found what he had been seeking, although (spoken in an aside, *sotto voce*) it took him a long, long time to do it! And besides, what good would it have done his readers to regale them with a scrupulously "historical" account of his rudimentary theology of grace from those early days?

That attempt to "save" him may not satisfy even the most ardent defenders of the truthfulness and "historicity" of Augustine's text. But the problem is real, and that is the best I can do to suggest a plausible settlement of it.

Onward, Christian Soldiers

Augustine brings the seventh book of his *Confessions* to a close by invoking a martial metaphor, setting it in the most somber hues of his *peregrinatio* image (27). The Neoplatonists may well have espied the supernal "land of peace," but life here below is unremitting warfare. They have not found the road leading to that land of peace, but wander about aimlessly through trackless barrens. In addition, they find themselves ambushed and assailed by the "fugitives and deserters" from the "heavenly army" who make up the hostile regiments of Satan, that "lion and dragon," the "prince" of these nocturnal regions.

Meanwhile, the army led by Christ, the "heavenly king," advances safely under His protective care. Its soldiers "hold fast" to the One Who is Himself the homeward Way, whereas the enemy robber-bands keep their distance from Him. His enemies avoid Him, in fact, as they would a punishment: the punishment, Augustine hopes we see, of crucifixion. For (in his companion metaphor to this one), our only safety, while traversing the treacherous seas of temporal life, lies in our "holding fast" to the "Wood" (*Conf* 1.25; *InJo* 2 4).

Even while composing the closing paragraphs of Book 7, therefore, Augustine was hinting at the need for "stability" he speaks of in the opening lines of Book 8. That lesson lies at the core of both his later view of the Incarnation and his "discovery" of grace. But the stability he yearns for is profoundly paradoxical, and at Milan he had not yet come to realize that: he still had to learn, both in theory and in spiritual attitude, to straighten up by first bowing down, to rise by first descending, to "stand" by first casting himself prostrate before the Incarnate Christ. Like a "little one," quite precisely like a suckling baby, he must practice to entrust himself unreservedly to the care of his touchingly "maternal" God.

WHAT HAPPENED IN THAT MILANESE GARDEN (*CONFESSIONS* 8)

To understand the sinuous turnings of the story Augustine is about to tell, the best place to begin is at the end. This formula is often a sound one for reading his early Dialogues, but it is especially helpful in providing the Ariadne's thread which leads through the maze we are about to enter. That thread, I suggest, is the text from Paul's Letter to the Romans which, if we are to believe Augustine, had such a thunderous effect upon him: it seems to have put an end to all his struggles, and written *finis* to the lengthy process of his conversion.

On the Capitulum Romans 13:11–14

Not every scholar would agree on the procedure I have just outlined. A number of them, in fact, would heap a generous dose of skeptical acid on any supposition that this notorious text casts any genuine illumination on the workings of Augustine's final conversion. Fr. Paul Henry, for example, years ago, saw Augustine as reading into these Pauline verses "a meaning they do not have"; this, Henry thought, had to be the reason why so relatively banal a passage could exert so disproportionate a power on him.[14] John O'Meara points to the "special circumstances"—the story of Antony, the conversion related by Ponticianus—that may have made Augustine's "happening on this particular text seem so remarkable, so providential."[15] We shall see that O'Meara brings us closer to an answer, but he also leaves us with the lurking suspicion that there must be more to the story than that.

But at least one scholar has, more recently, gone so far as to argue that as a matter of factual history this text did not figure at all in Augustine's conversion at Milan.[16] If it had, Dr. Ferrari reasons, we would certainly expect to find him citing it, or at least alluding to it, with some frequency during those years which followed closely on his conversion at Milan. But no; citations and allusions do occur, but only some years later, and they all cluster, suspiciously, in the years when Augustine was composing his *Confessions*! There was good reason for that, Ferrari's case continues; Augustine's growing interest in St. Paul's conversion is explained by the fact that he had resolved to take that conversion as a model for describing his own.[17]

Yet Augustine has, I think, furnished us with an elegant set of clues which point in a different direction. The first of them seems to have gone completely unnoticed. At the climax of the garden episode we are considering, he hears that child's voice telling him to "take, and read" (*tolle, lege*); he does so, and then proceeds to quote two verses from the thirteenth chapter of Romans: verses 13 and 14. But he tells us quite expressly that he read, in silence, not only those two verses but also the *capitulum* on which his eyes first fell, the "chapterlet," or chapter-subdivision, the sense-unit containing those two verses.[18] Augustine's habitual employment of the term *capitulum*[19] makes it clear that he used the term this way, and if we look for the appropriate sense-unit in this case, we must infer that his reading began with verse 11, included verse 12, and only then ran on to the verses he actually quotes, 13 and 14.[20]

On the assumption that our inference is sufficiently plausible to be accepted as a working hypothesis, what did Augustine read?

Allow me to give as brutally literal a translation of the Latin as I am able to concoct; I work from the version he was familiar with:[21]

> 11: And knowing that this is the time [*hoc scientes tempus*] because the hour has now come [*hora est jam*] for us to rise up from sleep [*de somno surgere*]. For our salvation is nearer now [*nunc*] than when we [first] believed. 12: Night precedes, but day approaches. Let us cast aside [*abjiciamus*] the works of darkness, therefore, and garb ourselves [*induamur*] in the armor of light.

Now we come to the verses Augustine actually quotes; again, I shall be brutally literal:

> 13: Let us walk honorably, as though in daylight; not in rioting and drunkenness, not in chambering and [acts of] shamelessness, not in contention and emulation—[or, less brutal but perhaps more exact, "not in a spirit of contentiousness and mutual rivalry": *non in contentione et aemulatione*], 14: but garb yourselves—[*induite* again]—in the Lord Jesus Christ, *et carnis providentiam ne feceritis in concupiscentiis.*

This closing phrase, I am persuaded, Augustine understood as chiding him to:

> exercise no carnal (or human) providence amid [or: in view of, on behalf of] your concupiscences.

Scriptural Associations of the Romans Capitulum

Now, Mlle Anne-Marie La Bonnardière has not yet published her study of Augustine's employment of Paul's Letter to the Romans, but her book on First Thessalonians has already confirmed what a close reading of the *Confessions* would lead one to surmise.[22] By the year 400, if not before, Augustine had come to associate this same *capitulum* from Romans with "matching" elements drawn from another Pauline text, 1 Thessalonians 5:4–8. "You, however," Paul says there,

> are not in darkness . . . 5: for you are all children of light and sons of God; we are not of the night nor of darkness. 6: Therefore let us not sleep like those others, but stay awake and be sober. 7: For those who get drunk, get drunk by night, and those who sleep, sleep by night; 8: we who are of the day are sober, having put

on faith and charity as a breastplate, and the hope of salvation as
a helmet.

Notice the image-elements which correspond to those found
in the text from Romans: night and day, sleeping and waking,
sobriety and drunkenness, and then, that final touch, "putting
on" (*induti*) the armor of the Christian soldiery—one can understand that Augustine associated the two texts. In his *Confessions*
(at 13.15), he explicitly quotes only verse 5:5 but in a context
studded with similar conversion imagery.

Now Augustine associates both those passages, in turn, with
elements drawn from Ephesians 5:8–14. At a crucial turning in
Book 8, in paragraph 22, he quotes from the first verse of this
passage: "You were at one time darkness, but are now light in the
Lord"; he then goes on to underline the same message as he does
in his tireless repetitions of the key phrases of the same verse: we
were, indeed, once "darkness," but now, are light *in Domino*: "in
the Lord," not "in ourselves," despite what the Manichees persist
in thinking (9.10; 13.3, 9, 13, 15). Again, to understand his theology of conversion, this point must be accorded central importance: it is all God's doing.

Verses 11–12 of the Ephesians text warn against doing the
"vain" and "shameful" deeds which are done in "darkness"; but
a more striking analogue to the text from Romans occurs at verse
14, where Paul quotes what was evidently an ancient Christian
hymn: "Awake, sleeper, and arise from the dead, and Christ will
enlighten you." We shall see Augustine quote this verse in the
course of elaborating his own masterful meditation on slumber
and waking. Again, though, the fact that he makes this text so
frequent a companion to the one from Romans suggests what
elements they had in common for his imagination, and, so, what
elements of the Romans text held importance for him. The emergence from night to day, from darkness to light, from sleep to
waking—conversion was all these things, and all of them tran-
spired *in Domino*, not on account of anything we were or did,
except that we surrendered totally to the workings of God's grace.

We may reasonably suppose, I suggest, that the elements common to these three texts point to at least some of the features of
the Romans *capitulum* which, in John O'Meara's words, Augustine
must have found shatteringly "apposite"; it would further seem

plausible that those elements converged to make his sheer chancing on this precise passage seem utterly "remarkable," indeed, nothing less than "providential." Accept this last affirmation, for the moment, as a next step toward refining our working hypothesis; what would that hypothesis look like when spelled out in detail?

The Impact of Verses 13:11–12

First of all, notice how many of the elements contained in the texts from First Thessalonians and Ephesians correspond to matching elements from the first two verses (11–12) of our *capitulum*. These are the verses which Augustine fails to quote, and which scholars, consequently, when trying to understand the impact of the Romans text, have uniformly left out of consideration. Yet look at them: from darkness to light, night to day, sleeping to waking, and, finally, that mention of "putting on" (*induere*) the armor of a soldier of Christ—these elements all are found in the two texts which Augustine habitually uses as "sidelighting" for the text from Romans. But, to repeat, when it comes to the Romans *capitulum* itself, they are found, not in the verses (13–14) Augustine actually quotes in his *Confessions* account, but in the two verses (11–12) which precede them in the same *capitulum*. Since these are the verses which our working hypothesis postulates that he read at the same time, we are entitled to think that one step has been taken toward converting that hypothesis into a thesis.

One might object that the term *induere* occurs where Paul speaks of "putting on Christ" in verse 14. But Henry found that expression so vague that he was compelled to speculate it meant "putting on Christ" in some indeterminate "mystical" sense or other. Having fixed his attention exclusively on verses 13 and 14, he never came to suspect that the implied direct object of *induere*, in Augustine's mind, was the "armor" proper to a soldier of Christ; instead of being mystical, the association was military. Henry's quandary shows that such an idea would never occur to an alert researcher, unless he expanded his attention to take verse 12 into consideration. But the story of this *capitulum* is by no means over; a closer examination of Augustine's account furnishes an abundance of evidence to further confirm the contribution which verses 11 and 12 made to his way of imaging God's work in his conversion.

Striking Features in the Romans Text

Turning, now, to a direct examination of the *capitulum* from Romans 13, I submit that we may speak of five distinct image-elements which Augustine detected there, each of which affected him; but the convergence of all of them struck him with galvanizing power. Some, but not all, of those elements are also present in the two "sidelighting" texts we have just examined.

The first of those images—to start with the most obvious of them—is contained in that warning against "chambering and [acts of] shamelessness." This is the portion of the Pauline quotation which is regularly exploited by those who are convinced that Augustine's chief, if not exclusive, spiritual problem was his hot-blooded sexuality. Henry, though, was right in claiming that this interpretation of the text had something trite and banal about it. Yet it must be said that, read from this standpoint, virtually every other feature of Paul's *capitulum* can be ignored, or at least dismissively played down; there is something invitingly neat about that. Another result is that the dramatic apparition of Lady Continence, just before the famous *tolle, lege* moment, is given a perfectly obvious interpretation: she brings healing to those unruly sexual urges of his. What else, after all, would any self-respecting Lady Continence be concerned with?

But was Augustine thinking all that neatly? And is this how he himself understood that reality, *continentia*? We shall have to probe more deeply into both those questions, shortly.

The second element in the Romans text may come as a surprise. It is lodged in that curious phrase which I have translated as "and exercise no carnal providence amid your concupiscences." Dr. Ferrari admits that we have here an exception to his basic contention, for Augustine both quotes and comments on this portion of the Romans text in paragraphs 76–77 of his *Exposition of Some Propositions from the Epistle to the Romans*, written in or about the year 394—hence, well before he composed his *Confessions*.[23] But so convinced is Ferrari that the liberation from sexual attachment is of near-exclusive importance in Book 8[24] that he fails to see this particular fragment as carrying any weight in Augustine's conversion story.

But the interpretation which Ferrari attributes to the Augustine of A.D. 394 is very akin to the one which emerges from reading

Book 8 in the light of my hypothesis.[25] Ironically, though, Ferrari's preoccupation with the sexual aspect of Augustine's conversion stands in the way of his making anything of it. To anticipate that interpretation for a moment: assume that Augustine was coming to realize that his desire for womanly embraces, even in the perfectly legitimate setting of Christian marriage, had as its inescapable consequence that he had to "provide," work for a living, in order to afford the "pleasures and delights" he desired, to say nothing of supporting his wife and any children that might be born from their union. In that case, he would have taken this segment of Paul's text as a scalding reminder that his "concupiscences" imposed on him the burden of "exercising" this "carnal" sort of "providence." And in order to ensure that providence, he had no alternative but to engage in the busy life, the *negotium*, of worldly "action."

This mention of the life of "action" serves to recall a connected feature of the Romans text which is usually ignored: that mention of "contentiousness and rivalry." We have seen how insistently Augustine underlines the fact that the "vain" *negotium* of the professional *rhetor* committed him to unremitting competition by means both fair and foul; his "insides," Augustine tells us, were torn apart by this spirit of "rivalry and contentiousness"; the term "rat-race" was never more aptly applied. But there was more: the chafing distress which the "burden" of his career imposed on him only sharpened his realization that his heart was not really in all this, and that the kind of life he most deeply longed for was the life of peaceful leisure, the *otium*, the utter *vacatio* of contemplation.

The third image-element in this *capitulum*, and in the associated texts from Ephesians and Thessalonians, is that contrast between darkness and light, along with the peremptory command to "rise up" (*surgere*) from sleeping to waking, from night to day.

But in order to "rise up"—*surgere*, exactly as the Prodigal did and then "returned" to his Father[26]—Augustine must shuck off everything which until now has been "weighing" him down. In terms of the familiar *pondus* image, he must "cast away" (Paul in this *capitulum* uses the energetic term *abjicere* instead of the milder Gospel term *relinquere*: to "leave behind") all the pompous vesture of worldly vanity, all those burdening "works of darkness," and "garb himself" instead in the "armor" of light—the armor which Thessalonians describes as "the breastplate of faith and charity" and the "helmet" that is our "hope of salvation." He is being summoned to strip away (*exuere*) his cumbersome worldly garb and exchange it (*induere*) for what he will call, in the *Contra Academicos*, the "light armor" proper to the *militia Christi* (*Acad* 3.15).[27] He has come to recognize that he is being called to that precise form of the contemplative life which consists in being a *servus Dei*, a servant of God and a "soldier of Christ."

But he recognizes keenly that he has been hearing that far trumpet, and desperately blocking his ears to it, for days and months and years. We saw how he dilates, in Book 6, on the agony his compromising delaying tactics were causing him. Now, at last, the best of his heart aches to say yes, to cut away everything and follow that call. Tomorrow, perhaps? or maybe sometime next week, or next month? His dilatory postponements have come to disgust, even torment, him. Why can he not do it *now*?

And here the opening words of that text from Romans came crashing out of the heavens with a command that was also promise. While writhing in the agony of his self-imposed delays, he is driven in desperation to pray to his God: "Give what You command, and command what You will." And God's own word replies: "*This* is the time," "*Now, now* is the hour." Salvation is closer now, indeed, salvation is at hand. *Iam*: now!

Again, Dr. Ferrari has furnished unwitting confirmation of this suggestion: he points out that, in the very same locus where Augustine commented on "carnal providence," he chose also to comment on verse 11. That choice, of course, holds no more significance for Ferrari than does the comment on "carnal providence." But from the moment one assumes that the unquoted verses of Paul's *capitulum* bear as much weight as their quoted partners, Augustine's illumination of verse 11 could not be more apposite. He is obviously thinking directly of that peremptory "*this* is the time" when he assures us that verse 11 "looks to what is said" (in 2 Corinthians 6:2): *Ecce nunc tempus acceptabile, ecce nunc dies salutis*: "Behold, *now* is the time, *now* is the day of salvation"— the same *nunc* which we shall see punctuating the climactic sections of Augustine's account of what happened to him in that garden.

To sum up, accordingly: Paul's words from Romans did, in fact, speak to the "chains" of Augustine's sexual attachments—an application of Augustine's familiar *pondus* image. But there was a second focus of the Romans text as well: it spoke to those sexual attachments as precisely binding Augustine to the "yoke," the "burden" (*iugum, onus*), of "making provision," exercising human, "carnal providence" for them, by a life of secular activity; it also added that further note, that his activity as a *rhetor* was torn by "contention and rivalry." Those two negative factors are pulling against a third, Augustine's smoldering desire, going back to his reading of Cicero's *Hortensius*, to embrace the contemplative life. Only now he has come to identify that form of life with "military service" in the army of Christ. But, fourthly, he images that step as a "stripping off" and "casting away" of his encumbering baggage and a donning of the lighter armor of a soldier of Christ, as "rising up" from night to day, darkness to light, sleeping to waking. And, fifthly, he aches to do it *now, now,* with no further delay.

This, therefore, in finished form, is the working hypothesis I am proposing: the *capitulum* from Romans, reinforced by the associated texts from Ephesians and First Thessalonians (Augustine *has* told us he had been reading St. Paul), provides us with five thematic "keys" to identify the image-motifs that subtly interweave throughout the eighth Book of Augustine's *Confessions*. It was not simply a string of outer circumstances; it was outer circumstances viewed through the prism of Augustine's interior agony of soul which charged the Romans text with its extraordinary power. So much for the lines of my hypothesis; now it is time to test that hypothesis against the detail of Augustine's account.

IMAGES FROM ROMANS IN AUGUSTINE'S CONVERSION ACCOUNT

I have already stressed how Augustine begins Book 8 by assuring us that his desire was no longer to become "more certain" (*certior*) about God, but to arrive at a firmer "stand" in Him (*stabilior in te esse*). In his "temporal life," however, in both his personal and his professional lives, he experienced nothing but instability (*nutabant omnia*). Now, in a resumption of the military metaphor with which he terminated Book 7, and which features prominently in the Romans text, he proposes to narrate how God "laid siege" to him (*circumvallabar abs te*). It is God's action that "broke the chains" which formerly shackled him to earthly desires (l),[28] and, consequently, tied him to "this-worldly" occupations, *in saeculo*.

The desires (*cupiditates*) he once had for honors and money no longer inflame him, no longer contribute their share of impetus for engaging in those activities; consequently, he has come to resent these activities like a "heavy slavery" (*servitutem gravem*); they have become a "ponderous burden" to him (*oneri mihi erat valde*). The "sweetness" (*dulcedo*) of God and the "beauty" (*decus*) of His lofty dwelling place have begun to exercise that *delectatio victrix*, that "conquering delight," by which grace draws the soul upward; but he was still "bound" (*conligabar*) by the love of woman (2). The images are remarkably consistent: the life of secular action weighs him down, whereas the attachment to sexual activity ties him up!

The Visit to Simplician

Now Augustine resolves to go to consult the old priest Simplician. And his reason for doing so is perfectly in line with what he has just told us. He has come to realize that he must make a radical decision concerning the conduct of his "temporal life"; to be precise, he has actually come to question his former resolve to marry.

He wants his readers (and especially his Manichee adversaries) to be perfectly clear on the way he envisaged this question: Paul's Epistles have assured him that marriage is one legitimate way of life a Catholic may choose; whatever the Manichees might think, there is nothing wrong with a good Christian's marrying. And yet, Paul would prefer us all to choose the "better" course, to be celibate, "as he was." In the face of that challenge, Augustine now sees himself as a "weakling" (*infirmior*), "held in thrall to a woman"; he has chosen to occupy a "softer place," far from the firing line (*molliorem locum*). But the consequence is inexorable: he is "languid and consumed by the exhausting cares" (*curis marcidis*) of "secular" activities.

Not only St. Paul, but Christ Himself, had made it clear: there are "eunuchs" who make themselves such for the kingdom of God. Yet that may not be the way for everyone, as the same Christ made clear by adding, "He that can take it, let him take it." The Church, accordingly, permitted her sons freely to choose—"this one went this way," *alius sic ibat* (in Paul's expression), *alius autem sic*, "and another went that way": married or celibate as the case might be. But what others might do was their business; Augustine is resolved to consult Simplician *precisely on this issue*: Which of the two, for an individual disposed exactly as *he* was (*sic affecto ut ego eram*), was the "fit way" (*aptus modus*) for *him* to "walk"?

Augustine now briefly reviews those dispositions of his. He had gone beyond the "vanity" of those who had not "found" God and His creative Word by means of the "witness" of all creation; again, certainties of that sort were not his problem. And God's "right hand" had "taken [him] up" and drawn him out of the ranks of those who, though knowing God, have failed to glorify and give thanks to Him; he has been placed, now, where he could recover his strength (*ubi convalescerem*). But that recovery of strength must follow the pattern of becoming a "little one"; he has to learn not to "wish to seem wise," for those who "claimed to be wise were made foolish." The wisdom he seeks must be one with "piety." This was the "good pearl" he had already found (*inveneram*: as far back as his reading of the *Hortensius*?), and he ought to have been ready, long since, to sell all he had and purchase it. And still, he quailed before taking that step (*et dubitabam*) (8.2).

An Exemplum: *Humility*

At this point Augustine credits Simplician with remarkable insight. This same old priest would later provoke him to review Paul's Letter to the Romans, and so come around to realize that God's grace had vastly more to do with converting us than human will-power ever could. Now, as if dimly anticipating that later insight, Simplician perceives that what Augustine needs is a lesson—in just that form a professional *rhetor* would appreciate, a stirring *exemplum*—of humility. And what more apposite example could he choose than that of another learnèd *rhetor*, especially since Augustine himself had furnished the man's name.

For in recounting his "wanderings" of mind and soul, Augustine has mentioned that he has recently been reading certain Platonic books which Marius Victorinus had translated into Latin. Victorinus had been a famous *rhetor* in Rome some years earlier, and had, Augustine was told, died a Catholic. Simplician congratulates him, in passing, on his choice of philosophical readings: far better he should read the Platonists than those of their rivals whose thinking was full of materialist explanations "according to the elements of this world." In the Platonists' writings, on the other hand, "God and His Word" were allusively introduced in every way possible.

This is the single theoretical remark the *Confessions* records as coming from Simplician.[29] Augustine makes the reason for that clear in his very next sentence. Simplician realizes that Augustine has not come to him for speculative tutoring, but he has also sensed, with the sagacity of an experienced spiritual counselor, that Augustine needs to be "exhorted to adopt the humility of Christ, which is hidden from the wise and revealed to little ones."

To that end, Simplician recounts the tale of Marius Victorinus' conversion to Christianity. The parallels with Augustine are striking: Victorinus had been, in the first place, an African; he had also been a distinguished *rhetor*, immensely learnèd in all the liberal arts, but especially in philosophy. He had gained everything that a foreigner like him could hope for in the way of reputation and worldly eminence, including ("what this world's citizens deem an outstanding honor") a statue erected in his honor in the Roman forum. At the height of his career he had been, in short, all that the unconverted side of Augustine's heart still aspired to become. Simplician, one suspects, was acute enough to sense that Augustine was not unmoved by prospects of worldly honors!

And yet, there was about Victorinus the subtlest taint of pride. It had previously shown in the way he thunderously defended the worship of Rome's multifarious idols by which the Roman nobles of his time were "puffed up" (8.3). It showed, as well, in the way he later claimed to be a Christian, privately, though not publicly; "walls, after all," he joked away Simplician's protests, "do not make the Christian, do they?" For he "feared," Augustine estimates, "to offend his friends, who were proud worshippers of demons" (*superbos daemonicolas*), and wanted to avoid incurring the enmity of those in high places. So, as Victorinus himself later came to realize, he had been guilty of the great crime of being, in effect, a proud follower of the proud demons, a man ashamed of Christ's "humility."

The Firmitas *of a Little One*

Gradually, however, through reading and waxing desire, he drank
in strength enough (*firmitatem*: one thinks of the "stability" still
wanting in Augustine) to submit to the siege God was laying to
him. In the end he consented to become a "child of Christ, an
infant of [God's baptismal] font." Like a vanquished warrior, he
bent his neck "to the yoke of humility" (3).

The Violence of Love

Finally, despite the offer that it could be done privately in order
to save him embarrassment, in a crowning gesture of humility,
Victorinus refused to "look back on vanities" (4); he was publicly
baptized a Catholic. As he rose to make his profession of faith,
his fellow-Christians whispered, then shouted, their joy to one
another: "and they all wanted to bear him away [*rapere*] into their
hearts. And bear him away they did [*rapiebant*], loving and rejoicing; these were the hands they used to bear him away" (*hae rapientium manus erant*) (5).

We have noticed how the image of military warfare threads it
way through these paragraphs. Augustine's preached works show
how naturally that *militia* theme summons up the note of force,
violence: *vis, violentia*, those are, after all, the soldier's stock in
trade (*SS 351* 4–5, *302* 15; *Enn 131* 6, *142* 9, *86* 6). But the Gospel
variant of that theme is visibly surfacing here, and, again, with
the paradoxical twist Augustine frequently applies. Very soon he
will exclaim exasperatedly to Alypius that even "the unlearnèd
rise up [*surgunt*] and," like the "violent" of Matthew's Gospel,
"bear heaven away" (*caelum rapiunt*) (8.19).

Rapere, rapiebant, rapientium: we have to excuse his insistence.
For Augustine does not want us to miss the radical transformation
"violence" must undergo in order to harmonize with the Christian
universe of love and grace. The applauding throng at Victorinus'
baptism were being violent, but with the sweet violence of charity: they would, all of them, have wished to lay hold of him and
bear him away, but the "hands" of that violence were the spiritual
hands of love and rejoicing (*amando et gaudendo; hae rapientium
manus erant*) (5). In a partner-text to the ones from Ephesians and
Thessalonians which we saw resonating with our *capitulum* from

Romans, Paul insists that the "soldier of Christ" must garb himself in the vesture of warfare, in greaves and breastplate and helmet; but over all these, Paul insists, he must "put on charity" (Col
3:14). For charity, Augustine is convinced, is the only appropriate
vehicle for Christian violence; love is the most powerful and enduring form of influence any heart can exert upon another.

On Bliss Refound

Augustine here departs from his line of development by introducing a meditation (6–8) on the special sweetness joy has for us
when it is found, or, rather, "re-found," after having been lost.
So it was with the Prodigal, the sheep that went astray, the
drachma that the woman of the Gospel had lost; so it is with
victory and peace after battle, with health restored after life-
threatening illness. "What is happening in the soul," Augustine
begs God to tell him, "that takes greater delight when things it
loves are found, or given back to it [inventis aut redditis], than if
the soul had kept them constantly in its possession" (7)? God
Himself is sheer uninterrupted joy; and there are heavenly beings
gathered about Him whose joy is equally uninterrupted. "Why is
it that this, our part of creation, alternates between decline and
progress, affronts and reconciliations?" Is it enough to answer that
this is simply the "mode of being" which God accorded to the
realities of our lower world when He created the variegated Omnia, with its strata of beings unequal in their perfection, each appointed its proper place and time? No, Augustine hints; for the
fuller answer recognizes that we have been meditating on joys
recovered, found after being lost. The Prodigal, the erring sheep,
returned: that is the dark enigma the Gospel would have us acknowledge. And yet, vix redimus ad Te, "how reluctant we are to
return" to God (8)!

Now, in a return to the "violence" image, Augustine exclaims:
"Act, Lord! Do it, rouse us and call us back, inflame and bear us
away [rape], draw us by Your sweetness [dulcesce]: let us love, let
us run" as lovers do toward the embrace of their belovèd. Once
more, we recognize the erotic imagery from the Hortensius episode, but we also detect more clearly now the language of grace
as that "sweet violence" of love, by which God draws us through
"conquering delight."

A Triumph for Christ's Soldiery

Augustine once again takes up his meditation on Victorinus' conversion. Briefly, he evokes the image of light and darkness: God's "call" summons many to "return" (*redire*), but to return from the deep Tartarus of blindness to "receive the Light," from spiritual darkness to the brightness of day.

Augustine now reflects on how Paul, the very Apostle who insisted on that Christian preference for the "weak things of this world," especially valued the "victory" which he, soldier of Christ that he was, had gained in "warfare" over the proud proconsul Paul: he, too, in the end, *per . . . militiam debellata superbia*, was brought to "pass under the sweet yoke of Christ." Augustine continues with the *militia* image: Victorinus' conversion was similar to the proconsul Paul's: the "enemy" had held him in an "impregnable bastion," and employed his skilled tongue as a "weapon" to slaughter many through worship of Rome's false gods. Christ's victory in this campaign was tantamount to the liberation of many whom Victorinus' prestigious influence formerly held in bondage (9).

Vacare Deo

With this story, Augustine admits, Simplician accomplished exactly what he had intended: the young *rhetor* is set "on fire" to imitate his forebear. *Ad hoc enim et ille narraverat*: this, and not some speculative discussion of Christian Neoplatonism, was the point both of Augustine's visit and of Simplician's response. Augustine recalls that, sometime after Victorinus' baptism, the emperor Julian published an edict which forbade Christians like him to continue teaching. What a welcome liberation that must have been, Augustine muses, affording the man "free time," a contemplative "vacation" as it were, to devote only to God (*occasionem vacandi tibi*). We have already seen Augustine ring the changes on that term *vacare*; we shall presently see more of it. It introduces a motif which will assume increasing importance as Book 8 proceeds. Augustine will use it to express the kind of liberation from toil, the leisure (*otium*) or "time off" as opposed to busy-ness (*negotium*), which a person longs for in order to reflect, study, contemplate, or simply be with God. But that same term will also convey something far more powerful and distinctively religious: the Isaian *cessatio* from restless striving which leaves room for God to act, for God to "be God." *Vacate et videte*, Psalm 45:11 commanded, "Be still, and know that I am God" (see *SS 103* 3, 6, *78* 3; *En 45* 14–15).

The Bondage of the Flesh

Although he is longing for just such an *occasio vacandi*, Augustine finds himself still "bound [*ligatus*], not by some enemy's iron, but by [his] own iron will." And yet, that will of his had in fact been fashioned into an enemy's chains, the enemy being Satan. He had lured Augustine to forge, through act upon lustful act, the "habit" that now, "link by interconnected link," prevented him from doing what he had lately come to desire at a deeper level of his will: to serve, and enjoy, God alone (10).

Augustine dilates on how this inner warfare between "flesh and spirit" was tearing him asunder. Once again, as he did earlier, he firmly excludes the lack of intellectual certainties as his reason for "not despising the *saeculum*." The time for that excuse is past and gone. Yet here he is, still "tied down to the earth" (*terra obligatus*), refusing to "serve," refusing to strip off his extra baggage, his *impedimenta*, and enter, light-armed, into God's "military service" (*militare tibi*) (11).

Awake, Sleeper

Enter once again the image of sleeping and waking. Augustine is approaching the climactic phase of his struggle. He compares the "worldly burden," the *sarcina saeculi* which "pressed down sweetly" upon him, to the pleasurable lethargy in which "sleep" is wont to fold us. We have all known the feeling, and to read Augustine's brilliant evocation of it is to remember it forever. We know it is time to get up; who in his right mind would want to sleep the whole day through? And yet, and yet—oh, what a nest of cosiness, our bed, especially when some "lethargic heaviness," the *gravis torpor* that comes with influenza, for instance, deliciously penetrates our every joint and muscle. (The image pointedly recalls those "delightful languors," *deliciosae lassitudines*, which one would expect Augustine to associate more explicitly with sexual activity; surprisingly, though, the entire context encases this image in a setting of worldliness and "vanity."[30]) Augustine hears those chiding words, already familiar from the fifth chapter of Ephesians, *"surge, qui dormis et exsurge a mortuis."* "Awake, sleeper," it is time to arise and walk out into daylight, time to shake off the weight of past habits and answer to God's summons. But all Augustine can do is murmur a soft and drowsy *modo, ecce modo, sine paululum*: oh, please, in a minute, let me have just one more minute! But a minute soon becomes five, and five minutes stretch to fifteen, and fifteen to . . . but then, we all know the story too painfully well. And yet, we know too, as Augustine reminds us, that there is always something vaguely troubled, something unsatisfying about those stolen extra minutes; just as those "delightful languors" are simultaneously "restless," *inquietae lassitudines*, this kind of sleep "is not wholly pleasing"; when half of us wants to doze on, our better half keeps nagging us to *"Get with it!* You *know* you want to be up and doing" (12).

The paradox is that in moments like these, the word we most sluggishly resist is at the same time the word we most deeply yearn to obey: *"now"*!

Disquieting Action, Restful Contemplation

Augustine is still not ready to leap to the command contained in that peremptory "now." But he is about to learn that only God can "release" his slumbering will, and both break the "chain" that binds him to sexual pleasure and liberate him from his "enslavement" to worldly occupations (*saecularium negotiorum*). His "anxiety" becomes even more tormenting; his wordly occupations "weigh" more and more heavily upon him. He snatches at every free moment of *vacatio*, spending it in church. He even imagines that both his dear friends, Alypius and Nebridius, are unintentionally mocking his own situation: for while Alypius is *otiosus*, enjoying the leisurely break between court sessions, Nebridius manages studiously to avoid all "disquieting" involvement in worldly affairs; his mind remains free, *liber, feriatus*, his life one unbroken "holiday" of reading and intellectual discussion (13).

This studied contrast, between the disquieting cares of the active life and the contemplative's untroubled peace, is punctuated now by a visit from a fellow-African, Ponticianus. He himself is a symbolic embodiment of those contrasts: he holds a high post in the service, the secular *militia*, of the emperor, and yet, he frequently takes time out for extended periods of prayer in church. He glimpses the codex of St. Paul's Letters on the "gaming table" before him, expresses his pleased surprise, and opens a lengthy recital about a conversion—another *exemplum* for Augustine to chew on—but this time the conversion of that paradigm of the contemplative life, Antony of Egypt. He is amazed that neither Augustine nor Alypius knows anything about such matters (14); they know nothing of the numerous desert monasteries, nothing, even, about the one, flourishing under Ambrose's patronage, just outside Milan.

Deeply shaken, his two listeners remain both amazed and engrossed as Ponticianus now drones on about two of his own former companions in the emperor's *militia*. They were both of them *agentes in rebus*, a technical term meaning "special agents." But surely Augustine hoped we would catch the deeper implication of his pun: they were, very much as he himself was, deeply involved in the "secular activities" incumbent on anyone in the service of a worldly emperor.

The two of them are walking one day, in a garden—fateful places, gardens, no one knew that better than Augustine![31] They chance upon a simple dwelling, inhabited by some poor servants of Christ. There they come upon a book recounting the life of Antony of Egypt. We may assume that it told of what Augustine mentions some moments later (29): how Antony one day opened the Gospel at random, read the first passage on the page before him, found it telling him directly and powerfully to "sell everything" he had and "follow," and was converted on the spot.

Now! At This Very Moment!

The *agens in rebus* doing the actual reading begins to contemplate giving up his service in the secular *militia* in order to *arripere*, "take hold" with Christian violence, upon the kind of life Antony had embraced before him. The prospect makes him explode in anger against himself. "What are our highest hopes from this kind of life"? he exclaims to his companion: to become, perhaps, at some uncertain, future time, one of the emperor's intimate friends? A chancy and dangerous prospect. Yet think of it: "if I but choose to be God's friend, I become it *now! Nunc fio.*"

And so it happens; there and then he makes the break: *iam*

abrupi, he tells his companion. Augustine cannot get over the marvel of it: the man decided on the very spot, *hoc loco*. And from that very hour, *ab hac hora*, he was "stripped of this world" (*exuebatur mundo*) and he donned the armor of Christ. And what of his companion? "I will stick with you," he announces, "for so great a reward, and in so glorious a *militia*." They had both been betrothed, Augustine quietly adds; their fiancées, when they heard the news, dedicated their virginity to Christ (15).

A Head Twisted About

There ensues the most dramatic exhibition of divine violence in the *Confessions*. Ponticianus drones on and on with his narration, blind and deaf to the series of spiritual detonations he has set off. Meanwhile, God wrenches Augustine's gaze about (*retorquebas, inpingebas me in oculos meos*). He forces Augustine to look at the unlovely self he had hoped to keep hidden behind his back. As though housebreaking a squirming puppy who has dirtied the rug, God forces him to gaze again and again at—or does He plunge Augustine's nose into?—the filth that is his doing (16).

Why Not Now?

How ardently he has suddenly been pierced with love for these men he has just heard about; they "gave themselves over totally to [God] for healing." As for himself, alas (that insistent memory comes flooding back once more), how many years has it been, twelve whole years, since Cicero's *Hortensius* ignited that burning desire to leave behind all earthly delights and worldly ambitions, in order to *vacare*, to devote himself without reserve to the "pursuit of Wisdom" in a life of philosophic contemplation. "Give me chastity," he had prayed as a youth, "*and* continence," (the "and" insinuates that Augustine sees a distinction between them). But even then he hedged his petition with the sleeper's drowsy protest, "not quite yet" (*noli modo*) (17). Now at last, he is aching to do it at this very instant.

To Cast Off, Violently

He returns again to that familiar theme: from day to day and year to year, he had kept putting off the resolve to "cast away" his "burden of vanity" (*abicere sarcinam vanitatis*): not simply "leave it behind" (*relinquere*), but, in the stronger term Paul uses at Romans 13:12 (and which, significantly, soon replaces the Gospel *relinquere* as a regular feature of Augustine's own vocabulary), "cast it away" (*abicere*). All those years he had pleaded that he possessed no certainties to guide him; now, however, he berates himself fiercely, that excuse is a thing of the past. Why can he not do what Ponticianus' companions did, "grow wings on shoulders set free" from all such burdens (18)?

Now he falls prey to the same temptation which had once ensnared Alypius—he begins to imagine he could accomplish his conversion by vigorous efforts of his own. Why, he cries out to Alypius, why, with all his learning, can he not be man enough at least to imitate these "unlearnèd" types who are "bearing away [*rapiunt*] the kingdom of heaven"? His companion stares incredulously at the change in him; all at once Augustine tears himself away (*abripuit*) and, followed closely by a concerned Alypius, plunges out into the garden adjoining their dwelling (19).[32]

Why, Augustine keeps berating himself, why can he not exert one forceful, one single strenuous, act of his will, and so shake off, once for all, the "weighty chain" of sinful habit, snap himself out of this drowsy "languor" (20)? What a "monstrous" situation, Augustine is momentarily tempted to call it: the will can command the leg, the arm, the hand, and they obey, but the will commands the will, and nothing happens! But perhaps it is not a *monstrum* after all, but only a proof that the will does not wholly will: too weighed down by sinful habit (*praegravatus*), it issues its commands only in a maimed and sickly fashion (21).

THE MECHANICS OF WILLING

At this juncture, Augustine enters a parenthetical refutation of how Manichee theory would explain this phenomenon of inner conflict precisely as the *monstrum* of "two substances" he has just briefly entertained and rejected (22–24). For our purposes here, there are two features of this refutation which are of interest. First, Augustine quotes the text from Ephesians 5:8 which we saw earlier as resonating the "light *vs.* darkness" image from the

Romans *capitulum*: "You were once darkness, but now you are light in the Lord." Augustine accuses the Manichees, with their view that the soul is identical with God, of wishing "to be light, not 'in the Lord,' but in themselves." That accusation gives us some notion of the bearing which that text from Ephesians held for him.

The second feature of this section is its conclusion, which sums up Augustine's understanding of the will's operation up to the point which his analysis has reached at the end of paragraph 24. "When eternity delights from above [*delectat superius*]," he writes,

and the pleasure to be had from some temporal good holds us fast from below [*retentat inferius*], it is the same soul which is willing [*volens*] the one or the other, but with a will [*voluntate*, that is, an act of willing] that is not entire. And so the soul is torn apart with grave vexation as long as it prefers the former for its truth, but habit does not let it put aside the latter.

Augustine is speaking here of "willing" (*volens, voluntas*), which he presumably thinks of as taking the form "command," as he indicated earlier. And yet, when compelled to be more explicit on how "willing" and "commanding" actually operate, his summary here remains consistent with the kind of language he has been using in his refutation of the Manichees. It is always a question of the will's being "drawn" or "led" (*ducta, reducta*) (23) or "borne" (*fertur*) (24) to or away from objects which are "desired" (*cupiuntur, appetuntur*) because they promise some (usually inferior) pleasure (*voluptas*) or (usually higher) "delight" (*delectatio*). Put these these terms together, and Augustine's "picture" of will-action is as follows: he imaginatively envisages the will as being effectively "drawn"—literally at-tracted—by the promised "delight" of the higher world, whenever, that is, divine grace so enlightens the mind that the mind presents that higher world to the will as more intensely and enduringly delightful than any competing pleasures the lower world can promise. So, it comes as no surprise when the ultimate act of "willing" involved in Augustine's description of "conversion" will resemble nothing more than a *cessatio*, a "cessation" of all human efforts of "willing" in a more positive sense of that term, in favor of a yielding, a total surrender, to God's "drawing" attraction.[33]

Last Efforts at Dis-Burdening the Self

Meanwhile, however, God secretly prods his exertions from deep within him. Augustine twists and turns in his efforts to break the chains which still hold him: they hold him more weakly now, but hold him nonetheless. He is afraid that if he lets up (*ne rursus cessarem*) his chains will grow strong again.

Or, in another image, like a man straining to leap over a wall,[34] he tries, tries again, falls back a bit, catches his breath, comes closer on the next try. He heartens himself with that familiar word, but whispers it now in a different key: *ecce modo fiat, modo fiat*, soon, soon—any second, and we'll have done it! "Just that little bit more; *now, now—iam iamque—that* did it!" But no, that didn't do it after all. Once again, Augustine sees the paradox: the thing he wants most is what most repels him; he is terrified by the very prospect of succeeding. Still, his terror fails to deflect or drive him back; it only keeps him suspended, as it were, in mid-air.

Vanity's Last Appeal

Now, in a densely concentrated image, he describes what still held him back, as though by silken threads:

> those toys, those playthings, those vanities of the vain, my past darlings [*nugae nugarum et vanitates vanitantium, antiquae amicae meae*]. They plucked at my garment of flesh and softly whispered, "Would you *really* dismiss us?" [*Dimittisne nos?*] And: "From this moment on shall we never more be with you? Forever? and ever?" [*Ultra in aeternum?*]

They flood his mind with vile suggestions, "You mean we shall never do *this* again? or *that?*" Filthy, shameful deeds (*sordes, dedecora*). And yet Augustine less than half-hears them now; they can only whisper from behind him, hoping to make him look back: *respicere*.[35] Still, they slow his progress, for he hesitates to "tear himself" away from them (*abripere*) and like David "leap over" the wall (*transilire*)[36] to where he was being "called" to go (*quo vocabar*) (26).

It has become a general, if not universal, assumption, that the *antiquae amicae* Augustine mentions here refer to his "past mistresses," so that the dominant attachment he is depicting is to the *sordes* and *dedecora*, the filth and shamefulness of sexual indulgence. That consensus has received a large measure of encouragement, of course, from the standard portrait of the youthful Augustine as sexual roué. But we have seen how generally questionable that portrait becomes under close scrutiny; more particularly, it seems unlikely that the relatively brief interval beween Augustine's arrival in Carthage and his common-law marriage would have permitted him to accumulate a very impressive list of *amicae* in the sexual sense.

Now it must be conceded that if Augustine is referring here to the attractions of sexual indulgence, he is doing so in a remarkably roundabout way. He begins, for one thing, by calling his tempters "toys" and "playthings," terms alike drawn from his lexicon of "vanity." A few lines later, they strive to make him *respicere*, "look back"; the very term he drew from Psalm 39:5, a few moments earlier, to depict Marius Victorinus' unswerving advance toward baptism: "he did not look back on vanities," *non respiciebat in vanitates*. And at 7.20, God closed Augustine's eyes "lest they look upon vanity" (Ps 118:37).

Recall, too, in this connection, that Augustine's imagination consistently distinguishes between the "yoke" or "burden" of secular occupations, and the "chains" or "bonds" of sexual attachment. As I mentioned earlier, he almost invariably images the first group (*iugum, onus, sarcina*) as weighing him "down," the second (*vincula, catena, ligationes*) as (forgive the expression) "tying him up." It is significant, then, that his *amicae* are pictured as striving to prevent his "leaping over" a wall or rampart (*transilire*) to where God's call is summoning him: an effect of "weighing down" which pertains to the "burdensomeness" of secular activity rather than to the "chains" of sexual attachment.

These, I suggest, are a set of distinctions which Augustine was making subconsciously, indeliberately; the works of imagination are not so subject to tampering, after-the-fact manipulation, as conscious and deliberate conceptualized distinctions can be. Hence, we do not need to be quite so guarded in accepting their testimony. Nothing could be clearer: these are all terms normally belonging to his vocabulary of "vanity," and therefore "secular" activity!

The very least one can conclude, then, is this: if Augustine is talking here about sexual attachments, he is imagining those

attachments as included in the larger class of worldly "vanities."
Why not take the next logical step, accordingly, and squarely
admit that Augustine is here depicting himself as being held
"down" by his attachment to worldly vanities, and that, in *this*
particular image, he may, *or may not*, have been thinking of sexual
attachments in that same connection?

One might object that the intervention of personified "Continence" in the very next paragraph makes much more sense as
replying to sexual rather than to worldly attachments. But that,
we shall come to see, implies a seriously questionable interpretation of what Augustine means by continence.

THE VISION OF CONTINENCE

In any case, that is when he glimpses her, supernal Continence in
all her radiant beauty. She is paradox itself: joyful and gay—*hi-
laris*—but, "serenely, not dissolutely" so; "alluring" as any courte-
san could be, but *honeste*, "honorably" so; Augustine feels her
beauty drawing him, "to come to her and hesitate no longer"; he
sees her reach out her hands to "take him up and embrace" him
(*ad suscipiendum et amplectendum*). She is chaste (*casta*) as any virgin,
but far from "barren" (*sterilis*), a mother teeming with children
sired by her husband, the Lord Himself. This Virgin Mother's
hands are peopled with inspiring *exempla*, boys, girls, virgins, and
widows. And every one of them has succeeded in making the leap
which he, grown man that he prides himself on being, has failed
to accomplish.

She laughs at him, does Continence, but she is laughing at the
same time at the death-knell tones of his onetime darlings; the
tone of her laughter is meant to hearten, not discourage, as though
it meant: "So you, you cannot do what these boys and girls have
done? But then, did they in fact achieve it of themselves, or,
rather, in the Lord their God," and through the power of His
grace?

Now she reminds Augustine of what he himself proclaimed, at
the outset of this book: what was still wanting to him was not to
be *certior* about God, but to be *stabilior in* Him. But, she chides
him, if he truly wants to take a "stand" and so find his "stability"
in God, why does he persist in standing in himself, with the

inevitable result that he cannot manage to stand at all (*quid in te stas et non stas*)?[37] "Cast yourself upon Him," Continence urges him, and summons up that familiar image of a weary, fretful child tossing itself onto its mother's lap. "Don't be scared, He won't pull back and let you fall; trust Him, cast yourself on Him! He will catch you up [*excipiet*], and make you well again" (*sanabit*).

Surrender to Grace

Here was the true "asses' bridge," the ultimate, the utterly radical, gesture of "humility." Augustine must become completely a "little one." This, he has come to suspect, is what the old Simplician had in view, however dimly, when he sketched the dramatic *exemplum* of Marius Victorinus. Augustine had mistakenly imagined that *he* must "strip himself" of all the weights that held him down to earth, in order to "rise up" like the Prodigal (*surgere*), and return to his Father; that *he* must shed his worldly garb, shake off his carnal *impedimenta*, before he could put on the lighter armor of the *miles Christi*, and then "leap over the wall." All this *he* must do, by a vigorous effort of his own will. So he was tempted to think.

In order to arrive at where he is heading, Continence now advises him, there *is* something he must do. But observe carefully what it implies: he must close his ears to the urging of his "unclean earthly members," to the "whisperings of those playthings" (*nugarum*) he has almost resolved to give up. "They speak to you of delights, but not like the delights you will find in the Law of your God"—in the vision of that Beauteous Wisdom he has longed to behold. Think, rather, Continence is urging him, think on those loftier delights to be found in the radiant world of Eternal Truth: let that *delectatio victrix*, that conquering delight, overpower and replace your former, earthly "weight"; let yourself be drawn, not downward, but upward (27).

This, Augustine is suggesting, is the only true way of viewing the process of conversion: instead of presuming that by some muscular effort of our will we can, by our own power, "take heaven by violence," we must consent to be "drawn"; instead of striving to conquer, we must learn to surrender: to the sublime allure of a Continence which, Augustine insinuates, is ultimately the feminine face of God.[38]

Augustine "rises up" (*surrexi*: that verb from the Prodigal story occurs twice within five lines of text) and flees to another part of the garden; he would not have even Alypius beside him now. He throws himself down "beneath a fig-tree, somehow, anyhow,"[39] and, choking with sobs, he prays. He conveys the "sense" of his prayer in the words of the Psalmist: "And You, Lord, how long? How long will You be angry? [*Usquequo, Domine, irasceris—in finem?*] . . . How long, how long? Tomorrow, and tomorrow? [*Quare non modo?*] Why not now? Why not *in this very hour* . . ." (28)? But then he heeds the mysterious summons of a little child's voice, opens the book of Paul's Epistles at random, and hits upon that *capitulum* from Romans. And, immediately, God's answer comes as deafening as a thunderclap: NOW, this very hour!

With that, Augustine tells us, a "luminous feeling of security flooded my soul, and all my murky hesitations fled away." *Securitas*: he had been straining to "leap over the wall" by man's strength, but had ignored King David's humble boast that it was only "through [God's] power" that it could be done: *in Deo meo transiliam murum* (2 Kings 22:30). Earlier, Augustine had succeeded to some small extent in "letting go" (*cessavi de me paululum*) (7.21) and allowing God to work; he had been rewarded by that thrilling glimpse of the universe nestling in the Hand of God, upholding all created reality. That lesson has not penetrated thoroughly; just now he had still been striving to "stand" on his own; he still lacked the childlike trust to cast himself on and find his stability "in God." This is what prompted Lady Continence to chide him on his fear of falling. Now, at last, the text from Paul has succeeded in breaking through his presumptuous determination to "provide" for himself, to ensure his "security" by his own human efforts. Now, at last, Augustine is convinced, he has found that security in the only way a once-rebellious Prodigal can: like a helpless little one, he has placed himself finally, unreservedly, into that infinitely careful *omnitenens*, God's All-upholding Hand (29).

AUGUSTINE'S CONVERSION: FROM WHAT, TO WHAT?

It was much more than a quasi-accidental instance of image-recession; it was, rather, perfectly typical of Augustine's superb artistry that the most shattering, the most imperative yet liberating, word he read in that Pauline *capitulum*, he sedulously abstained from actually quoting: "now." He regales us with all manner of synonyms: there need be no more *modo, modo*, "soon, soon, in a minute." "*This* is the time"! No more *cras, cras*, "tomorrow, or maybe the next day": "*this* is the very hour." But nowhere does he utter that simple word he found in Paul, *nunc*.

His performance here recalls the reticence which kept him from naming those two whose names must have been closest to the tip of his pen: the mother of his son, and that friend of his youth who died so untimely. With admirable finesse, he observes on a similar paradox: during his final struggle, it was the fear of success which most paralyzed him from succeeding. Now the reverse of that has taken place: the very word he was most terrified of hearing came to his ears, when it came, with a thrill of liberating relief.

Trust in God's Providence

A second suggestion concerning that *capitulum* would be this: at the time he wrote his *Confessions*, Augustine had come to see that the next most important phrase he read there was the one that admonished him to give up striving to "provide" for himself. Fixation on the sexual dimension of his conversion has tended to block scholars' view of this. And true it is, as Ferrari points out, that Augustine's earliest textual citation from the Romans *capitulum* (in A.D. 394) interprets what Paul terms "carnal providence" in explicitly "carnal"—meaning sexual—terms: true, but hardly surprising.[40]

But there are excellent reasons for thinking that, earlier on, Augustine thought of the "providence" Paul mentions in much broader, more radical terms. In his *De Genesi contra Manichaeos* (2.22), from the year 388/389, he explains that the core of our first parents' sin consisted in their proud refusal to remain "under God"; they wanted, rather, to "be in their own power [*in sua potestate*] without God." But that desire to be in their own power amounted, Augustine immediately goes on to say, to "using their own providence [*utentes propria providentia*], as they would use their own eyes, to distinguish between good and evil."

Here, too, Augustine has given us a clue to deciphering that sybilline counsel that Reason imparts when finishing the first book of the *Soliloquies*. Sybilline it may be, but the context shows it had importance for Augustine. *Noli esse velle quasi proprius et in tua potestate*, Reason urges: "Do not choose to be your own possession, as it were, and under your own power." Avoid that form of pride, Reason goes on to add, and the Lord will provide for you; "He will not cease raising you up to Himself; nor will He permit anything to happen to you except what profits you, even if you know it not" (*te ad Se sublevare non desinet, nihilque tibi evenire permittet, nisi quod tibi prosit, etiam si nescias*) (1.30). From the Cassiciacum Dialogues, up to the *Confessions*, Augustine is convinced that the worst kind of pride, the kind that brought on humanity's original fall, takes the form of distrusting God's providence and putting our human providence in its place. The only providence on which any of us may truly rely is God's enveloping, all-encompassing, God's literally maternal, care for us. That All-upholding Hand will always "lift [us] up," even when we "know it not."

By the time he wrote his *Confessions*, there is not the faintest doubt of that conviction: to "stand in himself" was not to stand at all; to presume that he could effect his own conversion by the un-graced power of his will verged on self-idolatry. He could not rouse himself from the sinful, drowsy lethargy that weighed him down, could not strip himself of the baggage that kept him earth-bound; he must let God strip, awaken, and enlighten him, humble him utterly, and only then "lift him up." This is what he announced in the opening paragraph of Book 8, announced and then repeated: *dirupisti vincula mea*. God was the one who "broke the chains" that bound him.

The Role of Continence

Meantime, we must also keep alert to a possible objection to the view I am proposing: that while the question of "providence" may have been crucial for him, it could have been important precisely to the extent that he had to cease employing his human providence in a strictly "carnal" way—in order to satisfy, among other things, his sexual "concupiscences." But I must again lay stress on that qualification, "among other things"; for Augustine makes it clear that he still relished the taste of applause and honors, reputation, the thrill of competitive triumph—and the first two verses of the Romans *capitulum* (which were at least as important to Augustine as the ones he actually quoted) are directed far more pointedly against these "vanities" than against sexual activity.

Now, the interpretation I am espousing would have it that Augustine located the most urgent imperative of his conversion not so much in the avoidance of "chambering and impurities" and the need for cutting sexual attachments as in a more fundamental and all-embracing need: the need for placing himself entirely into God's upholding Hand. But that Hand was not only *omnitenens* (7.20). We have seen it operate as *erigens, fovens, medicans, suscipiens, sublevans*: Eternal Son of the Father, He upholds us along with all creation, stands us upright from our fallenness, heals us when we are infirm and weak, lifts us up to become one again with Him. In a word, He—or perhaps more accurately "She"— takes exquisite care of us. But, we are about to see, Augustine also thinks of that same "Hand" as *Continens*, literally, as "Containing" us. But what does he mean by that?

In order to appreciate the way Augustine envisages Continence, one must first avoid the mistake of thinking he is uniformly talking about continence as a human virtue, continence "lower-case," if I may. For just as the human virtue of wisdom is a participation in Divine Wisdom, so, Augustine is convinced, the human being is continent by sharing in Divine Continence, Continence "upper-case."

Nor must we identify the human virtue of continence with that of chastity. By recalling his youthful prayer for "continence *and* chastity," Augustine already implies that there is a distinction between them. The same thing is implied when he describes the Lady Continence he beholds in that Milanese garden as *casta*; that would be mindless tautology if continence and chastity were identical.

A third mistake would be to catalogue Continence upper-case as a mere poetic personification and have done with it; what might be mere personification for another author regularly turns out to be, for Augustine, a hypostatic reality of the Platonic kind. Think, in this connection, of how Wisdom functions in the *Hortensius* account, or *Philosophia* in the early Dialogues. Both those hypostases turn out to be identical with Christ, whether Eternal or Incarnate Christ, or both. The same, we shall shortly see, is true of Continence.

What, then, is Continence? Augustine answers by describing

"Her" function, as when he writes that: "Through Continence we are collected [*colligimur*] and brought back into the One [*in unum*], from Whom we flowed down [*defluximus*] into [the realm of] the many" (10.40). Here Augustine is employing one of the classic Neoplatonic images for the soul's "fall" from contemplative eternity into time: it is as though we had originally been both stable and "solid," but we liquefied and spilled downward into the fluidities of time. In a slight variant on that image, both angels and human souls "flowed downward" (*defluxit angelus, defluxit anima hominis*) from contemplative union with the Eternal One (13.9), with the result that their interior powers became "cast abroad" (*sparsa*) and only God could "collect" them again (*colligantur*) (10.65).

This is the background for Augustine's depiction of Continence as exercising the identical "collecting" function as he attributes to Christ, the Father's own "Right Hand": just as we are "collected and brought back to the One" by Continence (11.40), so too, in the very same context, God's own *dextera* is described as doing the very same thing (11.39). True it is that at one juncture Augustine also attributes the reversal of this scattered condition to the enflaming action of the Holy Spirit; he pictures himself as "liquefied [*liquidus*] by the fire" of God's love, so that he "flows together into [Him]" (*confluam*) (11.39), with the result that he can (paradoxically!) attain to that ultimate form of the "stability" he had been searching for: to "stand and solidify in [God]" (*stabo atque solidabor in Te*) (11.40). But whether he attributes this action to the Second or to the Third Person of the Trinity—to Continence as identical with God's Right Hand, or to the Holy Spirit as the fire of Divine Love—the important point is that it is God Himself Who must "contain" us, literally be "Continence" for us, by imparting to us the human virtue of "continence" which— Augustine has finally learned—we can possess only if He make it His "gift" to us (10.40).

Often, though, we have seen that, in place of the images of liquefaction and solidification, Augustine evokes the image of the soul's becoming "distended" and "swelling up" like a diseased tumor, until it eventually bursts open and "spews forth its insides" (7.22, 11.39). For this, Augustine came to think, was the fundamental form which humanity's original sin assumed: far less a fall into body and the pleasures of bodily existence, much more crucially the fall of a contemplative soul into the fleeting distractions of time and temporal activity. This is why the most telling description of the "fall" occurs precisely at the climax of Augustine's famous meditation on Eternity and Time (11.39). *Ego in tempora dissilui*, Augustine exclaims there, "I leapt down *into* times." The accusative case implies that prior to that "leap" Augustine was "out of" time, hence "at home" in God's own eternity (4.31).

That "leap," moreover, was a leap which tore the soul's "insides" asunder (*dilaniantur . . . intima viscera animae meae*): again, that striking *tumor* image from Ecclesiasticus! Or, in a kindred image, it was a leap which resulted in his soul's being "pulled part" into the temporal multiplicity of past, present, and future (*ecce distentio est vita mea*) (11.39).

Finally, to correct once for all any assumption that he thinks of continence as having uniquely to do with sense pleasures, like those of sex, he makes it clear that God commands us to "contain" (*continere*)—hold in bounds, as it were—*all three* species of the triadic sin, meaning pride, carnal concupiscence, and curiosity (10.41)! For in warning us against the triadic sin, Augustine tells us, St. John is warning us to "contain ourselves" (*continere se*) from "love of this world" (*ab amore huius saeculi*) in all the three fundamental forms that that sinful love can assume (13.29).

Continence, then, is an absolutely fundamental virtue for Augustine, and chastity is only one of several forms such "self-containment" can take. The desire for sensual pleasures was only one of the lures which attracted human souls to desert the contemplative heights for the dust of temporality. But now Augustine can praise his God for having reached down with His Right Hand and "taken [him] up" (*suscepit*) from that scattered state: for as mediator between the "many" and God the "One," He "collects" (*colligar*) us so that we are able to "follow the One" and arrive (once again) at the contemplation of God's "delightfulness which neither comes [to be] nor passes away" (*et contempler delectationem tuam nec venientem nec praetereuntem*) (11.39).

Fall: Into Time and Mortal Body

Thus, the fall of the soul into the mortal body is itself, when appreciated at sufficient depth, identical with this fall into time.

This is the reason, I suggest, why at the climactic moment of his conversion, Augustine insinuates that sexual pleasures, his *antiquae amicae*, are only a species, a segment, of that more general class of *nugae nugarum*, "vanities of the vain." For like all things temporal, they lure us to "spew forth our insides," whether out of pride, curiosity, or carnal concupiscence. And yet, all such "vanities" can exercise only a surface attraction, can pluck away at our clothing: like praise and honors and the thrill of competitive triumph, they are, at bottom, only deceptive counterfeits of eternal happiness. They may whisper solemnly of "ever and forever"—*ultra in aeternum*—but that, too, is a lying deception: their writ runs only in the temporal world "under the sun," whereas *aeternum* bespeaks that "other, vastly other" higher world which vanity would convince us is vacuous, empty—literally, a "nothing."

This, too, is why the Continence who initially appears, in Book 8, to be the "bride" of Christ, eventually dissolves into identity with Christ Himself. The perspective Augustine once brought to reading the *Hortensius* has sunk deep roots; the gift of Continence is one with the gift of Divine Wisdom, and they both enflame the soul with the transcendent allure of feminity.

What Augustine Was Converted To

Finally, I suggest that this way of reading Book 8 of the *Confessions* makes it clear how Augustine thought of his "conversion," or, if you will, the successive phases of his lifetime process of conversion: the entire process aimed at, and reached temporal fulfillment in, his total surrender to God's call that he "put on Christ," in the precise sense that he enlist and serve in the *militia Christi*. That vocation was initially prefigured when he read Cicero's *Hortensius*; at that time it took the form of a conversion to the contemplative style of life comported by the term *philosophia*. But even then, Augustine insinuates, the "Wisdom" he dreamt of pursuing, a Wisdom he knew could be found only *apud Deum*, had strong religious, and specifically Christian, characteristics. This is why he is warranted in recalling that *Hortensius* experience not only in Book 8, but in Book 6 as well; in both instances, what barred him from fulfilling that youthful dream was his commitment to secular service of an earthly emperor.

Not only did that secular life of action hold out promise of forensic triumphs, reputation, honors, and even political power, it was also required of him by his marital responsibilities, whether actual or prospective. His option for celibacy remains an important and integral element in his conversion, but that option springs from the more radical decision he feels called to make: to yield, at long last, to this new version of the *Hortensius'* invitation to embrace the contemplative life. But that contemplative life he has now come to see in specifically Christian terms: as service in the *militia Christi*.

All this Augustine saw reflected, with powerful compression, in that four-verse *capitulum* from Paul's Letter to the Romans. But one large question about his employment of the Romans *capitulum* still calls for attention. While it may be considered proven that Augustine constructed the account of his conversion in Book 8 by means of allusions to the various images evoked by that passage, it still remains possible that this text assumed that importance for him only much later than that conversion year, A.D. 386. We shall take up that question in the closing part of this study; but we shall see that, to be dealt with satisfactorily, it must first be situated as one of a nest of questions about Augustine's earliest Dialogues.

What Augustine Was Converted From

But if his conversion was *to* the life of contemplation, Augustine's penchant for artistic symmetry was strong enough to suggest that his original "aversion" must have been *from* that same kind of life. That same circularity is insinuated by the models of aversion–conversion to which he refers repeatedly: whether Prodigal Son, Odysseus, or the lost sheep, return is always to the point of original departure.

It has sometimes been thought that the *Confessions* recounts Augustine's conversion from "paganism"; but we have seen that even as early as his nineteenth year he was a seriously religious person, whose religiosity—not excluding his time as a Manichee—was stamped with the "name" of Christ.

Could it be, then, that he is recounting his "re-conversion" from Manichaeism to the *Catholica* of his childhood? In that case, it would be puzzling that he makes it clear he had been de-converted from Manichaeism some years before the dramatic events at Milan in A.D. 386. Besides, that view of the matter ignores the striking fact that Augustine was brought to view his conversion to Manichaeism as a religiously progressive step, and not the reverse. For whatever inadequacies he eventually discovered in Manichaeism, and they were serious, that religion did represent an advance toward a faith which did not resist, but positively encouraged, the quest for "understanding." And Augustine always viewed understanding, not as some vaguely humanist value, but as an authentically religious exigency; it was a halfway house on our way to the recovery of Vision. This is why he identified the Manichees with those "mercenaries" who worked in the house of the Father. Heretics they might be; nonetheless, they actually fostered the Prodigal's conversion.

For the same reason, he depicts the *Hortensius*, Manichaeism, and even the *Catholica*, as so many *stabula*, travelers' way-stations, on his homeward road. This, too, was very probably his motive for climaxing his "autobiography," in Book 9, with the contemplative ascent at Ostia; it also explains why his meditation on "memory" in Book 10 (29) culminates in his "recall" of the contemplative "life of happiness." That happiness, Books 12 and 13 assure us, all of us once lived in the company of the angels in the Heaven of Heaven.[41]

How, then, came we here? Book 11 (39), as we saw, answers by describing our "fall" from the contemplative eternity we once enjoyed, into the dispersion and distention of temporal action. Book 13 underlines the same message while describing the divine economy of our "return." The Prodigal's story, then, is Augustine's; when he tells us that, on the occasion of reading the *Hortensius*, he had already begun to "rise up" and "return" to God, he puts this much at least beyond question: he situates his "aversion" from God as occurring *before* his reading of the *Hortensius*, hence before his joining the Manichees. Indeed, the first Book of the *Confessions* seriously raises the question whether he "was anywhere or anybody" even before entering his mother's womb (1.9; see 7–10), and broadly hints at a positive answer by recalling that we are all "conceived in iniquity" (1.12), all of us, accordingly, *aversi* from God from the moment of, or perhaps even *before*, our very conception.

Augustine's story, then, the Prodigal's story, is also Everyman's: we must all "rise up" (*surgere*) and journey back to our

Father's House. Augustine means it: we must literally "return" (*redire*) to the Eternal Day of that Heavenly Jerusalem we originally inhabited, before that primal *aversio* which sent us straying off into this "far country," this nocturnal region of unlikeness.

NOTES

1. See Paul Henry, s.j., *The Path to Transcendence: From Philosophy to Mysticism in Saint Augustine*, trans. Francis F. Burch (Pittsburgh: Pickwick Press, 1981), pp. 65–68 (henceforth: *Transcendence*) [this is a translation of Henry's *La Vision d'Ostie: Sa Place dans la vie et l'oeuvre de saint Augustin* (Paris: J. Vrin, 1938)]; Courcelle, *Recherches*, pp. 168–74; Goulven Madec, "Une lecture de *Confessions* VII, ix, 13—xxi, 27," REA, 16 (1970), 79–137 (esp. 135–36). See also my *St. Augustine's Platonism* (Villanova, Pa.: Villanova University Press, 1984), pp. 4–9, 31–38; and Ferrari, *Conversions*, pp. 69–70.

2. *Soundings*, pp. 23–24, 46.

3. *Soundings*, pp. 95–139.

4. *Soundings*, pp. 21–68.

5. *Soundings*, pp. 104–12.

6. Augustine's choice of this translation would be another topic which would repay some researcher's trouble.

7. See, most recently, Ferrari, *Conversions*, pp. 62–63; he reposes considerable confidence in Vincenz Buchheit's "Augustinus unter dem Feigenbaum (Zu *Conf* VIII)," VC, 22 (1968), which proves satisfactorily that a break with sexuality was at issue—but *only* that? See, for instance, p. 271, where Buchheit quotes *Conf* 8.30 to this effect, but wins his point by chopping off Augustine's coordinate mention of his break with *spem saeculi* as well! (Ironically *Spes Saeculi* figures as the title under which Lepelley [cited in note 8 of Part I above] has vigorously demonstrated the importance of this aspect of Augustine's conversion.

8. *Audacia*, even more than *superbia*, makes the near-ideal translation for Plotinus' *tolma*, the primary root of the soul's fall; see N. J. Torchia, "St. Augustine's Treatment of *Superbia* and Its Plotinian Affinities," AS, 18 (1987), pp. 66–81, esp. 71–73.

9. It is significant that in his earliest Dialogues Augustine attributes so many things to the working of Providence: the teaching power of the Church, the authority of Scripture, Plotinus' role in the history of philosophy, the liberating force of his own life's setbacks, etc., etc.

10. On Augustine's "Photinianism," see the Madec article cited in note 1 above, 106–23.

11. See my "*Confessions* VII, ix, 13—xxi, 27: Reply to Fr. Madec,"

REA, 19 (1973), 87–100 (henceforth: "Reply"). In his "The Incarnation in Augustine's Conversion," RA, 15 (1980), 80–98, William Mallard focuses on the Cassiciacum writings rather than on the texts from A.D. 389–390; if what I have claimed here is true, scil., about dating the insights expressed in this section, then those later texts are even more relevant to the issue.

12. See also Alberto Pincherle, "Intorno alla genesi delle *Confessioni* di S. Agostino," AS, 5 (1974), 167–76 (henceforth: "Genesi"), and Ferrari, *Conversions*, pp. 70–84.

13. *Soundings*, pp. 231–32.

14. See *Transcendence*, pp. 92–93.

15. *Young Augustine*, pp. 180–82.

16. Ferrari, *Conversions*, pp. 50–68 (building on the series of articles he cites there) claims that Augustine simply did not read this text in the garden at Milan in A.D. 386; Paula Fredriksen, in "Paul and Augustine: Conversion Narratives, Orthodox Tradition, and the Retrospective Self," JTS, N.S. 37, No. 1 (April 1986), 3–34 (henceforth: "Conversion Narratives"), builds partially on Ferrari's conclusions toward her own view that the "Pauline" characteristics of Augustine's conversion narrative were later adaptations.

17. In "Paul at the Conversion of Augustine (*Conf.* VIII, 29–30)," AS, 11 (1980), 5–20 (henceforth: "Paul at the Conversion") and "Saint Augustine on the Road to Damascus," AS, 13 (82), 151–70, Ferrari argues that Augustine became interested in the text from Romans only some years later, and, when writing his *Confessions*, employed the text to give his own conversion a Pauline cast.

18. This, at least, is the language he uses in the Skutella version of the text, dated 1934, which appears in the 1962 BA 14 edition, Book 8, paragraph 29, Skutella page 178, line 10. Line 1 of the same page has *caput*, but here, also, Skutella gives *capitulum* as an alternate in the manuscript tradition. Both mentions of *capitulum* have vanished from the Verheijen version, used in CC 27, dating from 1981, which leaves one with the question: How did it ever pass into Skutella's edition in the first place? Verheijen's omission, at any rate, does not destroy the power of Skutella's version to suggest this working hypothesis: suppose Augustine did write, and intend, *capitulum* instead of *caput*, does his text confirm that assumption?

19. A few examples from many: SS *55* 1, *83* 1; En *139* 18; InJo *101* 4, *93* 1, *53* 2.

20. Some modern editions still reflect the divisions into *capitula*. The *Jerusalem Bible* (London: Darton, Longman & Todd; Garden City, N.Y.: 1966), for example, prints Romans 13:11–14 as a single paragraph, and a careful reading shows that it constitutes a sense-unit.

21. The version I use has been recovered from Augustine's own quotations of the text.

22. *Biblia Augustiniana: Les Épîtres aux Thessaloniciens, à Tite, et à Philémon* (Paris: Études Augustiniennes, 1963), pp. 21–23.

23. In *Conversions*, p. 65, Ferrari refers erroneously to paragraphs 16–17.

24. See "Paul at the Conversion," 13–14.

25. Looking only for the sexual aspect of Paul's admonition, Ferrari can make little or nothing out of Augustine's stress on "providence."

26. See above, Part I, pp. 55–56.

27. Augustine claims to have donned *armatura levis*, presumably having exchanged his former "heavy armor" for lighter.

28. I assume that *terrena* here refers to both sexual and worldly attachments, as it did above; see p. 74.

29. Courcelle adduces a text from *Civ* to "prove" that Augustine went to Simplician at least several times precisely with such speculative discussions in view, but he has to doctor his translation of that text so maladroitly that his effort is more saddening than anything. See my "Reply" to Madec's allusion to this "proof." It is difficult to think that a professional like Courcelle would make those blunders unwittingly; it is equally disconcerting to see a professional like Madec so uncritically countenance them.

30. Aside from the fact that Augustine, as we shall see, seems to think of sexual attachments as a subclass of "vain" attachments, it would also appear that he imagines sleep, *sopor*, particularly the exhausted sleep brought on by vain activities, to be a degenerate simulacrum of the true contemplative *otium* which results from the complete renunciation of "activity" in favor of contemplative *requies*. We shall see much the same set of associations below at 8.17–18.

31. See Leo C. Ferrari, "The Arboreal Polarization in Augustine's *Confessions*," REA, 25 (1979), 35–46; also Richard Luman, "Journeys and Gardens: Narrative Patterns in the *Confessiones* of St. Augustine," *Collectanea*, "Founder," pp. 141–58.

32. In hopes of proving something definite and limited about the Romans text and its role at Milan, I must pass on dealing with a number of ancillary issues touching on the broader question of the "historicity" of this episode.

33. The TA gives only the one instance of the peculiar formation which we remarked on at the "conversion-moment" in Book 7.20, *cessare de me*. But the context there, along with the contextual dynamic here, strongly suggests the kind of shift from activity to passivity, *nihil cessationi similius*, which Augustine describes in *Quant* 55 as the loftiest phase of the soul's ascent to vision. So, too, in *GenMan* 2.16, Augustine

interprets the sleep of Adam (*sopor*) as symbolizing a state of "interior and secret" contemplation of Christ as *Sapientia Dei*.

34. When the psalm which David sings in 2 Kings 22 was transposed to figure also as Psalm 17, the *transiliam* of 2 Kings 22:30 became *transgrediar* in Psalm 17:29. Here, Augustine is echoing the original *transiliam* from Kings, thus making the image of leaping over a wall especially vivid.

35. This is another Biblical cross-fertilization: Psalm 39:5 praises the one who *non respexit in vanitates*, who "does not look [back] upon vanities," while Psalm 118:37 asks God, *averte oculos meos ne videant vanitatem*, "turn my eyes away lest they look upon vanity." Augustine has expressed his conversion-moment at 7.20 by means of Psalm 118: he describes how God closed his eyes "lest they look upon vanity" (*ne viderent vanitatem*). Here he expresses a similar movement of soul by the image (from Psalm 39:5) of not "looking back" (*respicere*). We may, I suggest, safely infer from the consistency of Augustine's imaginative ways that the implied object of *respicere* here, as in both relevant psalms, is "vanity."

36. See note 34, above; also, observe that Psalm 17:30 proclaims that *non in me, sed in Deo meo transgrediar . . .* : only "in God," meaning (as Augustine understands it) only in and through the power of God's grace working "from within" him can he leap the wall that he must leap.

37. The new translation to which Augustine is alluding must, therefore, have run something like: *nisi in me stas, non stabis*, "unless you [take your] stand in Me, you shall not stand [at all]."

38. See below, where it becomes plain that *Continentia* is another name for the Eternal Christ.

39. Buchheit, "Feigenbaum," 269–70, writes as though *Continentia* were equivalent to *Castitas* in having to do specifically with sexual attachment. Patrice Cambronne, in *L'Imaginaire*, pp. 582–83, presents a wealth of evidence for a more complex view.

40. Even that concession to Ferrari's case calls for some hedging: first, it is human *providence* Augustine is talking about; and, second, the term *carnalis* develops, over time, to comport something much broader than "sexual."

41. See my "The Fall of the Soul in the *Confessions*," *Atti* II, pp. 45–58, where I argue that both Knauer and Pépin had discovered this before me, but somehow failed to recognize the fact.

IV

The *Confessions* at Cassiciacum

THE QUESTION OF THE "TWO AUGUSTINES"

THE FAMOUS ARTICLE which Gaston Boissier wrote more than a century ago started a scholarly brush-fire which burned hot for decades.[1] His contention was that if we scrutinized closely what Augustine himself has told us of his conversion, we are bound to conclude that there are marked differences, even contradictions, between the self-portrait which Augustine gives in the *Confessions* and the one we can extract from the earliest Dialogues he wrote at Cassiciacum. In the handy catch-phrase, there were really "two Augustines."

As represented in subsequent scholarly discussion, the essential differences boiled down to these: in the Dialogues written in A.D. 386, Augustine strikes the reader as more Neoplatonist than Christian, more preoccupied with philosophical than with properly theological and religious issues, still committed to literary studies. There is little sign, the argument went, of those specifically "Christian" features which are emphasized by the theologically minded Bishop who composed the *Confessions*: the tearful penitent, the sudden conversion—in a word, the powerful intervention of God's "grace." Hence, Boissier and those who followed him contended, the portrait to be gleaned from the early Dialogues must be considered historically more veracious than the one presented in the *Confessions*. There, quite evidently, Augustine the Bishop is concerned with purveying an edifying theological construct.

The "Two Augustines" in More Recent Scholarship

Later scholars have riddled a number of Boissier's claims and torpedoed many of the assumptions he brought to his reading of what Augustine has told us of himself. Pierre Courcelle's landmark works[2] were considered by many as putting paid to all future exercises in opposing Neoplatonism to Christianity, hence in contrasting the Dialogues and the *Confessions*. But recently Drs. Leo C. Ferrari and Paula Fredriksen have revived the "two Augustines" approach, on slightly altered bases.[3]

Ferrari has claimed that one essential mainstay of the "sudden, work-of-grace" view of Augustine's conversion has no historical value: in that Milanese garden, Augustine never actually read the famous text from Romans 13 to which he attributes such explosive power. Augustine became interested in that text, Ferrari argues, only around the time of composing his *Confessions*, at the very same epoch when he became interested in the conversion of St. Paul.

Dr. Fredriksen accepts Ferrari's claim about the Romans text, and crisply adds her condensed version of the "two Augustines" theory. She sees Augustine in the early Dialogues as concerned with evil more as a "philosophical" than as a theological problem, and as struck by a "vision" of *Philosophia* instead of the *Continentia* featured in the *Confessions*; generally speaking, therefore, the early Augustine envisages "conversion" as a business of progressing in "philosophy." The picture given in the *Confessions* is, of course, dramatically different on all three counts, so that Dr. Fredriksen may go on to make a contention similar to Ferrari's, that the entire picture of conversion in the *Confessions*, far from being historical, is actually a retrospective construct—as anachronistic as it is apologetic—modeled on St. Paul's conversion on the road to Damascus.[4]

A Pair of Questions

There are two questions involved here, distinct, yet partially overlapping. The first concerns how the Dialogues and the *Confessions* present the general shape of Augustine's conversion: Are the alleged differences real or largely fictive? The second question focuses on that text from Romans. I hope I have succeeded in showing that, contrary to what both Ferrari and Fredricksen suppose, the account in Book 8 of the *Confessions* is built on the lines, *not* merely of the two verses from Romans which Augustine actually quotes, but of the entire *capitulum* which runs from verse 11 of chapter 13, to verse 14. But showing that this *capitulum* influenced the *Confessions* account does not, of course, prove that it was actively influential on Augustine's mind in the year 386. And yet, I am convinced, that is the fact. But showing that it is a fact requires that one first become clear on the larger background issue: how "Christian" are the Cassiciacum Dialogues?

CHRISTIAN THEMES AT CASSICIACUM

It would be idle to deny that there are no significant differences between the Dialogues of A.D. 386 and the *Confessions*, which was written more than ten years later. Indeed, we have seen several instances where the *Confessions* alludes to features of the theory of grace which Augustine does not seem to have elaborated formally until his answer *To Simplician* around the year 396/397. Even on this point, however, it remains to be seen whether the Cassiciacum Dialogues are "philosophical" in the sense of being utterly bereft of any notion of divine grace and of its role in conversion.

But in any case, it is a strenuous leap from acknowledging what differences exist to generalizing that the Cassiciacum Dialogues are primarily "philosophical," whereas the author of the *Confessions* is informing his story with a specifically Christian theology. This does little justice, in the first place, to the vital importance we saw the Bishop Augustine accord to his unwearying quest for "understanding"; "philosophy," even in our meaning of it, will play a crucial supporting role in Augustine's theologizing to the very end of his life. But we have also learned much, since Boissier wrote, of the thoroughly religious and specifically Christian style of understanding which the recent convert labels with the term "philosophy." In short, the *Confessions* are far more "philosophical" and the early Dialogues far more "Christian" than tenants of the "two Augustines" view ordinarily admit.

Augustine's Early Notion of "Philosophy"

But that judgment merely indicts the "two Augustines" theorists of what a multitude of other writers on Augustine have been guilty of: a curious incomprehension of what Augustine is driving at in the Cassiciacum Dialogues. I have already mentioned Olivier Du Roy's contribution in this connection: his book is from start to finish one long object-lesson in how many Christian allusions scholars have missed when reading these early Dialogues. Nothing, surely, could be more specifically Christian than the doctrine of the Trinity, or more typical of Augustine's "philosophy" than his tenacious attempt to Christianize the so-called "secular" and "pagan" philosophy of his time by unearthing the Trinitarian analogues he finds lurking in their thought.

This is why Augustine's concern with the problem of evil (especially evident in his *De ordine*) is indeed "philosophical" as Dr. Fredricksen claims, but in his own very personal sense of that term. In order to show that the existence of evil (a major preoccupation for the later Bishop, also) does not contravene the universality of Divine Providence (to which he so radically entrusted himself, remember, in that garden in Milan), Augustine repeatedly makes appeal to the notion of *Ordo*. But Du Roy has convincingly shown why that term, like so many others, must be capitalized: *Ordo* is one of Augustine's Trinitarian code-words for the Eternal Word, "Wisdom and Power of God" (*Acad* 2.1) and universal Law (*Vita* 25) governing all that exists and acts.[5]

But (*pace* Fredriksen, again) the same is as true of the *Philosophia* who reveals herself to him at Cassiciacum as it was of the *Continentia* who appeared to him in that Milanese garden: they are both stand-ins for that erotically tinged, feminine *Sapientia* Whom Augustine had been searching after since his reading of the *Hortensius*. So he can say, in all sincerity, that the attraction *Philosophia* was now exerting on him emanated, in fact, from "that religion" which had penetrated to his very marrow as a child (*Acad* 2.5).

Finally, "progress" in *this* kind of "philosophy," Augustine argues against the "skepticism" of the Academics, must start with the confidence that certainty is accessible, perhaps not to sense perception, but to "understanding." "Seek and you shall find" is already his Gospel motto for what is the furthest thing from a religiously neutral venture in epistemology.[6] For what Augustine hopes to "find" is not this or that particular "truth" or human philosophical teaching, but no less than the supernal Wisdom he has always sought.

But, he is careful to argue, we must all begin in the "Catholic" manner, with "belief" in the teaching of "authority" (*Ord* 2.26), and labor through stages of purification, both intellectual and moral, to what ostensibly "pagan and secular" thinkers have always aspired to: the "life of happiness."[7] And this is where the Christian mystery of Incarnation plays a central role in the young convert's nascent synthesis: as pre-Christian thinkers were able to surmise only from afar, and as Augustine strives to demonstrate in the Dialogue devoted to that topic, *beata vita* consists precisely in the "vision" of the Trinitarian God (*Vita* 33–36). Indeed, one of the principal points of Augustine's teaching about the Academics is precisely this: that God's Providence, out of "compassion for the masses" (*popularis clementia*), has ordained that Divine Wisdom Him/Her-Self should enter our human world in order to indicate or, rather, *be* the "Way" to happiness for the "many" who are incapable of taking the philosophical road more appropriate to the "few" (*Acad* 3.37–45).

All this Augustine himself sums up in his description of how he, personally, uses the term "philosophy":

> Philosophy promises reasoned knowledge, and sets free only very few: those few it compels not alone not to despise those [Christian] mysteries, but also to understand them as they were meant to be understood. If it be Philosophy in the true and the authentic [*germana*] sense, so to speak, it has no other business than that of teaching what the Source without source [*Principium sine principio*] of all things is, how great is the Intellect [*Intellectus*] which abides [*maneat*] in that Source, and That Which has proceeded thence for our salvation, without any deterioration whatever: which our venerable mysteries teach is the one all-powerful God, Father, Son, and Holy Spirit, liberator of all who believe in Him sincerely and unshakeably . . . [*Ord* 2.16].

Particular Christian Elements: Wisdom, Truth, Philosophy

So much for the overarching Christian intention of Augustine's early Dialogues; Du Roy's painstaking labors almost makes us wonder why that intention never before seemed so obvious; as is so often true, someone had to *make* it obvious before it could seem so to everyone.

But what holds for Augustine's presiding intention holds also for his employment of individual elements. Here, I shall make it my specific concern to show that Augustine's language of imagery already predicts much of what we later find in his *Confessions*.

That term needs stressing: the "language of imagery." Dr. Frederiksen maintains that a later, retrospective document can never really tell us what a convert like Augustine really thought and felt at the time of his conversion: apologetic intentions inevitably intervene, and virtually guarantee that history yields to anachronism.[8] This may be true of communications which run on the conscious level; they are often, if not always, subject to manipulative distortion. But the imagination does not lie so skillfully as the deliberative mind. Compare Augustine's deployment of imagery in his *Confessions* with that in his earliest Dialogues, and it is astonishing how consistently the imagination stands to its own version of the truth. It might sometimes even help us catch the more conscious mind at its little deceptions.

The Images of Philosophia and Sapientia

Some of that detailed imagery has already been alluded to above, in a general way. But supporting detail is plentiful. When it comes to that term *Philosophia*, first of all, we have to relearn the lesson of capitalization: Augustine's imagination pictures *Philosophia*, not as some bland poetical "personification," but as a vivid hypostatic reality, and an unmistakably personal one at that. At first blush, she bears a striking resemblance to the feminine *Sapientia* of the *Hortensius* episode. To stay for the moment with references drawn from the *Contra Academicos*: she has a "face" (2.6), "breasts" (1.4), "bosom" (1.3), and "lap" (2.7); her "true lovers" come "burning" and "panting" with desire for her (1.1–4, 2.4–6). (Similar imagery occurs in *De beata vita* 4, along with explicit mention of the *Hortensius*.)

That resemblance is further enhanced by what Augustine tells us of *Sapientia*. To stay with the *Contra Academicos* again: Wisdom is (already) situated *apud Deum* (3.20) and remains "in itself," *in semetipso* (3.31), in the same "intelligible world," evidently, where Plato told us "Truth has her abode," *in quo ipsa Veritas habitaret* (3.37). In a more imaged mode, we have already examined the *Soliloquies'* (1.22) remarkable erotic evocation of Wisdom "unveiled," toward whom Augustine would fly "burning" and "afire," to "seek and sigh after," to "cling to and delight in." The soul at the end of its quest, accordingly, will at last "contemplate Wisdom once She has been has found" (*sapientiam contemplatur inventam*), "cling to Her" (*ad ipsam se tenet*), and in turn be held fast by the "embrace" of God Himself (*amplexus*) (*Vita* 33). For what, Augustine asks, is "wisdom," and in answering his own question discloses the equations which have guided his pen from start to finish: wisdom in the deepest sense of the term can be nothing else than "God's own Wisdom . . . the Son of God" Who is, as St. John's Gospel (14:6) assures us, Truth and Wisdom, both (*Vita* 34). So the *De ordine* (1.23) can speak of that "Truth" in the fullest sense as the very "face of God" which the Psalmist (79:8) praises, "the Belovèd after Whom we sigh, and to Whom we are giving ourselves back, made pure and beautiful" once again.

It is initially tempting to hypothesize that "Wisdom" and "*Philosophia*" may be distinct hypostases for Augustine's imagination. In that supposition Wisdom would represent the term of her lovers' desire, while *Philosophia*'s role would be that of assisting those lovers in their quest for Wisdom: they drink from her generous breasts (1.4, 2.18); she "nourishes" and "cares for" them (*nutrit et fovet*), already "shows" God to them through "luminous clouds," but "promises" both to lead them further on to a direct vision of Him (1.1, 3; see *Ord* 2.14) and, in doing so, to "make them free" (as Christ Himself also promised!) (1.9).

But that distinction eventually breaks down, for Wisdom, too, like Christ Himself, is depicted not only as term but also as assisting with the quest. And here Augustine is subtly building on Christ's own self-depiction in St. John's Gospel as "Way and Truth and Life": *Via, Veritas, et Vita*. He soon comes to delight in that paradox, that the Incarnate Christ is "Way" to Himself as Eternal "Truth and Life." So, the first definition proposed for "wisdom" identifies it as the "right way of life" (*recta via vitae*), but Augustine hopes his alert reader will translate that as, the "right Way *to* Life" (1.13). To abet that result, the next paragraph corrects the earlier definition to read: "Wisdom is the right Way which leads to Truth" (1.14).

Since we have here to do with the workings of imagination, it is not entirely clear whether Augustine reflected consciously on this relationship: nonetheless, it would appear that he envisages *Philosophia* as identical with *Sapientia*, but precisely insofar as Divine Wisdom takes human form in order to lead us along the "way" to the abode of Wisdom, Truth, and Life in the higher, spiritual world. If that suggestion is correct, the relationship is virtually identical with the one later depicted in the *Hortensius* episode in the *Confessions*. But even if that suggestion goes too far, this much is beyond question: *Philosophia* is already, for the Augustine of Cassiciacum, a thoroughly religious figure with what Augustine is convinced is an authentically "Christian" function. Like the Christ Who promised to makes us "free," she liberates the "believer" from the oppressive "yoke" (*iugum*) of any authority that would forbid personal reflection (*Acad* 1.9); she "leads" him along the upward road of "understanding," a road which eventually issues in "vision."

The Image of "Understanding"

Remarkably enough, too, the image of understanding as a species of filtered vision is already in play: Augustine, we saw, is beginning to catch sight of the Divine Light through "light-filled clouds" (*per lucidas nubes*) (*Acad* 1.3). But he has also espied Romanianus' interior virtue like a lightning flash surrounded by clouds (*nubibus quasi fulmen involvitur*) (*Acad* 2.2; see also *Sol* 1.27), somewhat as one might glimpse the mythical Proteus through the shifting appearances he hides behind (*Acad* 3.11–13), or penetrate to the central truth of their position which the Academics tend to hide behind mists (*nebulas*) of strategic pretense (*Acad* 3.14).

The "Food" of Vision: Esca

Still another of Augustine's *Confessions* images is already firmly in place: the presiding motif of the *De beata vita* depicts Divine Truth, beheld in direct vision, as the "food" for which the famished soul longs. The image of food, for body or soul or both, recurs in almost every paragraph of the work, but it also crops up in the *Contra Academicos* (1.4, 25; 2.10, 13–14; 2.7) as well as in the *De ordine* (1.24). Augustine associates it with the notion, familiar from Origen, that a "fastidious" kind of "satedness" with contemplation brought on the soul's loss of the vision it originally enjoyed (*Vita* 9, 11, 17, 22, 35; *Acad* 3.7). But, even more striking, the same evocation of images taken from the "*Oculi omnium*" verses of Psalm 144:15–16, which occurs several times in the *Confessions* (6.17, 24), is already in place (*Vita* 13, *Ord* 1.24, *Sol* 1.2): Augustine can pray "grace before meals" and fully expect his Christian readers to detect that he is really thinking of the vision which the *Confessions* called *cibus grandium*, "food of grown-ups"!

REHEARSALS AND CONVERSIONS

Another feature of the *Confessions* account which is already anticipated at Cassiciacum is Augustine's tendency to describe other people's conversions in terms that closely parallel his own; he seems convinced that, given the unity of our human nature, conversion must "work" along the same general lines for all of us.

So, in one example, he sympathizes with Romanianus for being too involved in "domestic affairs," yet at the same time indirectly chides him on the "anxiety" and "hesitations" which prevent him from adopting the philosophic way of life. It cannot, he submits, be question of moral apathy or lethargy (*socordia*) on Romanianus' part, for who could have been more "awake" (*vigilantior*) than he during their philosophical discussions (*Acad* 2.3)? Further, Romanianus has already demonstrated his capacity for making the sudden, radical decision required here. Who could forget that lightning-bolt of "temperance" he showed that day when he slew a passionate attachment (*libido*) which had long tormented him? Let that same *virtus* break out (*erumpet*) once again, and transform (*converteret*) the sneering laughter of skeptics into utter stupefaction (*Acad* 2.2)! Sleep and waking, domestic responsibilities, lethargy and drowsy postponement of a decision he deeply desired to make; at last, the sudden break with the sexual bondage he was known for; and then, to be greeted by sneers of incredulity—one cannot but guess that Augustine is reading the lines of his own conversion into his friend's experience.

But a moment later he is doing something very similar with Romanianus' adversary: he reminds his former patron of how he, too, along with his circle of friends, had "burned" with "panting" desire for the philosophical life, and of how those Platonic books had turned that flame into a conflagration: oh, if Augustine could only show the "visage of *Philosophia*" to Romanianus' courtroom adversary, how quickly would even he "cast aside and leave behind" (*abjiciens et relinquens*) all those deceptive forms of the happy life which now attract him, and "like a holy lover chastely impassioned, marveling, panting, burning, fly toward that beauty." For even he harbors a "seed" of "spiritual beauty," though it lurks, "deformed and twisted" (*tortuose ac deformiter*), beneath the thorny leafage of vice (*inter scabra vitiorum*). And still, that seed is even now blindly struggling to "break forth" into authentic beauty

(*erumpet*). If once he caught sight of her beauty, "with what pleasure would he cast himself on Philosophy's bosom" (*Acad* 2.6–7).

The erotic imagery of conversion is familiar from Augustine's
many self-descriptions; but alongside that, one cannot but recall
that dramatic vision of himself in the *Confessions, distortus et sor-
didus, maculosus et ulcerosus*, which Augustine fought desperately
to shove behind his back, while God insistently and violently
"twisted him around" to gaze at his twisted self (*retorquebas*)
(8.16). Striking, too, are those other images of violence: *erumpet*
(again), and not only the relatively mild *relinquere*, which described both how the Apostles "left behind" their nets, and Antony of Egypt "left all things" to follow Christ, but *abjiciens* as
well. Augustine has used that more energetic expression previously to describe his own conversion-decision: he "cast aside" his
"windy profession" and took refuge in the "bosom of philosophy"
(*Acad* 1.3; *Vita* 4). It is a verb to be watched; we shall see more
of it.

Sudden Conversion, and Doubts . . .

That phenomenon of sudden conversion, and its being met with
incredulity, seems to have bothered Augustine; he returns to it in
the *De ordine* (2.29). Alypius has just made some remarks which
prompt Augustine to remind him that we often fail to form an
accurate estimate of another's interior: this can lead us to think of
a good man as less good than he is, or fail to see that, even in a
man who is seriously flawed, there can be that "seed" of goodness
he detected in Romanianus' adversary. The result is that "some,
and not a few, convert themselves suddenly [*subito*] to a good and
even admirable life, but so long as that fact does not manifest
itself by means of notable acts, everybody believes that they are
still the way they were" (*quales erant esse creduntur*). One cannot
help conjecturing that some personal reminiscences must be surfacing in observations of this sort. In any event, they would discourage any factitious contrasts one might be tempted to draw
between the Cassiciacum writings and the *Confessions*, as if the
Dialogues depicted conversion as "gradual," while the *Confessions*
portrayed the work of grace as "sudden." There are lightning-
bolts and thunderclaps aplenty in these early Dialogues!

Augustine applies the same rehearsal technique to his young

student Licentius. At first, the familiar erotic imagery is used contrapuntally, so to speak, to describe the young lad's passion for poetry instead of philosophy (*Acad* 3.7). But after some further exposure to their discussions, Licentius reveals that a certain "divine reality" (*divina re*) is "beginning to show itself to [him], and [he has] become passionately attached to it" (*cui me inhiantem suspendo*). Poetry, he maintains, will not "turn him away" from philosophy (*avertere*). Now he switches to more violent imagery: he only hopes that some subtle sophistry will not succeed in "twisting him away and breaking off" that growing attachment (*detorqueat atque disrumpat*) (*Ord* 1.10). A short time later, the erotic images all point in this new direction: "Philosophy is more beautiful," Licentius confesses, than Thysbe, Pyramus, or any of the poetic charms which used to enthrall him; "there is something, I know not what, which I now see shining bright, but with another, far other kind of light" (*alia, longe alia nescio quid mihi nunc luce resplenduit*). "And with that, he sighed and gave thanks to Christ" (*cum suspirio gratias Christo agebat*) (*Ord* 1.21). And we recall that Augustine describes the Divine Light he himself had glimpsed in near-identical terms: it was *aliud, aliud valde*, "other, vastly other" than any light he had ever known (*Conf* 7.16).

THE PRODIGAL AND ODYSSEUS

This habit of "rehearsal" would argue that Augustine thought that conversion took a fundamentally similar form despite individual differences. He may also have thought he had good reason to hold that view, for the ancient world had its "models" of the wayfaring soul, notably, the classical Odysseus and the Prodigal of St. Luke's Gospel. These two figures relay each other in his *Confessions*, or, rather, they relay, interfuse, coalesce with similar models—the lost sheep, the man who "went down" from Jerusalem to Jericho, the Israelites wandering in the desert—and separate out to relay each other over and over again. Both of them already make their appearance in the Cassiciacum Dialogues: Odysseus' voyage of departure and return functions as the matrix for Augustine's own circular life-journey in both the *Contra Academicos* (1.1–2, 2.1) and the *De beata vita* (2–4), while the Prodigal functions in a parallel way in the *De ordine* (1.20, 2.14), and the *Soliloquies* (1.5, 15).

Augustine's use of both models varies, from clear evocations to allusions of such subtlety that one wonders what kind of audience he was writing for! But again, as in his *Confessions*, he seems perfectly comfortable with both, and the way he can interchange them, even fuse them into one, indicates that, early or late, he senses no "pagan-*vs.*-Christian" tensions between them.[9]

"Becoming Erect"

There is yet another striking image which we saw Augustine employ in the *Confessions*, and which is already functioning in the Cassiciacum Dialogues: the image of "becoming [or: 'being made'] erect." I have traced the details of its genesis and meaning elsewhere;[10] suffice it to say here that its derivation illustrates how closely linked the Prodigal and Odysseus images always were in Augustine's imagination. To "become erect" primarily means, for Augustine, to "rise up" as the Prodigal did, and start on the "return" to the Father's "house"—a journey out of time into eternity along the road of spiritual "understanding." But Augustine seems also to have associated the image, just as appropriately, with Odysseus' act of "standing up" amid the material treasure which his Phaeacian rescuers had spread about him, and gazing beyond that treasure upon his new-found homeland, the "spiritual world" which Ithaca represented.

The Platonic tradition emphasized that the human being's "erect" stature symbolized the fact that humans, alone among the animals of the earth, have been created to look upward toward higher, spiritual realities; we were not meant to keep our gaze fixed on the "earthly" realities of the sense world. Augustine agrees, reading the same message out of St. Luke's Gospel. But, he adds, nor were we meant to keep our necks bowed, submissive and unthinking, under the "yoke" of authority; faith should pass on to "understanding." Again, Platonism and Christianity were not opposed, but profoundly akin to each other: for both of them, the true kingdom is "not of this world" (*Acad* 3.42, *Ord* 1.32).

Additional Features Common to the Confessions *and Dialogues*

It is slightly surprising to note how firmly developed a shape certain themes from the *Confessions* already assume in the Cassiciacum Dialogues. This is notably true, as we remarked earlier, with

the device of *admonitio*: Du Roy has capably unveiled how thoroughly Christian its flavor was for Augustine: in the last analysis,
he views the role of the Holy Spirit as that of arranging the entire
sense-world into a providential pattern of salvific *admonitiones*, and
even accords Him that title: He is subsistent *Admonitio* (*Vita* 35).[11]

The *exercitatio animi* is already a formally developed teaching
technique, as well; Augustine explicitly compares it with the kind
of ensuppling "exercise" the recruit must submit to in order to
become the skillful *miles*, the "soldier" of Christ. Evidently, he is
already anticipating the dialectical battles his charges may have
to engage in to defend a right understanding of the faith (*Ord*
1.23, 27–28).

But there is a final cluster of images, thoroughly Christian in
import, whose presence in the Cassiciacum Dialogues we should
perhaps have expected, yet the vigorous force Augustine brings
to emphasizing them comes as something of a surprise. These are
the images of sinfulness as a kind of sickness, disease, even (again,
a *Confessions* term), a form of *insania*. Augustine applies these
images to stress that sinners stand in need of healing, and that
healing must come from the divine *Medicus*, Christ, Whose
"Hand" reaches out to heal them (*Vita* 5, 18, 20; *Ord* 1; *Sol* 1.5,
25, 27). We already detect hints that a moment of passivity must
intervene: the convert-to-be must recognize his own helplessness,
and *submit* to that healing operation (*Sol* 1.26, 30). We shall see
more such passages, where it almost seems that Augustine already
has his mature doctrine of grace well in hand!

And yet, we have already noticed a number of possible counter-
indications to that view: Augustine appeals to such vivid images of
voluntaristic energy to depict the crisis moment when the convert
"breaks free" and—not simply "leaves behind" but—"breaks out
of" and "casts aside" his habits of old that we might almost be
tempted to think we were reading a Pelagian tract. But we shall
see more of that "violence" imagery presently; then we shall be
in a better position to grapple with the issues it raises.

AMBROSE'S HYMNS

But whichever way one resolves that problem of *how* grace articulates with human will-power in the Cassiciacum Dialogues, this

much is clear: Augustine is, even this early, insisting *that* sinful man needs divine assistance; his message on that point, as well as all the others we have listed, is distinctively Christian. That list is about to grow longer; but even its length to this juncture in the argument would suffice to make one wonder how the myth of "two Augustines" ever got its start.

But let me lengthen the list even further, not so much in the interests of proving the Christian character of the Dialogues as in the interests of enhancing our understanding of those Dialogues and of Augustine's compositional techniques more generally.

Augustine tells us in his *Confessions* how affected he was by the hymns sung in the basilica at Milan. One of those hymns, the *Deus Creator omnium*, features most prominently in the *Confessions* (4.15, 9.32, 10.62, 11.35; cf. *Mus* 6.2, 23, 57). But it also features dramatically at the climax of the *De beata vita*, where (as Du Roy makes clear)[12] Augustine is finally unveiling the Trinitarian message of the entire Dialogue. That message is by no means lost on Monica: she evinces her recognition of it by quoting the final line of Ambrose's hymn *Fove precantes, Trinitas*: "God-Trinity, care for those who pray to You." But the same hymn also depicts our love for God in the phrase *castus amor*; we have seen Augustine ring several variations on that image; it could, admittedly, have come from a number of conventional sources. Yet his use of the expression would have been a signal to a number of Catholics familiar with the hymn, hinting at the Catholic nature of what he was about. There are also a number of allusions to sleep and waking, light and dark, day and night, to which we shall return in another connection.

But the *Deus Creator omnium* is not the only Ambrosian hymn recalled in Augustine's later writings. In his classic study of early Latin hymns,[13] A. S. Walpole finds that he was familiar with a number of others, and one of them was certainly the *Splendor Paternae gloriae*. Augustine cannot resist lifting an image from it to describe how Ambrose's ministry made his people "soberly drunk in the Spirit."[14] More to the point which concerns us here, Du Roy has astutely pointed to where a couplet from that same hymn occurs in the climax section (35) of the *De beata vita*, to characterize the work of the Holy Spirit.[15]

The hymn *Consors Paterni luminis*, moreover, prays that God liberate us from "darkness of mind . . . and drive away drowsiness, lest it plunge the indolent down to ruin":

> *Aufer tenebras mentium*
> *Fuga catervas daemonum*
> *Expelle somnolentiam*
> *Ne pigritantes obruat.*

Augustine is obviously alluding to these lines when, assuming that his companions are familiar with the expression, he explains that "darkness of mind" (*mentis tenebras*) means the moral–intellectual blindness for which he frequently uses the accepted philosophical term *stultitia* (*Ord* 2.10). But it also seems probable that he had the same lines still in mind when warning his companions away from "the lethargy of sleep and indolence" (*a torpore somni atque pigritiae*) (*Ord* 2.24).

Augustine's "Coded" Images

These remarks on Augustine's allusions to the Ambrosian hymns have purposely been limited to those instances which seem relatively incontrovertible. In the not-too-distant future, though, the resources of computerized texts and computer-search techniques will almost certainly permit us to expand the circle of those allusions. Allow me to finish by adducing one further example; it may initially seem slightly forced, but it will, at any rate, serve as a transition to the next set of observations I mean to make.

Some thirty years ago, when writing on the *Contra Academicos*,[16] I had already begun to suspect that Augustine's argument was studded with code-words and-images of the Incarnate Christ: Proteus, for one (3.11–13), and, for another, the "Wisdom" which the Academics purported to claim could not "fall into a man" (*non posse in hominem cadere sapientiam*) (3.19). The phrasing of that sentence seemed to call attention to itself, and to its recondite message, if only by sheer awkwardness. As my suspicions became more and more alerted, another such awkward image flashed the same attention-getting signal: whatever prompted Augustine to speak of some "Hercules" who will come to suffocate Carneades in his cave? Hercules seemed to me then a Christ-symbol, expressed in Augustine's "veiled language of Incarnation": for Christ, too, I argued then, came as someone more than merely human, in order to bring humanity the hope that Truth could be found, despite what Carneades may have said.[17] All that is true, but what now seems even more to the point is that Hercules was also a giant, *gigas*: and in his hymn *Veni Redemptor gentium*, Ambrose explicitly refers to Christ as *Geminae Gigas substantiae*, a "giant of twinned substance," both divine and human. Augustine betrays his familiarity with this Ambrosian image in his *In Joannem 59* 3; but even before that, in *Confessions* 4.19, he quotes extensively from Psalm 18, where he interprets verse 6 as depicting the Incarnate Word come "like a giant" to "run his course" (*Exultavit gigas ad currendam viam*).

That minor instance suggests that what might at first have seemed a somewhat strained suggestion can later gain additional plausibility as confirmatory details pile up to buttress it.[18] But it suggests something else as well: that the Augustine of the Dialogues may himself have strained a bit. In his ambitious efforts to exercise a literary artfulness which "conceals itself," his concealment may have succeeded only too well. It is very possible that we might more lucidly decipher the message of his Dialogues—and, while we are at it, appreciate their Christian intentions more justly—if we could confidently identify more of the terms and images which went into his "coded transmissions." Let me propose a few more such images which a suspicious mind might query.

We have already seen that Du Roy has unearthed the Trinitarian reference contained in the ostensibly "philosophical" language of *Modus-Veritas-Admonitio* which Augustine employs in *De beata vita* 34–35;[19] I had come quite independently to suspect the presence of similar Trinitarian allusions in *De ordine* 2.16 and 26–27, where *Principium* stands for the Father, *Intellectus* for the Son, and the mysterious *Quod manaverit*, which then becomes *Ratio*, for the Holy Spirit; it came almost as a disappointment to learn that Du Roy had also come to that conclusion.[20] Du Roy administered a milder blow to my pride by verifying independently the slightly more transparent Trinitarian bearing of the *Pater-Veritas-Quod Manat* triad threading its way through the very culminating sections of the *De ordine*, 2.47 and 50–51.[21] My point is, however, that each of these is an instance of Augustine's propensity for "coded" expression, and taken together they show how he could make that code more or less decipherable.

IMAGES OF INCARNATION

A similar coding technique applies to Augustine's imagery of Incarnation.[22] His reticence in this connection may have a great deal to do with his friend Alypius' opposition to having the name of Christ appear in the Dialogues (*Conf* 9.7).[23] This may well have been Alypius' strategy for making those Dialogues more, rather than less, effective as *apologias* for Christianity; in any case, coded references to the mystery of the Trinity and (as we shall see) the mystery of the Incarnation shoot like threads of gold through the three "public" Dialogues. Scarcely anyone will deny that the more intimate *Soliloquies* is far more transparently Christian than its companions.

But the Christ who is a Herculean "giant" is also a "Proteus": the Truth of His interior divinity is clothed in the shifting appearances of the changeable realm. This Christic symbolism (which Augustine supposes is transparent even to his youthful charges!) is what makes him rejoice when Alypius himself introduces Proteus into their discussion: it shows that the two friends are one in "religion" after all (*Acad* 3.5–11).

But the Incarnate Christ makes another discreet appearance, I suggest, when the discussion revolves—for a considerable time—about that intriguing character, the "infamous" Albicerius (*Acad* 1.17–22). Apparently he was, for the purposes of the Dialogue, anyway, a seer and wonder-worker whom all of them had known in Carthage. The overt question is raised whether Albicerius possesses that "knowledge of things both human and divine" which Augustine and his companions have accepted as a working definition of "Wisdom." Worthless though he seems to have been, he was the agent of "innumerable" marvels, and Licentius recounts three of them: he told where a ladle Augustine had lost somewhere about the house could be found; he discovered the theft a slave had committed, and compelled the man to give the stolen money back (*nummos reddere* is the expression used); and to a man who was negotiating for the purchase of a field, he revealed all the details of the transaction, even though they had up until then remained secret.

Now why, even a moderately suspicious reader is prompted to ask, why should Licentius be depicted as recounting, out of all the "innumerable" wonders attributed to this man, precisely these three, each of them a kind of distorting mirror of an episode from the Gospels? The lost ladle—or are we supposed to be reminded of the "groat" that woman lost, and scoured her house, and found again (Lk 15:8–10)? *Reddere nummos*: give the money back—or "render to Caesar"? And why is it precisely a question of "purchasing a field"—as the man did in the Gospel parable? Could it be that the overt question concerning Albicerius' "wisdom" covers a "real" question which runs deeper, and that Augustine hopes his readers will see that all sorts of false miracles are possible, and one should be suitably wary (we are discussing skepticism here) of credulously reposing trust in just anyone—as though he were truly another Christ?

Once the ear is attuned to such Gospel echoes, the reader instinctively perks up when Licentius sets about testing the definition of wisdom that has just been proposed: the "right way of (or to?) life" (*recta via vitae*). He concocts the example of a "traveler" who chooses to follow the "way" which permits him to circumvent a band of robbers (*latrones*), and so escape death: but does this, Licentius asks, make the "way" he "followed" fulfill the proposed definition of "wisdom"? It does, of course, Augustine hopes we will eventually see, if the "Way" being "followed" is Christ Himself, Wisdom and Life, and Way to both; but the *exercitatio animi* has a good distance to go before he can convince us that when we talk of "wisdom" we are ultimately talking about God's own "Wisdom," His Eternal Son (*Vita* 34). Only then will we be of a measure to "understand" such sybilline affirmations as that God's own Wisdom and Word and Eternal Law has also become the Way which, "if we keep to it in life, will lead us to God" (*perducet ad Deum*) (*Ord* 1.27).

The Christian Character of the Dialogues

One can scarcely fault proponents of the "two Augustines" for having overlooked the more tenuous traces of Christian import I have just presented for consideration: only the plethora of more obvious "coded messages" could possibly entitle one to look for, and find, such gossamer subtleties as occupied us here. But we may also be forgiven a frisson of annoyance that so many scholars, without really having looked very hard, have so confidently denied the existence, or significance, of the more obvious Christian hallmarks studding Augustine's early Dialogues. Certainly, it would be difficult to decide which "comes first," the recognition of Augustine's overarching intention, or the Christian "point" embedded in his expression of particular elements. Doubtless, one must open one's mind to one or the other, in order to find that both aspects reciprocally confirm each other.

But we have by no means finished with this topic: I am about to suggest that the specifically Christian character of these earliest Dialogues is doubly confirmed by the subterranean, but nonetheless powerful, influence of that notorious *capitulum* from Paul to the Romans.

THE *CAPITULUM* FROM ROMANS AT CASSICIACUM

We have seen that the *Confessions* portrays the *capitulum* Romans 13:11–14 as exercising a decisive influence at the climactic moment of Augustine's conversion. But do the Cassiciacum Dialogues confirm that view? Dr. Ferrari, we know, has answered that question, provisionally at least, in the negative. He has, however, implied that as support for the contrary view he would not require explicit citations; "allusions" would suffice.[24] How he means that term "allusions" remains somewhat hazy, but it is reasonable to suppose that he would admit that image-traces would qualify, particularly if they were of a clearly identifiable sort. It is also reasonable to assume that he would be all the more impressed if those traces did not simply form a random constellation of individual pieces, but fell naturally into a converging pattern of evidence.

In tackling this question, we have several advantages over Ferrari from the outset. First, we know more exactly than he did what we mean to look for: "allusions," yes—but in the form of image-traces. And we have seen in a number of instances that the original linguistic vehicles of Augustine's images can go into "recession" without implying for a moment that the underlying image has lost any of its power; indeed, the contrary is more often the case. So, an image-trace unaccompanied by the linguistic trace which was its original partner can sometimes testify more eloquently to the continuing vitality of the image than would the persistence of the original image-word pair; and, *a fortiori*, a "recessive" image may represent an even stronger form of "allusion" than the linguistic trace considered in isolation.[25] Consider, for example, the number of linguistic expressions we have seen Augustine give to the *tumor* image of the fallen soul's distending, swelling, and exploding outward. It seems obvious that it was the striking character of the original image (or, twinned images, from Ecclesiasticus and Plotinus) which charged it with the power to animate such a variety of linguistic vehicles.

Another advantage we have over Ferrari is that we know, now, that we have to deal with the entire *capitulum*—both its quoted and its unquoted verses—on which Augustine's eye fell in that Milanese garden. Indeed, our examination of the *Confessions* has furnished us with a starting hypothesis pointing to what precise image-elements appear to have impressed him. How reliably that hypothesis fits the Cassiciacum Dialogues we must allow events to prove.

A Problem of Method

St. Paul's *capitulum* opens, as we saw, on the image of a convert (as Augustine's situation prompted him to read the text) emerging from "night," and the nocturnal works of sin, to "day," from "darkness" to "light." This is a classic image, of course. It is common both to the Romans text and to the texts from Thessalonians and Ephesians which Augustine found resonating with it; but it is also an image that runs through ancient literature and philosophy, through Manichaeism, and through more than one of the Ambrosian hymns with which Augustine was familiar. To further complicate matters, Ambrose frequently associates it, as Paul did in the Romans *capitulum*, with the theme of sleeping and waking—quite naturally, one may think, since a number of his hymns were composed to be sung during the hours of night-vigil, when drowsiness would be the enemy of prayerfulness.[26]

The very universality of the light-dark, day-night image-couple would, on the face of it, make it difficult to "prove" that its presence in Augustine's Dialogues could confidently be tracked to its "source" in Paul's *capitulum* from Romans *rather than* to Ambrose, or to St. John's Gospel, or, for that matter, to Plotinus, or the Manichees. But, as we have had to recognize so often before, that hermeneutic requirement supposes an either/or kind of thinking which is totally unreal when it comes to tracing the workings of the imagination. It is entirely possible, indeed it is far more plausible, that one or all of Augustine's light-dark images might represent the distillate of several, or all, of those influences, working in concert.

But, however true that answer is, it does not make our task any easier. How can we "prove" that any or all of Augustine's light-dark image-clusters can be traced to the influence of the Romans *capitulum*, even if we do suppose that that *capitulum* may have been working in concert with other influences? Here, I suggest, the principle of convergence comes to our assistance. Our business is not to prove that this or that individual piece of evidence, taken by itself and in isolation from its companion pieces, can be traced to Paul's text; we are asking whether there exists an entire interconnected *pattern* of such pieces, and whether the most convincingly natural explanation for that pattern is that Augustine saw the matching pattern in Paul.

If I may appeal to an analogy from chess, everyone knows that a move like "knight to queen-bishop four," considered in total isolation from the moves which preceded and followed it, could be executed by any of a million chess-players, including Mr. Gary Kasparov. But re-situate that move into the flow of a particular chess-match with a particular opponent, and an accomplished chess-master might confidently see that move, taken as part of a pattern of preceding and following moves, as the unmistakable signature of Kasparov's uniquely slashing style of play. Perhaps it is not too much to hope that we have by now learned a few things about how Augustine's individual imagination plays this game of "image-clusters"!

Darkness and Light

We saw above how Augustine took occasion to interpret the "darkness of mind," taken from an Ambrosian hymn, as a species of moral blindness (*Ord* 2.10). But he offers this suggestion only when the argument of the Dialogues is already well-advanced. The *Contra Academicos* begins in an atmosphere ostensibly receptive to a purely intellectual explanation of error and ignorance; so, the first occurrence of "night" imagery takes the form of an innocent-enough question: Suppose someone were asked if it was "day" and too hastily replied that it was "night," would this be an error on his part? And Licentius has to agree that Augustine's "admonition" has point; the definition of error he had earlier proposed was a faulty one (*Acad* 1.11). But the image returns: this time Augustine suggests that the "star [*sidus*] of Wisdom may not be so visible to our minds as the sun is to our eyes" (*Acad* 2.1). Error and ignorance are next traced, tentatively, to some "darkness" in the very nature of things (*naturae tenebras*), or some "deceptive similarity" which obscures the truth (*Acad* 2.12).

In the midst of his explanation of Academic doctrine, Augustine pictures Carneades as "waking up" to object; but he fends him off with a contrast between philosophers and folk who walk in "the ordinary light of everyday." He then remarks (mysteriously) on the "darkness of the untutored which only certain divine eyes" can pierce (*Acad* 3.22). All this occurs in the context of a discussion which is gradually unfolding the insight that the cause of error and ignorance may be moral-religious in nature—the same atmosphere surrounding the image of mankind emerging from the darkness of its body-prison (*cavea*) (*Sol* 1.24–25, 2.23)—so that only the aid of some "star of Wisdom," some divine *Medicus*, can heal and deliver the multitudes from that darkness.

The point Augustine had in mind in developing this motif is fully unveiled when he explains the soul's "want" of Truth as equivalent to moral "foolishness" (*stultitia*) (*Vita* 29), which in turn is a species of "darkness" whereby the soul is rendered *vitiosa* and iniquitous (30). Hence, when Augustine speaks to Licentius of how "error" wraps us around in "darkness" (*Ord* 1.13), we are clearly authorized to place a moral–religious interpretation on both those terms, as well as on the term *stultitia* which threads its way through the argument of the *De ordine* (2.11ff.).[27] This, needless to say, brings Augustine's entire development of the darkness–light couple into resonance with the religious atmosphere of St. Paul's text from Romans.

Sleeping and Waking

But the kindred theme of sleeping and waking is even more emphatically present. For "this life" (Augustine can scarcely find synonyms enough for it) is a kind of "torpidity," "dopiness," "lethargic sleep"—a *torpor, sopor, somnum veternum* (*Acad* 1.3, 2.20; *Vita* 2; *Ord* 2.25), a numbing, heavy, sluggish *stupor, socordia, tarditas* (*Acad* 2.1, 3.12), in which skeptical sophisms can make us (as they once made Augustine) too "indolent and altogether lazy" (*piger et prorsus segnis*) in our search for truth (*Acad* 2.23, 3.18). Indeed, it fairly hypnotizes us into "insanely" mistaking the stuff of our dreaming for solid reality (*Acad* 3.25, 28).

This sleeping–waking theme fairly bursts on the reader in the introductory paragraphs of the *Contra Academicos*: Augustine suggests that there is something "divine" in Romanianus which "the sleep of this life had made lethargic," but Providence has now decreed to "rouse" it. "Wake up, wake up, I beg you," Augustine exclaims, *Evigila, evigila, oro te*! He is urging Romanianus to follow the pattern of his own conversion to the philosophic life, and, typically, he can think of no more appropriate image than the one which applied to his own case: the long-deferred move from the sluggishness of sleep to alert wakefulness. Perhaps, the thought occurs, that initial question we saw Augustine pose to Licentius, about the man who mistook "night" for "day," was not so innocent, after all. Augustine will later remind us (*Acad* 3.25, 28) that one of the classic skeptical arguments turned on the dreamer's illusion that he was, in truth, awake, that dream was reality and night really day! In any event, having raised the question in those terms, Augustine promptly hints at the Platonic reversal which lay at the heart of his conversion and his refutation of skepticism: he has learned to despise, as mere "likenesses" of reality, everything which his "senses" and "mortal eyes" once urged him to take as real, has learned that what he once thought "night" was really "day" (*Acad* 1.3).

Once again, not only Paul's Epistles, but also hymn after hymn of Ambrose's[28] stood warrant for the Christian legitimacy of this sleeping–waking theme. It is typical that when Monica recognizes the Trinitarian bearing of Augustine's remarks, and quotes that closing line of the *Deus Creator omnium*, she does so, Augustine tells us, *Evigilans in fidem suam*: "awakening to her faith" (*Vita* 35). And so his own prayer in the *Soliloquies* can address God as the "Father Who awakens and enlightens us" (*Pater evigilationis et illuminationis nostrae*), and as the Son Who admonishes us to "awaken" (*quo admonemur ut vigilemus*) (*Sol* 1.2–3).[29]

"Now"!

Moreover, Augustine insinuates in a number of ways the sudden-
ness of the typical convert's awakening from that slumbrous condition. His own cry to Romanianus—*Evigila, evigila!*—rings with
the stridency of a clanging alarm clock, and we have already noticed that he seems to be both chiding his patron on deferring his
embrace of the philosophical life, and at the same time reminding
him of his proven capacity for making the break required for a
sudden conversion. Moreover, those tantalizing indications we
saw earlier, that he was disturbed by the incredulity often provoked by such sudden conversions, may well have been an echo
of his own case.

But Augustine has other means of evoking the peremptory
sense of abruptness which he experienced on reading the *hoc
scientes tempus* and *hora est iam* of Paul's text. We have already seen
several instances where he employs one such means: he repeatedly
resorts to images which convey the energy of will which goes
into "breaking forth" and "casting aside" (*erumpere, abjicere*) the
long-standing habits of the past.[30] The "violent" bear the kingdom
away (*rapiunt*): Augustine pictures himself as having been "held
back" by the attractions of both "woman and honors," but now—
with a providential assist from a chest ailment which "took hold"
of him (*arripuit*)—he has finally "broken loose" (*rumpere*) and
"borne himself away" (*me raperem*) to find rest in the bosom of
Philosophia (*Vita* 4). And now, no tempest of ill fortune can tear
him (or anyone) loose (*eripi potest*) from the "ever-abiding" God
in Whom he has placed his happiness (*Vita* 11, 25, 26). But he
does fear that his young pupil Licentius may be "torn away" (*raper-
etur*) by his love for poetry from being fully "converted" to *Philosophia* (*Ord* 1.8). For the danger is that "false images" can "take
hold" (*rapiunt*) of our minds and keep them from mounting higher
(*Ord* 2.43). He has no such fears for his friend Alypius, however,
since Alypius has "seized upon" the rules for wise living "so av-
idly" (*tanta rapuisti aviditate*) that Augustine would be quite content
to become his disciple (*Ord* 2.28).

One can be "seized" and carried either downward or upward,
accordingly. So, Divine Reason has left traces of beauty in the
sense-world precisely to induce our soul to "seize hold" of them
(*rapit*) (*Ord* 2.34) so that they can "bear us away" (*rapere*) to the

most blessèd contemplation of God (*Ord* 2.39). And it is that same God, he implies, Whom his young companions would, like himself (*rapui*), voraciously "seize upon" (*quasi totum rapientes*), the way "madly rapacious guests" (*rapacissimi convivae*) might seize upon food for their famished souls (*Vita* 14, 16).

Military Violence

But this brings us to the "soldier of Christ" motif which is so prominent in Paul's *capitulum* and the texts which Augustine makes its companions. Augustine can accent the forcefulness implied in that root verb *rapere* by combining it with metaphors of military training and combat, as well as with allusions to the energy required for "standing up" (*erigere*) and "standing firm" (*stare*).

So the young Trygetius, who has just recently returned from a spell of military service (*Acad* 1.4), "straightens up" (*sese erexit*) with "generous spiritedness" when Licentius threatens his reasoned argument by an appeal to authority: he "snatched up [the sword] [*arripuit*] which had been violently struck out of his hand" (*violenter excussum*) and presses his case unswervingly (*Acad* 1.24). Yet Augustine is persuaded that neither of these young trainees would turn his attack against Wisdom herself (*oppugnat*), since both desire to possess her (*Acad* 1.16). Augustine intends to "exercise" them (*exercere*), putting their "nerve and spirit" to the test (*Acad* 1.25), since without such training they might be tempted to think that Zeno's famous definition of certainty has torn away all hopes of attaining the truth (*arripuisse*) (*Acad* 2.11). More generally, they might succumb to the fear that the argumentative "arms" the Academics wield must be invincible (2.1). But training in the liberal arts will "nourish" their souls, making them "soldiers of philosophy," indeed, "captains" (*duces*) capable of leading their fellows to the very summit of vision (*Ord* 2.14).

Indeed, Augustine at one juncture in their discussion is compelled to allay their fears that their adversaries have taken them "captive," and stiffen their resolve (*vires*) to bring the fight (*pugna*) to the enemy (2.18–19). In a similar key, some time later, Alypius accuses Augustine himself of being unable to "stand firm" (*stare*) against the onslaughts of Carneades (2.27–28). They might be better advised, he goes on to suggest, to "bend the neck" (*praebere colla*) in submission to the "authority" of such great thinkers, and admit that truth cannot be "found" (2.30). But Alypius prefers not to conduct himself like some angry battler (*perpugnax*) for his personal point of view; let Augustine explain his position more clearly, and Alypius will not protest at being tormented, like a captive, by whatever tiny arrows are shot at him (3.8).

Augustine admits that there is danger of rejecting, out of pride (*superbe*), the "authority" of thinkers like Cicero; but he trusts that the reasonability of his position will win the day (3.14). He had hoped that this period of "leisure" at Cassiciacum would allow him to find some "rest" in "light armor" (*levi armatura*), instead of being pressed into laborious service this way, but so be it: he only hopes not to be carried away (*ne concitatus rapiar*) to the detriment of his feeble health (3.15). He has signed up for this "service" (*inservire*) (3.43): the "soldier of Christ" is at the same time "servant of God." So, he sets about manfully battling—with Pauline sword and spear and helmet—the skeptical arguments of the Academics as they were conventionally viewed (3.22–23, 33).

Abjiciamus: "Let Us Cast Aside"

But there is still another verb of "violence" which we have seen Augustine employ, and it holds a very particular interest. When recounting his life's "odyssey" of departure and return, he tells how he finally arrived at the haven he longed for. Once there, he describes his "conversion" in a gesture strangely reminiscent of the first Apostles: he beached his "boat" (*navem*) and left "all things" (*omnia*) to take up the philosophic life.

At this point we would fully expect him to use the Gospel term *relinquere*, to "leave behind," but, instead, Augustine uses the more vigorous expression, *abjicerem omnia*: he "cast aside everything" (*Vita* 4). That term clearly associates in his imagination with the Gospel's milder *relinquere*, for in evoking the conversion of Romanianus' adversary, he uses both terms in tandem, *abjiciens et relinquens* (*Acad* 2.6). Yet earlier, when describing his break with his profession of *rhetor*, he again opts for the stronger verb *abjicere* (*Acad* 1.3). And later, he generalizes: it is only right, after using a "boat" to cross the sea and having arrived at one's destination, to "cast it aside with contempt" (*abjicere et contemnere*) (*Acad* 3.3).

All this recalls the intriguing development we traced in the *Confessions*:[31] in his earlier evocations of the crisis-moment of actual conversion, Augustine can use either the Gospel-term *relinquere*, or the more forceful term *abjicere*; but the closer he approaches the turning point in that Milanese garden, the more regularly his preference goes to that term *abjicere*. The reason, I suggest, is that this was the term, and the peremptory image, which he found leaping at him from the page when his eyes fell on that *capitulum* from Romans: "let us cast aside the works of darkness": *abjiciamus*! And, typically, it comes from one of the verses Augustine chose not to quote!

"Rivalries and Contentiousness"

The "debates" and "controversies" which the Academics waged against their adversaries, and those that divided them into opposing camps among themselves, are repeatedly described as fierce military campaigns; but—here a new motif is sounded—they were sometimes waged out of "obstinacy and opinionatedness" (*Acad* 3.41), less in the interests of truth than for the empty "glory" of dialectical victory (*Acad* 2.15). Indeed, it was from any lingering ambition for "honors" of that sort that *Philosophia* "bore [Augustine] away" to his new way of life (*rapiebat*) (*Acad* 2.5). He has come to believe that, after centuries of such contentious squabbling (*contentionibus*), Divine Authority Itself has condescended to enter our human world to bring us, with no further need for disputatious rivalries (*disputationum concertatione*), a peaceful glimpse back toward the longed-for "homeland" of Truth (*respicere patriam*) (3.42).

But "not in contentiousness," Paul had said, *non in contentione*: even though Augustine does quote this portion of the Romans *capitulum*, scholars have been so mesmerized by the sexual implications of those "chamberings and impurities" that no one, to my knowledge, has paid sufficient attention to it. Yet how frequently in his *Confessions*, how insistently, we have seen him excoriate himself and his "vain" fellow-*rhetor*s for their cut-throat competitiveness, their stop-at-nothing rapacity for praise, applause, triumphs and prizes, honors and advancement—their utterly unscrupulous pursuit of worldly "glory."[32] More than anything else, this ferocious spirit of "rivalry and contentiousness" appears to have been the reason why his profession laid such a burden of "anxiety" upon him (*onus, sarcina*). It was also one of the chief attractions of *Philosophia*, in Augustine's Christian sense of that term, that it championed the ideal, and held forth the promise, of a serene contemplative search for Wisdom where all parties would carry on the spirited clash of arguments, the lively thrust and parry of position and counterposition, but always in the pure hope that victory might go, not to one or another human participant or factional sect, but to Truth Itself (*sine disputationum concertatione*) (*Acad* 3.42).

Once this "contentiousness" theme catches one's attention, it is amazing to realize that it has gone so little noticed. We have seen how important it was for the Augustine of the *Confessions*; it is at least as important in the Cassiciacum Dialogues.

In the *Contra Academicos*, the opening bars of the actual discussion (1.7–8) sound this theme: Augustine hopes that his two young charges will conduct themselves without any "puerile vanity" but out of a sincere desire for arriving at the truth. Licentius expresses his agreement: it is not "victory" that counts in what they are setting out to do, but the mutual discovery of what is "right and true" (*recti verique*). A lofty ideal, that: even dedicated professionals like the Academics have not been entirely free of "sophistry, obstinacy, and opinionatedness" (*calumnia, vel pertinacia, vel pervicacia*) (*Acad* 2.1). It should hardly surprise, then, that the young Licentius should at one point receive a severe tongue-lashing for having succumbed to that spirit of "rivalry" (*aemulatio*) (*Ord* 1.29–30), and that Augustine has to remind both lads against such seizures of puerile levity (*Acad* 1.8; *Ord* 2.2).

Among philosophers, Antiochus comes in for special condemnation on this score (2.15). But the prime example of the contentious spirit, Augustine thinks, has to be Epicurus who, like a Prodigal son, wasted his patrimony in quarreling (*patrimonium . . . per jurgia dissipavit*) (3.23). Something of that lust for victory, Alypius insinuates, could possibly affect Augustine himself (2.10–12), and one form that spirit could take is quarreling over words rather than substance (2.24–26, 3.24; *Vita* 31; *Ord* 2.4, 21). Augustine is sensitive to the charge, and defends himself against it; moreover, he makes his point by deliberately dramatizing an imaginary dispute between himself and an Academic, conducted in a spirit of "puerile levity" for no other prize than the "basest of glories" (*vilissima gloria*) (3.17–18).

It is with a certain air of solemnity that Augustine iterates, when approaching the climactic section of his Dialogue, the same warning he had uttered in his opening remarks: their business in this entire discussion has been, "not to win glory, but to arrive at the truth" (*non enim de gloria comparanda, sed de invenienda veritate tractamus*) (3.30). Antiochus and his vain posturing are dismissed one final time, and with his departure from the scene Augustine is convinced that he can at last write *finis* to the spirit of dialectical "obstinacy and opinionatedness" (*omni pervicacia pertinaciaque demortua*). After all those "centuries" of "contentiousness," the Incarnation has brought peace and truth together (3.41–42), and it has become possible for Augustine and his companions to contemplate the order of reality "most serenely" (*serenissime intuenti*) (*Ord* 1.11), and discuss the most emotionally charged questions with the purest "serenity and sincerity" (*serenissime et sincerissime*) (*Vita* 23). Hence, it comes as no surprise when, among the rules of life he offers for his charges to observe (*Ord* 2.25), Augustine issues a warning against "the torpidity of sleep and indolence" (one of St. Paul's "works of darkness"), adding immediately afterward that they must also strive to avoid (another such "work") all "rivalry [*aemulatio*], slander, jealousy, ambition for honors and power, and all immoderate desire even for praise." *Non in contentione et aemulatione*, Paul's *capitulum* had read, and Augustine repeats that command almost to the letter.

It is richly suggestive that Augustine's little exhortation should restore that association between *aemulatio*, the various forms *contentio* can take, and the ambitious desire for "honors," "praise," and positions of power. We have seen that he himself had found that spirit of ambition rampant among his professional peers, and was not entirely immune to it himself.

The Romans Capitulum *at Cassiciacum: Summing Up*

But now, to summarize how these echoes of the Pauline *capitulum* from Romans are disposed in the Cassiciacum Dialogues: How substantially do they match the echoes we caught in the *Confessions*?

To begin with, all the same elements of that Pauline text are present: the evocation of slumber, torpidity, and long deferment; the sudden burst of energy, "seizing upon," "breaking out," and "casting aside," provoked by that peremptory "now"; the emergence from night into day, from darkness into light, from sickness and insanity into health; the stripping off of the encumbrances from a former life to don the "light armor" of the *miles Christi*; the act of trust which permits God to be our "providence" and healing; the snapping of attachments both sexual and mundane; and, finally, the liberation from all "rivalry and contentiousness" to pursue Christ's Wisdom and Truth in contemplative serenity.

Again, the more usual scholarly obsession with Augustine's sexual attachments has tended to eclipse this deliverance from the pursuit of "honors" and "power," from the "rivalry and contentiousness" which made his secular activity such a burden of anxiety.[33]

It is perhaps possible to read the *Confessions* as portraying Augustine's attachment to his profession as owing *less* to his ambitious desire for honors and high office, and as far *more* an instrumental thing—a way of earning the money needed to support his "marriage habit," so to speak. We saw that, in his *Confessions*, Augustine drops a number of hints pointing in that direction, but we have also seen that he invariably hedges them around with qualifications that blunt their point (see esp. 6.22 and 6.25).

When he is about to consult Simplician, for example, he tells us that his "secular activity" had become a heavy and disagreeable "burden," because his ambitious "desires for money and for honors" no longer burned with their former customary flame (*ut solebant*). This might suggest that he was continuing with that activity uniquely because, as he goes on to say, he was "tenaciously attached to woman" (8.2). Yet a flame may burn lower and not be entirely quenched; it is hard to believe that Simplician's pointed account of the honors heaped on Marius Victorinus was intended to leave Augustine unmoved (8.3ff.); or that the budding author, "puffed up with knowledge," who yearned to "appear wise" and "gabbled on like an expert" (7.26) in works which "breathed forth the pride of the schools" (9.7), had become entirely indifferent to praise. And Alypius was certainly not entirely off the mark in suggesting that the zest for competition, the eagerness for debating victories, might still be alive in him (*Acad* 2.10–12).

Yet even if one were to accept the hypothesis that Augustine's dominating attachment was to sexual satisfaction, and his professional activity a means to achieving that end, it would still remain true that "conversion" required of him not only that he rupture the "chain" which bound him to sex, but also that he strip himself of the "burden" of his secular activity. And that twinned act of self-divestment is precisely what the *Confessions* portrays, if we read it with reasonable care.[34] It is not without point that, after that scene in the garden, he and Alypius report to Monica that, from this time forward, Augustine would "seek neither wife nor anything one can hope for in this world" (*nec aliquam spem saeculi huius*) (8.30).

In the Cassiciacum Dialogues, moreover, the attachment to sex and the aspiration toward "honors" are repeatedly portrayed as on an equal footing, and from beginning to end. His early move from Thagaste to Carthage was, Augustine admits to Romanianus, motivated by professional ambition (*illustrioris professionis gratia*), but despite his own hometown loyalties, the older man had stood behind his protégé "on the make" (*meliora tendentis*). Romanianus had shown a similar indulgence when Augustine left Africa for Rome (*Acad* 2.3). In Italy, the siren song (*ista cantantem*) of "success" (*prosperitates*) came close to seducing him, but then a chest ailment compelled him to "cast aside" (*abjicere*) his windy profession (*Acad* 1.3; *Vita* 4). Now, at last, he has "flown free of the chains of superfluous desires, and laid aside the burdens of dead cares." Augustine's imagination has already forged this distinction between the *vincula* of sexual attachments and the *onera* of professional anxieties; but he makes no such distinction between the holds they had on him (*Acad* 2.4; *Vita* 2, 4).

The same thing is true when he describes the liberating effect of his Platonic readings: no *honor*, no human pomp, no lust for empty notoriety (*inanis famae*) could hold him back now; nor could any "dulcet attachment [*retinaculum*] of this mortal life" (*Acad* 2.5). The connection we found in the *Confessions*, between *vanitas* and "empty" praise, honor and glory, is already in place (*Acad* 3.17–18) and the *vanitas–veritas* antithesis already taking inchoate form, but the twinned mention of those two spiritual adversaries, "pleasures and honors" (*voluptatum honorumque, uxoris honorisque*), has almost the ring of a cliché (*Vita* 2, 4).

The self-examination to which Reason submits him in the *So-*

liloquies tells the same tale: he had shed his hopes for worldly "honors" only very recently, indeed, almost during "these days" at Cassiciacum (*modo, ac pene his diebus*) (*Sol* 1.17). If wealth, honors, or marriage, any or all of them, still hold out any attraction to him, it is the purely instrumental attraction of means to the end of attaining Wisdom. Hence, Augustine insists, it is Wisdom he now loves, not them (*Sol* 1.18–19). But he makes no such distinction between the wealth and honors promised by his profession, and the wife and marriage they would go to support. Even after the nocturnal discovery that the fires of sex are not yet totally extinguished, he does not alter this order of priorities (*Sol* 1.25–26).

Yet we have seen that some scholars tend to think that, in his *Confessions*, Augustine reduces his attachment to the rewards promised by success in his profession to just such an instrumental role—as though they had, in his own words, "no sweetness of their own" (*dulcedinem suam*) (6.19). As a result, these scholars cast his liberation from sexual attachments into such prominence as to make it the unique focus of the conversion recounted in Book 8. Then, as a further result, the only feature of the quotation from Romans which holds any importance for them is the part about "chambering and impurities," which also has the dubious merit of according with the canard that Augustine was some randy monster of sexual insatiability. But if the entire *capitulum* of Romans 13:11–14 is what dramatically influenced Augustine, this monochromatic picture of his conversion is complicated and enriched, immeasurably; the Cassiciacum account is brought into close accord with what the Bishop later wrote; and the myth of "two Augustines" dies another of its numerous deaths.

Grace at Cassiciacum

One last feature calls for attention: how much does the portrait in the Dialogues reflect a recognition of "grace" and of its vital role in conversion? This could conceivably be a major point at which the *Confessions* picture significantly differs from the one contained in the Cassiciacum Dialogues, and where the "two Augustines" theory has an important truth on its side. For on Augustine's own accounting in his *Retractationes*, the meditations which went into his writing the answers *To Simplician* (sometime around the year 396/397) compelled him to credit "God's grace" with effecting what he had formerly attributed to human "free will" (see again *Retr* 2.1.1). And it has been convincingly argued that one of the Bishop's main preoccupations in writing his *Confessions* was to dramatize this new perspective.[36]

Oddly enough, however, if one approaches the Cassiciacum Dialogues with the expectation that the recent convert thought of "conversion" as a process uniquely dependent on the convert's free will, Augustine has some jolting surprises in store. Just review, for a moment, the major themes we have seen traversing these Dialogues, and it becomes plain that, though the technical term "grace" is absent, the doctrine of God's providential help to souls, and of our need for that help, is one of the points which Augustine is determined to make unmistakably clear to his readers, and to his young charges.

So, he tells us, the Incarnation is God's providential act of "compassion for the multitude" (*popularis clementia*) (*Acad* 3.42) aimed at leading them—not merely to "the truth," but—to their *patria* of Eternal Truth.

The Incarnate Christ is also the God-sent *Medicus*, the divine "Hand" held out to us, and to Whom we must entrust ourselves in order to be healed (*Sol* 1.5, 25; *Ord* 1.24). He is also the Way God has given us to follow, if we would arrive at Truth and Life (*Acad* 2.9, 3.44; *Ord* 1.17, 27), the One Who will lead us from our prison of darkness into the Light of His Day (*Sol* 1.24). So, *Philosophia*, or (to call her by her other name) Eternal Wisdom, "nourishes" and lavishes her "care" (*nutrit et fovet*) on those whom she has enflamed to pursue her (*Acad* 1; *Vita* 4); she "liberates" (*Acad* 1.9) and "leads" them to Herself (*Acad* 1.14).

The Holy Spirit, divine *Admonitio*, has ordered the sensible universe into a panoply of "admonitions," to "bear [souls] away" to that Kingdom of spiritual Beauty (*Vita* 35; *Ord*, passim). Souls famished for their heavenly "food" need only pray, and God will "open his Hand" to fill them with the blessing of Himself (*Sol* 1.2; *Ord* 1.24).

These are only some of the hints which we have seen Augustine scatter throughout his Dialogues to remind his young charges of their need for divine aid and to urge them to pray God to confer it. *Deum colant, cogitent, quaerant*—they must "be devoted to God, think on Him, seek for Him," exactly as all Christians do, "in faith, hope, and charity" (*Ord* 2.25; *Sol* 1.13–24). If any doubt remains, one has simply to reread the prayer with which Augustine opens the *Soliloquies*: that prayer, particularly its fifth and sixth paragraphs (*Sol* 1.5–6), along with the prayer which later punctuates the discussion (2.9), is massive testimony to Augustine's belief in man's need for God's help, and God's readiness to respond to that need.

Reason sets the tone which prevails throughout the *Soliloquies* by counseling that he pray for "saving help" (*ora salutem et auxilium*), and Augustine begins by praying God to help him pray well (*praesta . . . ut bene rogem*) (*Sol* 1.1–2). "I am on my way back to You," he confesses to God, "and ask once more from You those things which are needed to make my way back to You" (*quibus rebus ad Te ambiatur, a Te rursus peto*). Even to ask for those things aright, he needs God's aid; yet he is confident that "everyone searches for You rightly if You make them rightly search" (*quem Tu recte quaerere fecisti*) (1.6). Clearly, Augustine already believes that God's help is necessary even in order for us to pray for, seek, and cooperate with, that help.

In fact, God's help may be needed even for our belief that He is ready to help us: "Yes, let us believe," says Reason (*credamus*), "if indeed even that is in our power" (*si vel hoc in potestate nostra est*). And Augustine replies that God Himself is our power (*Potestas nostra ipse est*) (2.1). This exchange prompts a closer rereading of the final piece of advice which closes Book I. "Entrust yourself entirely to Him, as far as you can" (*te totum committe, quantum potes*), Reason counsels; and, then, "do not wish to be your own [*proprius*] and in your own power" (*in tua potestate*). Augustine has already confessed that he has entrusted himself totally to the "merciful care" (*clementiae curaeque*) of the Divine Physician (1.26); now Reason reminds him that he must consider himself as only the "servant" of a God Who is "most merciful and most generous" (1.30).

This trust in the total prevenience of God's help, and the radical self-dispossession it entails, may well undergird those expressions where the *Soliloquies* seems to be anticipating the famous *da mihi quod jubes, et jube quod vis* which so scandalized Pelagius when he read it in the *Confessions*. "Command me," Augustine prays, "to be pure"—*jubeasque me*; and the supposition seems to be that when

God commands He also furnishes the help necessary for obeying that command (*Sol* 1.6). Once again, therefore, not only does this recent convert believe that grace is necessary, he appears already to believe that "all is grace."

A Difficulty: The Images of "Violence"

And yet there is one aspect of the Dialogues which might give one to suspect that Augustine attributes more to human free will than he does to God's help. Recall how often we have seen him evoke those images of the "violent" act of will which conversion would appear to require, in order to "break"—now, at last!—with the slumbrous surrender to long-standing habit. And yet, he never suggests, even remotely, that conversion requires such a forceful act of will *instead of* God's help.

Indeed, a more careful examination discloses that Augustine sees God's help as vividly accompanying all such acts, working in tandem, as it were, with the exercise of human resolve. He can pray that God "give" Romanianus "back to [him]self," yet urge his friend to "wake up" as though that were his own doing (*Acad* 1.1, 2.1).

There are, in fact, a number of intriguing glimmers which suggest that Augustine already "imagines" this tandem-operation of grace and free will after the pattern of the *delectatio victrix* which later became the patented "Augustinian" definition of grace. In the *De ordine*, for instance, he uses the very dense formula that *Deus agit omnia*, "God does [works, effectuates, accomplishes] everything" through the instrumentality of "order," and uses it in a way which would seem to entail that God's "doing everything" implies that He is responsible for the creation of evils; God seems to work so "interiorly" to the working of human agents as to become virtually the sole effective agency at work (*Ord* 1.28, 2.21). That formula, however, may have been injected into the discussion as one side of the truth which must be respected by any adequately satisfactory solution. Augustine's eventual solution will come, I suggest again, only after he has formally elaborated his pivotal concepts of "perversity" and "dismissal."[37]

The antithetic truth he seems even now to be keeping in view is that God's agency, however effective, does not annihilate human responsibility. So, for example, he can pray for Romanianus' con-

version, with full confidence that God will "not permit" that those
prayers be uttered in vain (*frustra*) (*Acad* 2.2), and he can still, as
we saw, urge his patron to exert himself and "wake up" (*Acad*
1.3). Indeed, Augustine is aware that his somewhat necessitarian
notion of "divine order" lends this problem an even keener edge;
accordingly, he urges his young disciples to persist in believing
that "everything necessarily occurs in order," and that *tamen*,
"nonetheless, it is not in vain [*frustra*] that God is begged" for
what we need toward our salvation (*Ord* 2.51).

An Inchoate Solution?

It is seriously doubtful that Augustine already has the lines of a
conceptualized solution firmly in view. But the way his imagination seems to have framed the problem is at least suggestive, and,
indeed, eerily suggestive, of the solution he eventually comes to.

To explain what I mean by that, the *Soliloquies* provides the
best place to start. Augustine has been engaged in a self-
examination, under Reason's tutelage, to test how ready he is for
the vision of beauteous Wisdom which he longs for. When they
have concluded, he bursts out with a sudden protest: how can he
be expected to despise inferior realities, he expostulates, "unless I
see that which is supposed to make these things so much dirt in
comparison" (*nisi videro illud in cujus comparatione ista sordescant* (*Sol*
1.24)? The objection has all the unstudied quality of the imagination's quicksilver workings: it permits us to catch, in mid-flight,
the modality under which Augustine spontaneously envisages the
mechanism of this fundamental choice between "higher" and
"lower" attractions. For the "higher" good to exercise its conquering attractiveness, it must be "seen," and seen as *more* attractive
than its inferior competitors. Then, in the manner of Augustine's
later *delectatio victrix*, it will draw the will in virtue of the "victori-
ous delight" it promises.

"No one can come to me unless the Father draw him," says the
Christ of St. John's Gospel (6:44), and the record shows how
pivotal a text that became in Augustine's explanation of how
"grace" works.[38] But we have already seen how impressed Augustine already was by similar gnomic utterances from St. John.
That is why his choice of that Johannine verb *trahere*, in so appropriate a context, may be more significant than first appears. He

is speaking of those who would choose to follow another way than the ascent to vision through the "liberal disciplines" he has been outlining; "let them," he counsels, "fortify themselves with faith, that chain by which He draws them to Himself" (*ad sese trahat*), He Who "does not permit anyone to be lost who rightly believes in Him through the mysteries" of Christianity (*Ord* 2.15).

Again we notice, as we did when analyzing analogous loci in the *Confessions*, that God's action to convert us, when at its most efficacious, takes the form of "drawing to," quite literally "ad-*tract*-ing." That insight now suggests a way of rereading how Augustine expresses those moments of forceful decision which might seem, *prima facie*, to place all the weight on the human will, and none on grace. How did he envisage the interrelation of the attracting "draw" of the higher, with the human respondent's will-command?

Augustine's autobiographical sketch in the Prologue to the *De beata vita* furnishes a striking example of that interrelationship. He tells the story of all his delaying tactics; then he tells that he read those books of the Platonists. The result he describes to Manlius Theodorus in that language of erotic fire which goes all the way back to the *Hortensius* episode: "so enflamed was I [*sic exarsi*] that I would have willed to break loose from all those anchor-chains [*vellem anchoras rumpere*] if my respect for certain men [to whom he was professionally obligated] had not stood in the way." But at just that moment, a providential ailment intervened to free him from those professional responsibilities, and "I cast aside everything" and took up the philosophical life. *Vellem rumpere, Abjicerem omnia*—both verbs convey exactly that sense of a forceful exercise of will-power; and yet, Augustine seems clearly to imagine that vigorous break with the past as energized, fueled, by the erotic attraction which has just set him ablaze. Much as the various forms of the verb *rapere* do, the verbs *rumpere* and *abjicere*—"rupturing" and "casting aside"—suggest a "command" on the part of a strong, even violent will; and yet, Augustine plainly imagines the "flame" of attraction as interior to, and imparting, the power, the vital "heat," which enables the will to issue that command effectively (*Vita* 4).

That example has every chance of being the implicit paradigm for what Augustine depicts elsewhere in the Dialogues. Just a few lines earlier, in the same erotic image, Augustine had depicted the feminine *Philosophia*'s lap (*gremium*) as drawing him to "bear [himself] away" (*me raperem*) to find rest on her bosom (*sinus*) (*Vita* 4). To Romanianus, he expresses himself in that same interlacing of action and erotic attraction. Though the fire lighted by the *Hortensius* had never quite been quenched, it burned with a "slower flame"; hence, it failed to stir him and his companions to any decisive action (*minus acriter agebamus*). But, after all those delays, the Platonist books had more lately kindled the most "intense" of "flames," an "incredible conflagration," in fact, which was destined to "bear [them] away" (*arreptura*)—by inspiring, presumably, the decisive action they had been deferring. But Augustine now realizes that what he thought of as Philosophy was really the "religion" of his childhood which was "bearing [him], all unknowing, away to herself" (*ipsa me ad se nescientem rapiebat*) (*Acad* 2.5). He imagines the same thing happening to Romanianus' adversary: if only *Philosophia*'s visage would appear to him as it has to Augustine, how he would "break forth [*erumpere*] into the true beauty" he now secretly harbors within, "cast aside [*abicere*] and leave behind everything" and, like an ardent lover, fly to embrace her in all her beauty (*Acad* 2.6). The paradigm works consistently. Even when the action of "casting aside" is spoken of without explicit reference to any higher attraction, it is motivated by a kind of counter-attraction: one comes to "see" the person or object cast aside as contemptible, repelling (*Acad* 3.3; *Ord* 1.13).

Letting God Be God

Notice, however, a vital point at which this relationship of will-command and grace differs from the one exhibited in the *Confessions*. We saw how, in the later work, Augustine portrays all of man's forceful exertions of "will-power" (acting in the form of "command") as ultimately ineffectual. In his own story, as in the "rehearsal" story about Alypius, those energetic displays of "standing on our own" had to yield, in the end, to the *cessare*-movement of surrendering, of "standing in God." As the Psalmist puts it, we must learn to *vacare*, to "be still, and know that I am God." Letting God be God, we must also let Him act with the sovereign independence of all human activity which alone (Augustine later came to think) befits Him as God: *vacate, et videte quod ego sum Deus* (Ps 45:11).

But that is the very reverse of the insight which Augustine conveys to his Cassiciacum companions, in his very final pieces of advice to them. As for us, he tells them, "we must bend our highest efforts toward arriving at a good manner of life [*optimis moribus*]; for, otherwise, our God will be unable to grant us what we pray for [*exaudire non poterit*]; but He will answer [*exaudiet*] with the greatest of ease [*facillime*] the prayers of those who live well" (*Ord* 2.52). Augustine could scarcely make himself clearer: God's dispensation of His aid is dependent on the human's exercise of virtue—precisely what his later rereading of Paul to the Romans, at Simplician's behest, compelled him to deny. This may be why, on the second occasion when his *Soliloquies* appears to be anticipating the famous *jube quod vis*, its flavor has altered ever so slightly. *Impera*, he exclaims, "Command!" And yet, command "whatever is in my power" (*quae tamen in mea potestate sint*) (*Sol* 1.24).

Despite all the striking similarities between them, this stands out as the point at which the Dialogues differ from the *Confessions*. Which comes down to saying that the recent convert has not yet become the "compleat Augustinian." That, unsurprisingly, will take him some time. But it may be quite enough to have shown, for the present, that the Augustine of Cassiciacum is already unquestionably a Catholic Christian, and that his long-deferred conversion to the *militia Christi* was indeed decisively triggered by a four-verse *capitulum* from Paul's Letter to the Romans (13:11–14). If there really exist "two Augustines," they are remarkably resemblant twins.

Confessions 7.16–26: The Fruit of a Development

Whatever reservations one may have about this or that detail of Olivier Du Roy's study of Augustine's understanding of the Trinity, one series of his findings is beyond dispute: the Dialogues of Cassiciacum must now be looked upon as thoroughly saturated with Christian Trinitarian features. I hope to have added some additional strands of evidence to show that, in other respects as well, those Dialogues are far more apologetic and theological, more specifically Christian in nature and intention, than they are secular and philosophical. Philosophy is there, assuredly, and in abundance, but it has been subordinated to an unquestionably theological venture. Augustine is already in the business of "understanding the faith," by which he means understanding reality in the twinned light of both faith and intelligence. I predict that one of these days someone will do a comparably careful study on the images and themes of "Incarnation" in those earliest Dialogues; by paying closer attention than has been paid before, he or she will turn up treasure by the cartload.

But what is true of the Cassiciacum Dialogues is equally true of all Augustine's early works, from the year of his conversion, A.D. 386, to the year of his ordination, in 391, and beyond. None of them is strictly "philosophical." They are uniformly aimed toward nothing else than what he eventually was able to produce by the time he composed his *Confessions*: a systematic "understanding of the faith" of the *Catholica*. That systematic understanding, I have tried to show, Augustine displays in summary form in that central section of the *Confessions*, 7.16–26. This, I remain convinced, is the most natural and plausible way of interpreting that central section: it articulates a connected series of "intel-lectual" insights which constituted Augustine's world-view at the time he wrote his *Confessions*.

What I hope to show now is this: that that world-view was one which Augustine was already beginning to construct at Cassiciacum, but only beginning. Observe that from the moment we understand his earliest Dialogues that way, we have implicitly claimed that Augustine did not formulate the complete world-view contained in that central section of his *Confessions* during the spring and summer of A.D. 386. We are contending, rather, that that world-view was the fruit of his developing thought, the product of persistent reading, conversation, reflection, and writing. And we are implying that such a process of synthesis would have taken him months, even a number of years. Indeed, given the intricacy and dialectical sophistication embodied in that synthesis, nothing could be less surprising.

One can, I believe, become even more precise about the probable duration of that process of development: it can be shown to have extended over a period stretching from even before his first acquaintance with Neoplatonist philosophy, in A.D. 386,[39] through the final redaction of his *De libero arbitrio* (in A.D. 395 or so), and up to that watershed work, his *Ad Simplicianum*, composed (as near as one can figure) in 396 or 397.[40] Only then was Augustine intellectually prepared to write his *Confessions* in the way he did, and to crystallize his Christian synthesis in the terms he chose. On this view, the central section of the *Confessions* represents the product of a synthetic activity which it took Augustine more than ten years to elaborate.

A Question of Method

But how can such a series of contentions be proved? First, let me repeat that in cases of historical knowledge, like this one, one cannot ask for anything remotely resembling mathematical certainty; the best one can hope to establish is that a given way of viewing matters makes sense of the evidence more naturally and plausibly than do its potential competitors; and if that "plausibility gap" separating one's view from competing views is sizable enough, one is entitled to claim as firm a certainty as can reasonably be demanded in such cases.

Instead of laboriously outlining an abstract statement of method, let me give a concrete illustration which is likelier to make my procedure sufficiently clear. We know that Augustine composed his Dialogues at Cassiciacum several months after first reading those Platonic writings at Milan. It is conceivable, then, that he possessed certain insights at Cassiciacum that he had not yet attained to at Milan, whereas the opposite is far from likely. Similarly, it is conceivable that he possessed certain insights when elaborating the world-view encased in *Confessions* 7.13–26 which he had not yet mastered at Cassiciacum, and which, *a fortiori*, he had not yet mastered during the preceding months at Milan. But if it can be shown that this crucial *Confessions* section contains a number of such "later" insights, and that Augustine would have been happy to employ them in his Cassiciacum Dialogues had they been at his disposal at that time, then it becomes the most natural and plausible conclusion that this world-view section does not, in fact, tell us what Augustine already "saw" at Cassiciacum, and, *a fortiori*, in the preceding months at Milan.

The Objection from "Historicity"

But in the interests of obtaining a hearing I must first anticipate an objection. As one critic has put it,[41] the conclusion I have suggested might appear to destroy the "historicity" of this important section of Augustine's *Confessions*. For everyone, including the most searching critics of Augustine, has always read this section as embodying Augustine's intention to tell us, factually, as a matter of "history," what he came to "see" at Milan. If that is in fact his intention, of course, my evacuation of "historicity" becomes tantamount to making Augustine out to be a liar!

That virtually everyone has interpreted Augustine the way my critic claims, I would not deny. I would simply suggest that this *could* conceivably be just one more of those instances where our "traditional" reading of Augustine's text has turned out to be inattentive, even lazy. This was precisely my reason, earlier on, for stressing the difference between the way Augustine introduces the two distinct sections that make up his account in Book 7 of the *Confessions*. When he tells us repeatedly, as he does in the earlier section, that he "read" something there, *ibi legi*, his authorial intention seems clearly to be that we accept the "historicity" of his statement; even when he makes no secret of expressing what he read in different terms, the most natural way of understanding his text is as telling us "factually" *what* he read, and read *at that time*.

But once he had been "admonished" by those readings, he tells us that he passed to a second stage: he "returned to himself," "entered into his inmost self," and no longer "read" but "saw," "came to know" (*vidi, cognovi*). This is Augustine's language for reflecting, thinking in a "spiritual" way, "intel-lecting," and (we may infer from the entire tenor of his report) drawing conclusions from that process.

We are very probably right in assuming, also, that the process of reflection *began* even while he was at Milan and enjoying his first contact with those readings; but how long did that process endure? Once we realize that he is speaking of a second-stage process, subsequent to his Milanese "readings," it becomes plain that Augustine's language gives us no warrant whatever for decreeing that the series of reflections he enumerates was limited to those spring and summer months at Milan; it leaves that question of duration entirely open. But when faced with an open question, the responsible scholar has no other resort but to look around for evidence to settle it, "close" it, one way or the other—exactly the sort of evidence I have been speaking about. Instead, therefore, of letting our unexamined assumptions induce us to depreciate the value of that evidence before any examination of it, scholarly probity obliges us to let the evidence illuminate our judgment on those assumptions.

My contention, accordingly, is this: a careful survey of the evidence will destroy any presumption that *Confessions* 7.13–26 represents a world-view which Augustine came to "see" at Milan in A.D. 386, or even at Cassiciacum in the months that followed. On the contrary, that world-view was elaborated only gradually, step by laborious step, so that its final insights did not dawn on Augustine until sometime around the year 395/396.

This is scarcely the occasion for going into exhaustive detail on the issue; it would easily merit a book-length treatment. It should be sufficient to present enough items of evidence to carry conviction. Some of those items have already been presented to the scholarly world, but often in piecemeal fashion and in studies devoted to more particular issues: I shall sometimes be doing little else than adding up the results of such studies to show that they come to an impressive total.

The Grades of Being

One of the first of such items makes its appearance in the first paragraph (16) of Augustine's account of what he came to "see." He came to understand that God alone "existed" whereas he himself "did not yet exist." He clarifies that statement in the following paragraph: along with all other changeable realities, he was an unstable amalgam of being and non-being (17). He goes on in subsequent paragraphs to coordinate these grades of "being" with the grades of Goodness, Truth, and Beauty. Now, Olivier Du Roy has capably shown that the complex insight which is implied in these assertions never came to firm articulation in the Cassiciacum writings, and did not become explicitly operative in Augustine's thinking until he returned to Milan and set to work on his *De immortalitate animae*.[42]

The Problem of "Nothing"

But I would add that it is not simply a question of that insight's being absent. The absence is a "positive" one, in the sense that Augustine *needed* it, and would certainly have been happier had

he been able to apply it in his Cassiciacum Dialogues. For it would
have spared him the blunder of equating "nothingness" with "all
that flows, that is dissolved, that melts and steadily perishes" (*Vita*
8): this, obviously, is a maladroit stab at formulating what the
Christian teaching on "creation from nothing," or creation from
"unformed matter," later came to mean for him. Du Roy traces
Augustine's progress on that theme through his *De moribus ecclesiae*
and, more particularly, in his *De Genesi contra Manichaeos*, and
Emilie Zum Brunn's more recent study permits us to gauge, with
considerable confidence, Augustine's progress toward a more acceptable understanding of "nothingness."[43] Indeed, Augustine lists
a cluster of questions in *De ordine* 2.44–46 which, he implies, still
require his closer investigation; it seems fairly clear that he was
then still in the dark about, among other questions, what precisely
"nothing" (*nihil*) and "unformed matter" (*informis materia*) might
be. Hence, during the spring or summer of A.D. 386, he would
have been simply unable to express the span of metaphysical views
implicit in *Confessions* 7.16–26.

The "Divinity" of Soul

That same grades-of-being insight, though, would have spared
Augustine another, more serious blunder: that of sympathetically
entertaining the concept that the soul was in some real sense "divine" and, at the very apex of its being, unchangeable.[44] Again,
the record of his early writings allows us to detect when he came
to realize that the soul was changeable, temporally though not
spatially (*Ep 18* 2), a realization to which we saw him explicitly
refer in *Confessions* 7.23 (*quae [ratio] se quoque in me inveniens mutabi-
lem* . . .). But there could have been no question of his giving
utterance to that realization as early as spring or summer of
A.D. 386.

Dimissio *and* Perversitas

Another key notion which Augustine came to formulate only after
a period of hesitant searching is the complex of insights encased
in those connected terms *dimissio* and *perversitas*. Our presence
amid the so-called "evils" of this lower world results from our
having been "dis-missed," not "sent" here; it is not, therefore, the
result of some willful edict of a God Who delights in punishment,

but the "natural" and inexorable outworking of our own *perversitas*, our voluntary "turn away" from Him. That insight would have served him well at two junctures in his *De ordine*. In both instances he confronts the question whether the principle that God accomplishes everything *in ordine* applies as well to the *stultitia* of the *stultus*: translate, the "sin" of the "sinner" (*Ord* 2.15–16 and 25–26). That would seem to make God responsible for the sinner's very act of sinning, and the Augustine of Cassiciacum is manifestly unable to think that question through to a satisfying conclusion. He takes refuge in two series of reflections outlining how the mind itself must be "ordered" before it becomes capable of dealing with such thorny issues. Only toward the end of the *De Genesi contra Manichaeos* and at the end of the second book of his *De libero arbitrio*[45] does he bravely launch his earliest formulations of these two connected insights—something which, once again, was evidently beyond his powers during those weeks preceding the stay at Cassiciacum.

Du Roy has pointed to a number of other themes where careful study shows that the Augustine of *Confessions* 7 lays claim to insights which he could not have attained at Milan in the year 386. Many of these have to do with Augustine's progressive search for satisfactory Trinitarian triads; but he points as well to a crucial shift in the authority–reason relationship, as well as to a sharpening of the notion of the soul's fall and return.[46] Doubtless, there are others, too, who, having traced his development on particular themes from the year 386 to 391 or later, have turned up evidence pointing toward the same conclusion. But let me conclude with two such themes which are of special importance.

The Omnia *Insight*

One of the questions the young Augustine found bothersome was that of explaining God's motive for creating the lower, visible world. Several of the sheaf of agenda items he lists in *De ordine* 2.44–46 relate in one way or another to the question of why and how the lower, corporeal world ever came into existence.[47] We saw earlier that a vital piece in Augustine's eventual reply to that question is what I have termed the *Omnia* insight: that an ordered, hierarchical *Omnia* of unequal realities, both spiritual *and corporeal*, is more worthy of God's sublime artistry than a world consisting of spiritual realities only. That expression of the insight involves a quite special interpretation of the creation account in the opening chapters of Genesis, where God is said to have beheld "all things," the *Omnia* which He had created, and found it not simply "good" but "very good."

The first expression of this insight occurs in the third book of his *De libero arbitrio* (3.12–13, 24–25),[48] and our best scholarly efforts date that portion of the work in the year A.D. 395. In any case, this introduction of the *Omnia* insight almost certainly dates from later than Augustine's *De Genesi contra Manichaeos* (388/389) and later, also, than his "incomplete" attempt at writing a *De Genesi* of the "literal" sort (393/394?). For in neither of those interpretations of the creation account does Augustine take occasion of Scripture's mention of the *Omnia* to make this observation; and yet, the insight would have furnished Augustine with an elegantly crafted weapon against the Manichaean dualism which strongly preoccupied him during those years. Witness the alacrity and frequency with which he reaches for it once he has made it part of his interpretive armory (see *Oros*; *Civ* 14.12).

Conversion and Grace

The final piece of evidence I mean to submit is contained in phrases like "since You were my leader" and "You became my helper" (7.16). Even more emphatically, however, I mean to stress that seldom-noticed *cessavi de me paululum*, which I have translated to preserve its Isaian flavor, "I let go a little bit from my self[-reliance]" (7.20). One could argue, and convincingly, that Augustine may conceivably have found encouragement to use the first two expressions from reading Plotinus' magnificent description of entry on "vision," in *Ennead* 5.8; there Plotinus insists on the need of an initial trustful "belief" in one's mystical guide, and speaks of Zeus as lending aid to those who attain to the vision.[49] But the interpretation the *Confessions* imposes of the *cessavi de me* seems far too Isaian in spirit to have come from a Neoplatonist; it is my conviction that the earlier two expressions were written in that same Isaian spirit.

The *locus* Augustine is alluding to is clearly Isaiah 9:7, which he has formerly appealed to, repeatedly, but in the translation which has the prophet saying: "Unless ye believe, ye shall not understand": *Nisi credideritis, non intelligetis.*[50] But the translation which (for whatever reason) Augustine chose to use when writing his *Confessions* has the prophet saying, "Unless ye [take your] stand in Me, ye shall not stand [at all]." The Lady Continence who "appears" to Augustine in the Milanese garden at the very climax of his conversion struggle comes very close to quoting that Isaian phrase: *Quid in te stas et non stas;* "Why do you stand in yourself, and so stand not at all?" she chides. Then she urges him to do what a trusting infant would do with his mother: "Cast yourself on Him, don't be scared; He won't draw back and let you fall; trust, cast yourself on Him, He will take you up and heal you" (8.27).

The lesson was one which, when it came to Augustine, came hard. But it did not sink in until he was writing those "replies" to the questions which the old Simplician had asked about Paul's Letter to the Romans. What accounted for the fact that God's election and grace came to this sinner rather than that? Augustine confesses that he was at first of a mind to give the answer he had implicitly embodied in all his writings heretofore, including the final book of his *De libero arbitrio*: God's choice depended crucially on man's free will. "But God's grace won out," he tells us almost with a shudder (*sed vicit Dei gratia*) (*Retr* 2.1.1); God's choice of whom He will grace and whom He will abandon is utterly free, sovereignly independent of all consideration of human merits, whether antecedent or divinely foreseen. Sinful man must "become a child again"; his cooperation must forgo all presumptuous efforts to accomplish his conversion by his own efforts; he must learn to *cessare de se*, confide himself to God's care as an infant tosses himself onto his mother's lap.

This may seem a great deal to elicit from that single phrase *cessavi de me*, and indeed it is. But count it as just one more indication of how artfully Augustine composed his *Confessions*: he meant to dissolve any doubts we might have about the force of that phrase, and about the deeper theology of his conversion, in the course of Book 8. Then, having illustrated the dynamics of conversion in that book, he has put us in a better position to detect how he had already "rehearsed" those conversion-dynamics, and called attention to this need for *cessatio* not only here (7.20), but even more especially when portraying the two stages in the "conversion" of his friend Alypius (6.11–16).

Conclusion: A More Plausible View

I hope, then, to have established this much: the world-view which Augustine proposes to his readers in *Confessions* 7.13–26 is far more advanced in technicity and synthetic power than any he could actually have held as early as those spring and summer months in Milan in A.D. 386. So advanced is it, in fact, that it compels us to review any previous suppositions we may have entertained about this section. Most notably, it makes it very doubtful that Augustine ever intended us to interpret his words as meaning that he came to "see" and "understand" all those sophisticated metaphysical intricacies in a kind of rapid-fire series of explosive insights. That presumption, for it has never been anything more than that, must yield to the evidence of Augustine's early writings: once "returned" to himself, he "entered" that inner sanctuary, but re-entered it again and again, over a number of years, before the exquisitely crafted synthesis he displays in his *Confessions* had at last come to maturity.

A moment of reflection, finally, suggests that this view of Augustine's intentions makes considerably more sense than the conventionally accepted one. We should scarcely be surprised that a zealous bishop, like Augustine, would write a book like his *Confessions* with dominantly apologetic intentions in mind. So, when he presents his readers with a world-view, it would be of a kind that he would hope they could safely adopt as their own. Hence, we should expect him to put as persuasive a face on that world-view as it could wear. He is not some Rousseauvian romantic who thinks that the way he looked at reality at a certain stage in his life must hold uniquely fascinating interest for his readers simply because, however rudimentary, it was *his* way of seeing things "then." Nor is he concerned (as scholars are sometimes in danger of thinking) with presenting future historians of thought a factual progress report to furnish grist for their discussions of his "development." And though he will stubbornly refuse to lie, we must not ask him to hew to scrupulous notions of "factuality" like some present-day historian. He simply has other fish to fry.

So, we should expect him to present as mature and finished a world-view as he is capable of fashioning. He will honestly advertise his indebtedness to "what [he] read there," in those Platonic writings, but then he will warn his readers that what they are about to read resulted from his having entered into the inner space of personal reflection and come to "see" what he hopes some of them, too, may succeed in seeing. How long did it take him to spin out and interlace the varicolored threads he wove into the tapestry of that synthesis? We would love to know; but who will fault Augustine for counting that a secondary question, one which only the *curiosi* would insist on asking? In any event, his writings were there, open for consultation, by anyone genuinely interested in pursuing the matter.

NOTES

1. See Boissier, "Conversion." Courcelle, *Recherches*, pp. 7–12, gives a concise but fair summary of this controversy.

2. Not only *Recherches*, but *Tradition* as well. One should not forget earlier contributors who shed valuable light on Augustine's thought, notably Noerregaard, Boyer, and even that *enfant terrible* Prosper Alfaric.

3. Compare Ferrari's treatment in *Conversions* of *philosophia* (pp. 70–78) and of the *Hortensius* episode (pp. 10–17) with what I have presented above. He seems to me so often right, but he leaves the specifically religious aspects just enough out of focus that when he comes to the early Dialogues he fails to see the profound continuities linking them with the *Confessions*. And while Fredriksen, "Conversion Narratives," is surely correct in arguing (as Boissier did, with considerable finesse) that Augustine's shifting preoccupations over the years inevitably induced him as bishop to put a somewhat different interpretation on events than he did in the early Dialogues, I have to question whether she has accurately located and measured that difference. Both Fredriksen and Ferrari are agreed on one key point: that in that Milanese garden in A.D. 386 Augustine did not in fact read the text from Romans 13 which he claims finally catalyzed his conversion process.

4. See "Conversion Narratives," 20–21.

5. For a graphic summary of his findings in this connection, see the Trinitarian "triads" which Du Roy lists (along with page references) in *Trinité*, pp. 537–40.

6. The question about "seeking" and "finding" (*quaerere* and *invenire*) is posed in those Gospel terms at the outset (*Acad* 1.5) and commands the entire discussion until, only at 2.9, Augustine unveils what he has been doing by explicitly quoting the Gospel text (Matt. 7:7).

7. Augustine makes it clear that both *Vita* and *Acad* envisage the "seeking" for Truth as tantamount to the pursuit of the happy life.

8. "Conversion Narratives," 21–34.

9. One is sometimes led to wonder, however, whether certain "orthodox" Augustinians don't secretly harbor residual doubts about that compatibility.

10. See my "*Factus Erectior*," and, for fuller background, *Soundings*, pp. 198–219.

11. *Trinité*, pp. 161–65.

12. *Trinité*, pp. 167–68.

13. *Early Latin Hymns* (Cambridge: Cambridge University Press, 1922) (henceforth: *Hymns*).

14. *Hymns*, pp. 35–36, referring to *Conf* 5.23.

15. *Trinité*, p. 162n3; note the correction to Solignac's BA 13, p. 80n1, so that the third line of the first verse, referring to God the Son, actually reads: *Lux lucis et Fons luminis*. Compare, together with the line preceding, *De luce lucem proferens*, the interpretation given to Augustine's expressions discussed above, pp. 170–74.

16. See my "The *Enneads* and St. Augustine's Image of Happiness," VC, 17 (1963), 129–64, esp. 150, 155–64 (henceforth: "Happiness").

17. "Happiness," 159.

18. See Brian E. Daley, S.J., "The Giant's Twin Substance: Ambrose and the Christology of Augustine's *Contra Sermonem Arianorum*," *Collectanea*, "Marquette," 473–91.

19. *Trinité*, pp. 154–63.

20. *Trinite*, p. 125n1.

21. *Trinité*, p. 142–43.

22. Given his Trinitarian perspective, Du Roy is understandably less interested in Augustine's expressions for the Incarnate than those he uses for the Eternal Christ.

23. Does his "coded" language and imagery betray that Augustine was in part heeding Alypius' advice to be "discreet" in this regard? Or is he already applying his persuasion that the reader profits more from deciphering a message that is allegorical, parabolic, in any case not all that plain?

24. See "Paul at the Conversion," 10–12; in any event, Ferrari seems effectively to have limited his search to explicit citations.

25. Recall the remarks on this phenomenon of "recession" in the Preface above: the influence of the image is regularly more, rather than less, powerful when the linguistic correlate has gone into recession.

26. For this set of associations, see Ambrose's *Aeterne rerum Conditor, Deus Creator omnium, Somno refectis artibus*, and *Consors Paterni luminis*.

27. See *Lib* 3.71–74, and my *The Origin of the Soul in St. Augustine's Later Works* (New York: Fordham University Press, 1987), pp. 49–61 (henceforth: *Origin*).

28. See note 26 above. Notice that in *Conf* 9.32 Augustine actually quotes the *Deus Creator omnium* at length, as a hymn of praise for the God-given blessing of sleep!

29. *Trinité*, pp. 196–206.

30. See above, p. 271.

31. See above, pp. 215–16, 231–33, 237–38.

32. See above, pp. 238–39.

33. Ferrari and Buchheit are simply two more recent examples of this.

34. One needs, of course, to check on the most reliable of translators by close comparison with the Latin.

35. I mean this for now only as a hypothesis for exploration.

36. See Pincherle, "Genesi."

37. See above, pp. 240–42.

38. Eugene TeSelle, *Augustine the Theologian* (New York: Herder & Herder, 1970), pp. 333–38.

39. We saw that some of the elements of that synthesis dated back to insights incorporated into the *De pulchro et apto*.

40. See G. Bardy, *Les Révisions*, BA 12, pp. 575–76.

41. See Van Fleteren's "Reply to Fr. O'Connell," esp. 129–31.

42. *Trinité*, pp. 183–96.

43. See *Trinité*, 209–36, 269–97; Zum Brunn's headings, in *Augustine on Being and Nothingness*, mark the stages of Augustine's development clearly.

44. *Early Theory*, pp. 123–31.

45. *Early Theory*, pp. 169–82.

46. See *Trinité*, pp. 109–48, on Authority and Reason; pp. 230–36, on Fall and Return of the Soul; and pp. 269–277, on subsequent developments.

47. His questions include: What is nothing? What is unformed matter (2.44)? How can God be all-powerful, create no evil, and yet evil come into being? Did evil always exist, or did it come into being with time (46)? And so forth. There seems to be a Manichaean source for virtually each one of these questions.

48. See also *Origin*, pp. 139–45.

49. See note 16 above.

50. See *Lib* 2.6, the first time Augustine seems to have employed this text.

Bibliography

Archambault, Paul J. "Augustine's *Confessiones*: On the Uses and Limits of Psychobiography." *Collectanea,* "Founder." Pp. 83–99.

Bardy, Gustave, ed. and trans. *Les Révisions.* Bibliothèque Augustinienne 12. Paris: Desclée de Brower, 1950.

Beatrice, Pier Franco. "*Quosdam platonicorum libros*: The Platonic Readings of Augustine in Milan." VC, 43 (1989), 248–81.

——. *Tradux peccati: Alle fonti della dottrina agostiniana del peccato originale.* Milan: Vita e pensiero, 1978.

La Bonnardière, Anne-Marie. *Biblia Augustiniana: Les Épîtres aux Thessaloniciens, à Tite, et à Philémon.* Paris: Études Augustiniennes, 1964.

Bochet, Isabelle. *Saint Augustin et le désir de Dieu.* Paris: Études Augustiniennes, 1982.

Boissier, Gaston. "La Conversion de saint Augustin." *Revue des Deux Mondes,* 85 (1888), 43–69.

Bourke, Vernon J. *Augustine's View of Reality.* Villanova, Pa.: Villanova University Press, 1964.

——, trans. *Saint Augustine: Confessions.* New York: Fathers of the Church, 1953.

Bréhier, Émile. *Études de philosophie antique.* Paris: Press Universitaires de France, 1955.

Brown, Peter. "Augustine and Sexuality." *Colloquy,* 46 (1983), 1–13.

——. *Augustine of Hippo.* Berkeley: University of California Press, 1967.

——. *The Body and Society: Men, Women, and Sexual Renunciation in Early Christianity.* New York: Columbia University Press, 1988.

Buchheit, Vincenz. "Augustinus under dem Feigenbaum (Au *Conf* VIII)." VC, 22 (1968).

Cambronne, Patrice. *Recherches sur la structure de l'imaginaire dans les* CONFESSIONS *de saint Augustin.* 3 vols. Paris: Études Augustiniennes, 1979. Microfiche.

Capps, Donald. "Augustine as Narcissist: Comments on Paul Rigby's 'Paul Ricoeur, Freudianism and Augustine's *Confessions.*'" *Journal of the American Academy of Religion*, 53 (1985), 115–17.

Chadwick, Henry. *St. Augustine's* CONFESSIONS. Oxford: Oxford University Press, 1991.

Chevalier, Louis, s.j., and Rondet, Henri, s.j. "L'idée de la vanité dans l'oeuvre de saint Augustin." REA, 3 (1957), 221–34.

Courcelle, Pierre Paul. *Les* CONFESSIONS *dans la tradition littéraire: Antécédents et posterité.* Paris: Etudes Augustiniennes, 1963.

——. *Recherches sur les* CONFESSIONS *de saint Augustin,* 2nd ed. Paris: E. de Boccard, 1968.

Daley, Brian E., s.j. "The Giant's Twin Substance: Ambrose and the Christology of Augustine's *Contra Sermonem Arianorum.*" *Collectanea,* "Marquette." Pp. 473–91.

Dittes, Joseph E. "Augustine: Search for a Fail-Safe God to Trust." *Journal for the Scientific Study of Religion,* 25 (1986), 57–63.

Doignon, Jean. "*Factus Erectior* (*B. Vita* 1, 4): Une Étape de l'Évolution du jeune Augustin à Carthage." VC, 27 (1990), 79–93.

——. "La praxis de l'*admonitio* dans les Dialogues de Cassiciacum." VC, 23 (1986), 21–37.

——. "Le symbolisme des Sirènes dans les premiers Dialogues de saint Augustin." *Hommage à R. Chevalier.* Tours, 1986. Pp. 113–20.

——. "Sur l'enseignement de l'*Hortensius.* . . ." *L'Antiquité Classique,* 51 (1982), 193–206.

Dudden, F. Homes. *The Life and Times of Saint Ambrose.* 2 vols. Oxford: Clarendon, 1935.

Du Roy, Olivier. *L'Intelligence de la foi en la Trinité selon saint Augustin: Genèse de sa théologie trinitaire jusqu'en 391.* Paris: Études Augustiniennes, 1966.

Dutton, Marsha. "When I Was a Child. . . ." *Collectanea,* "Founder." Pp. 113–40.

Eliot, T. S. "The Dry Salvages." *Four Quartets.* London: Faber, 1963.

Ferrari, Leo C. "The Arboreal Polarization in Augustine's *Confessions.*" REA, 25 (1979), 35–46.

——. "Augustine's Nine Years in the Manichees." *Augustiniana,* 25 (1975), 208–15.

——. *The Conversions of Saint Augustine*. Villanova, Pa.: Villanova University Press, 1984.

——. "Paul at the Conversion of Augustine (*Conf.* VIII, 29–30)." *AS*, 11 (1980), 5–20.

——. "Saint Augustine on the road to Damascus." *AS*, 13 (1982), 151–70.

Fredriksen, Paula. "Augustine and His Analysts: The Possibility of a Psychohistory." *Soundings*, 61 (1978), 206–27.

——. "Paul and Augustine: Conversion Narratives, Orthodox Tradition, and the Retrospective Self." *JTS*, N.S. 37, No. 1 (April 1986), 3–34.

Gay, Volney. "Augustine: The Reader as Self-Object." *Journal for the Scientific Study of Religion*, 25 (1986), 64–76.

Gilson, Étienne. *The Christian Philosophy of St. Augustine*. New York: Random House, 1960.

Glare, P. G. W., ed. *The Oxford Latin Dictionary*. Oxford: Clarendon, 1982.

Harder, R. "Eine neue Schrift Plotins." *Kleine Schriften*. Bonn: Forschungsstelle für Buchwissenschaft an der Universitätsbibliothek Bonn, 1960. Pp. 303–13.

Henry, Paul, S.J. *The Path to Transcendence: From Philosophy to Mysticism in Saint Augustine*. Trans. Francis F. Burch. Pittsburgh: Pickwick Press, 1981. Originally published as *La Vision d'Ostie: Sa Place dans la vie et l'oeuvre de saint Augustin*. Paris: J. Vrin, 1938.

——. *Plotin et l'Occident*. Louvain: "Spicilegium Sacrum Lovaniense," 1934.

The Jerusalem Bible. London: Darton, Longman & Todd; Garden City, N.Y.: Doubleday, 1966.

Lafont, Ghislain. *Peut-on connaître Dieu en Jésus Christ?* Paris: Les Éditions du Cerf, 1969.

Lepelley, Claude. "*Spes Saeculi.*" *Atti* I. Pp. 99–117.

Lieu, Samuel N. C. *Manichaeism in the Later Roman Empire and Mediaeval China*. Manchester: Manchester University Press, 1985.

Loehrer, Magnus. *Der Glaubensbegriff des hl. Augustinus*. Einsiedeln: Benzinger, 1955.

Luman, Richard. "Journeys and Gardens: Narrative Patterns in the *Confessiones* of St. Augustine." *Collectanea*, "Founder." Pp. 141–58.

Madec, Goulven. Review of Beatrice, Pier Franco. *Tradux peccati: Alle fonti della dottrina agostiniana del peccato originale.* "Bulletin Augustinien." REA, 36 (1990), 406.

———. "Une lecture de *Confessions* VII, ix, 13—xxi, 27." REA, 16 (1970), 79–137.

Mallard, William. "The Incarnation in Augustine's Conversion." RA, 15 (1980), 80–98.

Mandouze, André. *Saint Augustin: L'Aventure de la raison et de la grâce.* Paris: Études Augustiniennes, 1968.

Marrou, H. I. Review of Pierre Courcelle. *Recherches sur les CONFESSIONS de saint Augustin.* REL, 29 (1951), 406.

Masai, François. "Les Conversions de saint Augustin et les débuts du spiritualisme en Occident." *Moyen Age,* 67 (1961), 1–40.

Miles, Margaret. "Infancy, Parenting, and Nourishment in Augustine's *Confessions.*" *American Academy of Religion,* 50 (1982), 349–64.

Nock, Arthur Darby. *Conversion: The Old and the New in Religion from Alexander the Great to Augustine of Hippo.* Oxford: Oxford University Press, 1933.

O'Connell, Robert J., s.j. *Art and the Christian Intelligence in the Works of St. Augustine.* Cambridge: Harvard University Press, 1978.

———. "*Confessions* VII, ix, 13—xxi, 27: Reply to Fr. Madec." REA, 19 (1973), 87–100.

———. "*Ennead* VI, 4–5 in the Works of St. Augustine." REA, 9 (1963), 1–39.

———. "The *Enneads* and St. Augustine's Image of Happiness." VC, 17 (1963), 129–64.

———. "Faith, Reason, and Ascent to Vision in St. Augustine." AS, 21 (1990), 83–126.

———. "The Fall of the Soul in the *Confessions.*" Atti II. Pp. 45–58.

———."The God of St. Augustine's Imagination." *Thought,* 57 (1982), 30–40.

———. *Imagination and Metaphysics in St. Augustine.* Milwaukee: Marquette University Press, 1987.

———. "Isaiah's Mothering God in St. Augustine's *Confessions.*" *Thought,* 58 (1983), 188–206.

———. "On Augustine's 'First Conversion': *Factus Erectior (De Beata Vita* 4)." AS, 17 (1986), 15–30.

———. *The Origin of the Soul in St. Augustine's Later Works*. New York: Fordham University Press, 1987.

———. *Saint Augustine's* CONFESSIONS: *The Odyssey of Soul*. 2nd ed. New York: Fordham University Press, 1989.

———. "St. Augustine's Criticism of Origen in the *Ad Orosium*." REA, 30 (1984), 84–99.

———. *St. Augustine's Early Theory of Man, A.D. 386–391*. Cambridge: Harvard University Press, 1968.

———. *Saint Augustine's Platonism*. Villanova, Pa.: Villanova University Press, 1984.

———. *Soundings in Augustine's Imagination*. New York: Fordham University Press, 1994.

———. "Where the Difference Still Lies." AS, 21 (1990), 139–52.

O'Donovan, Oliver. *The Problem of Self-Love in St. Augustine*. New Haven: Yale University Press, 1980.

O'Meara, John J. *The Young Augustine: The Growth of Augustine's Mind Up to His Conversion*. London: Longmans, Green, 1954.

Otto, Rudolf. *The Idea of the Holy: An Inquiry into the Non-Rational Factor in the Idea of the Divine and Its Relation to the Rational*. Trans. John W. Harvey. Oxford: Oxford University Press, 1958.

Pagels, Elaine. *Adam, Eve, and the Serpent*. New York: Random House, 1988.

Pellegrino, Michele. *Les* CONFESSIONS *de saint Augustin: Guide de lecture*. Paris: Études Augustiniennes, 1961.

Pépin, Jean. *Ex Platonicorum persona: Études sur les lectures philosophiques de saint Augustin*. Amsterdam: A. M. Hakkert, 1977.

Peters, Maria. "Augustins erste Bekehrung." *Harnack-Ehrung: Beiträge zur Kirchengeschichte*. Leipzig: Hinrichs, 1921. Pp. 195–211.

Peza, Elgardo de la. *El significado de "cor" en San Augustin*. Paris: Études Augustiniennes, 1962.

Pincherle, Alberto. "Intorno alla genesi delle *Confessioni* di S. Agostino." AS, 5 (1974), 167–76.

———. *Vita di sant' Agostino*. Rome: Laterza, 1980.

Pine-Coffin, R. S., trans. *Saint Augustine's* CONFESSIONS. Harmondsworth: Penguin, 1961.

Plotinus. *Plotini Opera*. Ed. Paul Henry, s.j. and Hans-Rudolph Schwyzer. 3 vols. Brussels: Desclée de Brouwer, 1951.

Poque, Suzanne. *Le Langage symbolique dans la prédication d'Augustin d'Hippone.* 2 vols. Paris: Études Augustiniennes, 1984.

Russell, Robert A., o.s.a. "Cicero's *Hortensius* and the Problem of Riches in St. Augustine." AS, 7 (1976), 59–68.

Ryan, John K., trans. *The Confessions of Saint Augustine.* Garden City, n.y.: Doubleday Image, 1960.

Schwyzer, H. R. "Plotinos." RE 21, cols. 547–48.

Sweetnam, J., s.j. "A Note on *In Idipsum* in St. Augustine." *Modern Schoolman,* 30 (1953), 328–31.

TeSelle, Eugene. "Augustine as Client and Theorist." *Journal for the Scientific Study of Religion,* 25 (1986), 92–101.

———. *Augustine the Theologian.* New York: Herder & Herder, 1970.

———. "Porphyry and Augustine." AS, 5 (1974), 113–47.

Testard, Maurice. *Saint Augustin et Cicéron,* 2 vols. Paris: Études Augustiniennes, 1958.

Thesaurus Augustinianus. Turnhout: Brepols, 1989.

Torchia, N. J. "St. Augustine's Treatment of *Superbia* and Its Plotinian Affinities." AS, 18 (1987), 66–81.

Tréhorel, Eugene, and Bouissou, Guilhen, trans. *Les Confessions.* Bibliothèque Augustinienne 13–14. Paris: Desclée de Brouwer, 1962.

Van Bavel, Tarcisius. "The Double Face of Love in St. Augustine." *Atti* III. Pp. 69–80.

———. "L'humanité du Christ comme *lac parvulorum.* . . ." *Augustiniana,* 7 (1957), 245–81.

Van Fleteren, Frederick. "Augustine's Ascent of the Soul: A Reconsideration." AS, 5 (1974), 29–72.

———. "Authority and Reason, Faith and Understanding." AS, 4 (1973), 33–71.

———. "A Reply to Fr. O'Connell." AS, 21 (1990), 127–38.

Verbeke, G. "Augustin et le Stoicisme." RA, 1 (1958), 67–89.

Walpole, A. S. *Early Latin Hymns.* Cambridge: Cambridge University Press, 1922.

Weiser, Artur. *The Psalms: A Commentary.* Philadelphia: Westminster, 1962.

Zum Brunn, Emilie. *Augustine on Being and Nothingness.* Trans. Ruth Namad. New York: Paragon House, 1988.

INDICES

1. Index of Subjects and Names

2. SACRED SCRIPTURE

3. Works of St. Augustine

Contra Academicos

De beata vita

De ordine

Soliloquia

1.1–2	393	1.18–19	290
1.2	266, 291	1.22	9, 11, 50, 264
1.5	271, 291	1.24–25	280
1.5–6	292	1.24	291, 294
1.6	292	1.25–26	45
1.7	3	1.25	291
1.12–13	51	1.26	292
1.12–15	9	1.25	271
1.12	96	1.27	266, 271
1.13–24	292	1.30	246, 292
1.17	9, 11, 89n90, 290		
		2.1	292
		2.9	292

De quantitate animae

55	255n33	70–79	187, 188

De moribus ecclesiae

1.3	159	2.2	153
1.16	138	2.2–7	149
1.26–32	102		
1.65–67	187		

De Genesi contra Manichaos

2.16	255n33

De libero arbitrio

2.6	309n50	3.12–13	304
2.15–34	187	3.71–74	308n27

De utilitate credendi

2–3	48

De musica

6.2	272	6.29	172
6.8	159	6.39	xvii
6.23	272	6.57	272

De vera religione

18	189	95	170
68	170	101	202n72

Confessiones

1.1–3	99	2.3	63
1.1–6	17	2.5	22, 63
1.1	265	2.6–7	20
1.3	265	2.6–8	63
1.4	99, 265	2.8	21, 25
1.5	53	2.9	24
1.7–10	99	2.24	12
1.9	24, 252, 265		
1.11–13	99	3.1	31, 64
1.11	210	3.2–4	31, 64
1.12	24	3.3	12
1.13	2, 65	3.5–6	32
1.16	15, 61	3.5	32, 64
1.17	20, 23, 50	3.7	22, 64
1.18	20, 265	3.10–11	36, 66
1.19	19	3.16	58, 63
1.20–26	24		
1.20	61	4.1	66
1.21	15, 24	4.2	16, 33, 66
1.24	61	4.3	66
1.23–26	12	4.9–13	76
1.25	219	4.14–15	27
1.27	33, 61	4.15	272
1.28	62	4.18	211
1.29	62	4.18–19	209
1.30	62, 210	4.19	272
		4.20	108–9
2.1	16, 30, 31, 62	4.22–23	172
2.2	25, 30	4.27	209, 211

Libri duo quaestionum Evangeliorum

De praedestinatione

De Trinitate

De Genesi ad litterams

De civitate Dei

Retractationes

Epistulae

Ennarrationes

Contra Faustum

Tractatus in Joannis Evangelium

2 4	219	*40* 5	125
13 5	184	*53* 2	254n19
18 10	125	*59* 3	274
21 4	125	*73* 1	254n19
40 4	163	*101* 4	254n19
		102 4	95

Sermones

2 8	132	*120* 11	168
2 12	168	*126* 15	125
5 21–22	23	*158* 7	132
20 1	168	*158* 9	132
23 5	168	*166* 2–3	184
24 4	95	*207*	23
34 3	163	*208*	23
55 1	254n19	*209*	23
58 13	132	*213* 7	163
83 1	254n19	*214* 4–6	184
93 51	33	*252* 7	184
113 2	163	*302* 15	231
117 15	132	*346* 2	132
		351 4–5	231